D0018806

A
Consumer's
Dictionary
of
Food
Additives

A Consumer's Dictionary of Food Additives

NEW, THIRD REVISED EDITION

Ruth Winter, M.S.

Crown Publishers, Inc. New York

Published by Crown Publishers, Inc., 201 East 50th Street, New York, New York 10022.
Member of the Crown Publishing Group.

CROWN is a trademark of Crown Publishers, Inc.

Manufactured in the United States of America

Library of Congress Cataloging-in-Publication Data
Winter, Ruth
A consumer's dictionary of food additives.
Includes bibliographical references.
I. Food additives—Dictionaries.   I. Title.
TX553.A3W55   1989   664'.06'0321   83-26135

ISBN 0-517-57262-1

10   9   8   7   6   5

A
Consumer's
Dictionary
of
Food
Additives

INTRODUCTION

A food label is a contract between us and the manufacturer. Like most contracts, it may be difficult to understand and what is not included may be as important as what is. The food processors and vendors attempt to sell us what we demand. In our fast-paced and complicated world today, we are in the market for:

- Instant food
- Instant health

INSTANT FOOD

We want convenience, which by definition means ease and speed of preparation or use, and higher costs. If we spend the day on the job outside the home, we no longer have the time or energy to shop frequently or to spend hours preparing a meal. Households have shrunk in size and the traditional sit-down family dinner has gone the way of the hand-held can opener.

The growing use of the microwave oven has also encouraged the use of convenience foods. In 1978, only 11 percent of American homes had the quick-cooking devices. Now, an estimated 80 percent of homes have them, and processed food products for microwaving are burgeoning.[1]

Those foods that are easier to prepare pass through many hands to be mashed, mushed, mangled, and loaded with chemicals so that we can have cake mixes, and peeled and sliced potatoes, and instant everything.

Technology has advanced, or retreated, depending upon one's view, to the point that some foods are almost pure ersatz. One well-known orange-flavored drink that has on the label "100% Natural Flavor . . . No Preservatives" consists of (in descending order of ingredients) sugar, citric acid, potassium citrate, Vitamin C, orange juice solids, artificial colors including Yellow No. 5, natural orange flavor with other natural flavors, xanthan gum, cellulose gums, niacinamide, Vitamin A, Vitamin B_6 riboflavin, and folic acid. While hydrogenated coconut oil and BHT that had been in its original formula have been eliminated, no "natural" orange ever grew on that tree. One whipped topping consists of sodium caseinate, dextrose, corn sugar, polysorbate 60, sorbitan, monostearate, carrageenan, and guar gum. All these ingredients are listed on the labels.

---

[1] Ed Fitch, "Scouts Agree: It's Hot If It's Microwavable," Special Report, *Advertising Age* (May 9, 1988): p. S-16.

By law, the label must identify the product in a language the consumer can understand. It must indicate the manufacturer, the packer or distributor, and declare the quantity of contents either in net weight or volume, and the ingredients must be declared on the label in order of predominance. The label must be accurate in any statement about the product. Also, if a vignette or picture of the product is placed on the label, it is supposed to be truly representative of the container's contents. Can a packaged or processed food contain "instant health"?

INSTANT HEALTH

The idea that food could prevent diseases such as cancer and heart attacks had been assigned by health and government agencies to the health "nut" category when the first edition of this book was published in 1972. In 1980 the surgeon general's office issued a report setting nutritional objectives for the nation by 1990 for improving the health of Americans. Some of the specific objectives were weight control; reduction in the population's serum cholesterol levels; reduced daily sodium intake; reduced consumption of potentially carcinogenic foods; and increased promotion and awareness of United States Department of Agriculture Dietary Guidelines.

The National Food Processors Association reaction to the surgeon general's report was cited in an editorial in the March 1981 issue of *Food Product Development,* a trade journal:

It should not be government's role in a free society to intervene or interfere in the production of manufactured foodstuffs to ensure their nutritional quality and content, a "technologic measure" suggested in the report. Such a policy could lead to government control over the food processing industry, lessening of competition, and stagnation in the development of new products with attributes desired by the consumer.

Nor is the positioning of products in the supermarkets to make nutrition information readily apparent, also suggested in the report, a province of government. So many factors are involved in shelf positioning of products that it is absurd to suggest that the presentation of nutrition information might become the overriding consideration.

The food processing industry is opposed to promulgation of guidelines to maintain or improve the nutritional quality of the food supply. Again, development of food products should be unfettered by government regulation, even in the guise of guidelines, and left to the play of market forces.[2]

Now, many of the largest food processors have changed their collective minds. Health claims sell! As of this writing, labels are carrying health claims citing recommendations for cancer- and heart

---

[2] Fran LaBell, Editorial, *Food Product Development* (March 1981), p. 70.

disease-preventive diets from such staid organizations as the National Cancer Institute, the American Heart Association, and the American Cancer Society. In fact, the American Heart Association is prepared to stamp its approval on processed foods that are low in fat, cholesterol, and sodium as a means of lessening the risk of heart disease.

The Food and Drug Administration (FDA) began to tolerate health messages on food packages when in October 1984 the Kellogs Company began displaying "Preventive health tips from the National Cancer Institute" including high-fiber, low-fat foods. Of course, their bran flakes were high fiber, low fat. The campaign not only helped boost sales of the high-fiber cereals in general but also cut into the consumer purchase of low-fiber cereals.

In 1987, the FDA said that it "believes it is important to consider ways to improve the public's understanding about health benefits that can result from adhering to a sound and nutritious diet . . . the rapid growth of scientific and public interest in nutrition argues for recognition and dissemination of such new knowledge, and food labels offer one appropriate vehicle for this dissemination."[3]

The FDA cited three principal factors for proposing the change in its former policy:

• The growing amount of scientific evidence suggests that there is a link between diet and various illnesses, such as cancer and coronary heart disease, and that people can reduce their risk of those diseases by eating more or less of various types of foods.

• Consumer interest in learning more about how to improve their diets, avoid diet-related illnesses, and generally stay healthier.

• Food industry interest in marketing and promoting products for their potential health benefits.

The FDA lists four criteria to determine the "propriety of the health-related claims and information."

• The health message or claims made on food labels must be truthful and not misleading to consumers, and they "should not imply that a particular food [can] be used as part of a drug-like treatment or therapy-oriented approach to health care." Further, the information "must not overemphasize or distort the role of a food" in promoting good health.

• The claims must be supported by "valid, reliable, publicly available scientific evidence . . . and should conform to generally

[3] "Selling Nutrition: Should Food Packages Carry Health Messages?" *FDA Consumer* (November 1987): pp. 22–25.

recognized medical and nutritional principles" for a sound, total diet. The "weight of scientific evidence" must support a health claim to ensure that the "substance of the message has achieved sufficient scientific recognition to be appropriate and nonmisleading."

• The claims must indicate clearly that good nutrition is the result of the total diet and not a result of eating a specific food or foods. That requirement conforms to the traditional advice of most nutrition experts that people should eat a varied but balanced diet of nutritious foods.

• Nutrition labeling is mandatory on any product making a health claim. In general, the purpose of the nutrition label is to inform consumers about the calories, protein, carbohydrate, fat, sodium, and certain essential vitamins and minerals present in each serving of a product.

But should you "swallow" everything a food processor puts on the label about the health benefits of a product? A soup company, for example, created a conflict when it claimed: "You can get as much fiber from a serving of home style bean soup as you can from a serving of many bran cereals . . . and fiber is important because the National Cancer Institute says that a diet high in fiber and low in fat may help reduce the risk of some kinds of cancer."

The Cancer Institute found the advertisement misleading because the company's bean and pea soups contained 600 to 700 milligrams of sodium, much higher than the Department of Health and Human Services maintains is prudent. The institute's name was removed from the soup company's advertising.

Likewise, the Dairy Board highlighted the benefits of calcium, which is high in dairy products, but left out that they are also high in fat and sodium.

Even that old home remedy, chicken soup, is not immune. How about a product that is promoted as very low sodium? *Chicken* and *Bouillon* are in big letters on the package and in between, in smaller letters, is the word *flavor*. The ingredients in descending order of content are: dextrose, potassium chloride, hydrolyzed cereal solids, autolyzed yeast, chicken fat, onion powder, monoammonium glutamate, gelatin, natural chicken flavor, spices, garlic powder, tumeric, disodium inosinate, disodium guanylate, and carrot powder. Chances are neither your mother nor a chicken would recognize it. It's true very low sodium is desirable for persons with cardiovascular problems, but chicken fat and the largest ingredient, dextrose (a sugar), are not.

Another "instant" chicken soup aimed at the general public proclaims "no preservatives" but it not only has sugar, cotton seed oil, sodium pyrophosphate and potassium pyrophosphate (both questionable antioxidants considered preservatives), sodium carbonate, potassium carbonate, monosodium glutamate, but a whopping 1,435 *milligrams* of sodium.

The National Academy of Sciences, whose experts establish dietary guidelines, recommends that we ingest no more than 1,100 to 3,000 *milligrams* of sodium for the entire day. The average American ingests 5,000 to 7,000 *milligrams*. If the numbers for sodium look very low on a label, look again and be aware of the difference between *milligrams* (mg) and *grams* (gr). Some companies make you think there is less by saying 5 *grams* of sodium, for example, which is really 5,000 *milligrams*.

The FDA does have established regulations for listing sodium on the label:

• Sodium free—less than 5 mg per serving.

• Very low sodium—35 mg or less.

• Low sodium—140 mg or less.

• Reduced sodium—processed to reduce the usual level of sodium by 75 percent.

• Unsalted—processed without salt.

"No salt added" can signify the producer didn't put any additional salt in during processing, but the food itself may still be naturally high in sodium.

The basic sources of cereals, on the other hand, are salt free—wheat, corn, rice, and oats. Yet instant oatmeal contains about 360 mg per serving, instant corn grits 590 mg, and instant cream of wheat 180 mg. If you're willing to cook the cereals a little bit, you can avoid the high salt. It's providing the "instant" that dishes out the sodium.

Some 70 sodium compounds are used in foods, as you will see in this book.

Sugar also masquerades under a variety of names as you will also read in this book, and sometimes it is difficult to avoid. Common table sugar (sucrose), fructose, and corn syrup are among the types of calorie-containing sweeteners found in foods. A food can be labeled "sugar free" or "sugarless" and still contain calories from sugar alcohols (xylitol, sorbitol, and mannitol), provided the basis for the claim is explained (but not necessarily understood). Saccharin is a nonnutritive sweetener—that is, it has no calories. Aspartame has the same calories as sugar, but is so much sweeter that only small amounts are needed to provide the desired sweetness in a product.

We may even be getting more than we bargained for when we get our sweets from fruit juice. A popular brand of diet fruit juice has a beautiful picture of an open pineapple and a cut orange on its label proclaiming it to be "sugar free" and "low sodium." It is, however, artificially sweetened and flavored with FD and C Yellow No. 5 and No. 6, both recognized allergens, and benzoate of soda, a flavoring agent that's also a common allergen, saccharin, and aspartame. Now from what tree was that concoction harvested?

There are countless studies in progress to correlate diet and heart and blood vessel disease prevention, and a great many of them involve a waxy alcohol called cholesterol that's found in everyone's living tissue. But most experts do advise that lowering saturated fat in the diet is a way of lowering cholesterol.

You can figure out the percentage of calories in a food product that comes from fat. There are nine calories in a gram of fat. Therefore, the formula is:

$$\frac{\text{Grams of fat per serving} \times 9}{\text{Total Calories per serving}}$$

Here is an example of the formula using one tablespoon of mayonnaise (14 grams) that contains 11 grams of fat and 100 calories.

$$\frac{11 \text{ Grams of fat} \times 9 \text{ calories}}{100 \text{ calories}}$$

Therefore, the percentage of calories from fat is 99 percent.

No rules exist, as of this writing, for claims about the saturated fats or cholesterol, although the FDA is in the process of forming regulations. According to the agency's proposal, the following should be in the package when lower cholesterol claims are on the label:

• Cholesterol free—less than 2 mg per serving.

• Low cholesterol—less than 20 mg per serving.

Michael J. Klug, who works on consumer affairs for one of the nation's largest organizations, the American Association of Retired Persons, found that when members were asked their complaints about labeling, they almost all complained about "cholesterol" labeling.

"People with heart disease or high cholesterol levels in their blood are quite upset with the current labeling practices for oils," Klug says. "Their first complaint involves 'and/or' labeling where tropical oils (e.g., palm and coconut oils) are among the listed potential ingredients. Many indicate that their doctors have told them to avoid products containing these highly saturated fats.

"A second complaint involves the 'no cholesterol' or 'vegetable oil only' claims on many products. People complained about the deceptiveness of such claims where the oils involved may be high in saturated fats and thus lead to the body's production of serum cholesterol."[4]

If low-salt, sugar-free, and low-cholesterol labeling may mislead you, how about "lite"?

LIGHT OR LITE

Most of us think that *lite* means a product is lighter in calories or fat. However, in a study by Madelyn L. Wheeler, coordinator of research dietetics at the Diabetes Research and Training Center of Indiana University Medical Center, Indianapolis, she and her colleagues found that one vegetable oil producer used *light* because his oil was 25 percent paler in color but the calories were the same as any other. A light pancake mix had the same calories as any other except that it had no preservatives or artificial flavors and a "Taco Light" was used on the label of taco shells made with wheat flour rather than corn meal, although the calories were the same.[5]

The only time you can count on light foods probably being light—in calories—is when the label says "low calorie" or "reduced calories" since the FDA requires such products to have at least one-third fewer calories than a similar "regular" product. Since 1980, FDA has required foods labeled as "low calorie" to contain no more than 40 calories in a serving and no more than 0.4 calories per gram. A "reduced-calorie" food must be at least one-third lower in calorie content than the foods to which it is compared. Foods naturally low in calories cannot use these terms. Foods labeled as "diet" or "dietetic" products must meet the requirements for low- or reduced-calorie foods or must be clearly described as being useful for special dietary purposes other than for maintaining or reducing body weight.

Natural and *organic* are other terms that appear on many products, but they have no legal meaning. Food labels may claim that a product is "natural" and contains no preservatives or MSG. The very same product, packaged differently, may be next to it on the shelf, make no health claims, also contain no preservatives or MSG, and be a fraction of the price.

FOOD ADDITIVES

What do you want from your food? You are part of the market force. By using this book to understand the labels and by selecting wisely,

---

[4] Michael J. Klug, personal communication with author, August 1988.
[5] Madelyn Wheeler, et al., *Diabetes Forecast* (September–October, 1983).

you can help increase sales of wholesome foods and protect the health of your family.

There are approximately three thousand indirect and direct common food additives in our diet, nearly two thirds of them flavorings used to replace the flavors lost during processing.

It is more important than ever that you read and understand the labels on food and have enough knowledge about what is claimed to make an informed choice. This book tells you about the additives in your food, where they come from, how they are used and what is known about how they may affect your health.

Pick up a can, box, or any package of food. Do you understand the label? Do you know what is not on the label but may be added to the food even so?

What the food processor is offering has changed greatly since this book was first published in 1972. Then there were thirty-five widely used food additives that had been approved, but they have since been found unsafe and have been removed, most of them because they were determined capable of causing cancer. In 1978, food additives were a $1.3-billion-a-year business. Today, it is a more than $4.5 billion enterprise. In 1978, there were 164.1 million pounds of food additives in processed meat alone. Today, there are more than 363 million pounds.[6]

In order to get you to buy a product, it must be placed properly on the shelf, priced right, and packaged attractively, usually with the word "new" printed on it. Approximately eight thousand new food products are introduced in a year, some with new additives and many with new combinations of additives.[7]

For more than three hundred "standard" foods—including ice cream, catsup, and mayonnaise—no ingredients need be listed. For standard foods, processors follow the standard chemical recipes written out by the government. The manufacturer is given the option to choose among many alternative standard chemicals, and only if he substitutes or adds a nonstandard chemical or uses Yellow No. 5 and No. 6 (see both), common allergens, must he indicate the fact on the label. Ice cream, for example, which can have some thirty additives, need not list ingredients on the label. In still other products such as canned fruit and gelatin desserts, the processor need only state "artificial coloring" or "artificial flavoring" without specifically identifying it, again with the exception of Yellow No. 5 and No. 6.

---

[6] *Food Product Development* (December 1980), pp. 36–40.
[7] Ed Fitch, "Life in the food chain becomes predatory," Special report, *Advertising Age* (May 9, 1988); p. 5–16.

The law also does not require that chemicals added in small amounts during processing, such as calcium bromate (a maturing agent for dough), be stated on the label.

This book tells you about the additives in your food, where they come from, how they are used, and what is known about how they may affect your health.

A food additive is a substance or mixture of substances, other than basic foodstuffs, present in food as a result of any aspect of production, processing, storage, or packaging. The term does not include chance contaminants.

Food processors have in their armamentaria an estimated ten thousand chemicals they may add to what we eat. Some are deleterious, some are harmless, and some are beneficial.

Every one of these chemicals used in food processing must serve one or more of the following purposes:[8]

- Improve nutritional value.
- Enhance quality or consumer acceptability.
- Improve the keeping quality.
- Make the food more readily available.
- Facilitate its preparation.

The majority of food additives have nothing to do with nutritional value, but are used for other purposes.

Most of the chemicals added to enhance consumer acceptability are to feed our illusions. We want enhanced food because all our lives we have been subjected to the beautiful pictures of foods in our magazines and on television. We have come to expect an advertiser's concept of perfection in color and texture, even though Mother Nature may not turn out all her products that way. As a result, the skin of the oranges we eat are dyed bright orange to match our mental image of the ideal orange; our poultry is fed a chemical to turn the meat yellower and more appetizing, and our fruits and vegetables are kept unblemished by fungicides, pesticides, herbicides, and other antispoilants.

To improve the keeping quality of some products, processors embalm them. Bread has as many as sixteen chemicals to keep it feeling "fresh" to the touch. One type of bread, balloon bread, undergoes rigor mortis thanks to its additive, plaster of Paris. Ironically, when nothing is added to the foods, they cost us considerably

---

[8] According to the Food Protection Committee of the National Academy of Sciences, which evaluates the safety of additives.

more. Unbleached flour is four times as expensive as bleached; untreated tomatoes, five times as much as regular canned tomatoes; and unsulfured raisins are six times the cost of treated ones.

Food companies ostensibly test additives for acute toxicity. Additives are fed to animals in large amounts. Although most companies do not use control groups—animals not fed any additive—for comparison or perform autopsies to determine the effects on tissues, they observe the additive-fed animals for symptoms of ill effects. They also usually determine the lethal dose (if in fact the additive can be determined to be lethal) based on the amount that kills 50 percent of the animals (LD—Lethal Dose—50).

In subacute studies (*see* subacute), which have also been done for a number of food additives, the food chemical is fed to groups of animals in varying amounts, to some nearly to the point of death. These tests usually last a minimum of three months and are made on at least two species of animals, most often rats and dogs. The data collected during the study include appetite, thirst, growth rates, weight, blood and urine analyses, and behavior patterns. At the end of the study, all surviving animals are autopsied. These tests are expensive and time-consuming, often costing more than $250,000 for a single chemical.

In the mid-1970s, the FDA discovered that some of the 130 laboratories doing food-additive testing had serious deficiencies, and in the 1980s, several laboratory executives were indicted for fraud. The federal agency had relied on the basic accuracy of the data submitted to make decisions about approving food and color additives for the market. The FDA officials noted: "The submission of faulty, erroneous, or distorted data increases the potential for reaching invalid judgments about the safety of these additives."

In September 1980, the National Toxicology Program (NTP) contracted with the National Research Council (NRC) and the National Academy of Sciences for a study[9] with two principal charges:

1. To determine toxicity-testing needs for substances to which humans are exposed so that the federal agencies responsible for the protection of public health will have the information needed to assess the toxicity of such substances.

2. To develop and validate uniformly applicable and wide-ranging criteria by which to set priorities for research on substances with potentially adverse public-health impact.

The NRC considered 65,725 substances of possible concern, among them 8,627 food additives and 3,410 cosmetic ingredients approved

[9] "Toxicity Testing Strategies to Determine Needs and Priorities," National Research Council (U.S.), National Academy Press: Washington, D.C., 1984.

for use. Through a random-sample program, 100 of these substances were selected for screening because at least some toxicity information about them was available. An in-depth examination of this subsample led to the conclusion that there was enough evidence of toxicity and ill-effects resulting from exposure to the products for a complete health-hazard assessment to be conducted on only a small fraction of the subsample. For the great majority of the substances, data considered to be essential for conducting a health hazard assessment are lacking. The NRC drew the following conclusions:

• When judged against current standards for toxicity testing, 92 percent of the tests in the subsample were inadequate.

• Of 18 standard tests, only one—the oral administration in rodents—was judged to be adequate. The other 17 tests deemed necessary to meet the standards were either not done at all for 67 to 100 percent of the food additives, or required repetition for more conclusive results.

• For food additives, a large variety of test types were found to be needed, such as chronic studies and inhalation studies, and more complex studies, such as neurotoxicity, genetic toxicity, and effects on the fetus.

• There is no toxicity information available on 46 percent of the additives, and for only 5 percent is complete health hazard assessment possible.

The fact is that a large percentage of the food additives have not been tested over the long term, one of the great problems in determining chemical safety. Cancer, for instance, may take twenty years to develop in humans, and often more than two years in animals. Long-term safety is determined from rats, which live from eighteen to twenty-four months. However, researchers point out that laboratory animals are in a nonnatural, sterile environment and that in two years, 70 to 90 percent of them would be dead anyway and only two or three would be left for evaluation. Therefore, long-term tests may provide invalid assurances of safety.

One partial solution, although not accepted by all scientists, is the Ames test. In the early 1970s, Dr. Bruce Ames, a biochemist at the University of California at Berkeley, developed a simple test using common bacteria that reveals whether a chemical is a mutagen. The test can be done quickly and is relatively inexpensive. Mutagens act by changing the genetic material that is transferred to daughter cells when cell division occurs. Carcinogens also act by fouling up the genetic material within a cell. Almost all of the chemicals known to be carcinogenic have also been shown to be mutagenic in the Ames test. While the testing of additives in our food for carcinogenicity may be imperfect, little if any testing is being done to determine if food additives may be toxic to the brain and nerves, although a number of scientists believe that neurotoxins are even more of a problem in food than carcinogens.[10, 11]

Researchers at Albert Einstein College of Medicine in New York, for example, have been working with a substance isolated from chick peas that causes nerve damage similar to amyotrophic lateral sclerosis (ALS), Lou Gehrig's disease. They have been collaborating with Indian and Israeli scientists. The toxic component, BOAA, is chemically related to two approved food additives, glutamate and aspartate (the ingredients in the sweetener Aspartame).

Another great problem with testing additives is determining how they interact with each other and with the sixty-three thousand other chemicals in common use today. In 1976, *The Journal of Food Science* carried a report on a small-scale attempt to determine the extent of the problem. When three additives were tested one at a time on rats, the animals stayed well. Given two at a time, the rats became ill. And with a three-additive combination, all the animals died within fourteen days.

How valid are animal studies? All but two of the known human carcinogens—benzene and arsenic—are also carcinogenic in rodents. None of the approximately 143 "rodent" carcinogens have been proven *not* to cause cancer in humans. Animal assays have predicted several human carcinogens, including three which may be contaminants in food: the mold found on nuts, aflatoxin; the plastic used in packaging, vinyl chloride, and the hormone once used to increase the weight of meat, diethylstilbestrol.

Incidentally, the FDA has set a limit for aflatoxins in nuts of 15 parts per billion. If a batch exceeds that, the producers are able to add noncontaminated nuts to the batch to reduce levels, a system a number of food processors advocate for other undesirable additives such as low-potency carcinogens.[12]

The FDA's Bureau of Foods has set up a computerized data bank, Priority-Based Assessment of Food Additives (PAFA). It attempts to keep track of changes in the dietary patterns of society, as well as the

---

[10] Bernard Weiss, Ph.D., University of Rochester School of Medicine, *Nutrition Update:* Vol. 1, 1983, pp. 21–38.

[11] Charles Vorhees and R. E. Butcher, *Developmental Toxicology,* ed. by K. Snell (London: Croom Helm, 1982), pp. 247–98.

[12] "Public Issues, Private Medicine," symposium by Smith Kline Corp. and the College of Physicians of Philadelphia, December 6, 1978, in Philadelphia.

development of new and important knowledge of potential toxic effects that can be associated with any additive or group of additives.

When the FDA concludes that available data for a new additive or a new use of a regulated additive are sufficient to meet current criteria, the agency issues a food additive regulation approving the petitioned use of that specific substance. In the same way regulated additives, previously considered safe, might not be judged so favorably using current criteria. Questions about safety may be raised because of additional studies of exposures to these additives or new and expanded knowledge about their toxic potentials.

The PAFA has in the data base 1,586 substances out of 3,000 known to be added to our food supply. Alan Rulis, Ph.D., who heads the project says that thus far, not a single additive in use has been flagged as being too dangerous based on the information gathered, although saccharin has been shown again in several recent studies to be a cancer-causing agent and there are still questions about the benefits versus risks of the preservatives BHT and BHA (see both). He did note that sulfites were cited as dangerous but only after several unsuspecting restaurant customers died from eating fresh salads that had been laced with sulfites to prevent browning.

Dr. Rulis was optimistic about the results of the computerization of information about food additives. In 1978, he said they had little information about individual food additives, but now his department hopes to set up a system where food processors and scientists can tap into the data base and obtain the latest information on the chemicals used. To date, the problem has not only been setting up a government fee and retrieval system but dealing with some of the complaints about revealing trade secrets in data base information.[13]

Although officially the FDA claims to know the additives used throughout the food industry, FDA researchers report that it is impossible to check all the small manufacturers. Efforts have been made through the years to have food manufacturers register and provide the information, but as yet, there is no law requiring them to do so.

Consumer Complaints

The widespread distribution of food additives and consequent public safety concerns necessitate timely and reliable evaluation of suspected adverse reactions. However, once the products have been marketed few criteria exist to evaluate consumer-initiated reports of adverse medical reactions.

---

[13] Personal communication with author, August 1988.

Currently, consumer complaints related to food additives as well as other food products are monitored by passive surveillance, carried out primarily by the Food and Drug Administration. Therefore, it is very important that if you have an adverse reaction to a food product, you report it. To report such an incident or to ask questions about processed food ingredients, write to the office of Consumer Affairs, Food and Drug Administration, HFE-88, 5600 Fishers Lane, Rockville, MD 20857. For a question about meat or the storage of it, call the USDA's toll-free Meat and Poultry Hotline, 1-800-535-4555. It operates weekdays from 10:00 A.M. to 4:00 P.M. EST.

Contrary to public belief, food additives are not a modern innovation. Adding chemicals to food began in the dawn of civilization when people first discovered that by adding salt to meat, the meat would last longer.

The father of modern food additives laws was Dr. Harvey W. Wiley, who in the early 1900s led the fight against chemical preservatives such as boric acid, formaldehyde, and salicyclic acid. He dramatized the problem with his famous "Poison Squad" comprised of young men willing to be guinea pigs, who agreed to eat measured amounts of these chemicals to determine their toxicity.

As a result of Dr. Wiley's pioneering work, the first federal food and drug act was passed in 1906. However, as can be determined from the contents of this dictionary, not all the questions concerning food additive safety have been answered.

In the mid-1950s, when Food and Drug Administration scientists pushed for the passage of more regulatory laws, the FDA could not stop the use of a chemical simply because it was questionable or had not been adequately tested. It was necessary to be able to prove in court that the chemical was poisonous or deleterious. But on September 6, 1958, the Food Additives Amendment was passed. Food and chemical manufacturers, as of that date, would now be required to run extensive tests on additives before they could be marketed, and the results of these tests would have to be submitted to the FDA.

The famous (or infamous, depending on one's view) Delaney Amendment is part of the 1958 law. Written by Representative James Delaney, the law specifically states that no additive may be permitted in any amount if the tests show that it produces cancer when fed to man or animals or by other appropriate tests.

This part of the law has been severely attacked by food and chemical manufacturers, the Nutrition Council of the American Medical Association, and several FDA commissioners. The FDA commissioners claim it is unenforceable and point to the problem with saccharin, a proven though weak carcinogen. The artificial sweetener has been in use since 1879. When it was shown to cause cancer in laboratory animals in 1977, the FDA announced the use of saccharin in foods and beverages would be banned. There was a public outcry from dieters, led by the Calorie Control Council, a trade organization that spent over a million dollars in the first six months to stop the ban. Saccharin is still on the market, the FDA having postponed the ban several times in response to "public" pressure.

The food industry has been pushing for changes in the food laws. Among the new legislation they want is the following:

• Define the term "safe," since a zero-risk standard is neither realistic nor desirable, they claim.

• Allow the comparison of risks and benefits when issuing or revoking approval for an additive since there is no need to ban a product where risks have been shown to be small or are unproven, according to the industry. This is now being touted as the *de minimis* approach to carcinogens in the food supply. This legal term is generally interpreted as meaning that the law does not care for, or take notice of, very small or trifling matters. By not banning all the carcinogens or carcinogen-containing foods or food ingredients being used, the FDA has been applying a *de minimis* concept.[14, 15]

• Permit a gradual phaseout of a product, they ask, since immediately effective bans on food additives disrupt the food supply and can cause severe economic hardship.

The advocates of such changes point to nitrites as an example of risk and benefit. Nitrites combine with natural stomach chemicals to cause nitrosamines, powerful cancer-causing agents, but nitrites also prevent botulism, a potentially fatal illness caused by contaminated food. Since they claim there is no good substitute for nitrites, the benefits outweigh the risks.

Unfortunately, when it comes to potentially harmful food additives, we often take the risk while the food processors take the benefits. Food processors keep talking about "no-effect levels" and pointing out that one part per billion is equal to one inch in sixteen thousand miles. But how much exposure to a carcinogen does it take to damage a gene or to cause cancer in a child or adult? No one knows for certain. The FDA

---

[14] "Congress Eyes Major Rewrite of Nation's Food Safety Laws," *American Medical News*, June 24, 1983.

[15] Roger D. Middlekauf (partner in the law firm of McKenna, Conner and Cuneo, Washington, D.C.), "Delaney Meets De Minimis," *Food Technology*, November 1985, pp. 62–69.

estimates that exposure to DES—diethylstibestrol—as low as one part per trillion may be associated with the risk of one cancer per million consumer lifetimes. That's pretty low, except, of course, if you are that consumer.

The National Research Council reports that although the number and use of chemicals are high, very little is known about their hazards. A committee of the NRC found that no toxicity data are available for about 80 percent of forty-nine thousand commercially used chemicals. Toxicity data were either inadequate or nonexistent for 64 percent of eighteen hundred drugs, and 80 percent of eighty-six hundred food additives. The FDA's budget in 1989 for food safety was $132,265,000 for foods and cosmetics.[16] Of the 2,129 personnel assigned to the food and cosmetics divisions, there are 373 inspectors and 60 toxicologists that must cover the multibillion-dollar food and cosmetics industries with their hundreds of thousands of products. The FDA personnel, while well-intentioned, do not have the resources to prevent all potentially harmful food additives from reaching the market. Your knowledge is the best protection.

Generally Recognized as Safe (GRAS) List

The GRAS list was established in 1958 by Congress. Those substances that were being added to food over a long time which, under the conditions of their intended use, were generally recognized as safe by qualified scientists, would be exempt from premarket clearance. Congress had acted on a very marginal response—on the basis of returns from those scientists sent questionnaires. Approximately 355 out of 900 responded, and only about 100 of those responses had substantive comments. Three items were removed from the originally published list.

Since then, developments in the scientific fields and in consumer awareness brought to light the inadequacies of the testing of food additives and, ironically, the complete lack of testing of the generally recognized as safe category.

Cyclamates, the artificial sweeteners, were shown to be cancer-causing agents in laboratory animals and were removed from the market. They had been on the GRAS list. As a result, in 1969 President Richard Nixon directed the FDA to reevaulate all of the items on the GRAS list. The study of the GRAS substances has been conducted by an expert advisory group—the Select Committee on GRAS Substances of the Federation of American Societies for Experimental Biology.

---

[16] *FDA Talk Paper*, February 19, 1988, Washington, D.C.

By 1980, 415 substances that had been in use prior to the 1985 Food Additives Amendment to the Food, Drug, and Cosmetic Act were reviewed. The committee's evaluations were based on review of medical and scientific literature and unpublished reports. In some cases the research extended back sixty years. The number of references obtained for a given GRAS substance ranged from twenty-three reports for carnauba wax to two thousand for Vitamin A.

Of the 415 substances reviewed, 305 were given Class 1 status, which means they are considered safe for use at current levels and future anticipated levels under the conditions of good manufacturing practices.

Sixty-eight were placed in Class 2. They are considered safe for use at current levels, but the committee advised that more research is needed to determine whether a significant increase in consumption would constitute a dietary hazard. This category includes certain zinc salts, alginates, iron, tannic acid, sucrose, and Vitamins A and D.

Class 3 status was given to nineteen substances for which the committee recommended additional studies because of unresolved questions in research data. The FDA issued interim regulations for this class of ingredients requiring that certain safety tests be undertaken within a specific time but meanwhile permitting current use of the substances. Caffeine, BHA, and BHT were listed in this class.

Five substances—salt and four modified starches—were placed in Class 4, which means the committee recommended that FDA establish safer conditions for use or prohibit addition of the ingredients to food.

The committee said there is no evidence that salt hurts most people but suggested that a reduction of salt in processed foods would benefit the 10 to 30 percent of the United States population genetically predisposed to high blood pressure and might thus reduce the frequency of hypertension.

Restrictions were also recommended on some starches—distarch glycerol and hydroxypropyl, acetylated and succinyl distarch glycerol—used primarily as thickening agents.

In addition, the use of lactic acid and calcium lactate was placed in this category for exclusion from infant formulas because of reports of adverse effects. They are no longer used in infant formulas, except when needed in special medical compounds.

Class 5 had eighteen substances about which, the committee said, there were insufficient data to make any evaluation. These substances include some glycerides and certain iron salts. The FDA proposes removing these substances from the GRAS list unless sufficient data become available for evaluation.

Approximately 100 new flavoring substances were designated as GRAS between 1980 and 1985, bringing the total of GRAS flavoring substances to 1,750.[17]

The expert committee evaluations and the questions raised about food additives continue. In the meantime, over 31 million Americans who are allergic to even the tiniest amount of some chemicals in foods (such allergic reactions ranging from a mild skin rash to death) can't wait. The disturbing questions of long-term toxicity and carcinogenicity remain.

The purpose of this dictionary is to enable you to look up any additive under its alphabetical listing to determine whether to continue with the product because it is beneficial or reject it in favor of something healthier. The dictionary includes most of the food additives in common use. For the sake of clarity and ease of use, their nearly fifty functions are grouped under the following broad categories:

Preservatives

These "antispoilants" are used to help prevent microbiological spoilage and chemical deterioration. They are of many different types, of which about one hundred are in common use.

Preservatives for fatty products are called antioxidants, which prevent the production of off flavors and off odors. These include benzoic acid used in margarine and butylated hydroxyanisole (BHA) used in lard, shortenings, crackers, soup bases, and potato chips.

In bread, preservatives are "mold" and "rope" inhibitors. They include sodium and calcium propionate, sodium diacetate, and such acetic substances as acetic acid and lactic acid.

Sorbic acid and sodium and potassium salts are preservatives used in cheeses, syrups, and pie fillings.

Preservatives used to prevent mold and fungus growth on citrus fruits are called "fungicides."

Sequestering agents, still another type of preservative, prevent physical or chemical changes that affect color, flavor, texture, or appearance. Ethylenediaminetetraacetic acid (EDTA) and its salts, for instance, are used to prevent the adverse effects of metals present in such products as soft drinks, where metal ions can cause clouding.

Sequestrants used in dairy products to keep them "fresh and sweet" include sodium, calcium, and potassium salts of citric, tartaric, and pyrophosphoric acids.

[17] B. L. Oser, et al, "GRAS Substances," *Food Technology*, November 1985, Vol. 39 (11), pp. 107–108, 110, 112.

Other common multipurpose preservatives are the gas, sulfur dioxide, propyl gallate, and, of course, sugar, salt, and vinegar.

Irradiated Food. When food is irradiated, it is loaded onto a conveyor belt and passed through a radiation cell where it is showered with beams of ionizing radiation produced by high radioactive isotopes. The radiation can inhibit ripening and kill certain bacteria and molds that induce spoilage, so that food looks and tastes fresh for up to several weeks. The process does not make food radioactive and does not change the food's color or texture in most cases. Does it destroy nutrients? Does it create radiolytic products in food after exposure that may cause genetic damage? Is irradiation less dangerous than some of the other chemicals added to foods as preservatives? These questions are being hotly debated.

The FDA requires food that has been irradiated to display on the label this international logo (a flower in a circle) and the words "treated by (or "with") irradiation."

Fresh Refrigerated Products. Fresh refrigerated products now account for $500 million of the $450 billion U.S. food industry, and they are expected to grow at 14 percent per year. These processed foods are designed to offer the convenience of frozen and canned foods while providing homemade taste and appearance. Typically, they are cooked just enough to ward off spoilage for a short period of time. As a further aid to freshness, they are often sealed in packaging that contains little or no oxygen, which can extend shelf life for several weeks. Scientists, however, are concerned that some dangerous bacteria may not be killed during the minimal precooking and that microorganisms that cause botulism can flourish in an oxygen-free environment. One publicized outbreak of botulism associated with fresh refrigerated food products could devastate the industry.

Acids, Alkalies, Buffers, Neutralizers

The degree of acidity or alkalinity is important in many processed foods. An acid such as potassium acid tartrate, sodium aluminum phosphate, or tartaric acid acts on the leavening agent in baked goods and releases the gas that causes the desired "rising." The flavor of many soft drinks other than cola is modified by the use of an acid such as citric acid from citrus fruits, malic acid from apples, or tartaric acid, a component of grapes. Phosphoric acid is used to give colas their "tangy" taste. The same acids that are used in soft drinks are also used in churning cream to help preserve the flavor and keep the quality of butter. Alkalies such as ammonium hydroxide in cocoa products and ammonium carbonate in candy, cookies, and crackers are employed to make the products more alkaline. Buffers and neutralizing agents are chemicals added to foods to control acidity or alkalinity, just as acids and alkalies are added directly. Some common chemicals in this class are ammonium bicarbonate, calcium carbonate, potassium acid tartrate, sodium aluminum phosphate, and tartaric acid.

Moisture Content Controls

Humectants are necessary in the production of some types of confections and candy to prevent drying out. Without a humectant, shredded coconut, for example, would not remain soft and pliable. Substances used for this purpose include glycerine, which retains the soft, moist texture in marshmallows, propylene glycol, and sorbitol. On the other hand, calcium silicate is used to prevent table salt from caking due to moisture absorption from the air.

Coloring Agents

Food colors of both natural and synthetic origin are extensively used in processed foods, and they play a major role in increasing the acceptability and attractiveness of these products. However, the indiscriminate use of color can conceal damage or inferiority, or make the product appear better than it actually is. The World Health Organization, in delineating some 140 different kinds of colorants, found many to be unsafe. Coal-tar colors were subject to a special provision in a 1938 law that required every coal-tar color used in food to be listed with the government as "harmless and suitable for use." Every batch of the color intended for use in food had to be certified by a government agency as safe. Some of the colors originally listed as "harmless" were found to produce injury when fed to animals and were removed from the list.

In 1960, the federal government required manufacturers to retest all artificial colors to determine safety. At present there are nine permanently listed as safe. Among them, FD and C Blue No. 1 and FD and C Citrus Red No. 2 have been shown to cause tumors at the site of injection in animals, but the FDA does not consider this significant because the experiment concerned injection by needle and not ingestion by food consumption or application on the skin. FD and C Red No. 40, one of the most widely used colorings, is also being questioned because it is made from a base known to be carcinogenic and because many scientists feel that it should not have been given permanent listing based solely on the manufacturer's tests.

Among the natural colors used in foods are alkanet, annatto, carotene, chlorophyll, cochineal, saffron, and turmeric. Foods that are frequently colored include candies, baked goods, soft drinks, and such dairy products as butter, cheese, and cream.

Flavorings

A wide variety of spices, natural extractives, oleoresins, and essential oils are used in processed foods. In addition, the modern flavor chemist has produced many synthetic flavors. Both types of products are used extensively in soft drinks, baked goods, ice cream, and confectionery. Flavoring agents are the most numerous additive; of the three thousand food additives known to be added to our food supply, two thousand are flavorings to replace the flavors lost during processing. Of these, some five hundred are natural and the balance synthetic. They are usually employed in amounts ranging from a few to three hundred parts per million. Amyl acetate, benzaldehyde, carvone, ethyl acetate, ethyl butyrate, and methyl salicylate are typical compounds employed in the preparation of flavoring materials. However, many of the compounds used in synthetic flavorings are also found in natural products or derive from natural acids. Essential oils, such as oil of lemon and oil of orange, are natural flavors made by extraction of the fruit rind. There are also flavor enhancers, the commonest being monosodium glutamate (MSG) and maltol.

Physiologic Activity Controls

The chemicals in this group are added to fresh foods to serve as ripeners or antimetabolic agents. For instance, ethylene gas is used to hasten the ripening of bananas and maleic hydrazide is used to prevent potatoes from sprouting. Coming into increasing use are enzymes that are of natural origin and generally believed to be nontoxic. Of all food enzyme additives, amylases, which act on starch, have the most numerous applications. Various amylases from plant, animal, fungal, and bacterial sources have been used to break down the components of starch to make it more digestible. Enzymes are also used in the fermentation of sugar to make candy, in the brewing industry, and in the manufacture of artificial honey, bread, and frozen milk concentrates.

Bleaching and Maturing Agents/Bread Improvers

Fresh-ground flour is pale yellow. Upon storage, it slowly becomes white and undergoes an aging process that improves its baking qualities. For more than fifty years, processors have added oxidizing agents to the flour to accelerate this process, thus reducing storage costs, spoilage, and the opportunity for insect infestation. Compounds such as benzoyl peroxide bleach the flour without effect on baking qualities. Other compounds, such as oxide of nitrogen, chlorine dioxide, nitrosyl chloride, and chlorine have both a bleaching and maturing or "improving" ability. Bread improvers used by the baking industry contain oxidizing substances such as potassium bromate, potassium iodate, and calcium peroxide. They also contain inorganic salts such as ammonium or calcium sulfate and ammonium phosphates, which serve as yeast foods and dough conditioners. Quantities used are relatively small since these can easily result in an inferior product. Bleaching agents may also be used in other foods such as cheese to improve the appearance of the finished product.

Processing Aids

Many chemicals fall into this category. Sanitizing agents, for instance, to clean bacteria and debris from products, are considered such aids. So are clarifying agents which remove extraneous materials. Tannin, for instance, is used for clarifying liquids in the wine and brewing industries. Gelatin and albumen remove small particles and minute traces of copper and iron in the production of vinegar and some beverages. Emulsifiers and emulsion stabilizers help to maintain a mixture and assure a consistency. They affect characteristics such as volume, uniformity, and fineness of grain (bakery products have a softer "crumb" and slower "firming" rate). They influence ease of mixing and smoothness, such as the whipping property of frozen desserts and the smoothness of cake mixes. They help maintain homogeneity and quality in such products as mayonnaise, candy, and salad dressing. Some common emulsifiers are lecithin, the monoglycerides and diglycerides, and propylene glycol alginate. Sorbitan derivatives are used to retard "bloom," the whitish deposits of high-melting components of cocoa butter that occasionally appear on the surface of chocolate candy. Food chemists sometimes call emulsifiers "surfactants" or "surface active-agents."

Texturizers or stabilizers are added to products to give them "body" and maintain a desired texture. For instance, calcium chloride or some other calcium salt is added to canned tomatoes and canned potatoes to keep them from falling apart. Sodium nitrate and sodium nitrite are used in curing meats to develop and stabilize the pink color. Nitrogen, carbon dioxide, and nitrous oxide are employed in pressure-packed containers of certain foods to act as whipping agents or as propellants. The texture of ice cream and other frozen desserts is dependent on the size of the ice crystals in the product. By adding agar-agar, gelatin, cellulose gum, or some other gum, the size of the ice crystals is stabilized. Texturizer gums are also used in chocolate milk to increase the viscosity of the product and to prevent the settling of cocoa particles to the bottom of the container. Gelatin, pectin, and starch are used in confectionery products to give a desired texture. Artificially sweetened beverages also need processing products to give a desired texture. Artificially sweetened beverages also need body-enhancing agents because they do not contain the "thickness" normally contributed by sugar. The thickeners employed include such natural gums as sodium alginate and pectins. The foaming properties of brewed beer can also be improved by the addition of texturizers.

Nutrition Supplements

Enrichment of food means that the natural nutrients have been removed during processing and then replaced. Enrichment of cereal foods, much touted by the big producers, according to them is supposed to provide 12 to 23 percent of the daily supply of thiamine, niacin, and iron, and 10 percent of the riboflavin recommended for human consumption.

Fortification of food means that additional nutrients are added to the product to make it more nutritious than it was before. For instance, Vitamin C is added to orange drinks and Vitamin A to margarine. Vitamin D is used to fortify milk to prevent rickets, and potassium iodide is added to iodized salt to prevent goiter, a thyroid tumor caused by iodine deficiency.

Amino acids, the building blocks of protein, may become commonly used as additives. The major use of amino acids in the food industry today is monosodium glutamate, which enhances flavor. Actually, the human body needs certain amino acids not manufactured in the body in sufficient amounts, and some processors add certain amino acids to increase the protein component of their product.

A number of additional substances are employed for various purposes. Certain sugar substitutes are used in food for persons who must restrict their intake of ordinary sweets. Saccharin and sorbitol are commonly used for this purpose. Glazes and polishes such as waxes and gum benzoin are used on coated confections to give luster to an otherwise dull surface. Magnesium carbonate and tricalcium phosphate are employed as anticaking agents in table salt, and calcium stearate is used for a similar purpose in garlic salt.

While unique in content, this dictionary follows the format of most standard dictionaries. The following are sample entries with any explanatory notes that may be necessary.

MARJORAM, POT • Sweet Marjoram. The natural extract of the flowers and leaves of two varieties of the fragrant marjoram plant. The *oleoresin* (*see*) is used in sausage and spice flavorings for condiments and meats. The *seed* is used in sausage and spice flavorings for meats (3,500 ppm) and condiments. Sweet marjoram is used in sausage and spice flavorings for beverages, baked goods (2,000 ppm), condiments, meats, and soups. The *sweet oil* is used in vermouth, wine, and spice flavorings for beverages, ice creams, ices, candy, baked goods, and condiments. Also used in hair preparations, perfumes, and soaps. Can irritate the skin. The redness, itching, and warmth experienced when applied to the skin are caused by local dilation of the blood vessels or by contraction of the smooth muscles. May produce allergic reactions. Essential oils such as marjoram are believed to penetrate the skin easily and produce systemic effects. GRAS.

We have learned that marjoram is a natural flavoring extract and that there are two varieties called pot and sweet marjoram whose oleoresin, seed, and sweet oil are used in food and beverage flavorings and in other product fragrances. By looking up *oleoresin* we learn that it is "a thick, sticky product obtained when a substance is extracted from a plant by a solvent and the solvent is then removed." The ppm figures stand for parts for million, that is 3,500 parts of marjoram is added to a million parts of meat. However, because ppm amounts (they do not appear on labels) represent maximum rather than actual usage, they are not reliable estimates of consumption, and are included here only to show how amounts can be relatively quite large or small. "No known toxicity" is not necessarily an assurance that an additive is absolutely harmless but merely that no deleterious effects have been recorded in the literature. GRAS means, of course, that the item is on the government's generally recognized as safe list, without having undergone thorough laboratory testing. ("GRAS in packaging" means that even though substances from the containers may migrate into the food, they are assumed not harmful.)

WORMWOOD • Absinthium.   A European woody herb with a bitter taste, used in bitters and liquor flavoring for beverages and liquors. The *extract* is used in bitters, liquor, and vermouth flavorings for beverages, ice cream, candy, and liquors, and in making absinthe. The *oil* is dark green to brown and a narcotic substance. Used in bitters, apple, vermouth, and wine flavorings for beverages, ice cream, ices, candy, baked goods, and liquors. In large doses or frequently repeated doses, it is a narcotic poison, causing headaches, trembling, and convulsions. Ingestion of the volatile oil or of the liquor, absinthe, may cause gastrointestinal symptoms, nervousness, stupor, coma, and death.

Absinthium, of course, is another name for wormwood and is cross-referenced in the dictionary. Source material for the comments on toxicity are indicated in the notes at the end of the dictionary. A similar example is the entry for lye.

SODIUM SESQUICARBONATE • Lye. White crystals, flakes, or powder produced from sodium carbonate. Soluble in water. Used as a neutralizer for butter, cream, fluid milk, ice cream, in the processing of olives before canning, cacao products, and canned peas. Used as an alkalizer in bath salts, shampoos, tooth powders, and soaps. Irritating to the skin and mucous membranes. May cause allergic reaction in the hypersensitive. The final report to the FDA of the Select Committee on GRAS Substances stated in 1980 that it should continue its GRAS status with no limitations other than good manufacturing practices.

Under the entry *ACACIA. Gum Arabic. Catechu,* the first two terms are used interchangeably. *Catechu* (from the Latin *Acacia catechu*) is less commonly used. Under the entry *ACETALDEHYDE. Ethanal,* the term *ethanal* is used interchangeably with *acetaldehyde.*

Some chemicals that are derived from a natural source are considered synthetic because they represent only a portion of the original compound or because other chemicals have been added. For instance:

NONANAL • Pelargonic Aldehyde. Colorless liquid with an orange-rose odor. A synthetic flavoring that occurs naturally in lemon oil, rose, sweet orange oil, mandarin, lime, orris, and ginger. Used in lemon and fruit flavorings for beverages, ice cream, ices, candy, baked goods, chewing gum, and gelatin desserts. Used also in perfumery. No known toxicity. *See* Aldehyde.

Terminology generally has been kept to a middle road between technician and average interested citizen, while at the same time avoiding oversimplification of data. If in doubt, look up any terms, which, in the same manner as the additives, are listed alphabetically, such as *anhydride,* or *demulcent, emollient, extract, isolate* (used in its chemical context), *oleoresin, mutagenic, subacute, teratogenic* and so on.

With *A Consumer's Dictionary of Food Additives* you will be able to work with the current labels to determine the purpose and the desirability or toxicity of the additives listed. You will be able to assert your right to wholesome food along with a wholesome environment. By knowing the options in the marketplace, by rejecting those products that are needlessly costly or unsafe or unpalatable in favor of "clean" food, you strike back at the greed and ignorance of many in the food industry and reward those manufacturers who deserve your purchases.

Presently, some legislators and consumer groups are fighting for more pervasive and informed labeling. Consequently, more chemicals included in this dictionary may be expected to appear on food labels, their identities at last revealed.

Consumer groups are demanding that all foods, including standard foods, carry labeling showing all ingredients. The FDA has published a proposed regulation requiring manufacturers to list sources of fats in processed foods to allow consumers to avoid certain fats, such as polyunsaturated fats, in dietary foods, and requiring labels on baby foods to state the protein content. Consumer action groups want more They want nutritional labeling on all foods, including calories, protein content, mineral elements, vitamins, and fat levels. We hope they will succeed.

There is little doubt that what we eat affects our health. Our bodies are wonderful machines that can detoxify and render harmless many poisons we ingest; however, we don't want to overburden our bodies by taking unnecessary chances. Certainly, not all food additives are harmful. Some, in fact, are greatly beneficial. It is all a matter of judgment. This book is intended to take the guesswork out of the chemicals in the food we eat so that you can make wiser choices.

A

ABIES ALBA MILLS • *See* Pine Needle Oil.

ABIETIC ACID • Sylvic Acid. Chiefly a texturizer in the making of soaps. A widely available natural acid, water-insoluble, prepared from pine rosin, usually yellow, and comprised of either glassy or crystalline particles. Used also in the manufacture of vinyls, lacquers, and plastics. Employed to carry nutrients that are added to enriched rice in amounts up to .0026 percent of the weight of the nutrient mixture. Little is known about abietic acid toxicity; it is harmless when injected into mice but causes paralysis in frogs and is slightly irritating to human skin and mucous membranes. May cause allergic reactions.

ABSINTHIUM • Extract or Oil. *See* Wormwood.

ABSOLUTE • The term refers to a plant-extracted material that has been concentrated, but that remains essentially unchanged in its original taste and odor (*see* Jasmine Absolute). Often called "natural perfume materials" because they are not subjected to heat and water as are distilled products. *See* Distilled.

ACACIA • Gum Arabic. Catechu. Acacia is the odorless, colorless, tasteless dried exudate from the stem of the acacia tree grown in Africa, the Near East, India, and the southern United States. Its most distinguishing quality among the natural gums is its ability to dissolve rapidly in water. The use of acacia dates back 4,000 years, when the Egyptians employed it in paints. Its principal use in the confectionery industry is to retard sugar crystallization and as a thickener for candies, jellies, glazes, and chewing gum. As a stabilizer, it prevents chemical breakdown in food mixtures. Gum acacia is a foam stabilizer in the soft drink and brewing industries. Also used for mucilage, the gum gives form and shape to tablets. In 1976 the FDA placed acacia in the GRAS category as an emulsifier, flavoring agent, processing aid, and stabilizer in beverages at 2.0 percent, chewing gum at 5.6 percent; as a formulation aid, stabilizer, and humectant in confections and frostings at 12.4 percent; as a humectant, stabilizer, and formulation aid in hard candy at 46.5 percent; in soft candy at 85 percent; in nut formulations at 1.0 percent; and in all other food categories at 8.3 percent of the product. It is permitted as an optional ingredient in a standardized food (which are not required to list ingredients on the label). Medically, it is used as a demulcent to soothe irritations, particularly of the mucous membranes. It slightly reduces cholesterol in the blood. It can cause allergic reactions such as skin rash and asthmatic attacks. Oral toxicity is low. *See also* Vegetable Gums and Catechu Extract. GRAS.

ACENAPHTHYLENE • White needles derived from coal tar, insoluble in water. Used as a dye intermediate in pharmaceuticals, insecticides, fungicides, and plastics. *See* Coal Tar.

ACER SPICATUM LAM • *See* Mountain Maple Extract.

ACEROLA • Used as an antioxidant. Derived from the ripe fruit of the West Indian or Barbados cherry grown in Central America and the West Indies. A rich source of ascorbic acid. Used in Vitamin C. No known toxicity.

ACESULFAME K • Acesulfame Potassium. Sunette. In a petition filed in September 1982, the American Hoechst Corporation asked for approval to make this nonnutritive sweetener two hundred times sweeter than table sugar for use in chewing gum, dry beverage mixes, confections, canned fruit, gelatins, puddings, custards, and as a tabletop sweetener. The petition, including 15 volumes of research studies, said the sweetener is not metabolized and would not add calories to the diet. The FDA approved acesulfame K on July 27, 1988, for use in dry food products and for sale in powder form or tablets that can be applied directly by the consumer. It has about the same sweetening power as aspartame (*see*), but unlike aspartame, has no calories. As of this writing, Hoechst was seeking approval to use acesulfame K as an ingredient in liquids and baked goods and candies. The sweetener has previously been approved for use in twenty countries including France and Britain.

The Food and Drug Administration said that four long-term animal studies in dogs, mice, and rats had not shown any toxic effects that could be pinned on the sweetener. However, the Center for Science in the Public Interest, a Washington, D.C.–based consumer group, sent a warning to the FDA more than six months before the sweetener's approval saying that animals fed acesulfame K in two different studies suffered more tumors than others that did not receive the compound. In another study cited by CSPI, diabetic rats had a higher blood level of cholesterol when fed the sweetener.

The FDA said in a press release that it had considered the center's concerns and concluded that "any tumors found were typical of what could routinely be expected and were not due to feeding with acesulfame K."

Hoeschst said that Sunette is not metabolized by the body and is excreted unchanged by humans and animals.

ACETAL • A volatile liquid derived from acetaldehyde (*see*) and alcohol and used as a solvent in synthetic perfumes such as jasmine. Also used in fruit flavorings (it has a nutlike aftertaste) and as a hypnotic in medicine. It is a central nervous system depressant, similar in action to paraldehyde but more toxic. Paraldehyde is a hypnotic and sedative whose side effects are respiratory depression, cardiovascular collapse, and possible high blood pressure reactions. No known skin toxicity.

ACETALDEHYDE • Ethanal. An intermediate (*see*) and solvent in the manufacture of perfumes. A flammable, colorless liquid, with a characteristic odor, occurring naturally in apples, broccoli, cheese, coffee, grapefruit, and other vegetables and fruit and used as a flavoring. Also used in the manufacture of synthetic rubber and in the silvering of mirrors. It is irritating to the mucous membranes, and ingestion of large doses may cause death by respiratory paralysis. Its ability to depress the central nervous system is greater than that of formaldehyde (*see*), and ingestion produces symptoms of drunkenness. Acetaldehyde is thought to be a factor in the toxic effect caused by drinking alcohol after taking the anti-alcohol drug Antabuse. Inhalation, usually limited by intense irritation of lungs, can also be toxic. Skin toxicity not identified. GRAS.

ACETALDEHYDE PHENETHYL PROPYL ACETAL PETITAL • A synthetic fruit flavoring agent for beverages, ice cream, ices, candy, and baked goods. See Acetaldehyde for toxicity.

***p*-ACETAMIDOBENZOIC ACID** • *See* Benzoic Acid.

ACETANISOLE • A synthetic flavoring agent, colorless to pale yellow solid, with an odor of hawthorne or hay, moderately soluble in alcohol and most fixed oils. Acetanisole is used in butter, caramel, chocolate, fruit, nut, and vanilla flavorings, which go into beverages, ice cream, ices, candy, baked goods, and chewing gum. No known toxicity.

ACETATE • Salt of acetic acid (*see*) used in liquor, nut, coffee, vanilla, honey, pineapple, and cheese flavorings for beverages, ice cream, sherbets, cakes, cookies, pastries, and candy. Also used in perfumery. May be irritating to the stomach if consumed in large quantities.

ACETIC ACID • Solvent for gums, resins, and volatile oils. It stops bleeding and stimulates the scalp. A clear colorless liquid with a pungent odor, it is used in freckle-bleaching lotions, hand lotions, and hair dyes. It occurs naturally in apples, cheese, cocoa, coffee, grapes, skimmed milk, oranges, peaches, pineapples, strawberries, and a variety of other fruits and plants. Vinegar is about 4 to 6 percent acetic acid and essence of vinegar is about 14 percent. It is used as a pickling and curing agent and as a flavor enhancer in cheese, soda water, and animal feeds. Can be used in standardized foods and thus need not be listed on the label. In its glacial form (without much water) it is highly corrosive and its vapors are capable of producing lung obstruction. Less than 5 percent acetic acid in solution is mildly irritating to the skin. It caused cancer in rats and mice when given orally or by injection. GRAS.

ACETIC ANHYDRIDE • Acetyl Oxide; Acetic Oxide. Colorless liquid with a strong odor, it is derived from oxidation of acetaldehyde (*see*). It is used as a dehydrating and acetylating agent (*see* Dehydrated and Acetylated) and in the production of dyes, perfumes, plastics, food starch, and aspirin. It is a strong irritant and may cause burns and eye damage.

ACETIC ETHER • Ethyl Acetate. A synthetic agent, transparent, colorless liquid with a fragrant, refreshing odor, used in butter, butterscotch, fruit, nut, and spice flavorings for beverages, ice cream, ices, candy, baked goods (1,000 ppm) and chewing gum (4,000 ppm). Also a coating for vegetables. *See* Ethyl Acetate.

ACETOACETIC ESTER • *See* Ethyl Acetoacetate.

ACETOIN • Acetyl Methyl Carbinol. A flavoring agent and aroma carrier used in perfumery, it occurs naturally in broccoli, grapes, pears, cultured dairy products, cooked beef, and cooked chicken. As a product of fermentation and of cream ripened for churning, it is a colorless or pale yellow liquid or a white powder, has a buttery odor, and must be stored in a light-resistant container. It is used in raspberry, strawberry, butter, butterscotch, caramel, coconut, coffee, fruit, liquor, rum, nut, walnut, vanilla, cream soda, and cheese flavorings for beverages, ice cream, ices, candy, baked goods, margarine, gelatin desserts, cottage cheese, and shortenings. No known toxicity. GRAS.

ACETONE • A colorless ethereal liquid derived by oxidation or fermentation and used as a solvent for spices, in which not more than 30 ppm may be a residual in the product. It is also used in nail polish removers and nail finishes. It is obtained by fermentation and is frequently used as a solvent for airplane glue, fats, oils, and waxes. It can cause peeling and splitting of the nails, skin rashes on the fingers and elsewhere, and nail brittleness. Inhalation may irritate the lungs, and in large amounts it is narcotic, causing symptoms of drunkenness similar to ethanol (*see*).

ACETONE PEROXIDE • Acetone (*see*) to which an oxygen-containing compound has been added. A maturing agent for bleaching flour and dough. It has a sharp, acrid odor similar to hydrogen peroxide. A strong oxidizing agent, it can be damaging to the skin and eyes. The FDA is pursuing testing for short- and long-term mutagenic, teratogenic, subacute, and reproductive effects of this widely used additive. It is a regulated food additive and included in a specific food standard, which means it does not have to be listed on the label.

ACETOOLEIN • Obtained from fats and oils, it is one of the glycerides (*see*) that the Select Committee on GRAS Substances stated in 1980 should be GRAS with no limitations. *See also* Oleic Acid.

ACETOPHENONE • A synthetic agent derived from coal tar, with an odor of bitter almonds, used in strawberry, floral, fruit, cherry, almond, walnut, tobacco, vanilla, and tonka bean flavorings for beverages, ice creams, ices, candy, baked goods, gelatin desserts, and chewing gum. It occurs naturally in strawberries and tea and may cause allergic reactions.

ACETOSTEARIN • Obtained from fats and oils, it is one of the glycerides (*see*) that the Select Committee on GRAS Substances stated in 1980 should be GRAS with no limitations. It is used as a protective coating for food and as a plasticizer. *See also* Stearic Acid.

ACETYL BENZENE • *See* Acetophenone.

ACETYL BENZOYL PEROXIDE • White crystals decomposed by water and organic matter. Used in medicine as a germicide and disinfectant. It is used to bleach flour. Toxic when ingested.

ACETYL BUTYRYL • *See* 2, 3-Hexanedione.

ACETYL-*o*-CREOSOL • *See o*-Tolyl Acetate.

ACETYL-*p*-TOLYL ACETATE • See *p*-Tolyl Acetate.

ACETYL EUGENOL • *See* Eugenyl Acetate.

ACETYL FORMALDEHYDE • See Pyruvaldehyde.

ACETYL FORMIC ACID • *See* Pyruvaldehyde.

N-ACETYL-L-METHIONINE • (Free, Hydrated, Anhydrous, or Sodium or Potassium Salts). Nutrient supplement in foods except infant foods and products containing added nitrites/nitrates (*see* both). Also see Methionine.

ACETYL METHYL CARBINOL • *See* Acetoin.

ACETYL NONYRYL. • *See* 2, 3-Undecadione.

ACETYL PELARGONYL • *See* 2, 3-Undecadione.

ACETYL PENTANOYL • *See* 2, 3-Heptanedione.

ACETYL PROPIONYL • Yellow liquid. Soluble in water. Used as a butterscotch or chocolate-type flavoring. *See* Propyl Propionate.

p-ACETYL TOLUENE. • *See* Tolyl Acetate.

ACETYL TRIBUTYL CITRATE • *See* Citric Acid.

ACETYL TRIETHYL CITRATE • A clear, oily, essentially odorless liquid used as a solvent. *See* Citric Acid.

ACETYL TRIOCETYL CITRATE PECTIN • Citrus Pectin. A jelly-forming powder obtained from citrus peel and used as a texturizer and thickening agent to form gels with sugars and acids. Light in color. It has no known toxicity.

ACETYL VALERYL • Yellow liquid used as cheese, butter, and miscellaneous flavors. *See* 2, 3-Heptanedione.

ACETYL VANILLIN • *See* Vanillin Acetate.

ACETYLATED • Any organic compound that has been heated with acetic anhydride or acetyl chloride to remove its water. Acetylation is used to coat candy and other foods to hold in moisture. Acetic anhydride produces irritation and necrosis of tissues in vapor state and carries a warning against contact with skin and eyes. *See* Acetic Anhydride.

ACETYLATED DISTARCH ADIPATE AND PHOSPHATE • Starches (*see*) that have been modified to change their solubility and digestibility. The Select Committee on GRAS Substances stated in 1980 that there is no available evidence that demonstrates or suggests a hazard to the public when they are used at levels now current and in the manner now practiced. However, it is not possible to determine, without additional data, whether a significant increase in consumption would constitute a dietary hazard. They can continue GRAS with limitations on amounts that can be added to food.

ACETYLATED DISTARCH PROPANOL • A starch (*see*) that has been modified to change its solubility and digestibility. The final report to the FDA of the Select Committee on GRAS Substances stated in 1980 that although no evidence in the available information on it demonstrates a hazard to the public at current use levels, uncertainties exist requiring that additional studies be conducted. GRAS status is continued while tests are being completed and evaluated, the FDA said in 1980. Since then, no action has been reported.

ACETYLATED HYDROGENATED COTTONSEED GLYCERIDE • *See* Cottonseed Oil.

ACETYLATED HYDROGENATED LARD GLYCERIDE • *See* Lard.

ACETYLATED HYDROGENATED VEGETABLE GLYCERIDE • *See* Vegetable Oils.

ACETYLATED MONOGLYCERIDES • Emulsifiers used in food, food processing, and food packaging restricted only according to good manufacturing practices.

ACETYLATED SUCROSE DISTEARATE • The acetyl ester of sucrose distearate (*see* Ester and Sucrose Distearate).

ACETYLISOEUGENOL • Isoeugenol acetate. White crystals with a spicy, clovelike odor, it is used as an aroma and flavor carrier in foods. In perfumery, it is used especially for carnation-type odors.

ACETYLMETHYLCARBINOL • Slightly yellow liquid or crystals used as an aroma and flavor carrier *See* Acetoin.

ACHILLEIC ACID • *See* Aconitic Acid.

ACID • An acid is a substance capable of turning blue litmus paper red and of forming hydrogen ions when dissolved in water. An acid aqueous solution is one that has a pH (*see*) of less than 7. Citric acid (*see*) is an example of a widely used acid in foods.

ACID-MODIFIED STARCHES • Usually made by mixing an acid—such as hydrochloric or sulfuric—with water and starch at temperatures too low for gelatinization. When the starch has been reduced in viscosity to the degree desired, the acid is neutralized and the starch is filtered, washed, and dried. It is done so that starches can be cooked and used at higher concentrations than unmodified starches. Acid-modified starches are often used for salad dressings and puddings and as inexpensive thickening agents. The final report to the FDA of the Select Committee on GRAS Substances stated in 1980 that acid-modified starches are GRAS with no limitations.

ACID POTASSIUM SULFITE • *See* Sulfites.

ACIDOPHILUS • A type of bacteria that ferments milk and has been used medically to treat intestinal disorders.

ACIDS • *See* Acidulants.

ACIDULANTS • Acids. An acid is a substance capable of turning blue litmus paper red and of forming hydrogen ions when dissolved in water. An acid aqueous solution is one with a pH (*see*) less than 7. Acidulants are acids that make a substance more acid and function as flavoring agents to acidify taste, to blend unrelated flavoring characteristics, and to mask any undesirable aftertaste. Acidulants are also used as preservatives to prevent germ and spore growths that spoil foods. Acidulants control the acid-alkali (pH) balance and are used in meat curings to enhance color and flavor and as a preservative. Among the most common acids added to foods are acetic, propionic, and sorbic (*see* all).

ACONITIC ACID • Citridic Acid. Equisetic Acid. Achilleic Acid. A flavoring agent found in beetroot and cane sugar. Most of the commercial aconitic acids, however, are manufactured by sulfuric acid dehydration of citric acid. It is used in fruit, brandy, and rum flavorings for beverages, ice cream, ices, candy, baked goods, liquors, and chewing gum. Also used in the manufacture of plastics and buna rubber. No known toxicity. GRAS.

ACRYLATE-ACRYLAMIDE RESIN • Acrylic Acid. Colorless, odorless crystals soluble in water and derived from acrylonitrile and sulfuric acid. It is used as a clarifying agent in beet sugar and cane sugar juice and liquor or corn starch hydrolyzate (5 ppm by weight of juice, 10 ppm by weight of liquor or hydrolyzate). The acid is the synthesis of this acrylic resin. It is also used in the manufacture of dyes, adhesives, and in permanent-press fabrics, nail enamels, and face masks. It is toxic if absorbed through the skin.

ACRYLATES • Salts or esters of acrylic acid used as thickening agents and protective coatings for fruits and vegetables. Strong irritants.

ACRYLIC RESINS • Polymers (*see* Polymer) of acrylics. Used in waxy oils, base coats, protective coatings, and waterproofing. Acrylates (*see*) if inhaled, can cause allergic reactions.

ACRYLONITRILE COPOLYMERS • Used in packaging for food on an "interim basis" according to the FDA. *See* Acrylic Resins.

ACTADECYLSILOXYDIMETHYLSIOLOXYPOLYSILOXANE • A component of defoamers (*see*) used in processing beets and yeast. No known toxicity.

ACTIVATED CHARCOAL (CARBON) • Used to remove impurities that cause undesirable color, taste, or odor in liquid. The major sources are lignite, coal, and coke. The Select Committee of the Federation of American Societies for Experimental Biology (FASEB), under contract to the FDA, concluded that it is not a hazard to human health at current or possible future use levels. However, the committee said because the substance is extensively used in the food industry, it would be prudent to have purity specifications for food-grade activated carbon to assure the absence of any cancer-causing hydrocarbons in food.

ACTIVATED 7-DEHYDROCHOLESTEROL • *See* Vitamin D_3.

ADENOSINE • White crystalline powder with mild saline or bitter taste. It is isolated by the hydrolysis of yeast nucleic acid.

ADENOSINE PHOSPHATE • *See* Adenosine Triphosphate.

ADENOSINE TRIPHOSPHATE • Adenylic Acid. An organic compound that is derived from adenosine (*see*). A fundamental unit of nucleic acid, it serves as source of energy for biochemical transformation in plants, photosynthesis, and also for many chemical reactions in the body, especially those associated with muscular activity.

ADIPIC ACID • Hexanedoic Acid. Colorless needlelike formations, fairly insoluble in water; found in beets. A buffering and neutralizing agent impervious to humidity. Used in flavorings for beverages and gelatin desserts (5,000 ppm) to impart a smooth-tart taste. Also used as a buffer and neutralizing agent in confections, but limited to 3 percent of contents; in the manufacture of plastics and nylons, and as a substitute for tartaric acid (*see*) in baking powders because it is impervious to humidity. No known toxicity. The final report to the FDA of the Select Committee on GRAS Substances stated in 1980 that it should continue its GRAS status with no limitations other than good manufacturing practices.

ADIPIC ANHYDRIDE • A starch-modifying agent, not to exceed 0.12 percent of the starch compound. No known toxicity. *See* Modified Starch.

AEROSOL • Small particles of material suspended in gas.

AGAR-AGAR • Japanese Isinglass. A stabilizer and thickener, it is transparent, odorless, and tasteless, and obtained from various seaweeds found in the Pacific and Indian oceans and the Sea of Japan. Agar was the first seaweed to be extracted, purified, and dried. Discovered by a Japanese innkeeper around 1658 and introduced in Europe and the United States by visitors from China in the 1800s as a substitute for gelatin, it goes into beverages, ice cream, ices, frozen custard, sherbet, meringue, baked goods, jelly, frozen candied sweet potatoes, icings, confections, and artificially sweetened jellies and preserves. It can be 1.2 percent of candy and 0.25 percent of frozen desserts, jelly, and preserves. Agar serves as a substitute for gelatin and is used for thickening milk and cream. It is also a bulk laxative. Aside from causing an occasional allergic reaction, it is nontoxic. The final report to the FDA of the Select Committee on GRAS Substances stated in 1980 that there is no evidence in the available information that it is a hazard to the public when used as it is now and it should continue its GRAS status with limitations on amounts that can be added to food.

AGAVE LECHUGUILLA • American Aloe. Native to the warm part of the United States, and known by its heavy, stiff leaf and tall panicle or spike of candelabralike flowers. The leaves are used for juice employed in cosmetics as an adhesive and in medicines as a diuretic. The fermented juice is popular in Mexico for its distilled spirit (mescal). Some species are cultivated for their fibers, which are used in thread and rope. No known toxicity.

AGRIMONY EXTRACT • An extract of *Agrimonia eupatoria,* an herb found in northern temperate regions. It has yellow flowers and bristly fruit.

ALANINE • Colorless crystals derived from protein. Believed to be a nonessential amino acid. It is used in microbiological research and as a dietary supplement in the L and DL forms. The FDA has asked for supplementary information. It is now GRAS for addition to food. It caused cancer of the skin in mice and tumors when injected into their abdomens.

ALAR[12] • *See* Diaminozides.

ALBUMIN (ALBUMEN) • A group of simple proteins composed of nitrogen, carbon, hydrogen, oxygen, and sulfur that are soluble in water. Albumin is usually derived from egg whites and employed as an emulsifier in foods and cosmetics. It may cause a reaction to those allergic to eggs. Large amounts can produce symptoms of lack of biotin, a growth factor in the lining of the cells.

ALCOHOL • Ethyl Alcohol. Ethanol. Alcohol as a solvent is widely used in the cosmetics and food fields. Alcohol is manufactured by the fermentation of starch, sugar, and other carbohydrates. It is clear, colorless, and flammable, with a somewhat pleasant odor and a burning taste. Medicinally used externally as an antiseptic and internally as a stimulant and hypnotic. *Absolute Alcohol* is ethyl alcohol to which a substance has been added to make it unfit for drinking. *Rubbing Alcohol* contains not less than 68.5 percent and not more than 71.5 percent by volume of absolute alcohol and a remainder of denaturants, such as perfume oils. Toxic in large doses.

ALDEHYDE, ALIPHATIC • A class of organic chemical compounds intermediate between acids and alcohols. Aldehyde contains less oxygen than acids and less hydrogen than alcohols. Formaldehyde (*see*), a preservative, is an example of an aldehyde widely used in cosmetics. Benzaldehyde and cinnamic aldehydes (*see* both) are used in flavorings. Most are irritating to the skin and gastrointestinal tract.

ALFALFA • Herb and Seed. Lucerne. Extract of *Medicago sativa*. A natural cola, liquor, and maple flavoring agent for beverages and cordials. Alfalfa is widely cultivated for forage and is a commercial source of chlorophyll (*see*). No known toxicity.

ALGAE, BROWN • Kelp. Ground, dried seaweed used to carry natural spices, seasonings, and flavorings. A source of alginic acid (*see*). Also used in chewing-gum base. All derivatives of alginic acid are designated "algin." The food industry is one of the major users of alginates (*see*) along with the pharmaceutical, cosmetics, rubber, and paper industries. The United States is the largest producer of alginates. Algae is claimed to prevent wrinkles and to moisturize the skin, but the American Medical Association denies any validity to claims for algae's therapeutic benefits. However, seaweed products are widely used in cosmetics for many purposes. The final report to the FDA of the Select Committee on GRAS Substances stated in 1980 that it should continue its GRAS status with no limitations other than good manufacturing practices. Nontoxic.

ALGAE MEAL, DRIED • Permanently listed to be used in chicken feed to enhance color of chicken skin and egg yolks. No known toxicity.

ALGAE, RED • A natural extract of seaweed used to carry natural spices, seasonings, and flavorings. Nontoxic. GRAS. *See* Alginates.

ALGIN • The sodium salt of alginic acid (*see*), it is used in cheeses, frozen desserts, soda water, jellies, and preserves as a stabilizer. GRAS.

ALGINATES • Ammonium, Calcium, Potassium, and Sodium. All derivatives of alginic acid are designated "algin." Gelatinous substances obtained from certain seaweeds and used as stabilizers and water retainers in beverages, ice cream, ices, frozen custard, emulsions, desserts, baked goods, and confectionery ingredients. A clarifying agent for wine, chocolate milk, meat, toppings, cheeses, cheese spreads, cheese snacks, salad dressings, and artificially sweetened jelly and jam ingredients. Alginates are used also as stabilizers in gassed cream (pressure-dispensed whipped cream). The alginates assure a creamy texture and prevent formation of ice crystals in ice creams. Alginates have been used in the making of ice pops to impart smoothness of texture by ensuring that the fruit flavors are uniformly distributed throughout the ice crystals during freezing, helping the pops to retain flavor and color, and to stop dripping. The final report to the FDA of the Select Committee on GRAS Substances stated in 1980 that there is no evidence in the available information that it is a hazard to the public when used as it is now and it should continue its GRAS status with limitations on the amounts that can be added to food. Alginates are also used as emulsifiers in hand lotions and creams, and as thickening agents in shampoos, wave sets, and lotions. They are also used to protect the skin from irritants in hand creams and lotions, in the manufacture of celluloid, as an emulsifier in mineral oil, and in mucilage. Sodium alginate from brown seaweed is used as a thickener in dentifrices, but the FDA is testing the sodium form (largely used in ice cream) for short-term mutagenic birth-deforming, reproduction, and subacute effects.

ALGINIC ACID • It is obtained as a highly gelatinous precipitate from seaweeds. It is odorless and tasteless and is used as a stabilizer in ice cream, frozen custard, ice milk, fruit, sherbet, water ices, beverages, icings, cheeses, cheese spreads, cheese snacks, French dressing, and salad dressing. It is also used as a defoaming agent in processed foods. Capable of absorbing two hundred to three hundred times its weight of water and salts. Also used in sizing paper and textiles and as a stabilizer in cosmetics. The sodium carbonate (*see*) extracts of brown dried seaweeds are treated with acid to achieve the result. Resembles albumin or gelatin (*see* both). Alginic acid is slowly soluble in water, forming a very thick liquid. No known toxicity.

ALKALI • The term originally covered the caustic and mild forms of potash and soda. Now a substance is regarded as an alkali if it gives hydroxyl ions in solution. An alkaline aqueous solution is one with a pH (*see*) greater than 7. Sodium bicarbonate (*see*) is an example of an alkali that is used to neutralize excess acidity in cosmetics.

ALKANET ROOT • A red coloring obtained from extraction of the herblike tree root grown in Asia Minor and the Mediterranean. Used as a copper or blue coloring (when combined with metals) for hair oils and other cosmetics. It is also used as a coloring for wines, inks, and sausage casings. May be mixed with synthetic dyes for color tints. Formerly used as an astringent. Formerly commonly used, the authorization for use was withdrawn by the FDA in 1988.

ALKANIN • A red powder and the principal ingredient of alkanet root (*see*).

ALKYL • Usually derived from alkane, an alkyl is any one of a series of saturated hydrocarbons such as methane. The introduction of one or more alkyls into a compound makes the product more soluble. The mixture is usually employed with surfactants (*see*), which have a tendency to float when not alkylated.

ALKYL BETAINES • *See* Alkyl Sulfates.

ALKYL ETHER SULFATES • *See* Alkyl Sulfates.

ALKYL SULFATES • Surfactants (*see*) used in foods, drugs, and cosmetics. These compounds were developed by the Germans during World War II when vegetable fats and oils were scarce. A large number of alkyl sulfates have been prepared from primary alcohols by treatment with sulfuric acid (*see*); the alcohols are usually prepared from fatty acids (*see*). Alkyl sulfates are low in acute and chronic toxicity but may cause skin irritation.

ALLERGEN • A substance that provokes an allergic reaction in the susceptible but does not normally affect other people. Plant pollens, fungi spores, and animal danders are some of the common allergens.

ALLERGIC REACTION • An adverse immune response following repeated contact with otherwise harmless substances such as pollens, molds, foods, cosmetics, and drugs.

ALLERGY • An altered immune response to a specific substance, such as ragweed or pollen, on reexposure to it.

ALLOMALEIC ACID • See Fumaric Acid.

ALLSPICE • A natural flavoring from the dried berries of the allspice tree. Allspice is used in liquor, meat, and spice flavorings for beverages, ice cream, ices, candy, baked goods (1,400 ppm), chewing gum, condiments (1,000 ppm), and meats. *Allspice oleoresin* (a natural mixture of oil and resin) is used in sausage flavoring for baked goods, meats, and condiments. *Allspice oil* is used in sausage, berry, cola, peach, rum, nut, allspice, cinnamon, ginger, nutmeg, and eggnog flavorings for beverages, ice cream, ices, candy, baked goods, chewing gum (1,700 ppm), condiments, pickles, meats, liquors, and soups. Nontoxic. GRAS.

ALLYL ANTHRANILATE • A synthetic citrus fruit and grape flavoring agent for beverages, ice cream, ices, candy, baked goods, and gelatin desserts. No known toxicity.

ALLYL BUTYRATE • A synthetic butter, fruit and pineapple flavoring agent for beverages, ice cream, ices, candy, baked goods, and gelatin desserts. No known toxicity.

ALLYL CINNIMATE • A synthetic fruit and grape flavoring agent for beverages, ice cream, ices, candy, baked goods. No known toxicity.

ALLYL CYCLOHEXANE ACETATE • A synthetic pineapple flavoring agent for beverages, ice cream, ices, candy, baked goods. No known toxicity.

ALLYL CYCLOHEXANE BUTYRATE • A synthetic pineapple flavoring agent for beverages, ice cream, ices, candy, baked goods. No known toxicity.

ALLYL CYCLOHEXANE HEXANOATE • A synthetic fruit flavoring agent for beverages, ice cream, ices, candy, baked goods. No known toxicity.

ALLYL CYCLOHEXANE PROPIONATE • A synthetic, liquid and colorless with a pineapplelike odor, used in pineapple flavorings for beverages, ice cream, ices, candy, baked goods, gelatin desserts, puddings, chewing gum, and icings. No known toxicity.

ALLYL DISULFIDE • Found naturally in garlic and leeks, but considered a synthetic flavoring. It is used in garlic, onion, and spice flavorings for meats and condiments. No known toxicity.

ALLYL ENANTHATE • *See* Allyl Heptanoate.

ALLYL 2-ETHYLBUTYRATE • A synthetic berry, fruit, and brandy flavoring agent for beverages, ice cream, ices, candy, baked goods, gelatin desserts, and puddings. No known toxicity. GRAS.

ALLYL 2-FUROATE • A synthetic coffee and pineapple flavoring agent for beverages, ice cream, ices, candy, baked goods, and gelatin desserts. No known toxicity. GRAS.

ALLYL HEPTANOATE • A synthetic berry, fruit, and brandy flavoring agent for beverages, ice cream, ices, candy, baked goods, gelatin desserts, and chewing gum. No known toxicity. GRAS.

ALLYL HEXANOATE • A synthetic orange, strawberry, apple, apricot, peach, pineapple, and tutti-frutti flavoring agent for beverages, ice cream, ices, candy, baked goods, gelatin desserts, and toppings. No known toxicity. GRAS.

ALLYL a-IONONE • Cetone V. A synthetic agent, yellow, with a strong fruity, pineapplelike odor, used in fruit flavorings for beverages, ice cream, ices, candy, baked goods, gelatin desserts, and toppings. No known toxicity. GRAS.

ALLYL ISOTHIOCYANATE • Mustard Oil. A naturally occurring agent in mustard, horseradish, and onion used in meat and spice flavorings for beverages, ice cream, ices, candy, condiments, meat, and pickles. Colorless or pale yellow with a very pungent irritating odor and acrid taste. It is used also in the manufacture of war gas. Can cause blisters and other skin problems. Toxic.

ALLYL MERCAPTAN • A synthetic spice flavoring agent for beverages, ice cream, ices, candy, baked goods, and meats. No known toxicity.

4-ALLYL-2-METHOXYPHENOL • *See* Eugenol.

ALLYL NONANOATE • A synthetic fruit and wine flavoring agent for beverages, ice cream, ices, candy, baked goods, and meats. No known toxicity.

ALLYL OCTANOATE • A synthetic pineapple flavoring agent for beverages, ice cream, ices, candy, baked goods, and gelatin desserts. No known toxicity.

ALLYL PELARGONATE • A liquid with a fruity odor, used in flavors and perfumes.

ALLYL PHENOXYACETATE • Acetate PA. A synthetic fruit and grape flavoring agent for beverages, ice cream, ices, candy, baked goods, and gelatin desserts. No known toxicity.

ALLYL PHENYLACETATE • A synthetic pineapple and honey flavoring agent for beverages, ice cream, ices, candy, baked goods. No known toxicity.

ALLYL PROPIONATE • A synthetic pineapple flavoring agent for beverages, ice cream, ices, candy, baked goods. No known toxicity.

ALLYL SORBATE • A synthetic fruit and grape flavoring agent for beverages, ice cream, ices, candy, baked goods, and gelatin desserts. No known toxicity.

ALLYL SULFHYDRATE • *See* Allyl Mercaptan.

ALLYL SULFIDE • A synthetic fruit and grape flavoring agent for beverages, ice cream, ices, candy, baked goods, condiments, and meats. Occurs naturally in garlic and horseradish. Produces irritation of the eyes and respiratory tract. Readily absorbed through the skin. Acute exposure can cause unconsciousness. Long-term exposure can cause liver and kidney damage.

ALLYL TIGLATE • A synthetic fruit and grape flavoring agent for beverages, ice cream, ices, candy, baked goods. No known toxicity.

ALLYL 10-UNDECENOATE • A synthetic fruit flavoring agent for beverages, ice cream, ices, candy, baked goods. No known toxicity.

p-ALLYLANISOLE • *See* Estragole.

ALLYLTHIOL • *See* Allyl Mercaptan.

4-ALLYLVERATROLE • *See* Eugenyl Methyl Ether.

ALMOND OIL • Bitter Almond Oil. A flavoring agent from the ripe seed of a small tree grown in Italy, Spain, and France. Colorless or slightly yellow, strong almond odor, and mild taste. Used in cherry and almond flavorings for beverages, ice cream, ices, candy, baked goods, chewing gums, maraschino cherries, and gelatin desserts. Used also in the manufacture of liqueurs and perfumes. It is distilled to remove hydrocyanic acid (prussic acid), which is very toxic. Nontoxic without the hydrocyanic acid. GRAS.

ALOE VERA • A compound expressed from the aloe plant leaf from a South African lilylike plant. Used for supposed softening benefits in skin creams. It contains 99.5 percent water, with the remaining .5 percent composed of some 20 amino acids (*see*) and carbohydrates. There is no scientific evidence that aloe vera has any benefits in cosmetics according to the American Medical Association. Used in bitters, vermouth, and spice flavorings for beverages (2,000 ppm) and alcoholic drinks. It has been used as a cathartic but was found to cause severe intestinal cramps and sometimes kidney damage. Cross reacts with benzoin and balsam Peru (*see* both) in those who are allergic to these ingredients.

ALPHA TOCOPHEROL • *See* Tocopherols.

ALTHEA ROOT • Marshmallow Root. A natural flavoring substance from a plant grown in Europe, Asia, and the United States. The dried root is used in strawberry, cherry, and root-beer flavorings for beverages. The boiled root is used as a demulcent in ointments to soothe mucous membranes. The roots, flowers, and leaves are used externally as a poultice. Nontoxic.

ALUM • Potash Alum. Aluminum Ammonium. Potassium Sulfate. A colorless, odorless, crystalline, water-soluble solid used in astringent lotions, after-shave lotions, and as a styptic (stops bleeding). A double sulfate of aluminum and ammonium potassium, it is also employed to harden gelatin, size paper, or waterproof fabrics. In concentrated solutions alum has produced gum damage and fatal intestinal hemorrhages. It has a low level of toxicity in experimental animals but ingestion of 30 grams (an ounce) has killed an adult human. It is also known to cause kidney damage. Concentrated doses have damaged gums. Liquid alum has been found by Penn State researchers to be capable of removing over 99 percent of phosphates from waste-water effluent. GRAS when used in packaging only.

ALUMINUM • Silvery white, crystalline solid. It is frequently used in food additives and cosmetics. Ingestion or inhalation of aluminum can aggravate kidney and lung disorders. Aluminum deposits have been found in the brains of Alzheimer's victims but its part, if any, in this degenerative brain disorder is not clear.

ALUMINUM AMMONIUM SULFATE • Odorless, colorless crystals with a strong astringent taste. Used in purifying drinking water; in baking powders; as a buffer and neutralizing agent in milling; and in the cereal industries. Used also for fireproofing and in the manufacture of vegetable glue and artificial gems. In medicine, it is an astringent and styptic (stops bleeding). Ingestion of large amounts may cause burning in mouth and pharynx, vomiting, and diarrhea. The final report to the FDA of the Select Committee on GRAS Substances stated in 1980 that it should continue its GRAS status with no limitations other than good manufacturing practices.

ALUMINUM CALCIUM SILICATE • Anticaking agent used so that it is 2 percent of table salt. Used also in vanilla powder to prevent caking. Essentially harmless when given orally. GRAS.

ALUMINUM DISTEARATE • A binder that holds loose powders together when compressed into a solid cake form. *See* Aluminum Stearates.

ALUMINUM HYDROXIDE • An alkali used as a leavening agent in the production of baked goods. Mild astringent and alkali used in antiperspirants, dentrifices, and dusting powders. A white gelatinous mass used as a drying agent, catalyst, adsorbent, and coloring agent in many cosmetic processes. Also used as a gastric antacid in medicine. Practically insoluble in water but not in alkaline solutions. Aluminum hydroxide has a low toxicity but may cause constipation if ingested. The final report to the FDA of the Select Committee on GRAS Substances stated in 1980 that it should continue its GRAS status for packaging only with no limitations other than good manufacturing practices.

ALUMINUM ISOSTEARATES/LAURATES/STEARATES • The aluminum salt of a mixture of isostearic acid, lauric acid, and stearic acid (*see* all). Used as a gelling agent. No known toxicity.

ALUMINUM ISOSTEARATES/MYRISTATES • Myristates is the aluminum salt of a mixture of isostearic acid and myristic acid. Used as a gelling agent. No known toxicity. *See* Stearic Acid and Myristic Acid.

ALUMINUM ISOSTEARATES/PALMITATES • Palmitates is the aluminum salt of palmitic acid and isostearic acid. Used as a gelling agent. No known toxicity. *See* Palmitic Acid and Stearic Acid.

ALUMINUM LACTATE • The aluminum salts of lactic acid (*see* both).

ALUMINUM MYRISTATES/PALMITATES • Myristates is the aluminum salt of a mixture of palmitic acid and isostearic acid. Used as a gelling agent. No known toxicity. *See* Palmitic Acid and Stearic Acid.

ALUMINUM NICOTINATE • Used as a source of niacin in special diet foods, also as a medication to dilate blood vessels and to combine fat. Tablets of 625 milligrams are complex of aluminum nicotinate, nicotinic acid, and aluminum hydroxide. Side effects are flushing, rash, and gastrointestinal distress when taken in large doses.

ALUMINUM OLEATE • A yellow, thick, acidic mass, practically insoluble in water. Used in packaging, as lacquer for metals, in waterproofing, and for thickening lubricating oils. Low toxicity. The final report to the FDA of the Select Committee on GRAS Substances stated in 1980 that it should continue its GRAS status for packaging only with no limitations other than good manufacturing practices.

ALUMINUM PALMITATE • White granules, insoluble in water, used as a lubricant and waterproofing and packaging material. Also used to thicken petroleum and as an antiperspirant. The final report to the FDA of the Select Committee on GRAS Substances stated in 1980 that it should continue its GRAS status for packaging only with no limitations other than good manufacturing practices.

ALUMINUM PHOSPHIDE • Used to fumigate processed foods, the FDA requires that processors aerate the finished food for 48 hours before it is offered to the consumer. It further warns that under no conditions should the formulation containing aluminum phosphide be used so that it or its unreacted residues will come into contact with any processed foods. Reacts with moist air to produce the highly toxic phosphine. Residues of phosphine in or on processed food may not exceed .01 parts per million, according to the FDA. Phosphine may cause pain in the region of the diaphragm, a feeling of coldness, weakness, vertigo, shortness of breath, bronchitis, edema, lung damage, convulsions, coma, and death.

ALUMINUM POTASSIUM SULFATE • Colorless, odorless, hard, transparent crystals or powder with a sweet antiseptic taste used for clarifying sugar, and as a firming agent and carrier for leaching agents. It is used in the production of sweet and dill pickles, cereal, flours, bleached flours, and cheese. Ingestion of large quantities may cause burning in the mouth and throat and stomach distress. The final report to the FDA of the Select Committee on GRAS Substances stated in 1980 that it should continue its GRAS status with no limitations other than good manufacturing practices.

ALUMINUM SALTS OF FATTY ACIDS • Used as binders, emulsifiers, and anticaking agents. Regulated and used according to good manufacturing practices. See Aluminum Sodium Sulfate.

ALUMINUM SODIUM SULFATE • Firming agent and carrier for bleaching agents. (For other uses, see Aluminum Potassium Sulfate.) The final report to the FDA of the Select Committee on GRAS Substances stated in 1980 that it should continue its GRAS status with no limitations other than good manufacturing practices.

ALUMINUM STEARATES • Hard, plasticlike materials used in waterproofing fabrics, thickening lubricating oils, and as a chewing gum based component and a defoamer component used in processing beet sugar and yeast. Aluminum tristearate is a hard plastic material used as a thickener and coloring in cosmetics. No known toxicity.

ALUMINUM SULFATE • Cake Alum. Patent Alum. Colorless crystals, soluble in water. Odorless, with a sweet, mildly astringent taste. Used in producing sweet and dill pickles and as a modifier for starch. Also used as an antiseptic, astringent, and detergent in antiperspirants, deodorants, and skin fresheners; also purifies water. It may cause pimples under the arm when in antiperspirants and/or allergic reactions in some people but otherwise there is no known toxicity. The final report to the FDA of the Select Committee on GRAS Substances stated in 1980 that it should continue its GRAS status with no limitations other than good manufacturing practices.

AMARANTH • Red No. 2, banned by the FDA in 1976. The ban was reaffirmed in 1980.

AMARANTH FLOUR • A grain grown in Central and South America for thousands of years, it is high in protein and fiber. Because it costs more than other grains, it is usually found only in health food stores.

AMBERGRIS • Concretion from the intestinal tract of the sperm whale found in tropical seas. About 80 percent cholesterol, it is a gray to black waxy mass and is used for fixing delicate odors in perfumery. It is also used in a flavoring for food and beverages. No known toxicity. GRAS.

AMBRETTE • A natural flavoring agent from the seed of the hibiscus plant, clear yellow to amber as a liquid, with a musky odor. Seed used in berry and floral flavorings for beverages, ice cream, ices, candy, baked goods. The tincture is used in black walnut and vanilla flavorings for the same products and in cordials. The seed oil is used in fruit flavoring for beverages, ice cream, candy, and baked goods. No known toxicity. GRAS.

AMBRETTOLID • Formed in ambrette-seed oil. Used as a flavoring, perfume fixative. No known toxicity.

AMERICAN DILLSEED OIL • *See* Dill.

AMES TEST • Dr. Bruce Ames, a biochemist at the University of California, developed a simple, inexpensive test in the early 1970s using bacteria that reveals whether a chemical is a mutagen. Almost all chemicals that are known carcinogens have also been shown to be mutagenic on the Ames Test. Whether the test can identify carcinogens is still controversial.

AMINE OXIDES • Surfactants derived from ammonia (*see* both).

AMINO ACIDS • The body's building blocks, from which proteins are constructed. Of the twenty-two known amino acids, eight cannot be manufactured in the body in sufficient quantities to sustain growth health. These eight are called "essential" because they are necessary to maintain good health. A ninth, histidine, is thought to be necessary for growth only in childhood. Widely used in moisturizers and emollients because they are thought to help penetrate the skin. Certain amino acid deficiencies appear to have tumor-suppressing action. The amino acids of protein foods are separated by digestion and go into a general pool from which the body takes the ones it needs to synthesize its own personal proteins.

p-AMINOBENZOIC ACID • *See* Para-aminobenzoic Acid below.

PARA-AMINOBENZOIC ACID (PABA) • The colorless or yellowish acid found in Vitamin B complex and Brewer's yeast. In an alcohol and water solution with a little light perfume, it is sold under a wide variety of names as a sunscreen lotion to prevent skin damage from the sun. It is also used as a local anesthetic in sunburn products. It is used medicinally to treat arthritis. However, a product containing para-aminobenzoic acid applied to the skin can cause general allergic reactions. In susceptible people it can also cause a sensitivity to light so that the treated skin, once exposed to sunlight erupts with a rash, sloughing, and/or swelling.

6-AMINOCAPROIC ACID • See Amino Acids and Caproic Acid.

AMMONIA • Liquid used in the manufacture of surfactants (see) and hair bleaches. Obtained by blowing steam through incandescent coke. Ammonia is also used in the manufacture of explosives and synthetic fabrics. It is extremely toxic when inhaled in concentrated vapors, and is irritating to the eyes and mucous membranes. It may cause hair breakage when used in permanent waves and hair bleaches.

AMMONIATED GLYCYRRHIZIN • GRAS. See Licorice.

AMMONIUM ALGINATE • A stabilizer and water retainer. The report to the FDA of the Select Committee on GRAS Substances stated in 1980 that there is no evidence in the available information that it is a hazard to the public when used as it is now and it should continue its GRAS status with limitation on amounts that can be added to food. See Alginates.

AMMONIUM BICARBONATE • An alkali used as a leavening agent in the production of baked goods, confections, and cacao products. Usually prepared by passing carbon dioxide gas through concentrated ammonia water. Shiny, hard, colorless or white crystals; faint odor of ammonia. Used also in powder formulas in cooling baths. Used medicinally as an expectorant and to break up intestinal gas. Also used in compost heaps to accelerate decomposition. The final report to the FDA of the Select Committee on GRAS substances stated in 1980 that it should continue its GRAS status with no limitations other than good manufacturing practices.

AMMONIUM BITARTRATE • White crystals, soluble in water, derived from tartaric acid. Used in baking powder. No known toxicity.

AMMONIUM CARBONATE • A white solid alkali derived partly from ammonium bicarbonate (see) and used as a neutralizer and buffer in permanent wave solutions and creams. It decomposes when exposed to air. Also used in baking powders, for defatting woolens, in fire extinguishers, and as an expectorant. Ammonium carbonate can cause skin rashes on the scalp, forehead, or hands. The final report to the FDA of the Select Committee on GRAS Substances stated in 1980 that it should continue its GRAS status with no limitations other than good manufacturing practices.

AMMONIUM CASEINATE • The ammonium salt of casein, a protein occurring in milk and cheese. It is used in standard foods, particularly bakery products. Therefore, it does not have to be listed on the label. *See* Casein.

AMMONIUM CHLORIDE • Ammonium salt that occurs naturally. Colorless, odorless crystals or white powder, saline in taste, and incompatible with alkalies. Used as a dough conditioner and a yeast food in bread, rolls, buns, and so on. Saline in taste. Also used as an acidifier in permanent wave solutions, eye lotions, and as a cooling and stimulating skin wash. Industrially employed in freezing mixtures, batteries, dyes, safety explosives, and in medicine as a urinary acidifier and diuretic. Keeps snow from melting on ski slopes. If ingested, can cause nausea, vomiting, and acidosis in doses of 0.5 to 1 gram. Lethal as an intramuscular dose in rats and guinea pigs. As with any ammonia compound, concentrated solutions can be irritating to the skin. The final report to the FDA of the Select Committee on GRAS Substances stated in 1980 that it should continue GRAS status for packaging only with no limitations other than good manufacturing practices.

AMMONIUM CITRATE • The salt of citric acid (*see*), it is a natural constituent of plants and animals and dissolves easily in water, releasing free acid. Used as a sequestrant, flavor enhancer, and firming agent. The final report to the FDA of the Select Committee on GRAS Substances stated in 1980 that it should continue its GRAS status with no limitations other than good manufacturing practices.

AMMONIUM GLUCONATE • Prepared from gluconic acid with ammonia. It is used as an emulsifying agent for cheese and salad dressings. No known toxicity.

AMMONIUM HYDROXIDE • Ammonium Bicarbonate. Ammonia Water. A weak alkali formed when ammonia dissolves in water and exists only in solution. A clear colorless liquid with an extremely pungent odor. Used as a buffer and neutralizer in cocoa products and in animal feeds. Also used as an alkali (*see*) in metallic hair dyes, hair straighteners, and in protective skin creams. Also used in detergents and for removing stains. It is irritating to the eyes and mucous membranes. It may cause hair breakage. The final report to the FDA of the Select Committee on GRAS Substances stated in 1980 that it should continue its GRAS status for packaging only with no limitations other than good manufacturing practices.

AMMONIUM OLEATE • The ammonium salt of oleic acid (*see*) used as an emulsifying agent.

AMMONIUM ISOVALERATE • *See* Isovaleric Acid.

AMMONIUM PERSULFATE • Ammonium Peroxydisulfate. Odorless crystals or white powder. Used as an oxidizer and bleacher and as a modifier for food starch. *See* Modified Starch.

AMMONIUM PHOSPHATE • Monobasic and Dibasic. Ammonium salt. An odorless, white or colorless crystalline powder with a cooling taste used in mouthwashes. It is used as an acidic constituent of baking powder. Used as a buffer, leavening agent, and bread, roll, and bun improver up to 10 percent of product. Used in brewing industry. Also used in fireproofing textiles, paper, and wood and for purifying sugar, in yeast cultures, and in fertilizers. Monobasic is used as baking powder with sodium bicarbonate. Medically used for its saline action. It has a diuretic effect (reducing body water) and makes urine more acid. No known toxicity. The final report to the FDA of the Select Committee on GRAS Substances stated in 1980 that it should continues its GRAS status with no limitations other than good manufacturing practices.

AMMONIUM SACCHARIN • *See* Saccharin.

AMMONIUM SULFATE • Ammonium salt. A yeast food, dough conditioner, and buffer in bakery products. Colorless, odorless, white crystals or powder. A neutralizer in permanent wave lotions. Industrially used in freezing mixtures, fireproofing fabrics, and tanning. Used medicinally to prolong analgesia. No known toxicity when used cosmetically. Rats were killed when fed large doses. No known toxicity. The final report to the FDA of the Select Committee on GRAS Substances stated in 1980 that it should continue its GRAS status with no limitations other than good manufacturing practices. *See* Ammonium Phosphate for other uses.

AMMONIUM SULFIDE • A salt derived from sulfur and ammonium, it is used as a synthetic spice flavoring agent for baked foods and condiments. Also used as a neutralizer in permanent wave lotions, as a depilatory, to apply patina to bronze, and in film developers. May evolve into toxic hydrogen sulfide and a fatality has been reported from ingestion of ammonium sulfide "permanent wave" solution. Irritating to the skin when used in depilatories.

AMPHO • Means "double" or "both."

AMPHOTERIC • A material that can display both acid and basic properties. Used primarily in surfactants (*see*).

2-AMYL-59 or 60-KETO-1, 4-DIOXANE • A synthetic fruit flavoring agent for beverages, ice cream, ices, candy, baked goods, and shortening. No known toxicity.

AMYL ACETATE • Banana Oil. Pear Oil. Obtained from amyl alcohol, with a strong fruity odor. Used in nail finishes and nail polish remover as a solvent, and as an artificial fruit essence in perfume. Also used in food and beverage flavoring and for perfuming shoe polish.

Amyl acetate is a skin irritant and causes central nervous system depression when ingested. Exposure of 950 ppm for one hour has caused headache, fatigue, chest pain, and irritation of the mucous membranes.

AMYL ALCOHOL • A synthetic berry, chocolate, apple, banana, pineapple, liquor, and rum flavoring agent for beverages, ice cream, ices, candy, baked goods, gelatin desserts, and chewing gum. Used as a solvent in nail polish. It occurs naturally in cocoa and oranges and smells like camphor. Highly toxic and narcotic, ingestion of as little as 30 milligrams has killed humans. Inhalation causes violent coughing.

AMYL ALDEHYDE • *See* Valeraldehyde.

AMYL BUTYRATE • A synthetic flavoring agent, colorless, with a strong apricot odor. Occurs naturally in cocoa. Used in raspberry, strawberry, butter, butterscotch, fruit, apple, apricot, banana, cherry, grape, peach, pineapple, and vanilla flavorings for beverages, ice cream, ices, candy, baked goods, cherry syrup, and chewing gums. Used in some perfume formulas for its apricotlike odor. No known toxicity.

AMYL CAPRATE • *See* Cognac Oil

AMYL CINNAMIC ALDEHYDE • Liquid with a strong floral odor suggesting jasmine. Used in perfumes and flavorings. *See* Cinnamic Acid.

AMYL 2-FUROATE • A synthetic rum and maple flavoring agent for beverages, candy, baked goods, and condiments. No known toxicity.

AMYL GALLATE • An antioxidant obtained from nutgalls and from molds. No known toxicity.

AMYL HEPTANOATE • A synthetic lemon, coconut, fruit, and nut flavoring agent for beverages, ice cream, ices, candy, baked goods, gelatin desserts, puddings, and chewing gum. No known toxicity.

AMYL HEXANOATE • A synthetic citrus, chocolate, fruit, and liquor flavoring agent for beverages, ice cream, ices, candy, baked goods, and gelatin desserts. No known toxicity.

AMYL OCTANOATE • Occurs naturally in apples. A synthetic chocolate, fruit, and liquor flavoring agent for beverages, ice cream, ices, candy, baked goods, and gelatin desserts. No known toxicity.

a-AMYL-B-PHENYLACROLEIN BUXINE • *See* a-Amylcinnamaldehyde.

AMYL PROPIONATE • Colorless liquid with applelike odor used in perfumes, flavors, and lacquers. No known toxicity.

AMYLASE • An enzyme prepared from hog pancreas used in flour to break down starch into smaller sugar molecules. Then, in turn, the enzymes produced by yeast in the dough again split these sugar molecules to form carbon dioxide gas, which causes the dough to rise.

It improves crumb softness and shelf life. Used as a texturizer in cosmetics, it is also used medically to combat inflammation. Nontoxic.

A-AMYLCINNAMALDEHYDE • A synthetic agent, yellow, with a strong floral odor of jasmine, used in strawberry, apple, apricot, peach, and walnut flavorings for beverages, ice cream, ices, candy, baked goods, gelatin desserts, and chewing gum. Very susceptible to oxidation by air.

a-AMYLCINNAMALDEHYDE DIMETHYL ACETAL • A synthetic fruit flavoring agent for beverages, ice cream, candy, and baked goods. No known toxicity.

a-AMYLCINNAMYL ACETATE • A synthetic chocolate, fruit, and honey flavoring agent for beverages, ice cream, ices, candy, baked goods, and chewing gum. No known toxicity.

a-AMYLCINNAMYL ALCOHOL • A synthetic chocolate, fruit, and honey flavoring agent for beverages, ice cream, ices, candy, baked goods, and chewing gum. No known toxicity.

a-AMYLCINNAMYL FORMATE • A synthetic chocolate, fruit, nut and maple flavoring agent for beverages, ice cream, ices, candy, baked goods, and chewing gum. No known toxicity.

a-AMYLCINNAMYL ISOVALERATE • A synthetic chocolate, fruit, grape and nut flavoring agent for beverages, ice cream, ices, candy, baked goods, and chewing gum. No known toxicity.

AMYLOGLUCOSIDASE • An enzyme, derived from *Rhizopus niveus,* used in the modification of gelatinized starch, and in the production of distilled spirits and vinegar. No known toxicity. (*See* Modified Starch.)

AMYLOPECTIN • Amioca. A starch derived from corn that forms a paste with water. Used as a texturizer in foods and cosmetics. Produces a red color when mixed with iodine. No known toxicity.

AMYLOSE • Starches commonly processed from plants contain 18 to 27 percent amylose. It is the inner, relatively soluble portion of starch granules. Corn starch solutions often form opaque gels after cooking and cooling; this is because of the presence of amylose. It is used as a dispersing and mixing agent for oleoresins. Nontoxic.

AMYRIS OIL • Sandalwood Oil. The volatile oil obtained from a gummy wood and used as a flavoring agent in chewing gum and candy. It is a clear, pale yellow, viscous liquid with a distinct odor of sandalwood. No known toxicity.

ANCHUSIN EXTRACT • *See* Alkanet Root.

ANETHOLE • A flavoring agent used in fruit, honey, licorice, anise, liquor, nut, root beer, sarsaparilla, spice, vanilla, wintergreen, and birch beer flavorings for beverages, ice cream, ices, candy, baked goods, chewing gum (1,500 ppm) and liquors (1,400 ppm). Obtained from anise (*see*) oil, fennel, and other sources. Colorless or faintly yellow liquid with a sweet taste and a characteristic aniselike odor. Chief constituent of anise. Anethole is affected by light and caused irritation of the gums and throat when used in a denture cream. When applied to the skin, anethole may produce hives, scaling, and blisters. GRAS.

ANETHUM GRAVEOLENS L • *See* Dill.

ANGELIC ACID • *See* Angelica.

ANGELICA • Used in inexpensive fragrances, toothpastes, and mouthwashes. Grown in Europe and Asia, the aromatic seeds, leaves, stems, and roots have been used in medicine for flatus (gas), to increase sweating, and to reduce body water. When perfume is applied, skin may break out with a rash and swell when exposed to sunlight. The *bark* is used medicinally as a purgative and emetic. The *root oil* is used in fruit, gin, and rum flavorings for beverages, ice cream, ices, candy, baked goods, gelatin desserts, chewing gum, and liquors. The *root extract* is used in berry, liquor, wine, maple, nut, walnut, and root beer flavorings for the same foods, up to baked goods, plus syrups. The *seed extract* is used in berry, fruit, walnut, maple, and spice flavorings for beverages, candy, baked goods, syrups, and condiments. The *seed oil* is used for fruit and gin flavoring for beverages, ice cream, ices, candy, baked goods, gelatin, desserts, and liquors. The *stem oil* is used for fruit flavoring for the same foods as is seed oil, excepting liquors. Angelica can induce sensitivity to light. GRAS.

ANGOLA WEED • A weed from West Africa used as a flavoring agent in alcoholic beverages only. No known toxicity.

ANGOSTURA • Flavoring agent from the bark of trees, grown in Venezuela and Brazil. Unpleasant musty odor and bitter aromatic taste. The light yellow liquid extract is used in bitters, liquor, root beer, and spice flavorings for beverages and liquors (1,700 ppm). Formerly used to lessen fever. No known toxicity. GRAS.

ANHYDRIDE • A residue resulting from water being removed from a compound. An oxide—combination of oxygen and an element—that can combine with water to form an acid, or that is derived from an acid by the abstraction of water. Acetic acid (*see*) is an example.

ANHYDROUS • Describes a substance that contains no water.

ANISE • Anise Seed. Dried ripe fruit of Asia, Europe, and the U.S. used in licorice, anise, pepperoni sausage, spice, and vanilla flavorings for beverages, ice cream, ices, candy, baked goods, condiments (5,000 ppm), and meats (1,200). The *oil* is used for butter, caramel, licorice, anise, rum, sausage, nut, root beer, sarsaparilla, spice, vanilla, wintergreen, and birch beer flavorings for the same foods as above excepting condiments but including chewing gum (3,200) and liquors. Sometimes used to break up intestinal gas. Used in masculine-type perfumes, cleaners, and shampoos. Can cause contact dermatitis. GRAS. *See* Star Anise.

ANISIC ALCOHOL • *See* Anisyl Alcohol.

ANISOLE • A synthetic agent with a pleasant odor used in licorice, root beer, sarsaparilla, wintergreen, and birch beer flavorings for beverages, ice cream, ices, candy, and baked goods. Also used in perfumery.

ANISYL ACETATE • Colorless liquid with a lilac odor used in perfumery. *See* Anise.

ANISYL ALCOHOL • A synthetic berry, chocolate, cocoa, fruit, and vanilla flavoring agent for beverages, ice cream, ices, candy, baked goods, gelatin desserts, and chewing gum. No known toxicity.

ANISYL BUTYRATE • A synthetic fruit and licorice flavoring agent for beverages, ice cream, ices, candy, and baked goods. No known toxicity.

ANISYL FORMATE • Formic Acid. A synthetic raspberry, fruit, licorice, and vanilla flavoring agent for beverages, ice cream, ices, baked goods, and gelatin desserts. Also used in perfumery. Found naturally in currant and vanilla. No known toxicity.

ANISYL PHENYLACETATE • A synthetic honey flavoring agent for beverages, ice cream, ices, candy, and baked goods. No known toxicity.

ANISYL PROPIONATE • Occurs naturally in quince, apple, banana, cherry, peach, and pineapple. A raspberry, cherry, and licorice flavoring agent for beverages, ice cream, ices, candy, baked goods, and gelatin desserts. No known toxicity.

ANNATTO • Extract and Seed. A vegetable dye from a tropical tree, yellow to pink, it is used in dairy products, baked goods, margarine, and breakfast cereals. It is also used to color such meat-product casings as bologna and frankfurters. A spice flavoring for beverages, ice cream, baked goods (2,000 ppm), margarine, breakfast cereals (2,000 ppm), and baked goods. No known toxicity. Permanently listed in 1963 but Certification not necessary for use (*see* Certified).

ANOXOMER • A mixture of benzenes (*see*) and other coal-tar derivatives, it is one of the newer antioxidants in food and is used at a level of not more than 5,000 based on fat and oil content of the foods. *See* Phenol.

ANTHOCYANINS • Intensely colored, water-soluble pigments responsible for nearly all the reds and blues of flowers and other plant parts. Such color, which is dissolved in plant sap, is markedly affected by the acidity and alkalinity of substances: red at low pH (*see*) and blue at higher pH values. There are about 120 known anthocyanins, including those obtained from grapes, cranberries, cherries, and plums. They can be used to color acid compounds such as wines and cranberry juice cocktail. No known toxicity.

ANTIBODY • Protein in blood, formed in response to invasion by a germ, virus, or other foreign body. In sensitive individuals, a special antibody, IgE, is responsible for the allergic reaction.

ANTIGEN • Any substance that provokes an immune response when introduced into the body.

ANTICAKING AGENTS • These keep powders and salt free-flowing, such as calcium phosphate (*see*) in instant breakfast drinks and other soft drink mixes.

ANTIOXIDANTS • Substances added to food to keep oxygen from changing the food's color or flavor. Apples, for instance, will turn brown when exposed to air, and fats will become rancid after exposure. Among the most widely used antioxidants are butylated hydroxyanisole (BHA) and butylated hydroxytoluene (BHT) (*see* both). Vitamin E and Vitamin C are natural antioxidants.

APPLE ACID • *See* Malic Acid.

APRICOT • Fruit and Oil. Persic Oil. The tart orange-colored fruit is used as a natural cherry flavoring agent for beverages, ice cream, ices, candy, baked goods, and soups. The oil is used in brilliantine and the crushed fruit as a facial mask to soften the skin. No known toxicity. GRAS.

ARABIC GUM • *See* Acacia.

ARABINOGALACTAN • A polysaccharide extracted with water from larch wood used in the minimum quantity required to be effective as an emulsifier, stabilizer, binder, and or bodying agent in essential oils. Used in nonnutritive sweeteners, flavor bases, nonstandardized dressings, chewing gums, and pudding mixes. No known toxicity.

ARAMANTH • *See* FD and C Red No. 2.

ARACHIDIC ACID • A fatty acid, also called eicosanoic acid, that is widely distributed in peanut oil fats and related compounds. It is used in lubricants, greases, waxes, and plastics. No known toxicity.

ARACHIDONIC ACID • A liquid unsaturated fatty acid that occurs in liver, brain, glands, and fat of animals and humans. The acid is generally isolated from animal liver. Used essentially for nutrition and to soothe eczema and rashes in skin creams and lotions. No known toxicity.

ARACHIDYL PROPIONATE • The ester of arachidyl alcohol and N-propionic acid used as a wax. *See* Arachidic Acid.

ARGININE • An essential amino acid (*see*), strongly alkaline. The FDA has asked for further information on the nutrient, which plays an important role in the production and excretion of urea (*see*). It has been used for the treatment of liver disease. GRAS.

ARHEOL • *See* Sandalwood Oil, Yellow.

ARNICA • Wolf's Bane. The dried flowerhead has long been used as an astringent to treat skin disorders. It is used as a flavoring in alcohol beverages only. Ingestion can lead to severe intestinal upset, nervous disturbances, irregular heartbeat, and collapse. Ingestion of one ounce has caused severe illness but no death. Active irritant on the skin. Not recommended for use in toilet preparation and should never be used on broken skin.

ARNOTTA EXTRACT AND SEED • *See* Annatto.

AROMATIC • In the context of cosmetics, a chemical that has an aroma.

AROMATIC BITTERS • Usually made from the maceration of bitter herbs and used to intensify the aroma of perfume. The herbs selected for aromatic bitters must have a persistent fragrant aroma. Ginger and cinnamon are examples.

ARROWROOT STARCH • From the rhizome of *Maranta arundinacea,* a plant of tropical America. It is used in the diet of babies and invalids because it is easy to digest. An ingredient in dusting powders and hair dyes made from the root starch of plants. Arrowroot was used by the American Indians to heal wounds from poisoned arrows and is still employed today in plants and animals both free and combined with proteins. It is used as a culture medium and as a medicine. In cosmetics, it is used to help moisturizers penetrate the skin. The final report to the FDA of the Select Committee on GRAS Substances stated in 1980 that it should continue its GRAS status with no limitations other than good manufacturing practices. No known toxicity.

ARTEMISIA • Mugwaort. A shrub and herb native to north and south temperate climates having strongly scented foliage and small rayless flower heads. Used as a flavoring. *See* Wormwood.

ARTICHOKE LEAVES • A tall herb that resembles a thistle. Used as a flavoring in beverages only. No known toxicity.

ARTIFICIAL • In foods, the term follows the standard meaning: a substance not duplicated in nature. A flavoring, for instance, may have all natural ingredients but it must be called artificial if it has no counterpart in nature.

ASAFOETIDA EXTRACT • Asfetida. Devil's Dung. A gum or resin obtained from the roots or rhizome of *Ferula assafoetida,* any of several plants grown in Iran, Turkestan, and Afghanistan. The soft lumps or ''tears'' have a garlicky odor and are used as a natural flavoring. The fluid extract is used in sausage, onion, and spice flavorings for beverages, ice cream, ices, candy, baked goods, meat, condiments, and soups. The gum is used in onion and spice flavorings for beverages, ice cream, ices, candy, baked goods, and seasonings. The gums have also been used medicinally as an expectorant and to break up intestinal gas. The oil is used for spice flavoring in candy, baked goods, and condiments. Asafetida has a bitter taste, an offensive charcoal odor, and is particularly used in India and Iran as a condiment. No known toxicity. GRAS.

ASCORBATE • Calcium and Sodium.   Antioxidants used in concentrated milk products, cooked, cured, or pulverized meat food products, and in the pickle in which pork and beef products are cured or packed. Nontoxic.

ASCORBIC ACID • Vitamin C.   A preservative and antioxidant used in frozen fruit, particularly sliced peaches, frozen fish dip, dry milk, beer and ale, flavoring oils, apple juices, soft drinks, fluid milk, candy, artificially sweetened jellies and preserves, canned mushrooms, cooked, cured, and pulverized meat food products, and pickle in which beef or pork is cured or packed (75 ounces of Vitamin C per 100 gallons). Vitamin C is necessary for normal teeth, bones, and blood vessels. The white or slightly yellow powder darkens upon exposure to air. Reasonably stable when it remains dry in air, but deteriorates rapidly when exposed to air while in solution. Nobel Laureate Linus Pauling caused a run on Vitamin C in 1970 by endorsing it as a cold medicine. Although his theories were not widely accepted by the medical community, a great deal of work is now in progress studying Vitamin C and immunity. Vitamin C is known to affect the excretion of medications such as barbiturates and to make them more toxic. Pharmaceutically incompatible with sodium salicylate, sodium nitrate, theobromine, and methenamine. The final report to the FDA of the Select Committee on GRAS Substances stated in 1980 that it should continue its GRAS status with no limitations other than good manufacturing practices. Nontoxic.

ASCORBYL PALMITATE • A salt of ascorbic acid (*see*), it is used as a preservative and antioxidant for candy. Like ascorbic acid, prevents rancidity, browning of cut apples and other fruits, used in meat curing. Nontoxic. The final report to the FDA of the Select Committee on GRAS Substances stated in 1980 that it should continue its GRAS status with no limitations other than good manufacturing practices. Nontoxic.

ASCORBYL STEARATE • *See* Ascorbyl Palmitate.

ASPARAGINE • L Form.   A nonessential amino acid (*see*). It is widely found in plants and animals both free and combined with proteins. It is used as a dietary supplement, a culture medium, and a medicine. In cosmetics, it is used to help moisturizers penetrate the skin. No known toxicity.

ASPARTAME • Nutrasweet.® A compound prepared from aspartic acid and phenylalanine (*see* both), with about two hundred times the sweetness of sugar, discovered during routine screening of drugs for the treatment of ulcers. The G. D. Searle Company sought FDA approval in 1973. The FDA approved it in 1974, but objections that aspartame might cause brain damage led to a stay, or legal postponement, of that approval. Another problem arose. An FDA investigation of records of animal studies conducted for Searle drug approvals and for aspartame raised questions. The FDA arranged for an independent audit, which took more than two years and concluded that the aspartame studies and results were authentic. The agency then organized an expert board of inquiry and the members concluded that the evidence did not support the charge that aspartame might kill clusters of brain cells or cause other damage. However, persons with phenylketonuria, or PKU, must avoid protein foods such as meat that contain phenylalanine—one of two components of aspartame. The board did, however, recommend that aspartame not be approved until further long-term animal testing could be conducted to rule out a possibility that aspartame might cause brain tumors. The FDA's Bureau of Foods reviewed the study data already available and concluded that the board's concern was unfounded. Aspartame was approved for use as a tabletop sweetener in certain dry foods on October 22, 1981.

In 1984 news reports fueled by the announcement that the Arizona Department of Health Services was testing soft drinks containing aspartame to see if it deteriorated into toxic levels of methyl alcohol under storage conditions created alarm. The Arizona Health Department acted after the director of the Food Sciences and Research Laboratory at Arizona State submitted a study alleging that higher than normal temperatures could lead to a dangerous breakdown in the chemical composition. The author checked with representatives of the Food and Drug Administration. They said that there are higher levels of methyl alcohol in regular fruit juices, and as far as the agency was concerned, the fears about decomposition products were unfounded.

Aspartame lowers the acidity of urine and therefore reportedly makes the urinary tract more susceptible to infection.

In 1988, the Mexican government stopped soda and food processors from using *nutra* in the brand name because it was "misleading." The Mexicans also required labeling that carries the following warning: "This product should not be used by individuals who are allergic to phenylalanine. Consumption by pregnant women and children under 7 years is not recommended. Users should follow a balanced diet. Consumption by diabetics must be authorized by a physician."

ASPARTIC ACID • DL & L Forms. Aminosuccinate Acid. A nonessential amino acid (*see*) occurring in animals and plants, sugar cane, sugar beets, and molasses. It is usually synthesized for commercial purposes. No known toxicity.

ASPERGILLUS • A genus of fungi that includes many species of molds and spores, which produce the antibiotic aspergillic acid. An Aspergillus flavus-Oryzae Group of mold has been cleared by the U.S. Department of Agriculture's Meat Inspection Division to soften tissues of beef cuts, to wit: "Solutions containing water, salt, monosodium glutamate, and approved proteolytic enzymes applied or injected into cuts of beef shall not result in a gain of more than 3 percent above the weight of the untreated product." It is also used in bakery products such as bread, rolls, and buns. Toxicity is unknown but because of the use of the fungi-antibiotic with monosodium glutamate, allergic reactions would certainly be possible.

ATTAR OF ROSES • *See* Rose Bulgarian.

ATOPIC DERMATITIS • A chronic, itching inflammation of the skin also called eczema.

AUBERPINE LIQUID • *See* p-Methoxybenzaldehyde.

AVOIDANCE • Measures taken to avoid contact with allergy-producing substances. Since there are no cures for allergies, as of yet, avoiding allergens is the best way to combat them.

AZO DYES • A large category of colorings used in both the food and cosmetic industries, the dyes are characterized by the way they combine with nitrogen. These are a very large class of dyes made from diazonium compounds and phenol. The dyes usually contain a mild acid, such as citric or tartaric acid. Among the foods in which they are used are "penny" candies, caramels and chews, Life Savers, fruit drops, filled chocolates (but not pure chocolate); soft drinks, fruit drinks, and ades; jellies, jams, marmalades, stewed fruit sauces, fruit gelatins, fruit yogurts; ice cream, pie fillings, vanilla, butterscotch and chocolate puddings, caramel custard, whips, dessert sauces such as vanilla, and cream in powdered form; bakery goods (except plain rolls), crackers, cheese puffs, chips, cake and cookie mixes, waffle/pancake mixes, macaroni and spaghetti (certain brands); mayonnaise, salad dressings, catsup (certain brands), mustard, ready-made salads with dressings, remoulade, bearnaise, and hollandaise sauces, as well as sauces such as curry, fish, onion, and tomato, and white cream; mashed rutabagas, purees, packaged soups and some canned soups; canned anchovies, herring, sardines, fish balls, caviar, cleaned shellfish. Azo dyes can cause allergic reactions, particularly hives.

AZODICARBONAMIDE • A bleaching and maturing agent for flour, yellow to orange red, a crystalline powder, practically insoluble in water. Used in amounts up to 45 ppm. The FDA wants further study of this chemical for both short-term and long-term effects.

B

BABASSU OIL • A nondrying edible oil expressed from the kernels of the babassu palm, which grows in Brazil. Used in foods and soaps but it is expensive. No known toxicity.

BACTERIAL CATALASE • A catalase is an enzyme in plant and animal tissues. It exerts a chemical reaction that converts hydrogen peroxide into water and oxygen. Derived from bacteria by a pure-culture fermentation process, bacterial catalase may be used safely, according to the FDA, in destroying and removing the hydrogen peroxide that has been used in the manufacture of cheese—providing "the organism *Micrococcus lysodeikticus* from which the bacterial catalase is to be derived, is demonstrated to be nontoxic and non-pathogenic." The organism is removed from the bacterial catalase prior to the use of the catalase, the catalase to be used in an amount not in excess of the minimum required to produce its intended effect. No known toxicity.

BAKER'S YEAST PROTEIN • Saccharomyces Cerevisial. A yeast strain yielding high growth and used in leavening bakery products and as a dietary supplement.

BAKER'S YEAST GLYCAN • Used as an emulsifier, thickener, or stabilizer. Used in frozen desserts, sour cream, cheese spread, and flavored snack dips. *See* Baker's Yeast Protein.

BAKING POWDER • In baking, any powder used as a substitute for yeast, usually a mixture of sodium bicarbonate, starch (as a filler), and harmless acid such as tartaric. Cream of tartar is often used as the necessary acid. Nontoxic.

BAKING SODA • A common name for sodium bicarbonate (*see*).

BALM OIL • A natural fruit and liquor flavoring agent for beverages, ice cream, ices, candy, and baked goods. The balm leaves extract also is used in fruit flavors for beverages. Nontoxic. GRAS.

BALSAM PERU • Obtained from Peruvian balsam in Central America near the Pacific Coast. A dark brown viscous liquid with a pleasant lingering odor and a warm bitter taste extracted from a variety of evergreens. Used in strawberry, chocolate, cherry, grape, brandy, rum, maple, walnut, coconut, spice, and vanilla flavoring for beverages, ice cream, ices, candy, baked goods, gelatin desserts, chewing gum, and syrups. The *oil* is used in berry, coconut, fruit, rum, maple, and vanilla flavoring for beverages, ice cream, ices, candy, and baked goods. The *Balsam fir oil* is a natural pineapple, lime, and spice flavoring for beverages, ice cream, ices, candy, baked goods, and gelatin desserts. *Balsam fir oleoresin* is a natural fruit and spice flavoring for beverages, ice cream, ices, candy and baked goods. *Fir balsam* is a yellowish green, thick, transparent liquid with a pinelike smell and a bitter aftertaste. It is also used in the manufacture of chocolate. Used also in face masks, perfumes, cream hair rinses, and astringents. Mildly antiseptic and irritating to the skin and may cause contact dermatitis and a stuffy nose. It is one of the most common sensitizers and may cross-react with benzoin, rosin, benzoic acid, benzyl alcohol, cinnamic acid, essential oils, orange peel, eugenol, cinnamon, clove, Tolu balsam, storax, benzyl benzoate, and wood tars.

B-APO-8′-CAROTENAL • A coloring used at the rate of 15 mg/lb of solid or semisolid food or per pint of liquid food. Permanently listed since 1963. *See* Carotene.

BARLEY FLOUR • A cereal grass cultivated since prehistoric times. Used in the manufacture of malt beverages, as a breakfast food, and as a demulcent (*see*) in cosmetics. No known toxicity.

BASES • Alkalies, such as ammonium hydroxide (*see*), used to control the acidity-alkalinity balance of food products. *See* pH.

BASIL EXTRACT • Sweet Basil. The extract of the leaves and flowers of *Ocimum basilicum,* an herb having spikes of small white flowers and aromatic leaves used as a seasoning. A natural flavoring distilled from the flowering tops of the plant has a slightly yellowish color and a spicy odor. Used in sausage and spice flavorings for beverages, candy, ice cream, baked goods, condiments, and meats. The oleoresin is used in spice flavorings for baked goods and condiments. The oil is used in loganberry, strawberry, orange, rose, violet, cherry, honey, licorice, basil, muscatel, meat, and root beer flavorings for beverages, ice cream, ices, candy, baked goods. No known toxicity. GRAS.

BAY, SWEET • A natural flavoring native to a Mediterranean plant with stiff, glossy, fragrant leaves. Used in vermouth, sausage, and spice flavorings for beverages, ice cream, ices, candy, baked goods, condiments, and meats. The *oil,* from the laurel, is used in fruit and spice flavorings for beverages, ice cream, ices, candy, baked goods, chewing gum, condiments, and meats. No known toxicity.

BAY LEAVES • The West Indian extract is a natural flavoring used in vermouth and spice flavorings for beverages, ice cream, ices, candy, baked goods, meat, and soups. The *oil* is used in fruit, liquor, and bay flavorings for beverages, ice cream, ices, candy, baked goods, condiments and meats. The *oleoresin* (*see*) is used in sausage flavoring for meats and soups. No known toxicity.

BEEF TALLOW • *See* Tallow Flakes. GRAS for packaging.

BEESWAX • From virgin bees and primarily used as an emulsifier. Practically insoluble in water. Yellow beeswax from the honeycomb is yellowish, soft to brittle, and has a honeylike odor. White beeswax is yellowish white and slightly different in taste but otherwise has the same properties as yellow beeswax. Used as a candy glaze and polish. Also used in many cosmetics including baby creams, brilliantine hair dressings, cold cream, emollient creams, wax depilatories, eye creams, eye shadow, foundation creams and makeup, lipstick, mascara, nail whiteners, protective creams, and paste rouge. Can cause an allergic reaction on the skin. The final report to the FDA of the Select Committee on GRAS Substances stated in 1980 that it should continue its GRAS status with no limitations other than good manufacturing practices. *See* Beeswax, Bleached.

BEESWAX, BLEACHED • White Wax. Yellow wax bleached and purified from the honeycomb of the bee. Remains yellowish white, is solid, somewhat translucent, and fairly insoluble in water. Differs slightly in taste from yellow beeswax. Used in fruit and honey flavorings for beverages, ice cream, ices, baked goods, and honey. Nontoxic. The final report to the FDA of the Select Committee on GRAS Substances stated in 1980 that it should continue its GRAS status with no limitations other than good manufacturing practices.

BEET • Juice and Powder. Vegetable dye used to color dairy products. Listed for food use in 1967. No known toxicity.

BEETROOT JUICE POWDER • The powdered stem base of the beet used for its reddish color in powders and rouges. No known toxicity.

BENTONITE • A colloidal clay (aluminum silicate) that has a high swelling capacity in water. Used as a food additive as a thickener and colorant. Inert and generally nontoxic but when injected into rats it was lethal. GRAS.

BENZALDEHYDE • Artificial Almond Oil. A colorless liquid that occurs in the kernels of bitter almonds. Lime is used in its synthetic manufacture. As the artificial essential oil of almonds, it is used in berry, butter, coconut, apricot, cherry, peach, liquor, brandy, rum, almond, pecan, pistachio, spice, and vanilla flavoring. Occurs naturally in cherries, raspberries, tea, almonds, bitter oil, cajeput oil, cassia bark. Used in beverages, ice cream, ices, candy, baked goods, chewing gum, and cordials. Also used in cosmetic creams and lotions, perfumes, soaps, and dyes. May cause allergic reactions. Highly toxic. Produces central nervous system depression and convulsions. Fatal dose is estimated to be 2 ounces. GRAS.

BENZALDEHYDE DIMETHYL ACETAL • A synthetic agent used in fruit, cherry, nut, and almond flavorings for beverages, ice cream, ices, candy, baked goods, gelatin, and puddings. *See* Benzaldehyde for toxicity.

BENZALDEHYDE GLYCERYL ACETAL • A synthetic agent used in fruit, cherry, nut, and almond flavorings for beverages, ice cream, ices, candy, baked goods, and chewing gums. *See* Benzaldehyde for toxicity.

BENZALDEHYDE PROPYLENE GLYCOL ACETAL • A synthetic agent used in fruit, cherry, nut, and almond flavorings for beverages, ice cream, ices, candy, baked goods, and chewing gum. *See* Benzaldehyde for toxicity.

BENZENECARBONAL • *See* Benzaldehyde.

BENZENCARBOXYLIC ACID • *See* Benzoic Acid.

BENZENEMETHYLAL • *See* Benzaldehyde.

BENZOATE OF SODA • *See* Sodium Benzoate.

1, 2-BENZODIHYDROPYRONE • *See* Dihydrocoumarin.

BENZOE • *See* Benzoin.

BENZOIC ACID • A preservative that occurs in nature in cherry bark, raspberries, tea, anise, and cassia bark. First described in 1608 when it was found in gum benzoin. Used in chocolate, lemon, orange, cherry, fruit, nut, and tobacco flavorings for beverages, ice cream, ices, candy, baked goods, icings, and chewing gum. Also used in margarine and pickles. Also an antifungal agent. Used as a chemical preservative and a dietary supplement up to 0.1 percent. A mild irritant to the skin. It can cause allergic reactions such as asthma, red eyes, and skin rashes, especially in people sensitive to aspirin. Listed by the FDA as GRAS in a reevaluation of safety in 1976. The final report to the FDA of the Select Committee on GRAS Substances stated in 1980 that it should continue its GRAS status with no limitations other than good manufacturing practices.

BENZOIC ALDEHYDE • *See* Benzaldehyde.

BENZOIN • Gum Benjamin. Gum Benzoin. Any of several resins containing benzoic acid (*see*), obtained as a gum from various trees. Used as a preserving ointment for fumigating, in perfumes and cosmetics as a compound tincture of benzoin, as a skin protectant and respiratory inhalant. The resin is used as a flavoring agent in chocolate, cherry, rum, spice, and vanilla for beverages, ice cream, ices, candy, baked goods, and chewing gum. Benzoin also is a natural flavoring agent for butterscotch, butter, fruit liquor, and rum. Nontoxic. It was tested by the National Cancer Institute and found not to be a cancer-causing agent in rats and mice.

BENZOPHENONES (1–12) • At least a dozen different benzophenones exist. Synthetic agents used in berry, butter, fruit, apricot, peach, nut, and vanilla for beverages, ice cream, ices, candy, and baked goods. They are used as fixatives (*see*) for heavy perfumes (geranium, for example) and soaps (the smell of "new-mown hay"). Obtained as a white flaky solid with a delicate, persistent, roselike odor, and soluble in most fixed oils and in mineral oil. Also used in the manufacture of hairsprays, and in sunscreens. They help prevent deterioration of ingredients which might be affected by the ultraviolet rays found in ordinary daylight. May produce hives and contact sensitivity. In sunscreens they may cause immediate hives as well as other photoallergic reactions. Toxic when injected.

2,3-BENZOPYRROLE • *See* Indole.

BENZOYL BENZENE • A fixative for heavy perfumes such as geranium, used especially in soaps. *See* Benzophenones.

BENZOYL EUGENOL • *See* Eugenyl Benzoate.

BENZOYL PEROXIDE • A bleaching agent for flours, blue cheese, Gorgonzola, and milk. A catalyst for hardening certain fiberglass resins. A drying agent in cosmetics. Toxic by inhalation. A skin allergen and irritant. GRAS.

BENZYL ACETATE • A colorless liquid with a pear or flowerlike odor obtained from a number of plants, especially jasmine, for use in perfumery and soap. A synthetic raspberry, strawberry, butter, violet, apple, cherry, banana, and plum flavoring agent for beverages, ice cream, ices, candy, baked goods, chewing gum, and gelatin desserts. Can be irritating to the skin, eyes, and respiratory tract. Ingestion causes intestinal upset, including vomiting and diarrhea.

BENZYL ACETOACETATE • A synthetic berry and fruit flavoring agent for beverages, ice cream, ices, candy, baked goods, gelatin desserts, and chewing gum. *See* Benzyl Acetate for toxicity.

BENZYL ACETYL ACETATE • *See* Benzyl Acetoacetate.

BENZYL ALCOHOL • A flavoring that is derived as a pure alcohol and is a constituent of jasmine, hyacinth, and other plants. It has a faint sweet odor. Used in synthetic blueberry, loganberry, raspberry, orange, floral, rose, violet, fruit, cherry, grape, honey, liquor, muscatel, nut, walnut, root beer, and vanilla flavorings for beverages, ice cream, ices, candy, baked goods, gelatin desserts, and chewing gum. A solvent in perfumes, a preservative in hair dyes, and a topical antiseptic. Irritating and corrosive to the skin and mucous membranes. Ingestion of large doses causes intestinal upsets. It may cross-react in the sensitive with Balsam Peru (*see*).

BENZYL BUTYL ETHER • Synthetic fruit flavoring agent for beverages, ice cream, ices, candy, baked goods, gelatin desserts, and puddings. No known toxicity.

BENZYL BUTYRATE • Butyric Acid. A synthetic flavoring agent, colorless, liquid, with a plumlike odor. Used in loganberry, raspberry, strawberry, butter, apricot, peach, pear, liquor, muscatel, cheese, and nut flavorings for beverages, ice cream, ices, candy, baked goods, chewing gum, and gelatin desserts. No known toxicity.

BENZYL CARBINOL • *See* Phenethyl alcohol.

BENZYL CINNAMATE • Sweet Odor of Balsam. Colorless prisms, used to give artificial fruit scents to perfumes. A synthetic flavoring agent used in raspberry, chocolate, apricot, cherry, peach, pineapple, plum, prune, honey, liquor, and rum for beverages, ice cream, ices, candy, baked goods, chewing gum, and gelatin desserts. *See* Balsam Peru for toxicity.

BENZYL DIMETHYL CARBINYL ACETATE • *See* $a,a,$-Dimethylphenethyl Acetate.

BENZYL DIMETHYL CARBINYL BUTYRATE • *See* $a,a,$-Dimethylphenethyl Butyrate.

BENZYL DIMETHYL CARBINYL FORMATE • *See* $a,a,$-Dimethylphenethyl Formate.

BENZYL 2,3-DIMETHYLCROTONATE • A synthetic fruit and spice flavoring agent for beverages, ice cream, ices, candy, and baked goods.

BENZYL DIPROPYL KETONE • *See* 3-Benzyl-4-Heptanone.

BENZYL DISULFIDE • A synthetic fruit flavoring agent for beverages, ice cream, ices, and candy. No known toxicity.

BENZYL ETHYL ETHER. • Colorless, oily liquid; aromatic odor; insoluble in water; miscible in alcohol. Used in flavoring for beverages, ice cream, ices, candy, and baked goods. Narcotic in high concentrations. May be a skin irritant.

BENZYL FORMATE • Formic Acid. A synthetic chocolate, apricot, cherry, peach, pineapple, plum, prune, honey, and liquor flavoring agent for beverages, ice cream, ices, candy, baked goods, and chewing gum. Pleasant fruity odor. Practically insoluble in water. There are no specific data for toxicity but it is believed to be narcotic in high concentrations.

3-BENZYL-4-HEPTANONE • Synthetic fruit flavoring for beverages, ice cream, ices, candy, and baked goods. No known toxicity.

BENZYL o-HYDROXYBENZOATE • *See* Benzyl Salicylate.

BENZYL ISOAMYL ALCOHOL • *See* a-Isobutylphenethyl Alcohol.

BENZYL ISOBUTYL CARBINOL • *See* a-Isobutylphenethyl Alcohol.

BENZYL ISOBUTYRATE • A synthetic strawberry and fruit flavorings for beverages, ice cream, ices, candy, and baked goods. No known toxicity.

BENZYL ISOEUGENOL • A synthetic spice flavoring for beverages, ice cream, ices, candy, and baked goods. No known toxicity.

BENZYL ISOVALERATE • A synthetic raspberry, apple, apricot, banana, cherry, pineapple, walnut, and cheese flavoring agent for beverages, ice cream, ices, candy, baked goods, gelatin desserts, and chewing gum. No known toxicity.

BENZYL MERCAPTAN • A synthetic coffee flavoring agent used for beverages, ice cream, ices, candy, and baked goods. No known toxicity.

BENZYL METHOXYETHYL ACETAL • Synthetic fruit and cherry flavoring agent for beverages, ice cream, ices, candy, and baked goods. No known toxicity.

BENZYL PHENYLACETATE • A synthetic butter, caramel, fruit, and honey flavoring agent for beverages, ice cream, ices, candy, baked goods, and toppings. A colorless liquid with a sweet floral odor, it occurs naturally in honey. No known toxicity.

BENZYL B-PHENYLACRYLATE • *See* Benzyl Cinnamate.

BENZYL PROPIONATE • A synthetic flavoring substance, colorless liquid, with a sweet fruity odor. Used in berry, apple, banana, grape, pear, and pineapple flavorings for beverages, ice cream, ices, candy, baked goods, chewing gum, and icings. No known toxicity.

BENZYL SALICYLATE • Salicylic Acid. Used in floral and peach flavorings for beverages, ice cream, ices, candy, and baked goods. A fixative in perfumes and a solvent in sunscreen lotions. It is a thick liquid with a light pleasant odor and is mixed with alcohol or ether. As with other salicylates it may interact adversely with such medications as antidepressants and anticoagulants, and may cause skin to break out with a rash and swell when exposed to sunlight. *See* Salicylates.

BENZYLACETIC ACID • *See* Benzyl Acetate.

BENZYLACETONE • *See* 4-Phenyl-3-Buten-2-One.

BENZYETHYL ALCOHOL • *See* 3-Phenyl-1-Propanol.

1-BENZYLOXY (B-METHOXY) ETHOXY ETHANE • *See* Benzyl Methoxyethyl Acetal.

BENZYLPROPYL ACETATE • *See* a,a-Dimethylphenethyl Acetate.

BENZYLPROPYL ALCOHOL • *See* a,a-Dimethylphenethyl Acetate.

BENZYLPROPYL CARBINOL • *See* a-Propylphenethyl Alcohol.

BENZYLTHIOL • *See* Benzyl Mercaptan.

BERGAMOL • *See* Linalyl Acetate.

BERGAMOT • Bergamot Orange or Red. Oswego Tea. An orange flavoring extracted from a pear-shaped fruit, whose rind yields a greenish-brown oil much used in perfumery and brilliantine hairdressings. Used in strawberry, lemon, orange, tangerine, cola, floral, banana, grape, peach, pear, pineapple, liquor, spice, and vanilla flavorings for beverages, ice cream, ices, candy, baked goods, gelatin desserts, chewing gum, and icings. The oil can cause brown skin stains (berloque) when exposed to sunlight and is considered a prime photosensitizer (sensitivity to light). GRAS.

BETA-APO-8'-CAROTENAL • Coloring agent for solid or semisolid foods. Nontoxic.

BETA-CAROTENE • Provitamin A. Beta Carotene. Found in all plants and in many animal tissues. It is the chief yellow coloring matter of carrots, butter, and egg yolk. Extracted as red crystals or crystalline powder. It is used as a coloring in food and cosmetics. Also used in the manufacture of Vitamin A. Too much carotene in the blood can lead to carotenemia, a pale yellow-red pigmentation of the skin that may be mistaken for jaundice. It is a benign condition, and withdrawal of carotene from the diet cures it. Beta-Carotene has less serious side effects than Vitamin A and was given to 22,000 physicians as part of a five-year study to determine whether aspirin could protect against heart disease and beta carotene against tumors. It is nontoxic.

BETA-CITRAURIN • Excellent raw material for the extraction of carotenoids (*see* Carotene), or orange coloring. Found in tangerine and orange peels. Soluble in alcohol.

BETAINE • Used as a coloring and as a dietary supplement. Occurs in common beets and in many vegetables as well as animal substances. Used in resins. Has been employed to treat muscle weakness medically. No known toxicity.

BETAINE, ANHYDROUS • Betaine (*see*) with the water removed.

BHA • *See* Butylated Hydroxyanisole.

BHT • *See* Butylated Hydroxytoluene.

BIACETYL • *See* Diacetyl.

BILBERRY EXTRACT • The extract of *Vaccinium myrtillus,* a plant found in North America and the Alps that differ from the typical blueberries in having single flowers or very small buds.

BINDER • A substance such as gum arabic, gum tragacanth, glycerin, or sorbitol (*see* all), which dispense, swell, or absorb water, increase consistency, and hold ingredients together. For example, binders are used to make powders in compacts retain their shape; binders in toothpaste provide for the smooth dispensing of the paste.

BIOFLAVONOIDS • Vitamin P Complex. Citrus-flavored compounds needed to maintain healthy blood-vessel walls. Widely distributed among plants, especially citrus fruits and rose hips. Usually taken from orange and lemon rinds and used as a reducing agent (*see*). No known toxicity. Any claim for special dietary use, according to FDA regulations, renders the food misbranded.

BIOTIN • Vitamin H. Vitamin B Factor. A whitish crystalline powder used as a texturizer in cosmetic creams. Present in minute amounts in every living cell and in larger amounts in yeast and milk. Vital to growth. It acts as a coenzyme in the formation of certain essential fatlike substances, and plays a part in reactions involving carbon dioxide. It is needed by humans for healthy circulation and red blood cells. Nontoxic. GRAS.

BIRCH FAMILY • Betulaceae. Sweet Oil and Tar Oil. A flavoring agent from the bark and wood of deciduous trees common in the Northern Hemisphere. The oils are obtained by distillation. It is a clear, dark brown liquid with a strong leatherlike odor. *Birch sweet oil* is used in synthetic strawberry, pineapple, maple, nut, root beer, sarsaparilla, spice, wintergreen, and birch beer flavorings for beverages, ice cream, ices, candy, baked goods, gelatins, puddings (4,300 ppm), and syrups. *Birch tar oil,* which is refined, is used in chewing gum, and has also been used for preserving leather. Used as an astringent in creams and shampoos, it is an ancient remedy. The medicinal properties of the plant tend to vary, depending upon which part of the tree is used. It has been used as a laxative, as an aid for gout, to treat rheumatism and dropsy, and to dissolve kidney stones. It is supposedly good for bathing skin eruptions. The oil is used in food flavorings. No known toxicity.

BITTER ALMOND OIL • Almond Oil. Sweet Almond Oil. Expressed Almond Oil. A colorless to pale yellow, bland, nearly odorless, essential and expressed oil from the ripe seed of the small sweet almond grown in Italy, Spain, and France. It has a strong almond odor and a mild taste. Used as a flavoring and in the manufacture of perfumes and as an oil in hair creams, nail whiteners, nail polish remover, eye creams, emollients, soaps, and perfumes. Many users are allergic to cosmetics with almond oil. It causes stuffy nose and skin rashes.

BITTER ASH EXTRACT • *See* Quassia Extract.

BITTER WOOD EXTRACT • *See* Quassia Extract.

BITTER ORANGE OIL • The pale yellow volatile oil expressed from the fresh peel of a species of citrus and used in perfumes and flavorings. May cause skin irritation and allergic reactions.

BIXIN • Norbixin. The active ingredients of annatto, both carotenoidlike compounds, but with five times the coloring power of carotene, and with better stability. They impart a yellow coloring to food. *See* Annatto.

BLACK COHOSH • Cimicifuga. Snakeroot. Bugbane. Used in astringents, perennial herb with a flower that is supposedly distasteful to insects. Grown from Canada to North Carolina and Kansas. It has a reputation for curing snake bites. It is used in ginger ale flavoring. A tonic and antispasmotic. No known toxicity.

BLACK CURRANT EXTRACT • The extract of the fruit of *Ribes nigrum,* a European plant that produces hanging yellow flowers and black aromatic fruit.

BLACK CUTCH EXTRACT • *See* Catechu Extract.

BLACK WALNUT EXTRACT • Extract of the leaves or bark of the black walnut tree (*Juglans nigra*) found in eastern North America. It produces nuts with a thick oil and is used as a black coloring.

BLACKBERRY BARK EXTRACT • A natural flavoring agent extracted from the woody plant. Used in berry, pineapple, grenadine, root beer, sarsaparilla, wintergreen, and birch beer flavorings for beverages, ice cream, ices, candy, baked goods, and liquor. The leaves are used for a soothing bath. No known toxicity.

BLACKTHORN BERRIES • *See* Sloe Berries.

BLEACHING AGENTS • Used by many industries, particularly flour milling, to make dough rise faster. Certain chemical qualities, which pastry chefs call "gluten characteristics," are needed to make an elastic, stable dough. Such qualities are acquired during aging but in the process, flour oxidizes, that is, combines with oxygen, and loses its natural gold color. Although mature flour is white, it possesses the qualities bakers want. But proper aging costs money and makes the flour more susceptible to insects and rodents, according to food manufacturers. Hence, the widespread use of bleaching and maturing agents.

BLOOM INHIBITOR • Bloom is an "undesirable effect" caused by the migration of cocoa fat from the cocoa fibers to the chocolate's surface. Chocolate that has bloomed has a gray-white appearance. Nonbloomed chocolate has a bright, shiny surface, with a rich appearance. A bloom inhibitor—a surfactant (*see*) such as lecithin (*see*)—controls the size of the chocolate crystals and reduces the tendency of the fat to mobilize.

BLUE • *See* FD and C Blue.

BLUE NO. 1 • *See* FD and C Blue No. 1.

BOIS DE ROSE OIL • A fragrance from the chipped wood of the tropical rosewood tree obtained through steam distillation. The volatile oil is colorless, pale yellow, with a light camphor odor. Used in citrus, floral, fruit, meat, and spice flavorings for beverages, ice cream, ices, candy, baked goods, and chewing gum. No known toxicity. GRAS.

BOLDUS LEAVES • Flavoring from a Chilean fir tree with a sweet edible fruit used in alcoholic beverages only. No known toxicity.

BOLETIC ACID • *See* Fumaric Acid.

BORAGE EXTRACT • The extract of the herb *Borago officinalis.* Contains potassium and calcium and has emollient properties and is used in a "tea" for sore eyes.

BORIC ACID • An antiseptic with bactericidal and fungicidal properties used as a fungus control on citrus fruit (FDA tolerance: 8 ppm boron residues). Also used in baby powders, bath powders, eye creams, liquid powders, mouthwashes, protective creams, aftershave lotions, soaps, and skin fresheners. It is still widely used despite repeated warnings from the American Medical Association of possible toxicity. Severe poisonings have followed both ingestion and topical application to abraded skin.

BORNEO CAMPHOR • *See* Borneol.

BORNEOL • A flavoring agent with a peppery odor and a burning taste. Occurs naturally in coriander, ginger oil, oil of lime, rosemary, strawberries, thyme, citronella, and nutmeg. Toxicity is similar to camphor oil (*see*). Used as a synthetic nut or spice flavoring for beverages, syrups, ice cream, ices, candy, baked goods, chewing gum. Used in perfumery. Can cause nausea, vomiting, convulsions, confusion, and dizziness.

BORNYL ACETATE • It may be obtained from various pine-needle oils. Strong piney odor. As a yarrow herb and iva herb extract, it is used as synthetic fruit and spice flavorings for beverages, ice cream, ices, candy, baked goods, chewing gum, and syrups. Colorless liquid derived from borneol (*see*), it is also used in perfumery, and as a solvent.

BORNYL FORMATE • Formic Acid. A synthetic fruit flavoring agent for beverages, ice cream, ices, candy, baked goods, and syrups. Used in perfumes, soaps, and as a disinfectant. *See* Borneol.

BORNYL ISOVALERATE • A synthetic fruit flavoring agent with a camphorlike smell used for beverages, ice cream, ices, candy, baked goods, and syrups. Used in perfumes, soaps, and as a disinfectant. Also used medicinally as a sedative. No known toxicity. *See* Borneol.

BORNYL VALERATE • A synthetic fruit flavoring agent for beverages, ice cream, ices, candy, and baked goods. No known toxicity. *See* Borneol.

BORNYVAL • *See* Bornyl Isovalerate.

BORON SOURCES • Boric Acid. Sodium Borate. Boron occurs in the earth's crust (in the form of its compounds, not the metal) and borates are widely used as antiseptics even though toxicologists warn about possible adverse reactions. Used in modified hops extract. Boric acid and sodium borate are astringents and antiseptics. Borates are absorbed by the mucous membranes and can cause symptoms such as gastrointestinal bleeding, skin rash, central nervous system stimulation. The adult lethal dose is 30 grams (1 ounce). Infants and young children are more susceptible. Boron is used as a dietary supplement up to 1 milligram per day. Cleared for use by the FDA in modified hops extract up to 310 ppm.

BORONIA, ABSOLUTE • A synthetic violet and fruit flavoring agent extracted from a plant. Used as a flavoring for beverages, ice cream, ices, and baked goods. No known toxicity.

BOSWELLIA SPECIES • *See* Olibanum Extract.

BRAN • The outer indigestible shell of cereal grain that is usually removed before the grain is ground into flour. It provides bulk and fiber.

BRASSICA ALBA • *See* Mustard.

BREWER'S YEAST • Originally used by beer brewers, it is a good source of B Vitamins and protein. It can cause allergic reactions.

BRILLIANT BLUE • *See* FD and C Blue No. 1.

BROMATED • Combined or saturated with bromine, a nonmetallic, reddish, volatile, liquid element. *See* Bromates.

BROMATES • *Calcium bromate* is a maturing agent and dough conditioner in bromated flours and bromated whole wheat flour. *Potassium bromate* is a bread improver. Sugar contaminated with potassium bromate caused a food poisoning outbreak in New Zealand. The lethal dose is not certain but 2 to 4 ounces of a 2-percent solution causes serious poisoning in children. Death in animals and man apparently is due to kidney failure but central nervous system problems have been reported. Also used in permanent wave neutralizers. Topical application to abraded skin has also caused poisoning. Bromates may also cause skin eruptions.

BROMELIN • Bromelain. A protein-digesting and milk-clotting enzyme found in pineapple. Used for tenderizing meat, chill-proofing beer, and as an anti-inflammatory medication. The federal government rules say: "Solutions consisting of water, salt, monosodium glutamate, and approved proteolytic enzymes applied or injected into cuts of beef shall not result in a gain of more than 3 percent of the weight of the untreated product."

BROMINATED VEGETABLE OIL • Bromine, a heavy, volatile, corrosive, nonmetallic liquid element, added to vegetable oil or other oils. Dark brown or pale yellow, with a bland or fruity odor. These high-density oils are blended with low-density essential oils to make them easier to emulsify. Used largely in soft drinks, citrus-flavored beverages, ice cream, ices, and baked goods. The FDA has them on the "suspect list." *See* Bromates for toxicity.

BROOM EXTRACT • *See* Genet, Absolute.

BRYOMA ROOT • Flavoring agent from a plant used in alcoholic beverages only.

BUCHU LEAF OIL • A natural flavoring agent from a South African plant used in berry, fruit, chocolate, mint, and spice flavorings for beverages, ice cream, ices, candy, baked goods, liquors, and condiments. Has been used as a urinary antiseptic and mild diuretic. No known toxicity.

BUCKBEAN LEAVES • Flavoring in alcoholic beverages only.

BUCKTHORN • Frangula. A shrub or tree grown on the Mediterranean coast of Africa, it has thorny branches and often contains a purgative in the bark or sap. Its fruits are used as a source of yellow and green dyes. No known toxicity.

BUFFER • Usually a solution with a relatively constant acidity-alkalinity ratio, which is unaffected by the addition of comparatively large amounts of acid or alkali. A typical buffer solution would be a mixture of hydrochloric acid (*see*) and sodium hydroxide (*see*).

BUTADIENE-STYRENE COPOLYMER • A component for a chewing-gum base. Butadiene is produced largely from petroleum gases and is used in the manufacture of synthetic rubber. It may be irritating to the skin and mucous membranes and narcotic in high concentrations. Styrene, obtained from ethyl benzene, is an oily liquid with a penetrating odor. It has the same uses and toxicity.

BUTADIENE STYRENE RUBBER • Latex. A chewing gum base. No known toxicity.

BUTANAL • *See* Butyraldehyde.

BUTANDIONE • *See* Diacetyl.

BUTANE • N-butane. Methylsulfonal Bioxiran Dibutadiene Dioxide. A flammable, easily liquefiable gas derived from petroleum. A solvent, refrigerant, and food additive. Also used as a propellant or aerosol in cosmetics. The principal hazard is that of fire and explosion, but it may be narcotic in high doses and cause asphyxiation. It has been determined by the National Institute of Occupational Safety and Health to be an animal carcinogen. GRAS.

1,4-BUTANEDICARBOXYLIC ACID • *See* Adipic Acid.

BUTANOIC ACID • *See* Butyric Acid.

1-BUTANOL • *See* Butyl Alcohol.

2, 3-BUTANOLONE • *See* Acetoin.

(TRANS)-BUTENEDIOIC ACID • *See* Fumaric Acid.

BUTOXYPOLYETHYLENE • A synthetic antifoaming agent used in beet sugar manufacture. No known toxicity.

BUTRYIC ACID • A clear, colorless liquid present in butter at 4 to 5 percent. It has a strong, rancid butter odor, and is used in butterscotch, caramel, and fruit flavorings. It is used in chewing gums and margarines, as well as cosmetics. It is found naturally in apples, geraniums, rose oil, grapes, strawberries, and wormseed oil. It has a low toxicity but can be a mild irritant. It caused tumors when applied to the skin of mice in doses of 108 milligrams per kilogram of body weight and cancer when injected into the abdomen of mice in doses of 18 milligrams per kilogram of body weight. A NIOSH review has determined it is a positive animal carcinogen.

BUTTER FAT • The oily portions of the milk of mammals. Cow's milk contains about 4 percent butter fat.

BUTTERMILK • The fluid remaining after butter has been formed from churned cream. It can also be made from sweet milk by the addition of certain organic cultures. Used as an astringent right from the bottle. Apply liberally and let dry about 10 minutes. Rinse off with cool water.

BUTTERS • Acids, Esters, and Distillate. *Butter acids* are synthetic butter and cheese flavoring agents for beverages, ice cream, ices, candy (2,800 ppm), baked goods. *Butter esters* are synthetic butter, caramel, and chocolate flavoring agents for beverages, ice cream, ices, baked goods, toppings, and popcorn (1,200 ppm). *Butter starter distillate* is a synthetic butter flavoring agent for ice cream, ices, baked goods, and shortening (12,000 ppm). In cosmetology, substances that are solid at room temperature but that melt at body temperature are called "butters." Cocoa butter is one of the most frequently used in both foods and cosmetics. Newer butters are made from natural fats by hydrogenation (*see*), which increases the butter's melting point or alters its plasticity. Butters may be used in stick or molded cosmetics such as lipsticks or to give the proper texture to a variety of finished products. Nontoxic.

BUTYL ACETATE • Acetic Acid. Butyl Ester. A synthetic flavoring agent, a clear liquid with a strong fruit odor, prepared from acetic acid and butyl alcohol. Used in raspberry, strawberry, butter, banana, and pineapple flavorings for beverages, ice cream, ices, candy, baked goods, chewing gum, and gelatin desserts. Used in perfumery, nail polish, and nail polish remover. Also used in the manufacture of lacquer, artificial leather, plastics, and safety glass. It is an irritant and may cause eye irritation (conjunctivitis). It is a narcotic in high concentrations, and toxic to humans when inhaled at 200 ppm.

BUTYL ACETOACETATE • A synthetic berry and fruit flavoring agent for beverages, ice cream, candy, and baked goods. No known toxicity.

BUTYL ALCOHOL • A synthetic butter, cream, fruit, liquor, rum, and whiskey flavoring agent for beverages, ice cream, ices, candy, baked goods, cordials, and cream. A colorless liquid with an unpleasant odor, it occurs naturally in apples and raspberries. Used as a clarifying agent (*see*) in shampoos; also a solvent for waxes, fats, resins, and shellac. It may cause irritation of the mucous membranes, headache, dizziness, and drowsiness when ingested. Inhalation of as little as 25 ppm causes pulmonary problems in humans. It can also cause contact dermatitis when applied to the skin.

t-BUTYL ALCOHOL • *See* Butyl Alcohol.

BUTYL ALDEHYDE • *See* Butyraldehyde.

BUTYL ANTHRANILATE • A synthetic grape, mandarin, and pineapple flavoring agent for beverages, ice cream, ices, candy, and baked goods. No known toxicity.

BUTYL BUTYRYLLACTATE • A colorless, synthetic flavoring agent from butyl alcohol, with a fruity odor. Used in berry, butter, apple, banana, peach, pineapple, liquor, Scotch, and nut flavoring for beverages, ice cream, ices, candy, baked goods, chewing gum, and gelatin desserts. No known toxicity.

a-BUTYL CINNAMALDEHYDE • A synthetic fruit, nut, spice, and cinnamon flavoring agent for beverages, ice cream, ices, candy, and baked goods. No known toxicity.

BUTYL CINNAMATE • A synthetic chocolate, cocoa, and fruit flavoring for beverages, ice cream, ices, candy, baked goods, and liquor. No known toxicity.

BUTYL 2-DECENOATE • A synthetic apricot and peach flavoring agent for beverages, ice cream, ices, candy, baked goods, chewing gum (2,000 ppm). No known toxicity.

BUTYL DECYLENATE • *See* Butyl 2-Decenoate.

BUTYL DODECANOATE • *See* Butyl Laurate.

BUTYL ETHYL MALONATE • A synthetic fruit and apple flavoring for beverages, ice cream, ices, candy, and baked goods. No known toxicity.

BUTYL FORMATE • Formic Acid. A synthetic fruit, plum, liquor, and rum flavoring for beverages, ice cream, ices, candy, and baked goods. Caustic to the skin.

BUTYL HEPTANOATE • A synthetic fruit and liquor flavoring for beverages, ice cream, ices, candy, and baked goods. No known toxicity.

BUTYL HEXANOATE • A synthetic butter, butterscotch, pineapple, and rum flavoring agent for beverages, ice cream, ices, candy, and baked goods. No known toxicity.

BUTYL p-HYDROXYBENZOATE • Butyl Paraben. Butyl p-Oxybenzoate. Almost odorless, small colorless crystals or a white powder used as an antimicrobial preservative. No known toxicity.

BUTYL ISOBUTYRATE • A synthetic raspberry, strawberry, butter, banana, and cherry flavoring agent for beverages, ice cream, ices, candy, baked goods, and chewing gum (2,000 ppm). No known toxicity.

BUTYL ISOVALERATE • A synthetic chocolate and fruit flavoring for beverages, ice cream, ices, candy, puddings, and gelatin desserts. No known toxicity.

2-BUTYL-5 (OR 6)-KETO-1, 4-DIOXANE • A synthetic fruit and spice flavoring for beverages, ice cream, ices, candy, baked goods, and shortenings. No known toxicity.

BUTYL LACTATE • A synthetic butter, butterscotch, caramel, and fruit flavoring agent for beverages, ice cream, ices, candy, baked goods. No known toxicity.

BUTYL LAURATE • A synthetic fruit flavoring for beverages, ice cream, ices, candy, and baked goods. No known toxicity.

BUTYL LEVULINATE • A synthetic butter, fruit, and rum flavoring agent for beverages, ice cream, ices, candy, baked goods. No known toxicity.

BUTYL PARASEPT • *See* Butyl *p*-Hydroxybenzoate.

BUTYL PHENYLACETATE • Synthetic butter, honey, caramel, chocolate, rose, fruit, and nut flavoring agent for beverages, ice cream, ices, candy, baked goods, gelatin desserts, and puddings. No known toxicity.

BUTYL PROPIONATE • A synthetic butter, rum butter, fruit, and rum flavoring agent for beverages, ice cream, ices, candy, and baked goods. May be an irritant.

BUTYL RUBBER • A synthetic rubber used as a chewing gum base component. No known toxicity.

BUTYL SEBACATE • *See* Dibutyl Sebacate.

BUTYL STEARATE • A synthetic antifoaming agent used in the production of beet sugar. Also a synthetic banana, butter, and liquor for beverages, ice cream, ices, candy, baked goods, chewing gum, and liqueurs. No known toxicity.

BUTYL SULFIDE • A synthetic floral, violet, and fruit flavoring for beverages, ice cream, ices, candy, baked goods. No known toxicity.

BUTYL 10-UNDECENOATE • A synthetic butter, apricot, cognac, and nut flavoring agent for beverages, ice cream, ices, candy, baked goods, chewing gum, icing, and liquor. No known toxicity.

BUTYL VALERATE • A synthetic butter, fruit, and chocolate flavoring agent for beverages, ice cream, ices, candy, baked goods, puddings, and gelatin desserts. No known toxicity.

BUTYLATED HYDROXYANISOLE (BHA) • A preservative and antioxidant in many products, including beverages, ice cream, ices, candy, baked goods, chewing gum, gelatin desserts, soup bases, potatoes, glacéed fruits, potato flakes, sweet potato flakes, dry breakfast cereals, dry yeast, dry mixes for desserts, lard, shortening, unsmoked dry sausage, and in emulsions for stabilizers for shortenings. It is a white or slightly yellow, waxy solid with a faint, characteristic odor. Insoluble in water. Total content antioxidants is not to exceed 0.02 percent of fat or oil content of food; allowed up to 1,000 ppm in dry yeast; 200 ppm in shortenings; 50 ppm in potato flakes; and 50 ppm with BHT (*see* Butylated Hydroxytoluene) in dry cereals. Can cause allergic reactions. BHA affects the liver and kidney functions (the liver detoxifies it). BHA may be more rapidly metabolized than BHT and in experiments at Michigan State University it appeared to be less toxic to the kidneys of living animals than BHT. Can cause allergic reactions. The final report to the FDA of the Select Committee on GRAS Substances stated in 1980 that while no evidence in the available information on it demonstrates a hazard to the public at current use levels, uncertainties exist, requiring that additional studies be conducted. The FDA said in 1980 that GRAS status should continue while tests on BHA are being completed and evaluated. As of this writing, nothing further has been reported.

BUTYLATED HYDROXYMETHYLPHENOL • A new antioxidant, a nearly white, crystalline solid, with a faint characteristic odor. Insoluble in water and propylene glycol; soluble in alcohol. No known toxicity but the formula, 4-hydroxymethyl-2,6-di-tert-butylphenol, contains phenol which is very toxic.

BUTYLATED HYDROXYTOLUENE (BHT) • A preservative and antioxidant employed in many foods. Used as a chewing gum base, added to potato and sweet potato flakes, and dry breakfast cereals, an emulsion stabilizer for shortenings, used in enriched rice, animal fats, and shortenings containing animal fats. White, crystalline solid with a faint characteristic odor. Insoluble in water. Total content of antioxidants in fat or oils not to exceed 0.02 percent. Allowed up to 200 ppm in emulsion stabilizers for shortenings, 50 ppm in dry breakfast cereals and potato flakes. Used also as an antioxidant to retard rancidity in frozen fresh pork sausage and freeze-dried meats up to 0.01 percent based on fat content. Can cause allergic reactions. Loyola University scientists reported on April 14, 1972, that pregnant mice fed a diet consisting of one half of one percent of BHT (or BHA, butylated hydroxyanisole) gave birth to offspring that frequently had chemical changes in the brain and subsequently abnormal behavior patterns. BHT and BHA are chemically similar but BHT may be more toxic to the kidney than BHA (*see* Butylated Hydroxyanisole), according to researchers at Michigan State University. The Select Committee of the American Societies for Experimental Biology, which advises the FDA on food additives, recommended further studies to determine "the effects of BHT at levels now present in foods under conditions where steroid hormones or oral contraceptives are being ingested." They said the possibility that BHT may convert other ingested substances into toxic or cancer-causing agents should be investigated. BHT is prohibited as a food additive in England. The FDA is pursuing further study of BHT. GRAS

1,3-BUTYLENE GLYCOL • A clear, colorless, viscous liquid with a slight taste. A solvent and humectant most resistant to high humidity and thus valuable in foods and cosmetics. It retains scents and preserves against spoilage. When ingested may cause transient stimulation of the central nervous system, then depression, vomiting, drowsiness, coma, respiratory failure, and convulsions; renal damage may proceed to uremia and death. One of the few humectants not on the GRAS list, although efforts to place it there have been made through the years.

BUTYLPARABEN • Widely used in food and cosmetics as an antifungal preservative, it is the ester of butyl alcohol and *p*-hydroxybenzoic acid (*see* both). No known toxicity.

BUTYRALDEHYDE • A synthetic flavoring agent found naturally in coffee and strawberries. Used in butter, caramel, fruit, liquor, brandy, and nut flavorings for beverages, ice cream, ices, candy, baked goods, alcoholic beverages, and icings. Used also in the manufacture of rubber, gas accelerators, synthetic resins, and plasticizers. May be an irritant and a narcotic.

BUTYRIC ACID • N-Butyric Acid. Butanoic Acid. A clear, colorless liquid present in butter at 4 to 5 percent with a strong penetrating rancid-butter odor. Butter, butterscotch, caramel, fruit, and nut flavoring agent for beverages, ice cream, ices, candy, baked goods, gelatin desserts, puddings, chewing gum, and margarine. Found naturally in apples, butter acids, geranium, rose oil, grapes, strawberries, and wormseed oil. It has a low toxicity but can be a mild irritant. GRAS.

BUTYRIC ALDEHYDE • *See* Butyraldehyde.

BUTYRIN • *See* (tri-) Butyrin.

(tri-)BUTYRIN • A synthetic flavoring agent found naturally in butter. Butter flavoring for beverages, ice cream, ices, candy (1,000 ppm), baked goods, margarine, and puddings. No known toxicity.

BUTYROIN • *See* 5-Hydroxy-4-Octanone.

BUTYRONE • *See* 4-Heptanone.

BUXINE® • *See* a-Amylcinnamaldehyde.

BUXINOL • *See* a-Amylcinnamyl Alcohol.

BUTYROLACTONE • Butanolide. Liquid lactone used chiefly as a solvent for resins. It is also an intermediate (*see*) in the manufacture of polyvinylpyrrolidone (*see*) and as a solvent for nail polish. Human toxicity is unknown.

C

**CACAO SHELL • ** Cocoa shells of the seeds of trees grown in Brazil, Central America, and most tropical countries. Weak chocolatelike odor and taste, thin and peppery with a reddish-brown color. Used in the manufacture of caffeine (*see*); also theobromine, which occurs in chocolate products and is used as a diuretic and nerve stimulant. Occasionally causes allergic reactions from handling. GRAS.

**CACHOU EXTRACT • ** *See* Catechu Extract.

**CACTUS ROOT EXTRACT • ** *See* Yucca Extract.

**CADINENE • ** A general fixative that occurs naturally in juniper oil and pepper oil. It has a faint, pleasant smell. Used in candy, baked goods (1,200 ppm), and chewing gum (1,000 ppm). No known toxicity.

**CAFFEINE • ** Guaranine. Methyltheobromine. Theine. An odorless white powder with a bitter taste that occurs naturally in the coffee, cola, guarana paste, tea, and kola nuts. Caffeine is the number-one psychoactive drug. Obtained as a by-product of caffeine-free coffee. Used as a flavor in root beer beverages and other foods. It is a central nervous system, heart, and respiratory system stimulant. Caffeine can alter blood sugar release and cross the placental barrier. It can cause nervousness, insomnia, irregular heartbeat, noises in ears, and in high doses, convulsions. It has been linked to spontaneous panic attacks in persons sensitive to caffeine. Because of its capability to cause birth defects in rats, the FDA proposed regulations to request new safety studies and to encourage the manufacture and sale of caffeine-free colas. One regulation would make the food industry's continued use of caffeine as an added ingredient in soft drinks and other foods conditional upon its funding of studies of caffeine's effects on children and the unborn. Under present regulations, a soft drink, except one artificially sweetened, must contain caffeine if it is to be labeled as "cola" or "pepper" and the FDA wants soda producers to be able to use this name when caffeine is not used. The FDA has asked for studies on the long-term effects of the additive to determine whether it may cause cancer or birth defects. The final report to the FDA of the Select Committee on GRAS Substances stated in 1980 that while no evidence in the available information demonstrates a hazard to the public at current use levels, uncertainties exist, requiring that additional studies be conducted. GRAS status continues while tests are being conducted.

CAJEPUT OIL • A spice flavoring from the cajeput tree native to Australia. The leaves yield an aromatic oil. Used for beverages, ice cream, ices, candy, and baked goods. No known toxicity.

CAJEPUTENE • *See* d-Limonene.

CAJEPUTOL • *See* Eucalyptol.

CALCIUM ACETATE • Brown Acetate of Lime. A white amorphous powder that has been used medicinally as a source of calcium. It is used in the manufacture of acetic acid and acetone and in dyeing, tanning, and curing skins as well as a corrosion inhibitor in metal containers. Used cosmetically for solidifying fragrances and as an emulsifier and firming agent. Low oral toxicity. The final report to the FDA of the Select Committee on GRAS Substances stated in 1980 that it should continue its GRAS status with no limitations other than good manufacturing practices.

CALCIUM ACID PHOSPHATE • See Calcium Phosphate.

CALCIUM ALGINATE • A stabilizer, thickener, gelling agent, and texturizer. Also used as a solvent and vehicle for flavorings. Found in ice creams and popsicles, soft and cottage cheeses, cheese snacks, dressings and spreads, fruit drinks, beverages, and instant desserts. GRAS. *See* Alginates.

CALCIUM ASCORBATE • A preservative and antioxidant prepared from ascorbic acid (Vitamin C) and calcium carbonate (*see*). Used in concentrated milk products; in cooked, cured, or pulverized meat products; in pickles in which pork and beef products are cured and packed (up to 75 ounces per 100 gallons). *See* Ascorbic Acid for toxicity. The final report to the FDA of the Select Committee on GRAS Substances stated in 1980 that it should continue its GRAS status with no limitations other than good manufacturing practices.

CALCIUM BENZOATE • *See* Benzoic Acid.

CALCIUM BROMATE • A maturing agent and dough conditioner used in bromated flours. *See* Bromates.

CALCIUM CARBONATE • Chalk. Absorbent that removes shine from talc. A tasteless, odorless powder that occurs naturally in limestone, marble, and coral. Used as a white food dye, an alkali to reduce acidity in wine by up to 2.5 percent, a neutralizer for ice cream and in cream syrups up to 0.25 percent, in confections up to 0.25 percent, and in baking powder up to 50 percent. Employed as carrier for bleaches. Once widely used as a white coloring in foods and cosmetics, the authorization by the FDA was withdrawn in 1988. Calcium carbonate is also used as an alkali to reduce acidity, and as a neutralizer and firming agent. Also used in dentifrices as a tooth polisher, in deodorants as a filler, in depilatories as a filler, and in face powder as a buffer. A gastric antacid and antidiarrhea medicine, it may cause constipation. Female mice were bred after a week on diets supplemented with calcium carbonate at 220 and 880 times the human intake of this additive. At all dosage levels, the first and second litters of newly weaned mice were lower in weight and number, and mortality was increased. The highest level caused heart enlargement. Supplementing the maternal diet with iron prevented this, so the side effects were attributed to mineral imbalance due to excessive calcium intake. In humans, 500 milligrams per kilogram of body weight was fed to ulcer victims for three weeks. The amounts ingested were 145 times the normal amount ingested as an additive. Some patients developed an excess of calcium in the blood and suffered nausea, weakness, and dizziness. Calcium carbonate can cause constipation.

CALCIUM CARRAGEENAN • *See* Carrageenan.

CALCIUM CASEINATE • Used as a nutrient supplement for frozen desserts, creamed cottage cheese. *See* Casein.

CALCIUM CHLORIDE • The chloride salt of calcium. Used in its anhydrous (*see*) form as a drying agent for organic liquids and gases. Used as a firming agent for sliced apples and other fruits, in apple pie mix, as a jelly ingredient, in certain cheeses to aid coagulation, in artificially sweetened fruit jelly, and in canned tomatoes. An emulsifier and texturizer in cosmetics and an antiseptic in eye lotions. Also used in fire extinguishers, to preserve wood, and to melt ice and snow. Employed medicinally as a diuretic and a urinary acidifier. Ingestion can cause stomach and heart disturbances. The final report to the FDA of the Select Committee on GRAS Substances stated in 1980 that it should continue its GRAS status with no limitations other than good manufacturing practices.

CALCIUM CITRATE • A fine, white, odorless powder prepared from citrus fruit. Used as a buffer to neutralize acids in confections, jellies, jams, and in saccharin at the rate of 3 ounces per 100 pounds of the artificial sweetener. It is also used to improve the baking properties of flour. *See* Citrate Salts for toxicity. The final report to the FDA of the Select Committee on GRAS Substances stated in 1980 that it should continue its GRAS status with no limitations other than good manufacturing practices.

CALCIUM DIACETATE • A sequestrant used in cereal. GRAS. *See* Calcium Acetate.

CALCIUM DIOXIDE • Used in cereal flours. *See* Calcium Peroxide.

CALCIUM DISODIUM EDTA • Edetate Calcium Disodium. Calcium Disodium Ethylenediamine Tetraacetic Acid. A preservative and sequestrant. A white, odorless powder with a faint salty taste. Used as a food additive to prevent crystal formation and to retard color loss.

Used in canned and carbonated soft drinks for flavor retention; in canned white potatoes and cooked canned clams for color retention; in crab meat to retard struvite (crystal formation); in dressings as a preservative; in cooked and canned dried lima beans for color retention; in fermented malt beverages to prevent gushing; in mayonnaise and oleomargarine as a preservative; in processed dried pinto beans for color retention; and in sandwich spreads as a preservative. Used medically as a chelating agent to detoxify poisoning by lead and other heavy metals. May cause intestinal upsets, muscle cramps, kidney damage, and blood in urine. On the FDA priority list of food additives to be studied for mutagenic, teratogenic, subacute, and reproductive effects.

CALCIUM GLUCONATE • Odorless, tasteless, white crystalline granules, stale in air. Used as a buffer, firming agent, sequestrant. It is soluble in water. May cause gastrointestinal and cardiac disturbances. The final report to the FDA of the Select Committee on GRAS Substances stated in 1980 that it should continue its GRAS status with no limitations other than good manufacturing practices.

CALCIUM DI-L-GLUTAMATE • The salt of glutamic acid (*see*). A flavor enhancer and salt substitute. Almost odorless white powder. The FDA says that it needs further study. As of this writing, nothing has been reported.

CALCIUM GLYCEROPHOSPHATE • A fine, white, odorless, nearly tasteless powder used in dentifrices, baking powder, and as a food stabilizer and dietary supplement. A component of many over-the-counter nerve-tonic foods. Administered medicinally for numbness and debility. *See* Calcium Sources. The final report to the FDA of the Select Committee on GRAS Substances stated in 1980 that it should continue its GRAS status with no limitations other than good manufacturing practices.

CALCIUM 5'-GUANYLATE • Flavor potentiator. Odorless white crystals or powder having a characteristic taste. *See* Flavor Potentiators.

CALCIUM HEXAMETAPHOSPHATE • An emulsifier, sequestering agent, and texturizer used in breakfast cereals, angel food cake, flaked fish (prevents struvite), ice cream, ices, milk, bottled beer, reconstituted lemon juice, puddings, processed cheeses, artificially sweetened jellies and preserves, potable water supplies to prevent scale formation and corrosion, and in pickle for curing hams. No known toxicity. The final report to the FDA of the Select Committee on GRAS Substances stated in 1980 that it should continue its GRAS status with no limitations other than good manufacturing practices.

CALCIUM HYDROXIDE • Slaked Lime. Calcium Hydrate. Limewater. Lye. An alkali, a white powder with a slightly bitter taste. Used as a firming agent for various fruit products, as an egg preservative, in water treatment, and for dehairing hides. Used in cream depilatories; also in mortar, plaster, cement, pesticides, and fireproofing. Employed as a topical astringent and alkali in cosmetic solutions or lotions. Accidental ingestion can cause burns of the throat and esophagus; also death from shock and asphyxia due to swelling of the glottis and infection. Calcium hydroxide also can cause burns of the skin and eyes. The final report to the FDA of the Select Committee on the GRAS Substances stated in 1980 that it should continue its GRAS status with no limitations other than good manufacturing practices.

CALCIUM HYPOCHLORITE • A germicide and sterilizing agent, the active ingredient of chlorinated lime, used in the curd washing of cottage cheese, in sugar refining, as an oxidizing and bleaching agent, and as an algae killer, bactericide, deodorant, disinfectant, and fungicide. Sterilizes fruits and vegetables by washing in a 50-percent solution. Under various names, dilute hypochlorite is found in homes as laundry bleach and household bleach. Occasionally cases of poisoning occur when people mix household hypochlorite solution with various other household chemicals, which causes the release of poisonous chlorine gas. As with other corrosive agents, calcium hypochlorite's toxicity depends upon its concentrations. It is highly corrosive to skin and mucous membranes. Ingestion may cause pain and inflammation of the mouth, pharynx, esophagus, and stomach, with erosion particularly of the mucous membranes of the stomach.

CALCIUM HYPOPHOSPHITE • Crystals of powder that is slightly acid in solution, and practically insoluble in alcohol. It is a corrosion inhibitor and has been used as a dietary supplement in veterinary medicine. The final report to the FDA of the Select Committee on GRAS Substances stated in 1980 that it should continue its GRAS status with no limitations other than good manufacturing practices.

CALCIUM 5'-INOSINATE • *See* Inosinate.

CALCIUM IODATE • White odorless or nearly odorless powder used as a dough conditioner and oxidizing agent in bread, rolls, and buns. It is a nutritional source of iodine in foods such as table salt, and used also in a topical disinfectant and as a deodorant. Low toxicity, but may cause allergic reactions.

CALCIUM LACTATE • White, almost odorless crystals or powder used as a buffer and as such is a constituent of baking powders and is employed in confections; also used in dentifrices and as a yeast food and dough conditioner. In medical use, given for calcium deficiency; may cause gastrointestinal and cardiac disturbances. The final report to the FDA of the Select Committee on GRAS Substances stated in 1980 that it should continue its GRAS status with no limitations other than good manufacturing practices.

CALCIUM LACTOBIONATE • A calcium salt (*see*) used as a firming agent in dry pudding mixes. *See* Calcium Salts.

CALCIUM LIGNOSULFONATE • Made from calcium and sodium salts, it is used as a dispersing agent and stabilizer for pesticides used on bananas. *See* Calcium Sources.

CALCIUM METASILICATE • White powder, insoluble in water, used as an absorbent, antacid, filler for paper coatings, and as a food additive. Use in food restricted to 5 percent in baking powder and 2 percent in table salt. Irritating dust.

CALCIUM ORTHOPHOSPHATE • Buffer and neutralizing agent used in noncarbonated beverages. No known toxicity.

CALCIUM OXIDE • Quicklime. Burnt Lime. A hard, white or grayish white odorless mass or powder that is used as a yeast food and dough conditioner for bread, rolls, and buns. It is also an alkali for neutralizing dairy products (including ice cream mixes) and alkalizes sour cream, butter, and confections, and is used in the processing of tripe. Industrial uses are for bricks, plaster, mortar, stucco, dehairing hides, fungicides, insecticides, and for clarification of beet and cane sugar juices. A strong caustic, it may severely damage skin and mucous membranes. The final report to the FDA of the Select Committee on GRAS Substances stated in 1980 that it should continue its GRAS status with no limitations other than good manufacturing practices. *See* Calcium Sources.

CALCIUM PANTOTHENATE • Pantothenic Acid Calcium Salt. A B-complex vitamin, pantothenate is a white, odorless powder with a sweetish taste and bitter aftertaste. Pantothenic acid occurs everywhere in plant and animal tissue, and the richest common source is liver; jelly of the queen bee contains six times as much. Rice bran and molasses are other good sources. Acid derivatives sold commercially are synthesized. Biochemical defects from lack of calcium pantothenate may exist undetected for some time but eventually manifest themselves as tissue failures. The calcium chloride double salt of calcium pantothenate has been cleared for use in foods for special dietary uses. The final report to the FDA of the Select Committee on GRAS Substances stated in 1980 that it should continue its GRAS status with no limitations other than good manufacturing practices. *See d-*Pantothenamide.

CALCIUM PEROXIDE • White or yellowish, odorless, almost taste-less powder that is derived from an interaction of a calcium salt and sodium peroxide with subsequent crystallization. Used in bakery products as a dough conditioner, for bleaching of oils and modification of starches, and as a seed disinfectant. Irritating to the skin.

CALCIUM PHOSPHATE • Dibasic, Monobasic, and Tribasic. White, odorless powders used as yeast foods, dough conditioners, and firming agents. *Tribasic* is an anticaking agent used in table salt, powdered sugar, malted milk powder, condiments, puddings, meat, dry-curing mixtures, cereal flours, and vanilla powder. It is tasteless. Used as a gastric antacid mineral supplement and a clarifying agent for sugars and syrups. *Dibasic* is used to improve bread, rolls, buns, cereal flours; a carrier for bleaching; used as a mineral supplement in cereals, in dental products, and in fertilizers. *Monobasic* is used in bread, rolls, and buns, artificially sweetened fruit jelly, canned potatoes, canned sweet peppers, canned tomatoes, and as a jelling ingredient. Employed as a fertilizer as an acidulant, in baking powders, and in wheat flours as a mineral supplement. Nontoxic. The final report to the FDA of the Select Committee on GRAS Substances stated in 1980 that it should continue its GRAS status with no limitations other than good manufacturing practices.

CALCIUM PHYTATE • Used as a sequestering agent (*see*). When 300 milligrams per kilogram of body weight was fed to rats as a diet supplement, it successfully provided calcium for bone deposition, and the animals remained healthy. The final report to the FDA of the Select Committee on GRAS Substances stated in 1980 that it should continue its GRAS status with no limitations other than good manufacturing practices.

CALCIUM PROPIONATE • Propanoic Acid, Calcium Salt. White crystals or crystalline solid with the faint odor of propionic acid. A mold and rope inhibitor in breads and rolls and poultry stuffing, it is used in processed cheese, chocolate products, cakes, cupcakes, and artificially sweetened fruit jelly. It is used as a preservative in cosmetics and as an antifungal medication for the skin. GRAS.

CALCIUM PYROPHOSPHATE • A fine white, odorless, tasteless powder used as a nutrient, an abrasive in dentifrices, a buffer, and as a neutralizing agent in foodstuffs. No known toxicity. The final report to the FDA of the Select Committee on GRAS Substances stated in 1980 that it should continue its GRAS status with no limitations other than good manufacturing practices. *See* Calcium Sources.

CALCIUM 5'-RIBONUCLEOTIDES • Flavor potentiators (*see*), in odorless, white crystals or powder, with a characteristic taste. *See* Inosinate.

CALCIUM SACCHARIN • *See* Saccharin.

CALCIUM SALTS • Acetate, Chloride, Citrate, Diacetate, Gluconate, Phosphate (monobasic), Phytate, Sulfate. Emulsifier salts used in evaporated milk, frozen desserts, and enriched bread. Firming agents in potatoes and canned tomatoes. May be gastric irritants, but they have little oral toxicity. GRAS. *See* separate listing for Calcium Sulfate and Calcium Phosphate.

CALCIUM SALTS OF FATTY ACIDS • Used as binders and anticaking agent in foods. No known toxicity.

CALCIUM SALTS OF PARTIALLY DIMERIZED ROSIN • Used as a coating on free citrus fruits. *See* Calcium Salts.

CALCIUM SILICATE • Okenite. An anticaking agent, white or slightly cream-colored, free-flowing powder. It is used up to 5 percent in baking powder and 2 percent of table salts. Absorbs water. Used in face powders because it has extremely fine particles and good water absorption. Also used as a coloring agent. Constituent of lime glass and cement, used in road construction. Practically nontoxic orally, except inhalation may cause irritation of the respiratory tract. On the FDA list of additives that need further study for mutagenic, teratogenic, subacute, and reproductive effects. Used in baking powder, in road construction, and in lime glass. The final report to the FDA of the Select Committee on GRAS Substances stated in 1980 that it should continue its GRAS status with no limitations other than good manufacturing practices.

CALCIUM SORBATE • A preservative and fungus preventative used in beverages, baked goods, chocolate syrups, soda-fountain syrups, fresh fruit cocktail, tangerine puree (sherbet base), salads (potato, macaroni, cole slaw, gelatin), cheesecake, pie fillings, cake, cheese in consumer-size packages, and artificially sweetened jellies and preserves. No known toxicity. The final report to the FDA of the Select Committee on GRAS Substances stated in 1980 that it should continue its GRAS status with no limitations other than good manufacturing practices.

CALCIUM SOURCES (Harmless calcium salts) • Carbonate, Citrate, Glycerophosphate, Oxide, Phosphate, Pyrophosphate, Sulfate (see all). Calcium is a mineral supplement for breakfast cereals, white corn meal, infant dietary formula, enriched flour, enriched bromated flour (*see* Bromates), enriched macaroni, noodle products, self-rising flours, enriched farina, cornmeal and corn grits, and enriched bread and rolls. Calcium is a major mineral in the body. It is incompletely absorbed from the gastrointestinal tract when in the diet so its absorption is enhanced by calcium normally present in intestinal secretions. Vitamin D is also required for efficient absorption of calcium. Recommended daily requirements for adult females is 1.5 grams, for adult males 1.2 grams, and for children 0.8 grams. Calcium and phosphorus are the major constituents of teeth and bones. The ratio of calcium to phosphorus in cow's milk is approximately 1.2 to 1. In human milk the ratio is 2 to 1. The final report to the FDA of the Select Committee on GRAS Substances stated in 1980 that it should continue its GRAS status with no limitations other than good manufacturing practices.

CALCIUM STEARATE • The calcium salt of stearic acid (*see*), it is an emulsifier, a coloring agent, and a flavoring agent. It is used as an emulsifier in hair grooming products and in paints and printing ink. Nontoxic. The final report to the FDA of the Select Committee on GRAS Substances stated in 1980 that it should continue its GRAS status with no limitations other than good manufacturing practices.

CALCIUM STEAROYL LACTYLATE • Calcium Stearyl-2 Lactylate. A mixture of sodium salts and stearoyl lactylic acids and other sodium salts, it is manufactured from stearic acid and lactic acid (*see* both). It is used as a dough conditioner, emulsifier, or processing aid in baked products, pancakes, and waffles in amounts not to exceed 0.5 part for each 100 parts of flour used. It is also used as a surface-active agent, emulsifier, or stabilizer in icings, fillings, puddings, and toppings in amounts not to exceed 0.2 percent by weight of the finished food. It is also used as an emulsifier or stabilizer in fat and water emulsions that are substituted for milk or cream in beverage coffee, at a level not to exceed 0.3 percent by weight of the edible fat-water emulsion. It is also used as an emulsifier, stabilizer, or texturizer in snack dips, cheese substitutes, and prepared mixes. No known toxicity.

CALCIUM SULFATE • Plaster of Paris. A fine, white to slightly yellow, odorless, tasteless powder used as a firming agent and yeast food and dough conditioner. Utilized in brewing and other fermentation industries, in Spanish type sherry, as a jelling ingredient, in cereal flours, as a carrier for bleaching agents, in bread, rolls, and buns, in blue cheese and Gorgonzola cheese, in artificially sweetened fruit, jelly, canned potatoes, canned sweet peppers, and canned tomatoes. Used also in creamed cottage cheese as an alkali, in toothpaste and tooth powders as an abrasive and firming agent, and in cosmetics as a coloring agent. Employed industrially in cement, wall plaster, and insecticides. Because it absorbs moisture and hardens quickly, its ingestion may result in intestinal obstruction. Mixed with flour, it has been used to kill rodents. No known toxicity on the skin. GRAS.

CALCIUM SULPHIDE • A yellow powder formed by heating gypsum with charcoal at 1,000° F. Employed in depilatories. Used in acne preparations. Also used as a food preservative and in luminous paints. It can cause allergic reactions.

CALCIUM TARTRATE • White crystals soluble in acids derived from cream of tartar. Used as a food preservative and antacid. No known toxicity.

CALENDULA • Dried flowers of pot marigolds grown in gardens everywhere. Used as a natural flavoring agent. *See* Marigold, Pot, for foods in which it's used. Formerly used to sooth inflammation of skin and mucous membranes, now used in "natural" creams, oils, and powders for babies. No known toxicity. GRAS.

CALORIE • A unit used to express the heat output of an organism and the fuel or energy value of food. The amount of heat required to raise the temperature of one gram of water from 14.5 to 15.5° C. at atmospheric pressure.

CALUMBA ROOT • Flavoring used in alcoholic beverage only.

2-CAMPHANOL • *See* Borneol.

CAMOMILE • *See* Chamomile.

CAMPHENE • A synthetic spice and nutmeg flavoring agent for beverages, ice cream, ices, candy, and baked goods. Occurs naturally in calamus oil, citronella, ginger, lemon oil, mandarin oil, myrtle, petitgrain oil, and juniper berries. No known toxicity.

CAMPHOR OIL. JAPANESE WHITE OIL • Camphor Tree. Distilled from trees at least fifty years old grown in China, Japan, Formosa, Brazil, and Sumatra. Camphor tree is used in spice flavorings for beverages, baked goods, and condiments. Used in emollient creams, hair tonics, eye lotions, preshave lotions, after-shave lotions, and skin fresheners as a preservative and to give a cool feeling to the skin. It is also used in horn-rimmed glasses, as a drug preservative, in embalming fluid, in the manufacture of explosives, in lacquers, as a moth repellent, and topically in liniments, cold medications, and anesthetics. It can cause contact dermatitis. In 1980, the FDA banned camphorated oil as a liniment for colds and sore muscles because of reports of poisonings through skin absorption and because of accidental ingestion. A New Jersey pharmacist had collected case reports and testified before the Advisory Review Panel on Over the Counter Drugs of the FDA in 1980. Camphor is readily absorbed through all sites of administration. Ingestion of 2 grams generally produces dangerous effects in an adult. Ingestion by pregnant women has caused fetal deaths. As of this writing, nothing new to report.

CANANGA OIL • A natural flavor extract obtained by distillation from the flowers of the tree. Light to deep yellow liquid with a harsh, floral odor. Used in cola, fruit, spice, and ginger ale flavoring for beverages, ice cream, ices, candy, baked goods. May cause allergic reactions. No known toxicity. GRAS.

CANDELILLA WAX • Obtained from candelilla plants. Brownish to yellow brown, hard, brittle, easily pulverized, partially insoluble in water. Hardens other waxes. Used as a coating for foods. No known toxicity. GRAS.

CANE SUGAR • *See* Sucrose.

CANOLA • A low erucic acid rapeseed oil (*see*) used in salad oils because it contains 50 percent less saturated oils than other popular oils.

CANTHAXANTHIN • A color additive derived from edible mushrooms, crustaceans, trout and salmon, and tropical birds. It produces a pink color when used in foods. FAO/WHO said that up to 25 milligrams per kilogram of body weight is acceptable. Permanently listed in 1969 for human food and permanently listed in 1985 in chicken feed to enhance the yellow color of chicken skin. It is exempt from certification. Oral intake may cause loss of night vision.

CAPERS • A natural flavoring from the spiny shrub. The picked flower bud is used as a condiment for sauces and salads. No known toxicity. GRAS.

CAPRALDEHYDE • *See* Decanal.

CAPRIC ACID • Obtained from a large group of American plants. Solid crystalline mass with a rancid odor used in the manufacture of artificial fruit flavors. Also used to flavor lipsticks. No known toxicity. *See* Decanoic Acid.

CAPRIC ALDEHYDE • *See* Decanal.

CAPRINALDEHYDE • *See* Decanal.

CAPROALDEHYDE • *See* Hexanal.

CAPROIC ACID • Hexanoic Acid. A synthetic flavoring that occurs naturally in apples, butter acids, cocoa, grapes, oil of lavender, oil of lavandin, raspberries, strawberries, and tea. Used in butter, butterscotch, fruit, rum, and cheese flavorings. Used also in the manufacture of "hexyl" derivatives such as hexyl alcohol (*see*). No known toxicity. The final report to the FDA of the Select Committee on GRAS Substances stated in 1980 that it should continue its GRAS status with no limitations other than good manufacturing practices.

CAPRYL BETAINE • *See* Caprylic Acid and Betaine.

CAPRYLAMINE OXIDE • *See* Caprylic Acid and Capric Acid.

CAPRYLIC ACID • An oil liquid made by the oxidation of octyl alcohol (*see*) for use in perfumery. Occurs naturally as a fatty acid in sweat, fusel oil, in the milk of cows and goats, and in palm and coconut oil. Cleared for use as a synthetic flavoring. No known toxicity. The final report to the FDA of the Select Committee on GRAS Substances stated in 1980 that it should continue its GRAS status with no limitations other than good manufacturing practices.

CAPRYLIC ALCOHOL • *See* Octyl Alcohol.

CAPSICUM • African Chilies. Cayenne Pepper. Tabasco Pepper.

The dried fruit of a tropical plant used as a natural spice and ginger ale flavoring for beverages, ice cream, ices, candy, baked goods, chewing gum, and meats and sauces. The oleoresin form is used in sausage, spice, ginger ale, and cinnamon flavorings for beverages, ice cream, ices, candy, baked goods, chewing gum, meats, and condiments. Used internally as a digestive stimulant. Irritating to the mucous membranes, it can produce severe diarrhea and gastritis. May cause a "hot" sensation and sweating. *See* Cayenne Pepper for toxicity. GRAS.

CAPSORUBIN • Coloring from paprika (*see*).

CARAMEL • A chemically ill-defined group of material produced by heating carbohydrates. Burnt sugar with a pleasant, slightly bitter taste. Made by heating sugar or glucose and adding small quantities of alkali or a trace mineral acid during heating. Caramel color prepared by ammonia process has been associated with blood toxicity in rats. Because of this, the joint FAO/WHO Expert Committee on Food Additives temporarily removed the acceptable daily intake for ammonia-made caramel. It was found to inhibit the metabolism of B_6 in rabbits. Caramel is widely used as a brown coloring in ice cream, baked goods, soft drinks, confections. As a flavoring, it is used in strawberry, butter, butterscotch, caramel, chocolate, cocoa, cola, fruit, cherry, grape, birch beer, liquor, rum, brandy, maple, black walnut, walnut, root beer, spice, ginger, ginger ale, vanilla, and cream soda beverages (2,200 ppm), ice cream, candy, baked goods, syrups (2,800 ppm), and meats (2,100 ppm). Used as a coloring in cosmetics and a soothing agent in skin lotions. The FDA has given caramel priority for testing its mutagenic, teratogenic subacute, and reproductive effects as a food additive. Sulfite ammonia caramels tested on humans produced soft to liquid stools and increased bowel movements. The final report to the FDA of the Select Committee on GRAS Substances stated in 1980 that it should continue its GRAS status with no limitations other than good manufacturing practices. Permanently listed in 1963 as a coloring. Certification not required.

CARAWAY SEED AND OIL • The dried ripe seeds of a plant common to Europe and Asia and cultivated in England, Russia, and the U.S. A volatile, colorless to pale yellow liquid, it is used in liquor flavorings for beverages, ice cream, baked goods, and condiments; also used as a spice in baking. The oil is used in grape licorice; anisette, kummel, liver, sausage, mint, caraway, and rye flavorings for beverages, ice cream, ices, candy, baked goods, chewing gum, meats, condiments, and liquors. The oil is used to perfume soap. Can cause contact dermatitis. A mild carminative from 1 to 2 grams to break up intestinal gas. No known toxicity. GRAS.

CARBON BLACK • Several forms of artificially prepared carbon or charcoal, including animal charcoal, furnace black, channel (gas) black, lamp black, activated charcoal. Animal charcoal is used as a black coloring in confectionery. Activated charcoal is used as an antidote for ingested poisons, and as an adsorbent in diarrhea. The others have industrial uses. Carbon black, which was not subject to certification (*see* Certified) by the FDA, was reevaluated and then banned in 1976. It was found in tests to contain a cancer-causing by-product that was released during dye manufacture. It can no longer be used in candies such as licorice and in jelly beans or in drugs or cosmetics.

CARBON DIOXIDE • Colorless, odorless, noncombustible gas with a faint acid taste. Used as a pressure-dispensing agent in gassed creams. Also used in the carbonation of beverages and as dry ice for refrigeration in the frozen food industry. Used on stage to produce harmless smoke or fumes. May cause shortness of breath, vomiting, high blood pressure, and disorientation if inhaled in sufficient amounts. GRAS.

CARBONATE, POTASSIUM • *See* Potassium Carbonate.

CARBONATE, SODIUM • *See* Sodium Carbonate.

CARBONYL IRON • Iron which has been processed with carbon and oxygen. Used as a coloring. *See* Iron Salts. The final report to the FDA of the Select Committee on GRAS Substances stated in 1980 that there is no evidence in the available information that it is a hazard to the public when used as it is now and it should continue its GRAS status with limitations on the amounts that can be added to food.

CARBOXYMETHYL CELLULOSE • Sodium. Made from cotton by-products, it occurs as a white powder or in granules. A synthetic gum it is used as a stabilizer in ice cream, beverages, and other foods. It is employed in bath preparations, beauty masks, dentifrices, hair-grooming aids, hand creams, rouge, shampoos, and shaving creams. As an emulsifier, stabilizers, and foaming agent, it is a skin protectant. It is used medicinally as a laxative or antacid. It has been shown to cause cancer in animals when ingested. Its toxicity on the skin is unknown. The final report to the FDA of the Select Committee on GRAS Substances stated in 1980 that it should continue its GRAS status with no limitations other than good manufacturing practices.

CARDAMON OIL • Grains of Paradise. A natural flavoring and aromatic agent from the dried ripe seeds of trees common to India, Ceylon, and Guatemala. Used in butter, chocolate, liquor, spice, and vanilla flavorings for beverages, ice cream, ices, candy, baked goods (1,700 ppm), meats, and condiments. The seed oil is used in chocolate, cocoa, coffee, cherry liquor, liver, sausage, root beer, sarsaparilla, cardamon, ginger ale, vanilla, and cream soda flavorings for beverages, ice cream, ices, candy, baked goods, chewing gum, liquor, pickles, curry powder and condiments. Used also in perfumes and soaps. As a medicine, it breaks up intestinal gas. No known toxicity.

CARMINE • Cochineal. A crimson pigment derived from a Mexican and Central American species of a scaly female insect that feeds on various cacti. Carmine and Cochineal *extracts* are permanently listed. The colorings once used in red apple sauce, confections, baked goods, meats, and spices have been withdrawn by the FDA. Cochineal was involved in an outbreak of salmonellosis (an intestinal infection), which killed one infant in a Boston hospital, and made twenty-two patients seriously ill. Carmine, used in the diagnostic solution to test the digestive organs, was found to be the infecting agent. Also used in cosmetic colors.

CARMINIC ACID • Natural Red No. 4. Used in mascaras, liquid rouge, paste rouge, and red eye shadows. It is the glucosidal coloring matter from a scaly insect (*see* Carmine). Color is deep red in water and violet to yellow in acids. May cause allergic reactions. Not subject to certification by the FDA.

CARNAUBA WAX • The exudate from the leaves of the Brazilian wax palm tree used as a candy glaze and polish. The crude wax is yellow or dirty green, brittle and very hard. It is used in many polishes and varnishes, and when mixed with other waxes, makes them harder and gives them more luster. Used as a texturizer in foundation makeups, mascara, cream rouge, lipsticks, liquid powders, depilatories, and deodorant sticks. It rarely causes allergic reactions. It is on the FDA list for further study for mutagenic, teratogenic, subacute, and reproductive effects. The final report to the FDA of the Select Committee on GRAS Substances stated in 1980 that there were insufficient relevant biological and other studies upon which to base an evaluation of it when it is used as a food ingredient. GRAS.

CAROB BEAN • *See* Locust Gum Bean.

CAROTENE • Provitamin A. Beta Carotene. Found in all plants and many animal tissues, it is the chief yellow coloring matter of carrots, butter, and egg yolk. Extracted as red crystals or crystalline powder, it is used as a vegetable dye in butter, margarine, shortening, skimmed milk, buttermilk, and cottage cheese. It is also used to manufacture Vitamin A and is a nutrient added to skimmed milk, vegetable shortening, and margarine at the rate of 5,000 to 13,000 USP units per pound. Insoluble in water, acids, and alkalies. Too much carotene in the blood (exceeding 200 micrograms per 100 milliliters of blood) can lead to carotinemia—a pale yellow-red pigmentation of the skin that may be mistaken for jaundice. It is a benign condition and withdrawal of carotene from the diet cures it. The final report to the FDA of the Select Committee on GRAS Substances stated in 1980 that it should continue its GRAS status with no limitations other than good manufacturing practices. Beta Carotene has been permanently listed as a coloring since 1964.

CARRAGEENAN • Chondrus Extract. Irish Moss. A stabilizer and emulsifier, seaweedlike in odor, derived from Irish Moss, used in oils in cosmetics and foods. It is used as an emulsifier in chocolate products, chocolate-flavored drinks, chocolate milk, gassed cream (pressure-dispensed whipped cream), syrups for frozen products, confections, evaporated milk, cheese spreads, and cheese foods, ice cream, frozen custard, sherbets, ices, French dressing, and artificially sweetened jellies and jams. Completely soluble in hot water and not coagulated by acids. Salts of carrageenan, such as calcium, ammonium, potassium, or sodium, are used as a demulcent to soothe mucous membrane irritation. Carrageenan is on the FDA list for further study. Carrageenan stimulated the formation of fibrous tissue when subcutaneously injected into the guinea pig. When a single dose of it dissolved in saline was injected under the skin of the rat, it caused sarcomas after approximately two years. Its cancer-causing ability may be that of a foreign body irritant, because upon administration to rats and mice at high levels in their diet, it did not appear to induce tumors, although survival of the animals for this period was not good. Its use as a food additive is being studied. The final report to the FDA of the Select Committee on GRAS Substances stated in 1980 that while no evidence in the available information demonstrates a hazard to the public at current use levels, uncertainties exist, requiring that additional studies be conducted. The FDA continued the GRAS status while tests were being completed and evaluated. As of this writing, nothing has been reported.

CARROT JUICE POWDER • *See* Carrot Oil.

CARROT OIL • Either of two oils from the seeds of carrots. A light yellow essential oil which has a spicy odor and is used in liqueurs, flavorings, and perfumes. It is used as a violet, fruit, rum, and spice flavoring for beverages, ice cream, ices, candy, baked goods, gelatin desserts, puddings, condiments, and soups. Rich in Vitamin A, it is also used as a coloring and has been permanently listed since 1964. No known toxicity. GRAS.

CARROT SEED EXTRACT • Extract of the seeds of *Daucus Carota sativa*.

CARVACROL • A colorless to pale yellow liquid with a pungent, spicy odor, related to thymol but more toxic. It is found naturally in oil of origanum, dittany of crete oil, oregano, lavage oil, marjoram, and savory. It is a synthetic flavoring used in citrus, fruit, mint, and spice flavorings for beverages, ice cream, ices, candy, baked goods, and condiments. It is used as a disinfectant and is corrosive; one gram by mouth can cause respiratory and circulatory depression and cardiac failure leading to death.

CARVACRYL ETHYL ETHER • A synthetic spice flavoring agent for beverages, ice cream, ices, candy, and baked goods. Found naturally in caraway and grapefruit. No known toxicity.

CARVEOL • A synthetic mint, spearmint, spice, and caraway flavoring agent for beverages, ice cream, ices, candy, and baked goods. Found naturally in caraway and grape, baked fruit. No known toxicity.

CARVOL • *See d*-Carvone.

4-CARVOMENTHENOL • A synthetic citrus and spice flavoring for beverages, ice cream, ices, candy, and baked goods. Occurs naturally in cardamon oil, juniper berries. No known toxicity.

(d- OR l-) CARVONE • Oil of Caraway. *d*-Carvone is usually prepared by distillation from caraway seed and dill seed oil. It is colorless to light yellow with an odor of caraway. *1*-Carvone occurs in several essential oils. It may be isolated from spearmint oil or synthesized commercially from *d*-limonene. It is colorless to pale yellow with the odor of spearmint. Carvol is a synthetic liquor, mint, and spice flavoring agent for beverages, ice cream, ices, candy, and baked goods. Used also in perfumery and soaps. It breaks up intestinal gas and is used as a stimulant. No known toxicity. GRAS.

CARVYL ACETATE • A synthetic mint flavoring for beverages, ice cream, ices, candy, and baked goods. No known toxicity.

CARVYL PROPIONATE • A synthetic mint flavoring for beverages, ice cream, ices, candy, and baked goods. No known toxicity.

CARVYLOPHYLLENE ACETATE • A general fixative that occurs in many essential oils, especially in clove oil. Colorless, oily, with a clovelike odor. Used for beverages, ice cream, ices, candy, baked goods, and chewing gum. Practically insoluble in alcohol. No known toxicity.

BETA-CARYOPHYLLENE • A synthetic spice flavoring. Occurs naturally in cloves, black currant buds, yarrow herb, grapefruit, allspice, and black pepper. The liquid smells like oil of cloves and turpentine. Used beverages, ice cream, ices, candy, baked goods, chewing gum, and condiments. No known toxicity.

CAROPHYLLENE ALCOHOL • A flavoring that occurs in essential oils, especially in clove oil. Colorless, oily, with a clovelike odor. Used as a synthetic mushroom flavoring for baked goods and condiments. No known toxicity.

CASCARA, BITTERLESS EXTRACT • A natural flavoring derived from the dried bark of a plant grown from northern Idaho to northern California. Cathartic. Used in butter, maple, caramel, and vanilla flavoring for beverages, ice cream, ices, and baked goods. Also used as a laxative. The freshly dried bark causes vomiting, and must be dried for a year before use, when the side effect has disappeared. It has a bitter taste and its laxative effect is due to its ability to irritate the mucosa of the large intestine.

CASCARILLA BARK • A natural flavoring agent obtained from the bark of a tree grown in Haiti, the Bahamas, and Cuba. The dried extract is added to smoking tobacco for flavoring and used in bitters and spice flavorings for beverages. The oil, obtained by distillation, is light yellow to amber, with a spicy odor. It is used in cola, fruit, root beer, and spice flavorings for beverages, ice cream, ices, candy, baked goods, and condiments. No known toxicity. GRAS.

CASEIN • Ammonium Caseinate. Calcium Caseinate. Potassium Caseinate. Sodium Caseinate. The principal protein of cow's milk. It is a white water-absorbing powder without noticeable odor. Used as a texturizer for ice cream, frozen custard, ice milk, fruit sherbets, and in special diet preparations. Also used in protective cream and as the "protein" in hair preparations to make the hair thicker and more manageable. It is also used to make depilatories less irritating and as a film-former in beauty masks. It is also used as an emulsifier in many cosmetics and in special diet preparations. Nontoxic. The final report to the FDA of the Select Committee on GRAS Substances stated in 1980 that it should continue its GRAS status with no limitations other than good manufacturing practices.

CASHOO EXTRACT • *See* Catechu Extract.

CASSIA OIL • Cloves. Chinese Oil of Cinnamon. Darker, less agreeable and heavier than true cinnamon. Obtained from a tropical Asian tree, it is used in bitters, fruit, liquor, meat, root beer, sarsaparilla, and spice flavorings for beverages, ice cream, candy, and baked goods (3,000 ppm). It is also used in perfumes, poultices, and as a laxative. It can cause irritation and allergy such as a stuffy nose.

CASSIA BARK • Padang or Batavia. GRAS. *See* Cassia Bark, Chinese.

CASSIA BARK, CHINESE • A natural flavoring extract from cultivated trees. Used in cola, root beer, and spice flavorings for beverages, ice cream, candy, and baked goods. The bark oil is used in berry, chocolate, lemon, coffee, cola, cherry, peach, rum, peppermint, pecan, root beer, cassia, ginger ale, and cinnamon flavorings for beverages, ice cream, ices, candy, baked goods, chewing gum, meats, and condiments. The buds are used in spice flavorings for beverages. Cassia bark can cause inflammation and erosion of the gastrointestinal tract. GRAS.

CASSIE, ABSOLUTE • A natural flavoring from the flowers of the acacia plant. Used in blackberry, violet, vermouth, and fruit flavorings for beverages, ice cream, ices, candy, baked goods, and gelatin desserts. No known toxicity.

CASSIS • *See* Currant Buds, Absolute.

CASTOR OIL • Palm Christi Oil. The seed of the castor-oil plant. After the oil is expressed from the beans, a residual castor pomace remains, which contains a potent allergen. This may be incorporated in fertilizer, which is the main source of exposure, but people who live near a castor bean processing factory may also be sensitized. A flavoring, pale yellow and viscous, it has a slight acrid, sometimes nauseating taste. Used in butter and nut flavorings for beverages, ice cream, ices, candy, and baked goods. Also a release and antisticking agent in hard candy products. The raw material is a constituent of embalming fluid, and a cathartic. It is also used in bath oils, nail polish removers, solid perfumes, face masks, shaving creams, lipsticks, and many men's hair dressings. It is also used as a plasticizer in nail polish. It forms a tough shiny film when dried. More than 50 percent of the lipsticks in the United States use a substantial amount of castor oil. Ingestion of large amounts may cause pelvic congestion and induce abortions. Soothing to the skin.

CASTOREUM EXTRACT • A natural plant extract used in gooseberry, raspberry, tutti-frutti, rum, wine, black walnut, and vanilla flavorings for beverages, ice cream, ices, candy, baked goods, chewing gum, toppings, and condiments. The liquid is used in loganberry, raspberry, orange, balsam, rose, violet, cherry, grape, honey, rum, muscatel, whiskey, and vanilla flavorings for beverages, ice cream, ices, candy, baked goods, gelatin desserts, chewing gum, and toppings. No known toxicity. GRAS.

CATALASE • An enzyme from bovine liver used in milk, for making cheese, and for the elimination of peroxide. It is used also in combination with glucose oxidase for treatment of food wrappers to prevent oxidative deterioration of food.

CATALYST • A substance that causes or speeds up a chemical reaction but does not itself change.

CATECHU EXTRACT • Black Cutch Extract. Cachou Extract. Cashoo Extract. Pegu Catechu Extract. A preparation from the heartwood of the *Acacia Catechu* (*see* Acacia) grown in India, Sri Lanka, and Jamaica. Used in bitters, fruit, and rum flavorings for beverages, ice cream, ices, candy, baked goods, and chewing gum. Used also in toilet preparations and for brown and black colorings. The powder is used in fruit, rum, and spice flavorings for beverages, ice cream, candy, baked goods, and chewing gum. Incompatible with iron compounds, gelatin, lime water, and zinc. Used as an astringent in diarrhea. May cause allergic reactions.

CAYENNE PEPPER • Pepper, Red. A condiment made from the pungent fruit of the plant. Used in sausage and pepper flavorings for beverages, ice cream, ices, candy, meats (910 ppm), soups, and condiments. Reported to retard growth of Mexicans, South Americans, and Spaniards who eat a great deal of these peppers. Rats fed the ingredient of pepper, a reddish-brown liquid called capsaicin, used in flavorings and pickles, were stunted in growth. A report by F. M. Gannett of the Eppley Institute for Research, University of Nebraska Medical Center, Omaha, at the 1988 American Chemical Society meeting, Toronto, Canada, said that capsaicin, the substance that makes these peppers hot, is not a low-level mutagen as earlier believed but is actually antimutagenic.

CEDAR • Cedar Wood Oil. The oil from white, red, or various cedars obtained by distillation from fresh leaves and branches. A colorless to yellow liquid, it is used in fruit and spice flavorings for beverages, ice cream, ices, candy, baked goods, chewing gum, and liquors. It is often used in perfumes, soaps, and sachets for its warm woodsy scent. Used frequently as a substitute for oil of lavender. There is usually a strong camphor odor that repels insects. Cedar oil can be a photosensitizer, causing skin reactions when the skin is exposed to light. Similar toxicity to camphor oil (*see*).

CEDAR WOOD OIL • *See* Cedar.

CEDRO OIL • *See* Lemon Oil.

CELERY SEED • A yellowish to greenish brown liquid, having a pleasant aromatic odor, distilled from the dried ripe fruit of the plant grown in southern Europe. Celery seed is used in sausage and celery flavorings for beverages (1,000 ppm), baked goods, condiments (2,500 ppm), soups, meats, and pickles. Celery seed solid extract is used in celery, meat, and spice flavorings for beverages, ice cream, ices, candy, baked goods, condiments, and maple syrup. Celery seed oil is used in fruit, honey, maple, sausage, nut, root beer, spice, vanilla, and cream soda flavorings for beverages, ice cream, ices, candy, baked goods, chewing gum, meats, soup, pickles, and condiments. Celery seed may cause a sensitivity to light. GRAS.

CELLULASE • An enzyme used to clarify (*see* Clarification) juice. No known toxicity.

CELLULOSE • Chief constituent of the fiber of plants. Cotton contains about 90 percent cellulose. It is the basic material for cellulose gums (*see*). Used as an emulsifier in cosmetic creams. No known toxicity.

CELLULOSE GUMS • Any of several fibrous substances consisting of the chief part of the cell walls of plants. Cellulose acetate is obtained by treating cellulose with food starch modifer. It is insoluble in water, alcohol, and ether. Used in the manufacture of rubber and celluloid substitutes, airplane dopes, varnishes, and lacquer. Ethylcellulose is a film-former in lipstick. Methylcellulose (Methocel^R) and hydroxy-ethylcellulose (Cellosize^R) are used as emulsifiers in hand creams and lotions. They are resistant to bacterial decomposition and give uniform viscosity to products. No known toxicity. The final report to the FDA of the Select Committee on GRAS Substances stated in 1980 that it should continue its GRAS status for packaging only with no limitations other than good manufacturing practices.

CENTAURY (CENTRUIUM) HERB • Flavoring in alcoholic beverages only.

CERTIFIED • Each batch of coal tar or petrochemical colors, with the exception of those used in food and cosmetic dyes, must be certified by the FDA as ''harmless and suitable for use.'' The manufacturer must submit samples of every batch for testing and the lot test number accompanies that colors through all subsequent packaging.

CETONE D • *See* Methyl *b*-Napthyl Ketone.

CETONE V • *See* Allyl *a*-Ionone.

CETYL- • Means derived from cetyl alcohol (*see*).

CETYL ALCOHOL • An emollient and emulsion stabilizer used in many foods and cosmetics preparations including baby lotion, brillian-tine hairdressings, deodorants and antiperspirants, cream depilatories, eyelash creams, and oils, foundation creams, hair lacquers, hair straighteners, hand lotions, lipsticks, liquid powders, mascaras, nail polish removers, nail whiteners, cream rouge, and shampoos. Cetyl alochol is waxy, crystalline, and solid, and found in spermaceti from sperm whales. It has a low toxicity for both skin and ingestion and is sometimes used as a laxative. Can cause hives.

CETYL ARACHIDATE • An ester produced by the reaction of cetyl alcohol and arachidic acid. The acid is found in fish oils and vegetables, particularly peanut oil. A fatty compound used as an emulsifier. Nontoxic.

CETYL ESTERS • Synthetic spermaceti, a waxy substance from sperm whales.

CETYLIC ACID • *See* Palmitic Acid.

CEYLON CINNAMON • *See* Cinnamon.

CEYLON CINNAMON LEAF OIL • *See* Cinnamon Leaf Oil.

CHAMOMILE • Roman, English, German, and Hungarian Chamomile. The daisylike white and yellow heads of these flowers provide a coloring agent known as apigenin. The essential oil distilled from the flower heads is pale blue and is added to shampoos to impart the odor of chamomile. Powdered flowers are used to bring out a bright yellow color in the hair. Also used in rinses and skin fresheners. Roman chamomile is used in berry, fruit, vermouth, maple, spice, and vanilla flavorings. English chamomile is used as a flavoring in chocolate, fruit, and liquor flavorings for beverages, ice cream, ices, candy, and baked goods. Roman chamomile oil is used in chocolate, fruit, vermouth, and spice flavorings for beverages, ice cream, ices, candy, baked goods, gelatin desserts, and liquors. Hungarian chamomile oil is used in chocolate, fruit, and liquor flavorings for beverages, ice cream, ices, candy, baked goods, chewing gum, and liquors. Chamomile contains sesquiterpene lactones which may cause allergic contact dermatitis and stomach upsets. GRAS.

CHECKERBERRY EXTRACT • *See* Wintergreen Oil.

CHECKERBERRY OIL • See Wintergreen Oil.

CHELATING AGENT • Any compound, usually one that binds and precipitates metals, such as ethylenediamine tetraacetic acid (EDTA), which removes trace metals. *See* Sequestering Agent.

CHERRY BARK (WILD) EXTRACT • A natural flavoring extracted from the pits of sweet and sour cherries used in cherry flavoring for beverages, ice cream, and ices. No known toxicity. GRAS.

CHERRY LAUREL LEAVES • A flavoring. *See* Cherry Bark Extract.

CHERRY PIT OIL • A natural flavoring and fragrance extracted from the pits of sweet and sour cherries. Also a cherry flavoring for beverages, ice cream, and condiments. No known toxicity.

CHERRY PLUM • Source of purplish red color. *See* Anthocyanins.

CHERVIL • A natural flavoring extracted from an aromatic Eurasian plant and used in spice flavorings for beverages, ice cream, ices, candy, baked goods, and condiments. A chewing gum base. No known toxicity. GRAS.

CHICLE • The gummy milky resin obtained from trees grown in Mexico and Central America. Rubberlike and quite soft at moderate temperatures. Used in the manufacture of chewing gum, insulation, and waterproofing. No known toxicity.

CHICORY EXTRACT • A natural flavor extract from a plant, usually with blue flowers and leaves. Used in butter, caramel, chocolate, coffee, maple, nut, root beer, sarsaparilla, vanilla, wintergreen, and birch beer flavorings for beverages, ice cream, ices, candy, and baked goods. The root of the plant is dried, roasted, and ground for mixing with coffee. No known toxicity.

CHILTE • A chewing gum base component of vegetable origin. No known toxicity.

CHINA BARK EXTRACT • *See* Quillaja Extract.

CHINESE CINNAMON • *See* Cinnamon.

CHINESE CINNAMON LEAF OIL • *See* Cinnamon Leaf Oil.

CHIVES • A member of the onion family, native to Eurasia. The leaves are used for a seasoning. No known toxicity. GRAS.

CHLORINE DIOXIDE • Flour bleacher and oxidizing agent. A yellow to reddish yellow gas, with an unpleasant odor, highly irritating and corrosive to the skin and mucous membranes of respiratory tract. Reacts violently with organic materials. It can kill.

CHLORINE GAS • Flour bleaching agent and an aging and oxidizing agent. Also used in water purification. Found in the earth's crust, it is a greenish-yellow gas with a suffocating odor. A powerful irritant, dangerous to inhale, and lethal. Thirty ppm will cause coughing. The chlorine used in drinking water often contains carcinogenic carbon tetrachloride, a contaminant formed during the production process. Chlorination has also been found to sometimes form undesirable "ring" compounds in water, such as toluene, xylene, and the suspected carcinogen styrene—they have been observed in both the drinking water and in waste-water plants in the Midwest.

CHLORITE • *See* Calcium Hypochlorite.

CHLORPENTAFLUOROETHANE • Alone or with carbon dioxide. Used as a propellant and aerating agent in foods. May no longer be used because of concerns about the ozone layer.

CHLOROPHYLL • The green coloring matter of plants, which plays an essential part in the plant's photosynthesis process. Used in antiperspirants, dentifrices, deodorants, and mouthwashes as a deodorizing agent. It imparts a greenish color to certain fats and oils, notably olive oil and soybean. Can cause a sensitivity to light.

CHLORTETRACYCLINE • Aureomycin. Biomycin. Biomitsin. A preservative, an antibiotic, used in a dip for uncooked poultry. One of the reasons for increased resistance to antibiotics in patients is believed to be the widespread use of antibiotics in food animals. In 1969, the British restricted the veterinary use of antibiotics. In 1972, the FDA-appointed committee to study the use of antibiotics in animals recommended curbs on use. Many strains of bacteria are known to be resistant to tetracycline. The use of this antibiotic has caused permanent discoloration of the permanent teeth in children given the drug prior to the eruption of the second teeth. The drug can also cause skin rash, gastrointestinal upsets, and inflammations in the ano-genital area.

CHOLIC ACID • A colorless or white crystalline powder that occurs in the bile of most vertebrates and is used as an emulsifying agent in dried egg whites and as a choleretic to regulate the secretion of bile. Bitter taste; sweetish aftertaste. No known toxicity. The final report to the FDA of the Select Committee on GRAS Substances stated in 1980 that it should continue its GRAS status with no limitations other than good manufacturing practices.

CHOLINE BITARTRATE • A dietary supplement included in the B complex and found in the form of a thick syrupy liquid in most animal tissue. It is necessary to nerve function and fat metabolism and can be manufactured in the body but not at a sufficient rate to meet health requirements. Dietary choline protects against poor growth, fatty liver, and renal damage in many animals. Choline deficiency has not been demonstrated in humans but the National Academy of Sciences lists 500 to 900 milligrams per day as sufficient for the average person. The final report to the FDA of the Select Committee on GRAS Substances stated in 1980 that it should continue its GRAS status with no limitations other than good manufacturing practices.

CHOLINE CHLORIDE • Ferric Choline Citrate. A dietary supplement with the same function as choline bitartrate (*see*). The final report to the FDA of the Select Committee on GRAS Substances stated in 1980 that it should continue its GRAS status with no limitations other than good manufacturing practices.

CHOLESTEROL • A fat-soluble crystalline steroid alcohol (*see*) occurring in all animal fats and oils, nervous tissue, egg yolk, and blood. Used as an emulsifier and lubricant in brilliantine hairdressing, eye creams, shampoos, and other cosmetic products. It is important in metabolism but has been implicated as contributing to hardening of the arteries and subsequently heart attacks. Nontoxic to the skin.

CHONDRUS EXTRACT • Used as a stabilizer. GRAS. *See* Carrageenan.

CINCHONA EXTRACT • The extract of the bark of various species of cinchona cultivated in Java, India, and South America. A natural flavoring, red cinchona bark is used in bitters, fruit, rum, vermouth, and spice flavorings for beverages, ice cream, ices, candy, liquors, and bitters (1,000 ppm). Yellow cinchona bark is a natural flavoring from the bark of a species of South American tree used in bitters, fruit, and vermouth flavorings for liquors and bitters. The yellow extract is used as a bitters flavoring for beverages. Quinine is derived from it. May rarely cause allergies.

CINENE • *See* d-Limonene.

CINEOLE • *See* Eucalyptol.

CINNAMAL • *See* Cinnamaldehyde.

CINNAMALDEHYDE • Cinnamic Aldehyde. A synthetic yellowish oily liquid with a strong odor of cinnamon isolated from a wood-rotting fungus. Occurs naturally in cassia bark extract, cinnamon bark, and root oils. Used in cola, apple, cherry, liquor, rum, nut, pecan, spice, cinnamon, vanilla, and cream soda flavorings for beverages, ice cream, ices, candy, baked goods, chewing gum (4,900 ppm), condiments, and meats. Also used in perfume industry and to flavor mouthwash and toothpaste. Also to scent powder and hair tonic. It is irritating to the skin and mucous membranes, especially if undiluted. Can cause inflammation and erosion of the gastrointestinal tract. One of the most common allergens. GRAS.

CINNALDEHYDE ETHYLENE GLYCOL ACETAL • Cinncloval. Spice, cassia, cinnamon, and clove flavorings for beverages, ice cream, ices, candy, baked goods, chewing gum, and condiments. *See* Cinnamaldehyde for toxicity.

CINNAMEIN • *See* Benzyl Cinnamate.

CINNAMIC ACID • A cherry, honey, spice, cassia, and cinnamon flavoring agent for beverages, ice cream, ices, candy, baked goods, and chewing gum. Also used in suntan lotions and perfumes. Occurs in storax, balsam Peru, cinnamon leaves, and coca leaves. Usually isolated from wood-rotting fungus. Used mainly in the perfume industry. It may cause allergic skin rashes.

CINNAMIC ALCOHOL • Fragrance ingredient. One of the most common allergens in fragrances and flavorings. Used in mouthwashes, toilet soaps, toothpastes, and sanitary napkins. *See* Cinnamaldehyde.

CINNAMIC ALDEHYDE • Found in cinnamon oil, cassia oil, cinnamon powder, patchouli oil, flavoring agents, toilet soaps, and perfumes. It cross-reacts with balsam of Peru and benzoin. May cause depigmentation and hives.

CINNAMON (CEYLON, CHINESE, SAIGON). • Obtained from the dried bark of cultivated trees. *See* Cinnamaldehyde for toxicity. Used in bitters, cola, apple, plum, vermouth, sausage, eggnog, cinnamon, and vanilla flavorings for beverages, ice cream, ices, candy (4,000 ppm), baked goods (1,900 ppm), condiments, meats, and apple butter. Used to flavor toothpaste and mouthwash and to scent hair tonic and powder. Extracts have been used to break up intestinal gas and to treat diarrhea, but can be irritating to the gastrointestinal system. GRAS.

CINNAMON BARK • Extract and Oil. From the dried bark of cultivated trees, the extract is used in cola, eggnog, root beer, cinnamon, and ginger ale for beverages, ice cream, baked goods, condiments, and meats. The oil is used in berry, cola, cherry, rum, root beer, cinnamon, and ginger ale flavorings for beverages, condiments, and meats. Can be a skin sensitizer in humans and cause mild sensitivity to light.

CINNAMON LEAF OIL • Oil of Cassia. Chinese Cinnamon. Yellowish to brown volatile oil from the leaves and twigs of cultivated trees. About 80 to 90 percent cinnamal. It has the characteristic odor and taste of cassia cinnamon and darkens and thickens upon aging or exposure to air. Used in cola, apricot, rum, root beer, cinnamon, and ginger ale flavorings for beverages, ice cream, ices, candy, baked goods, chewing gum, gelatin desserts, condiments, pickles, and sliced fruits. Cinnamon oil is used to scent perfumes and as a flavoring in dentrifices. Can cause contact dermatitis.

CINNAMYL ACETATE • A synthetic flavoring, colorless to yellow, liquid, with a sweet floral odor. Occurs naturally in cassia bark. Used in berry, apple, apricot, cherry, grape, peach, pineapple, cinnamon, and vanilla flavorings for beverages, ice cream, ices, candy, baked goods, chewing gum, and condiments. Can cause allergic reactions.

CINNAMYL ALCOHOL • A synthetic flavoring, white to slightly yellow, liquid with a balsamic odor. Occurs in storax, balsam Peru, cinnamon leaves, and hyacinth oil. Used in raspberry, strawberry, apricot, peach, plum, prune, grape, liquor, brandy, nut, black walnut, spice, and cinnamon flavorings for beverages, ice cream, ices, candy, baked goods, chewing gum, gelatin desserts, and brandy. Used also in synthetic perfumes and in deodorants. Can cause allergic reactions.

CINNYAMYL ANTHRANILATE • A synthetic flavoring agent and fragrance ingredient used since the 1940s as an imitation grape or cherry flavor. It is used as a fragrance in soaps, detergents, creams, lotions, and perfumes. United States sales equaled more than 2,000 pounds in 1976. The National Cancer Institute reported on December 20, 1980, that it caused liver cancer in male and female mice and caused both kidney and pancreatic cancers in male rats in feeding studies. Earlier studies showed it increased lung tumors in mice. The FDA banned the use of it in food in 1982. Most companies voluntarily stopped using it in cosmetics after publication of the NCI information.

CINNAMYL BENZOATE • A synthetic butter, caramel, and fruit flavoring agent for beverages, ice cream, ices, candy, baked goods, condiments, and chewing gum. No known toxicity.

CINNAMYL BUTYRATE • A synthetic citrus orange and fruit flavoring for beverages, ice cream, ices, candy, baked goods, and chewing gum. No known toxicity.

CINNAMYL CINNAMATE • A synthetic fruit flavoring agent for beverages, ice cream, ices, candy, and baked goods. No known toxicity.

CINNAMYL FORMATE • Formic Acid. A synthetic flavoring, colorless to yellow liquid with a faint cinnamon odor. Used in banana, cherry, pear, and spice flavorings for beverages, ice cream, ices, candy, baked goods, and chewing gum. Formic acid, from which cinnamyl formate is made, is a cancer-causing agent in mice and can adversely affect the human kidney.

CINNAMYL ISOBUTYRATE • A synthetic strawberry, citrus, apple, banana, grape, peach, pear, and pineapple flavoring agent for beverages, ice cream, ices, candy, baked goods, gelatin desserts, chewing gum, and toppings. No known toxicity.

CINNAMYL ISOVALERATE • A synthetic flavoring, colorless to yellow liquid with a spicy, fruity, floral odor. Used in strawberry, chocolate, apple, apricot, cherry, grape, maple nut, nut, spice, peach, pineapple, and plum flavorings for beverages, ice cream, ices, candy, baked goods, chewing gum, and gelatin desserts. No known toxicity.

CINNAMYL PHENYLACETATE • A synthetic flavoring, colorless to yellow liquid, with a fruity-floral odor. Used in berry, apple, chocolate, currant, grape, peach, pear, and pineapple flavorings for beverages, ice cream, ices, candy, and baked goods. No known toxicity.

CINNAMYL PROPIONATE· • A synthetic flavoring, colorless to yellow liquid with a fruity-floral odor. Used in berry, apple, chocolate, currant, grape, peach, pear, and pineapple flavorings for beverages, ice cream, ices, candy, baked goods, chewing gum, and gelatin desserts. No known toxicity.

CINNCLOVAL • *See* Cinnamaldehyde Ethylene Glycol Acetal.

CINOXATE • *See* Cinnamic Acid.

CIRE D'ABEILLE ABSOLUTE • *See* Beeswax, Bleached.

CITRAL • A light, oily liquid that occurs naturally in grapefruit, orange, peach, ginger, grapefruit oil, oil of lemon, and oil of lime. Either isolated from citral oils or made synthetically. Used in strawberry, lemon, lime, orange, apple, cherry, grape, spice, ginger, and vanilla flavorings for beverages, ice cream, ices, candy, baked goods, and chewing gum. Used in perfumes, soaps, and colognes for its lemon and verbena scents. Also used in the synthesis of Vitamin A. Causes discoloration of white soaps. Used in soaps and colognes for its lemon and verbena scents. Found also in detergents and furniture polish. The compound has been reported to inhibit wound healing and tumor rejection in animals. Vitamin A counteracts its toxicity but in commercial products to which pure citral has been added, Vitamin A may not be present. GRAS.

CITRAL DIMETHYL ACETAL • A synthetic citrus, lemon and fruit flavoring agent for beverages, ices, candy, and condiments. No known toxicity.

CITRATE, CALCIUM • *See* Calcium Citrate.

CITRATE, ISOPROPYL • *See* Isopropyl Citrate.

CITRATE, MONOGLYCERIDE • *See* Monoglyceride Citrate.

CITRATE SALTS • Softening agent for cheese spreads; emulsifier salts to blend pasteurized processed cheeses and cheese foods. Citrates may interfere with the results of laboratory tests including tests for pancreatic function, abnormal liver function, and blood alkalinity-acidity.

CITRATE, SODIUM • *See* Sodium Citrate.

CITRATE, STEARYL • *See* Stearyl Citrate.

CITRIC ACID • One of the most widely used acids in the cosmetics industry, it is derived from citrus fruit by fermentation of crude sugars. It is also extracted from citrus fruits and occurs naturally in coffee and peaches. It is a flavoring for beverages (2,500 ppm), ice creams, ices, candy (4,300 ppm), baked goods, and chewing gum (3,600 ppm). Citric acid is used to neutralize lye employed in peeling vegetables, as an adjuster of acidity-alkalinity in fruit juices, wines, jams, jellies, jelly candies, canned fruit, carbonated beverages, frozen fruit, canned vegetables, frozen dairy products, cheese spreads, sherbet, confections, canned figs, dried egg white, mayonnaise, salad dressing, fruit butter, preserves, and fresh beef blood. Employed in curing meats, for firming peppers, potatoes, tomatoes, and lima beans, and to prevent off flavors in fried potatoes. Removes trace metals and brightens color in various commercial products. Employed as a preservative, sequestering agent (*see*), to adjust acid-alkali balance; as a foam inhibitor and plasticizer in cosmetics and also used as an astringent alone or in astringent compounds. Among the cosmetic products in which it is frequently found are freckle and nail bleaches, bath preparations; skin fresheners, cleansing creams, depilatories, eye lotions, hair colorings, hair rinses, and hair-waving preparations. The clear, crystalline, water-absorbing chemicals are also used to prevent scurvy, a deficiency disease, and as a refreshing drink with water and sugar added. It has been used to dissolve urinary bladder stones. No known toxicity. The final report to the FDA of the Select Committee on GRAS Substances stated in 1980 that it should continue its GRAS status with no limitations other than good manufacturing practices.

CITRIDIC ACID • *See* Aconitic Acid.

CITROFLEX A-4 • *See* Tributyl Acetylcitrate.

CITRONELLA OIL • A natural food flavoring extract from fresh grass grown in Asia. It consists of about 60 percent geraniol (*see*), 15 percent citronellol (*see*), and 10 to 15 percent camphene (*see*). Almost colorless with a pleasant odor. Used in citrus, fruit, and ginger ale flavorings for beverages, ice cream, ices, candy, and baked goods.

Used in perfumes, toilet waters, and perfumed cosmetics; also an insect repellent. May cause allergic reactions such as stuffy nose, hay fever, asthma, and skin rash when used in cosmetics. Can cause vomiting when ingested, cyanosis, convulsions, damage to intestinal mucosa, and when taken in sufficient amounts, death. GRAS.

CITRONELLAL • A synthetic flavoring agent. The chief constituent of citronella oil (*see*). Also found in lemon and lemongrass oils. Colorless liquid with an intense lemon-rose odor. Used in citrus, lemon, cherry, and spice flavorings for beverages, ice cream, ices, candy, baked goods, chewing gum, and gelatin desserts. A mild irritant. *See* Citronella Oil for toxicity.

CITRONELLOL • A synthetic flavoring. Obtained from citronellal or geraniol, geranium rose oil or citronella oil (*see* all). Colorless liquid with a roselike odor. The *d* form is more oily and is the major ingredient of rhodinol (*see*). Used in berry, citrus, cola, fruit, rose, and floral flavorings for beverages, ice cream, ices, candy, baked goods, chewing gum, and gelatin desserts. Used in perfumes. A mild irritant. *See* Citronella Oil.

CITRONELLOXY ACETALDEHYDE • A synthetic floral, rose, and fruit flavoring agent for beverages, ice cream, ices, candy, and baked goods. *See* Citronella Oil for toxicity.

CITRONELLYL ACETATE • A synthetic flavoring agent, colorless liquid, with a fruity odor. Used in lemon, rose, apricot, banana, grape, pear, and raisin flavorings for beverages, ice cream, ices, candy, baked goods, chewing gum, and gelatin desserts. A major ingredient of rhodinyl acetate (*see*). No known toxicity.

CITRONELLYL BUTYRATE • A synthetic flavoring agent, colorless liquid, with a strong fruit-rose odor. Used in cola, floral, rose, apple, pineapple, plum, prune, and honey flavorings for beverages, ice cream, ices, candy, baked goods, chewing gum, and gelatin desserts. A major ingredient of rhodinyl acetate (*see*). No known toxicity.

CITRONELLYL FORMATE • Formic Acid. A synthetic flavoring agent, colorless liquid, with a strong fruity odor. Used in orange, apple, apricot, peach, plum, and honey flavorings for beverages, ice cream, ices, candy, baked goods. A major ingredient of rhodinyl acetate (*see*). Made from formic acid, which is in mice a cancer-causing agent and which can adversely affect the human kidney.

CITRONELLYL ISOBUTYRATE • A synthetic flavoring agent, colorless liquid, with a rose-fruit odor. Used in raspberry, strawberry, floral, rose, and grape flavorings for beverages, ice cream, ices, candy, baked goods, and gelatin desserts. A major ingredient of rhodinyl acetate (*see*). No known toxicity.

CITRONELLYL PHENYLACETATE • A synthetic butter, caramel, rose, fruit, and honey flavoring agent for beverages, ice cream, ices, candy, and baked goods. A major ingredient of rhodinyl acetate (*see*). No known toxicity.

CITRONELLYL PROPIONATE • A synthetic flavoring agent, colorless liquid, with a rose-fruit odor. Used in lemon and fruit flavorings for beverages, ice cream, ices, candy, baked goods, and chewing gum. A major ingredient of rhodinyl acetate (*see*). No known toxicity.

CITRONELLYL VALERATE • A synthetic flavoring agent for beverages, ice cream, ices, candy, and baked goods. No known toxicity.

CITRUS BIOFLAVONOIDS • Vitamin P complex nutrient supplement up to one gram per day. Occurs naturally in plant coloring and in the tonka bean; also in lemon juice. High concentrates can be obtained from all citrus fruits, rose hips, and black currants. Commercial methods extract rinds of oranges, tangerines, lemons, limes, kumquats, and grapefruit. P vitamin is related to healthy blood vessels and skin. At one time it was thought to prevent colds.

CITRUS PEEL EXTRACT • A natural flavor extract from the peel or rind of grapefruit, lemon, lime, orange, and tangerine. Color, odor, and taste characteristic of source. Used as flavoring agents in bitters, lemon, lime, orange, vermouth, beer, and ginger ale flavorings for beverages, ice cream, ices, candy, and baked goods. No known toxicity. GRAS.

CITRUS OILS • Eugenol. Eucalyptol. Anethole, Irone, Orris, and Menthol (*see* all). Used in flavoring food products and cosmetics and as odorants in special soaps.

CITRUS RED NO. 2 • Monoazo. Used only for coloring orange skins that are not intended for processing, and that meet minimum maturity standards established by or under laws of the states in which the oranges are grown. Oranges colored with Citrus Red No. 2 are not supposed to bear more than 2 ppm of the color additive calculated on the weight of the whole fruit. Citrus Red No. 2 toxicity is far from determined even though, theoretically, consumers would not ingest the dye in the peel as it is removed. The 2-naphthol constituent of the dye, if ingested in quantity, can cause eye lens clouding, kidney damage, vomiting, and circulatory collapse. Application to the skin can cause peeling, and even some deaths have been reported. Also may cause allergic reactions. *See* FD and C Colors.

CIVET, ABSOLUTE • Flavoring derived from the unctuous secretions from the receptacles between the anus and genitalia of both the male and female civet cat. Semisolid, yellowish to brown mass, with an unpleasant odor. Used in raspberry, butter, caramel, grape, and rum flavorings for beverages, ice cream, ices, candy, baked goods, gelatin desserts, and chewing gum. A fixative in perfumery. No known toxicity.

CLARIFICATION • Removal from liquid of small amounts of suspended matter, for example, the removal of particles and traces of copper and iron from vinegar and certain beverages.

CLARIFYING AGENT • A substance that removes from liquids small amounts of suspended matter. Butyl alcohol, for instance, is a clarifying agent for clear shampoos.

CLARY • Clary Sage. A well-known spice in food and beverages. A fixative (*see*) for perfumes. A natural extract of an aromatic herb grown in southern Europe and cultivated widely in England. The herb is a vermouth and spice flavoring agent in vermouth (500 ppm). Clary oil is used in butter, black cherry, grape, licorice, vermouth, wine, root beer, birch beer, spice, vanilla, and cream soda flavorings for beverages, ice cream, ices, candy, baked goods, condiments, and vermouth. No known toxicity.

CLAYS. KAOLIN • China Clay. Used to clarify liquids (*see* clarification) and as a filler for paper. Also used in the manufacture of porcelain and pottery, as an emollient, and as a poultice and gastrointestinal adsorbent. Nontoxic. The final report to the FDA of the Select Committee on GRAS Substances stated in 1980 that it should continue its GRAS status with no limitations other than good manufacturing practices.

CLOVE BUD EXTRACT • A natural flavor extract from the pungent, fragrant, reddish-brown dried flower buds of a tropical tree. Used in berry, fruit, meat, root beer, and spice flavorings for beverages, ice cream, candy, baked goods, condiments, and meats. Cloves are used also as a dental analgesic and germicide. They may cause intestinal upsets. Rats poisoned with clove oil have shown paralysis of hind legs and jaws, with prostration and eventually death. The FDA gave toxicity studies of clove additives top priority in 1980. As of this writing, nothing new has been reported. GRAS.

CLOVE BUD OIL • The volatile, colorless or pale yellow oil obtained by steam distillation from the dried flower buds of a tropical tree. A characteristic clove odor and taste. Used in raspberry, coffee, cola, banana, cherry, peach, plum, rum, sausage, eggnog, pecan, root beer flavorings for beverages, ice cream, ices, candy, baked goods, chewing gum (1,800 ppm), gelatin desserts, meats, liquors, spiced fruit (830 ppm), jelly, and condiments. Used as an antiseptic and flavoring in tooth powders and as a scent in hair tonics and to flavor postage stamp glue, as a toothache treatment, as a condiment, and as a flavoring in chewing gum. It is 82 to 87 percent eugenol (*see*) and has the characteristic clove oil odor and taste. It is strongly irritating to the skin and can cause allergic skin rashes. Its use in perfumes and cosmetics is frowned upon, although in very diluted forms it is innocuous. The final report to the FDA of the Select Committee on GRAS Substances stated in 1980 that it should continue its GRAS status with no limitations other than good manufacturing practices.

CLOVE BUD OLEORESIN • A natural resinous, viscous flavoring extract from the tree that produces clove buds. Used in fruit, meat, and spice flavorings for meat. *See* Clove Bud Extract for toxicity.

CLOVE LEAF OIL • The volatile pale yellow oil obtained by steam distillation of the leaves of the tropical tree that produces clove buds. Used in loganberry, cherry, root beer, sarsaparilla, and cinnamon flavorings for beverages, ice cream, ices, candy, baked goods, chewing gum, gelatin desserts, meats, pickles, apple butter, and condiments. *See* Clove Bud Extract for toxicity. The final report to the FDA of the Select Committee on GRAS Substances stated in 1980 that it should continue its GRAS status with no limitations other than good manufacturing practices.

CLOVE STEM OIL • The volatile yellow to light-brown oil obtained by steam distillation from the dried stems of the tropical tree that produces clove buds. Characteristic odor and taste of cloves. Used in berry, cherry, root beer, ginger ale, and ginger beer flavorings for beverages, ice cream, ices, candy, baked goods, and condiments. *See* Clove Bud Extract for toxicity. The final report to the FDA of the Select Committee on GRAS Substances stated in 1980 that it should continue its GRAS status with no limitations other than good manufacturing practices.

CLOVER • An herb, a natural flavoring extract from a plant characterized by three leaves and flower in dense heads. Used in fruit flavorings for beverages, ice cream, ices, candy, and baked goods. May cause sensitivity to light. GRAS.

CLOVER BLOSSOM EXTRACT • Trifolium Extract. The extract of the flowers of *Trifolium pratense*. Used in fruit flavorings. May cause sensitivity to light.

CLOVERLEAF OIL • Eugenia Caryophyllus Leaf Oil. The volatile oil obtained by steam distillation of the leaves of *Eugenia caryophyllus*. It consists mostly of eugenol (*see*).

COAL TAR • Used in adhesives, creosotes, insecticides, phenols, woodworking, preservation of food, synthetic flavors, and dyes to make colors used in cosmetics, including hair dyes. Thick liquid or semisolid tar obtained from bituminous coal, it contains many constituents including benzene, xylenes, naphthalene, pyridine, quinolineoline, phenol, and cresol. The main concern about coal-tar derivatives is that they cause cancer in animals but they are also frequent sources of allergic reactions, particularly skin rashes and hives.

COBALT SOURCES • Caprylate, Carbonate, Chloride, Gluconate, Sulfate, and Tallate. Cobalt is a metal occurring in the earth's crust; gray, hard, and magnetic. All here are used as mineral supplements at the rate of 1 milligram per day. Excess administration can produce an overproduction of red blood cells and gastrointestinal upset. In the 1960s, it was discovered that cobalt salts added to beer to maintain the "head" caused serious heart problems in beer drinkers. Cobaltous salts and its derivatives have been banned by the FDA for use in human food but are permitted in animal feed.

COCA LEAF EXTRACT (DECOCAINIZED). • Flavoring from the dried leaves of cocaine-containing plants grown in Bolivia, Brazil, Peru, and Java. Used in bitters and cola flavoring for beverages, ice cream, ices, and candy. Once a central nervous system stimulant. No known toxicity. GRAS.

COCHINEAL • See Carmine.

COCOA • A powder prepared from the roasted and cured kernels of ripe seeds of *Theobroma cacao* and other species of *Theobroma*. A brownish powder with a chocolate odor, it is used as a flavoring. May cause wheezing, rash, and other symptoms of allergy, particularly in children.

COCOA EXTRACT • Extract of *Theobroma cacao*. See Cocoa.

COCOAMPHODIACETATE • Widely used in cosmetics in the manufacture of toilet soaps, creams, lubricant, chocolate, and suppositories. *See* Coconut Oil.

COCOAMPHOCARBOXYPROPIONIC ACID • *See* Coconut Oil.

COCOAMPHODIPRIOPIONATE • *See* Coconut Oil.

COCONUT ACIDS • *See* Coconut Oil.

COCONUT ALCOHOLS • *See* Coconut Oil.

COCONUT OIL (REFINED) • The white, semisolid, highly saturated fat expressed from the kernels of the coconut. Used in chocolate, candies, in baking instead of lard, and in self-basting turkeys. A saturated fat that is not recommended for those worried about fat-clogged arteries. No known toxicity. Used in the manufacture of baby soaps, shampoos, shaving lathers, cuticle removers, preshaving lotions, hairdressings, soaps, ointment bases, and massage creams. Stable when exposed to air. Lathers readily and is a fine skin cleaner. Usually blended with other fats. May cause allergic skin rashes. The final report to the FDA of the Select Committee on GRAS Substances stated in 1980 that it should continue its GRAS status with no limitations other than good manufacturing practices.

COD-LIVER OIL • The fixed oil expressed from fresh livers used in skin ointments and special skin creams to promote healing. Pale yellow, with a bland, slightly fishy odor. Contains Vitamin A and D, which promote healing of wounds and abscesses. No known toxicity.

COGNAC OIL • Wine Yeast Oil. The volatile oil obtained from distillation of wine, with the characteristic aroma of cognac. Green cognac oil is used as a flavoring for beverages, ice cream, ices, candy, baked goods, chewing gum, liquors, and condiments. White cognac oil, which has the same constituents as green oil, is used in berry, cherry, grape, brandy, and rum flavorings for beverages, ice cream, ices, candy, baked goods, and gelatin desserts. No known toxicity. GRAS.

COLLOIDAL SILICON DIOXIDE • Practically insoluble in water. A free-flowing agent in salt, seasoned salt, and sodium bicarbonate. Also included in vitamin products, dietary products, spices, meat-curing compounds, flavoring powders, dehydrated honey, dehydrated molasses, and dehydrated nondiastatic malt. Percentages range from 1 percent in salt to 2 percent in dehydrated products. Prolonged inhalation of the silicon dust can cause fibrosis of the lungs. Increases susceptibility to tuberculosis. Chemically and biologically inert when ingested. *See* Silicon Dioxide.

COLORING • More than 90 percent of the food colorings now in use are manufactured, frequently from coal-tar colors. The coal-tar derivatives need to be certified, which means that batches of the dyes are chemically tested and approved by the FDA. As more and more food colors are banned, interest has grown in color derived from natural sources such as carotene (*see*) from carrots, which is used to color margarine, and beet juice, which provides a red color for some foods. *See* FD and C Colors for information on the synthetics now in use.

COLORS • *See* FD and C Colors.

CONTACT DERMATITIS • Skin "outbreaks" caused by direct contact with a substance.

COPOLYMER • Result of polymerization (*see* polymer), which includes at least two different molecules, each of which is capable of polymerizing alone. Together they form a new, distinct molecule. They are used in the manufacture of nail enamels and face masks.

COPOLYMER CONDENSATES OF ETHYLENE OXIDE AND PROPYLENE OXIDE • Stabilizers in flavor concentrates, processing and wetting agents in yeast-leavened bakery products, dough conditioners, surfactants, defoaming agents, and nutrient supplements in animal feed. No known toxicity.

COPPER • Gluconate, Sulfate. One of the earliest known metals. An essential nutrient for all mammals. Naturally occurring or experimentally produced copper deficiency in animals leads to a variety of abnormalities including anemia, skeletal defects, and muscle degeneration. Copper deficiency is extremely rare in humans. The body of an adult contains from 75 to 150 milligrams of copper. Concentrations are highest in the brain and liver and heart. A copper intake of 2 milligrams per day appears to maintain a balance in adults. An ordinary diet provides 2 to 5 milligrams daily. Copper itself is nontoxic, but soluble copper salts, notably copper sulfate, are highly irritating to the skin and mucous membranes and when ingested cause serious vomiting. Copper salts include copper carbonate, chloride, gluconate, hydroxide, orthophosphate, oxide, pyrophosphate, and sulfate. The final report to the FDA of the Select Committee on GRAS Substances stated in 1980 that it should continue its GRAS status with no limitations other than good manufacturing practices.

CORIANDER OIL • The colorless or pale yellow volatile oil from the dried ripe fruit of a plant grown in Asia and Europe. Used as a flavoring agent in raspberry, bitters, fruit, meat, spice, ginger ale, and vanilla flavorings for beverages, ice cream, ices, candy, baked goods (880 ppm), chewing gum, meats (1,300 ppm), liquors (1,000 ppm), and condiments. Used to flavor dentifrices. The oil is used in blackberry, raspberry, chocolate, coffee, cola, fruit, liquor, sausage, root beer, spice, ginger ale, and vanilla flavorings for beverages, ice cream, ices, candy, baked goods, chewing gum, condiments, meats, and liquors. Can cause allergic reactions, particularly of the skin. Coriander is used as weak medication (up to 1 gram) to break up intestinal gas. GRAS.

CORN • Corn Sugar. Dextrose. Used in maple, nut, and root beer flavorings for beverages, ice cream, ices, candy, and baked goods. The oil is used in emollient creams and toothpastes. The syrup is used as a texturizer and carrying agent in cosmetics. It is also used for envelopes, stamps, sticker tapes, ale, aspirin, bacon, baking mixes, powders, beers, bourbon, breads, cheeses, cereals, chop suey, chow mein, confectioner's sugar, cream puffs, fish products, ginger ale, hams, jellies, processed meats, peanut butters, canned peas, plastic food wrappers, sherbets, whiskeys, and American wines. It may also be found in capsules, lozenges, ointments, suppositories, vitamins, fritters, Fritos, frostings, canned or frozen fruit, graham crackers, gravies, grits, gum, monosodium glutamate, Nescafe, oleomargarine, pablum, paper, peanut butter, tortillas, vinegar, yeasts, bologna, baking powders, bath powders, frying fats, fruit juices, laxatives. May cause allergic reactions including skin rashes and asthma.

CORN ACID • *See* Corn Oil.

CORN COB MEAL • The milled powder prepared from the cobs of *Zea mays*.

CORN DEXTRIN • Dextri-Maltose. A white or yellow powder obtained by enzymatic action of barley malt on corn flours, and used as a modifier or thickening agent in milk and milk products. Nontoxic. The final report to the FDA of the Select Committee on GRAS Substances stated in 1980 that it should continue its GRAS status with no limitations other than good manufacturing practices.

CORN ENDOSPERM OIL • Used in chicken feed to enhance yellow color of chicken skin and eggs. Permanently listed since 1967.

CORN FLOUR • A finely ground powder. Used in face and bath powder. *See* Corn Oil.

CORN GERM EXTRACT • The extract of the germ of *Zea mays*.

CORN OIL • Used in emollient cream and toothpastes. Obtained as a by-product by wet milling the grain for use in the manufacture of cornstarch, dextrins, and yellow oil. It has a faint characteristic odor and taste and thickens upon exposure to air. No known toxicity, but can cause skin reactions in the allergic.

CORN POPPY EXTRACT • The extract obtained from the petals of the *Papaver rhoeas*.

CORN SILK • Fresh styles and stigmas of *Zea mays,* it is used as a natural flavoring extract in beverages and candy. The final report to the FDA of the Select Committee on GRAS Substances stated in 1980 that there were insufficient relevant biological and other studies upon which to base an evaluation when it is used as a food ingredient. It remains GRAS.

CORN SUGAR • *See* Corn Syrup.

CORN SYRUP • Corn Sugar. Dextrose. A sweet syrup prepared from cornstarch. Used in maple, nut, and root beer flavorings for beverages, ice cream, ices, candy, and baked goods. Also used for envelopes, stamps, and sticking tapes, aspirin, and many food products including bacon, baking mixes, powders, beer, bourbon, breads, breakfast cereals, pastries, candy, carbonated beverages, catsups, cheeses, cereals, chop suey, chow mein, confectioner's sugar, cream puffs, fish products, ginger ale, hams, jellies, processed meats, peanut butter, canned peas, plastic food wraps, sherbet, whiskey, and American wines. May cause allergic reactions. The final report to the FDA of the Select Committee on GRAS Substances stated in 1980 that there is no evidence in the available information that it is a hazard to the public when used as it is now and it should continue in GRAS status with no limitations on amounts that can be added to food.

CORNSTARCH • Many containers are powdered with cornstarch to prevent sticking. The dietetic grade is marketed as Maizena®, Mondamin®. It is an absorbent dusting powder and a demulcent for irritated colons. May cause allergic reactions, including skin rashes and asthma. The final report to the FDA of the Select Committee on GRAS Substances stated in 1980 that it should continue its GRAS status with no limitations other than good manufacturing practices.

CORPS PRALINE • *See* Maltol.

COSTMARY • Virgin Mary. A natural flavoring derived from an herb native to Asia. Its yellow aromatic flowers are shaped like buttons. Used as a pot herb and salad plant. Infrequently used today as a flavoring in beer and ale. Regarded as sacred to the Virgin Mary. No known toxicity.

COSTUS ROOT OIL • The volatile oil is obtained by steam distillation from dried roots of an herb. Light yellow to brown viscous liquid, with a persistent violetlike odor. A natural fruit and vanilla flavoring for beverages, ice cream, ices, candy, baked goods, chewing gum, and gelatin desserts. No known toxicity.

COTTONSEED FLOUR • Cooked, partly defatted, and toasted flour used for pale yellow coloring. Sometimes used to make gin. It is permanently listed as a coloring. It is known to cause allergies and because it is used in a wide variety of products without notice, it may be hard to avoid. More often, exposures to the allergens arise from the use of cottonseed meal, which may be found in fertilizers and as a constituent of feed for cattle, hogs, poultry, and dogs. Symptoms usually result from inhalation but allergic reactions also can occur from ingesting cottonseed meal used in pan-greasing compounds and in foods such as some fried cakes, fig bars, and cookies.

COTTONSEED OIL • The fixed oil from the seeds of the cultivated varieties of the plant. Pale yellow, oily, odorless liquid used in the manufacture of soaps, creams, baby creams, nail polish removers, and lubricants. The oil is used in most salad oils and oleomargarines and most mayonnaises and salad dressings. Lard compounds and lard substitutes are made with cottonseed oil. Sardines may be packed in it. Most commercial fried products such as potato chips and doughnuts are fried in cottonseed oil, and restaurants use it for cooking. Candies, particularly chocolates, often contain this oil, and it is used to polish fruits at stands. It is also used in cotton wadding or batting in cushions, comforters, mattresses, and upholstery, varnishes, fertilizers, and animal feeds. Known to cause many allergic reactions, but because of its wide use in cosmetics, foods, and other products, it is hard to avoid.

COUCHGRASS • *See* Dog Grass Extract.

COUMARONE-INDENE RESIN • This is a coal-tar additive used as a protective coating on grapefruit, lemons, limes, oranges, tangelos, and tangerines. The FDA says that resin remaining on the fruit shall not exceed 200 ppm on a fresh-weight basis. *See* Coal Tar.

CRANBERRY JUICE CONCENTRATE • Bright red coloring from the juice of the red acid berry, produced by any of several plants of the genus *Vaccinium* grown in the United States and Europe. Food manufacturers may substitute this natural coloring for the synthetic reds that were banned. No known toxicity.

CRANBERRRY POMACE • Source of natural red coloring. *See* Anthocyanins.

CREAM OF TARTAR • *See* Tartrate.

CREOSOL • *See* 2-Methoxy-4-Methylphenol.

p-**CRESOL** • A synthetic nut and vanilla flavoring agent. Obtained from coal tar. It occurs naturally in tea, and used in beverages, ice cream, ices, candy, and baked goods. It is more powerful than phenol and less toxic. Phenol is an extremely toxic acid obtained from coal tar which has many industrial uses, including use as a disinfectant for toilets and as an anesthetic.

4-CRESOL • *See p*-Cresol.

o-**CRESYL ACETATE** • *See o*-Tolyl Acetate.

p-**CRESYL ACETATE** • See *p*-Tolyl Acetate.

CRETAN DITTANY • *See* Dittany of Crete.

CROCETIN • Yellow coloring from saffron (*see*).

CROCUS EXTRACT • *See* Saffron.

CROSS-REACTIVITY • When the body mistakes one compound for another of similar chemical composition.

CRYPTOXANTHIN • A natural yellow coloring from corn and marigolds. *See* Xanthophyll.

CUBEBS • Tailed Pepper. Java Pepper. The mature, unripe, sun-dried fruit of a perennial vine grown in South Asia, Java, Sumatra, the Indies, and Sri Lanka. It has a strong, spicy odor and is used in fruit flavoring for beverages (800 ppm). The volatile oil is obtained by steam distillation from the fruit and is colorless to light green with the characteristic spicy odor and a slightly acrid taste. It is used in berry, fruit, and ginger flavorings for beverages, ice cream, ices, candy, baked goods, meats, and condiments. Java pepper was formerly used to stimulate healing of mucous membranes. The fruit has been used as a stimulant and diuretic and sometimes is smoked in cigarettes. No known toxicity.

CUCUMBER JUICE • From the succulent fruit of the vine and used as an astringent by many ''natural'' cosmetic fans. It has a pleasant aroma and imparts a cool feeling to the skin. Nontoxic.

CUMALDEHYDE • *See* Cuminaldehyde.

CUMIN • Cummin. A natural flavoring obtained from the seeds of an Old World plant. Used in spice and sausage flavorings for baked goods (2,500 ppm), condiments (3,900 ppm), and meats. A volatile oil, light yellow to brown, with a strong, disagreeable odor, it is distilled from the plant. It is used in berry, fruit, sausage, and spice flavorings for beverages, ice cream, ices, candy, chewing gum, baked goods, meats, pickles, and condiments. No known toxicity. GRAS.

CUMINAL • *See* Cuminaldehyde.

CUMINALDEHYDE • It is a constituent of eucalyptus, myrrh, cassia, cumin, and other essential oils, but often is made synthetically. Colorless to yellowish, oily, with a strong lasting odor. It is used as a synthetic flavoring in berry, fruit, and spice flavorings for beverages, ice cream, ices, candy, baked goods, chewing gum, and condiments. Used in perfumery. No known toxicity.

CUMINIC ALDEHYDE • *See* Cuminaldehyde.

CUPRIC CHLORIDE • Copper Chloride. A copper salt used in hair dye. A yellow to brown water-absorbing powder that is soluble in diluted acids. It is also used in pigments for glass and ceramics and as a feed additive, disinfectant, and wood preservative. Irritating to the skin and mucous membranes. Irritating when ingested, causing vomiting. *See* Copper.

CUPRIC ACETATE • The copper salt of acetic acid and copper (*see* both).

CUPRIC HYDROXIDE • Copper Hydrate. A blue-green gel used as a coloring and in fungicides, insecticides, in staining paper, and as a feed additive.

CUPRIC OXIDE • *See* Copper.

CUPRIC SULFATE • Copper sulfate occurs in nature as hydrocyanite. Grayish white to greenish white crystals. Used as agricultural fungicide, herbicide, and in the preparation of azo dyes (*see*). Used in hair dyes as coloring. Very irritating if ingested. No known toxicity on the skin and is used medicinally as a skin fungicide. *See* Copper.

CUPROUS IODIDE • The final report to the FDA of the Select Committee on GRAS Substances stated in 1980 that it should continue its GRAS status with no limitations other than good manufacturing practices. *See* Iodine Sources.

CURACAO PEEL EXTRACT • A natural flavoring extracted from a plant native to the Caribbean island. Used in orange and liquor flavorings for beverages (1,700 ppm). GRAS.

CURACAO PEEL OIL • A natural flavoring extracted from a plant native to the Caribbean island. Used in berry, lime, and liquor flavorings for beverages, ice cream, ices, candy, and baked goods. No known toxicity.

CURCUMIN • The orange-yellow colorant derived from turmeric (*see*) and used as a natural food coloring. It does not require certification because it is a natural product but the Expert Committee on Food Additives of the FDA recommended that the acceptable daily intake of curcumin (and turmeric) be limited to 0 to 0.5 milligrams per kilogram of body weight.

CURING AGENTS • These include salt, nitrites (*see*), and other compounds used to stabilize color, give flavor, and/or preserve.

CURRANT BUDS, ABSOLUTE • A natural flavoring from a variety of small raisins grown principally in Greece. Used in fruit, berry, and raspberry flavorings for beverages, ice cream, ices, candy, and baked goods. No known toxicity.

CURRANTE BLACK, BUDS AND LEAVES • *See* Currant Buds.

CUSPARIA BARK • Essential oil from the bark of Angostura used as a flavoring. *See* Angostura. GRAS.

CYANOCOBALAMIN • Vitamin B_{12}. Produced by intestinal micro-organisms, it is found also in soil and water. Necessary for healthy blood.

CYANODITHIOIMIDOCARBONATE, DISODIUM • Bacteria-killing component in the processing of sugar cane. Many organic cyano compounds are decomposed in the body to yield highly toxic cyanide.

CYCLAMATES • Sodium and Calcium. Artificial sweetening agent about 30 times as sweet as refined sugar, removed from the food market on September 1, 1969, because they were found to cause bladder cancer in rats. At that time 175 million Americans were swallowing cyclamates in significant doses in many products ranging from chewing gums to soft drinks.

CYCLAMIC ACID • Fairly strong acid with a sweet taste. It is the acid from which cyclamates (*see*) were derived.

CYCLODEXTRIN • A sugary substance produced by certain strains of bacteria developed by U.S. Department of Agriculture Research Service as a potential substitute for sulfites to prevent browning in fruit juices and vegetables.

CYCLOHEXANEACETIC ACID • A synthetic butter and fruit flavoring for beverages, ice cream, ices, candy, and baked goods. Cyclohexane in high concentrations may act as a narcotic and skin irritant.

CYCLOHEXANE ETHYL ACETATE • A synthetic fruit and honey flavoring for beverages, ice cream, ices, candy, and baked goods. *See* Cyclohexaneacetic Acid for toxicity.

CYCLOHEXYL ANTHRANILATE • A synthetic apple, banana, and grape flavoring for beverages, ice cream, ices, candy, baked goods, and gelatin desserts. Some cyclohexyl compounds are irritating to the skin.

CYCLOHEXYL CINNAMATE • A synthetic apple, apricot, peach, and prune flavoring for beverages, ice cream, ices, candy, and baked goods. Some cyclohexyl compounds are irritating to the skin.

CYCLOHEXYL FORMATE • Formic Acid. A synthetic cherry flavoring for beverages, ice cream, ices, candy, and baked goods. Some cyclohexyl compounds are irritating to the skin.

CYCLOHEXYL ISOVALERATE • A synthetic strawberry and apple flavoring for beverages, ice cream, ices, candy, and baked goods. Some cyclohexyl compounds are irritating to the skin.

CYCLOHEXYL PROPIONATE • A synthetic fruit flavoring for beverages, ice cream, ices, candy, and baked goods. Some cyclohexyl compounds are irritating to the skin.

CYCLOPENADECANOLIDE • *See* Pentadecalactone.

o-**CYMEN-3-OL** • *See p*-Cymene.

p-**CYMENE** • A synthetic flavoring, a volatile hydrocarbon solvent that occurs naturally in star anise, coriander, cumin, mace oil, oil of mandarin, and origanum oil. Used in fragrances; also in citrus and spice flavorings for beverages, ice cream, candies, and baked goods. Its ingestion pure may cause a burning sensation in the mouth and nausea, salivation, headache, giddiness, vertigo, confusion, and coma. Contact with the pure liquid may cause blisters of the skin and inflammation of mucous membranes.

CYMOL • *See p*-Cymene.

CYMOPHENOL • *See* Carvacrol.

CYSTEINE • L-Form. An essential amino acid (*see*), it is derived from hair and used in hair products and creams. Soluble in water, it is used in bakery products as a nutrient. It has been used to promote wound healing. On the list of FDA additives to be studied. As of this writing, no new evaluation has been made public. GRAS.

CYSTINE • A nonessential amino acid (*see*) found in urine and in horsehair. Colorless, practically odorless, white crystals, it is used as a nutrient supplement and in emollients. On the FDA list for further study. As of this writing, no new evaluation has been made public. GRAS.

D

DAMIANA LEAVES • The dried leaves of a plant of California and Texas used as a flavoring. Formerly used as a tonic and aphrodisiac. No known toxicity.

DANDELION LEAF AND ROOT • Lion's Tooth. Used as a skin refreshing bath additive. Obtained from *Taraxacum* plants that grow abundantly in the United States. The common dandelion weed eaten as a salad green was used by the Indians for heartburn. Rich in Vitamin A and C, it is also used as a flavoring. Dandelion coffee is made from the dried roots of the plant. The root extract is used in bitters, butter, caramel, floral, fruit, root beer, and vanilla flavorings for beverages, ice cream, ices, candy, and baked goods. The fluid extract is used in butter, caramel, fruit, maple, and vanilla flavorings for beverages, ice cream, ices, candy, and baked goods. No known toxicity. GRAS.

DAUCUS CAROTA • See Carrot Oil.

DAVANA OIL • A plant extract used in fruit flavoring for beverages, ice cream, ices, candy, baked goods, and chewing gum. No known toxicity.

DAVANA OIL • A plant extract used in fruit flavorings for beverages, ice cream, ices, candy, baked goods, and gelatin desserts. No known toxicity.

o-DECALACTONE • A synthetic flavoring agent. Occurs naturally in butter, cream, and milk. Colorless with a fruity odor. Used in coconut and fruit flavorings for beverages, ice cream, ices, candy, baked goods, oleomargarine (10 ppm), and toppings. No known toxicity.

γ-DECALACTONE • A synthetic flavoring agent, colorless, with a fruity odor, used in citrus, orange, coconut, and fruit flavorings for beverages, ice cream, ices, candy, baked goods, and gelatin desserts. No known toxicity.

DECANAL • A synthetic flavoring agent. Occurs naturally in sweet orange peel, sweet mandarin oil, grapefruit oil, orris, and coriander. Colorless to light yellow, with a definite fatlike odor that becomes florallike when diluted. Used in berry, citrus, lemon, orange, fruit, and honey flavorings for beverages, ice cream, ices, candy, baked goods, chewing gum, and gelatin desserts. No known toxicity. GRAS.

DECANAL DIMETHYL ACETAL • A synthetic flavoring agent. Occurs naturally in anise, butter acid, oil of lemon, and oil of lime. Used in butter, coconut, fruit, liquor, whiskey, and cheese flavorings for beverages, ice cream, ices, candy, baked goods, chewing gum, and gelatin desserts. No known toxicity. GRAS.

DECANOIC ACID • A synthetic flavoring agent that occurs naturally in anise, butter acids, oil of lemon, and oil of lime, and is used to flavor butter, coconut, fruit, liquor, and cheese flavorings for beverages, ice cream, ices, candy, baked goods, chewing gum, gelatin desserts, puddings, and shortenings. No known toxicity.

1-DECANOL • A synthetic flavoring agent. Occurs naturally in orange and ambrette seed. Used in butter, lemon, orange, coconut, and fruit flavorings for beverages, ice cream, ices, candy, baked goods, and chewing gum. No known toxicity.

DECANYL ACETATE • See Decyl Acetate.

2-DECENAL • A synthetic fruit flavoring for beverages, ice cream, ices, candy, and baked goods. No known toxicity.

DECENALDEHYDE • *See* 2-Decenal.

DECYL ACETATE • A synthetic berry, orange, apple, peach, plum, and honey flavoring agent for beverages, ice cream, ices, candy, baked goods, and chewing gum. No known toxicity.

DECYL ALCOHOL • An intermediate (*see*) for surface-active agents, an antifoam agent, and a fixative in perfumes. Occurs naturally in sweet orange and ambrette seed. Derived commercially from liquid paraffin wax (*see*). Colorless to light yellow liquid. Used also for synthetic lubricants and as a synthetic fruit flavoring. Low toxicity in animals. No known toxicity for the skin.

DECYL BUTYRATE • A synthetic citrus and fruit flavoring agent for beverages, ice cream, ices, candy, and baked goods. No known toxicity.

DECYL PROPIONATE • A synthetic citrus and fruit flavoring agent for beverages, ice cream, ices, candy, and baked goods. No known toxicity.

DECYLIC ACID • *See* Decanoic Acid.

DECYLIC ALCOHOL • *See* 1-Decanol.

DEFATTED • Meaning the fat has been partly or totally removed from a product. If partly removed there is no minimum percentage set by the Food and Drug Administration.

DEFATTED COTTONSEED OIL • From cottonseed flour (*see*) with the fat removed.

DEFOAMER • Antifoamer. Foam Inhibitor. Any number of surfactants (*see*), such as liquid glycerides (*see*), which are used to control the amount of foam produced in the processing of baked goods, coffee, whiteners, candies, milk products, jams, jellies, and fruit juices. They remove the "head" from processed drinks, such as orange and pineapple juice.

DEHYDRATED • With the water removed.

DEHYDROACETIC ACID • DHA. Sodium Dehydroacetate. A weak acid that forms a white odorless powder with an acrid taste. Used as a preservative in cut or peeled squash. Used as an antienzyme agent in toothpastes to prevent tooth decay and as a preservative for foods and shampoos. Also used as a fungi and bacteria-destroying agent in cosmetics. The presence of organic matter decreases its effectiveness. Not irritating or allergy-causing, but it is a kidney-blocking agent and can cause impaired kidney function. Large doses can cause vomiting, imbalance, and convulsions.

DELANEY AMENDMENT • Written by Congressman James Delaney, the amendment was part of the 1958 law requested by the Food and Drug Administration. The law stated that food and chemical manufacturers had to test additives before they were put on the market and the results had to be submitted to the FDA. Delaney's amendment specifically states that no additive may be permitted in any amount if the tests show that it produces cancer when fed to man or animals or by other appropriate tests. Ever since it was enacted, the food and chemical industries have tried to get it repealed.

DEMULCENT • A soothing, usually thick oily or creamy substance used to relieve pain in inflamed or irritated mucous surfaces. The gum acacia, for instance, is used as a demulcent.

DENATURANT • A substance that changes another substance's natural qualities or characteristics. For example, denatonium benzoate is added to the alcoholic content in cosmetics to make it undrinkable.

DERMATITIS • Inflammation of the skin.

DESOXYCHOLIC ACID • An emulsifying agent, white, crystalline powdered, almost insoluble in water. Used in dried egg whites up to 0.1 percent. No known toxicity. The final report to the FDA of the Select Committee on GRAS Substances stated in 1980 that it should continue its GRAS status with no limitations other than good manufacturing practices.

DEXTRAN • A term applied to polysaccharides produced by bacteria growing on sugar. Used as a foam stabilizer for beer, in soft-center confections, and as a substitute for barley malt. It has also been used as a plasma expander for emergency treatment of shock. Has caused cancer in rats. The final report to the FDA of the Select Committee on GRAS Substances stated in 1980 that there is no evidence in the available information that it is a hazard to the public when used as it is now and it should continue its GRAS status with limitations on amounts that can be added to food.

DEXTRIN • British Gum. Starch Gum. White or yellow powder produced from starch and used as a foam stabilizer for beer, a diluting agent for dry extracts and pills, in polishing cereals, for preparing emulsions and dry bandages, for thickening industrial dye pastes, and in matches, fireworks, and explosives. Also used as a thickener in cream and liquid cosmetics. May cause an allergic reaction. The final report to the FDA of the Select Committee on GRAS Substances stated in 1980 that it should continue its GRAS status with no limitations other than good manufacturing practices.

DEXTROSE • The final report to the FDA of the Select Committee on GRAS Substances stated in 1980 that there is no evidence in the available information that it is a hazard to the public when used as it is now and it should continue its GRAS status with no limitations other than good manufacturing practices. *See* Corn Syrup.

DHC • *See* Dihydrochalcones.

DIACETIN • A mixture of the diesters (*see*) of glycerin (*see*) and acetic acid (*see*), used as a plasticizer, softening agent, or as a solvent for cellulose derivatives, resins, and shellacs. No known toxicity.

DIACETYL • It occurs naturally in cheese, cocoa, pears, coffee, raspberries, strawberries, and cooked chicken, but is usually prepared by a special fermentation of glucose. It is a yellowish-green liquid. Also used as a carrier of aroma of butter, vinegar, and coffee. Also used in blueberry, raspberry, strawberry, butter, buttermilk, butterscotch, caramel, chocolate, coffee, fruit, cheese, cherry, liquor, rum, wine, nut, almond, spice, ginger ale, vanilla, and cream soda flavorings for beverages, ice cream, ices, candy, baked goods, gelatin desserts, chewing gum, and shortening. Cleared by U.S. Department of Agriculture (Meat Inspection Division) to flavor oleomargarine in "amount sufficient for the purpose." Diacetyl compounds have been associated with cancer when ingested by experimental animals. GRAS.

DIACETYL TARTARIC OF MONOGLYCERIDES AND DIGLYCERIDES • An emulsifying agent used to improve volume and uniformity in bakery products allowed up to 20 percent by weight of the combination of such a preparation and the shortening. The final report to the FDA of the Select Committee on GRAS Substances stated in 1980 that it should continue its GRAS status with no limitations other than good manufacturing practices.

DIALLYL DISULFIDE • *See* Allyl Disulfide.

DIALLYL SULFIDE • *See* Allyl Sulfide.

DIAMINOZIDE • Alar®. In 1989 the Environmental Protection Agency proposed banning its use in enhancing the growth and appearance of apples. It was reported to be carcinogenic.

1, 4-DIANILINOANTHRAQUINONE • *See* Coal Tar.

DIASMOL • *See* 1, 3-Nonanediol Acetate (mixed esters).

DIATOMACEOUS EARTH • Kieselguhr. A porous and relatively pure form of silica formed from fossil remains of diatoms—one-celled algae with shells. Inert when ingested. Used in dentifrices, as a clarifying agent, as an absorbent for liquids because it can absorb about four times its weight in water, and as a buffer for acid-proofing food packaging. Also used in nail polishes and face powders. The dust can cause lung damage after long exposure to high concentrations. Not recommended for use on teeth or skin because of its abrasiveness. The final report to the FDA of the Select Committee on GRAS Substances stated in 1980 that it should continue its GRAS status with no limitations other than good manufacturing practices.

DIAZO- • A compound containing two nitrogen atoms such as diazolidinyl urea, one of the newer preservatives, or diazepam, a popular muscle relaxant.

DIBENZYL ETHER • A synthetic fruit and spice flavoring agent for beverages, ice cream, ices, candy, baked goods, and chewing gum. No known toxicity.

2, 2-DIBROMO-3-NITRILOPROPIONAMIDE • Preservative used alone for control of microorganisms in raw cane sugar in cane and beet-sugar mills (2–10 ppm). No information on toxicity from available sources.

4, 4-DIBUTYL-γ-BUTYROLACTONE • A synthetic butter, coconut, and nut flavoring agent for ice cream, candy, ices, and baked goods. No known toxicity.

DIBUTYL SEBACATE • Sebacic Acid. A synthetic fruit flavoring usually obtained from castor oil and used for beverages, ice cream, and baked goods. Also used for sealing food packages. Used in fruit-fragrance cosmetics. No known toxicity.

DIBUTYL SULFIDE • *See* Butyl Sulfide.

DIBUTYLENE TETRAFURFURAL • Derived from bran, rice hulls, or corn cobs, it is used in the manufacture of medicinals and as a solvent and flavoring in cosmetics and food. Toxic when absorbed by the skin. Irritating to the eye.

DICHLORODIFLUOROMETHANE • Colorless, odorless gas used to freeze foods by direct contact and for chilling cocktail glasses. Narcotic in high doses.

DICHLOROMETHANE • *See* Methylene Chloride.

DIESTER- • A compound containing two ester groupings. An ester is formed from an alcohol and an acid by eliminating water. It is usually employed in fragrant liquids for artificial fruit perfumes and flavors.

DIETARY FOOD SUPPLEMENT • Any food product to which enough vitamins and minerals have been added to furnish more than 50 percent of the recommended daily allowance in a single serving, according to the FDA. Such foods must, of course, have ingredients identified on the label.

DIETHYL ASPARTATE • The diester of ethyl alcohol and aspartic acid (*see* both).

DIETHYL GLUTAMATE • *See* Glutamate.

DIETHYL PALMITOYL ASPARTATE • *See* Aspartic Acid.

DIETHYL PYROCARBONATE (DEP) • A fermentation inhibitor in still wines, beer, and orange juice added before or during bottling at a level not to exceed 200 to 500 parts per million. DEP was widely used because it supposedly did its job of preserving and then decomposed within 24 hours. However, instead of disappearing, it reacted with the ammonia in beverages to form urethane, according to University of Stockholm researchers. They said that DEP caused urethane concentration of 0.1 to 0.2 milligrams per liter in orange juice and approximately 1 milligram per liter in white wine and beer. Since 1943 urethane has been identified as a cancer-causing agent. The FDA had not required listing of DEP on the label and therefore did not know how many beverages were actually treated with this additive. The FDA banned the use of DEP in 1976.

DIETHYL MALATE • Malic Acid. A synthetic apple and rum flavoring agent for beverages, ice cream, ices, candy, baked goods, gelatin, and puddings. No known toxicity.

DIETHYL MALONATE • A synthetic berry, fruit, apple, grape, peach, and pear flavoring for beverages, ice cream, ices, candy, and baked goods. No known toxicity.

DIETHYL SEBACATE • Sebacic Acid. A synthetic butter, coconut, apple, melon, peach, and nut flavoring for beverages, ice cream, ices, candy, baked goods, chewing gum, and gelatin desserts. No known toxicity.

DIETHYL SUCCINATE • A synthetic raspberry, butter, orange, and grape flavoring for beverages, ice cream, ices, candy, and baked goods. No known toxicity.

DIETHYL TARTRATE. • *See* Tartaric Acid.

DIETHYL GLYCOL • Made by heating ethylene oxide and glycol. A clear, water-absorbing, almost colorless liquid; it is mixable with water, alcohol, and acetone. Used as a solvent, humectant, and plasticizer in foods, cosmetic creams, and hair sprays. A wetting agent (*see*) that enhances skin absorption. Can be fatal if swallowed. Not usually irritating to the skin, but can be absorbed through the skin and the use of glycols on extensive areas of the body is considered hazardous.

DIETHYLENE GLYCOL DIBENZOATE • Used as a plasticizer. *See* Diethylene Glycol.

DIETHYLSTILBESTROL (DES) • Stilbestrol. A synthetic estrogen fed to cattle and poultry to "fatten them." A proven carcinogen, hormonal in nature, according to the FDA, which has given top priority to the study of the safety of DES. The FDA stipulates a zero tolerance for the compound after a proper withdrawal period. In 1971, three Harvard scientists linked DES to a rare form of vaginal cancer in the daughters of women who had taken DES during pregnancy. An estimated 100,000 to 150,000 head of cattle containing residues of the hormones are apparently getting to market. The European Common Market, Italy, and Sweden have forbidden the use of DES in cattle. It was banned by the FDA but showed up in some meat as late as 1986.

DIGLYCERIDES • Emulsifiers. *See* Glycerides.

2, 3-DIHYDRO-3-OXO-BENZISOSULFONAZOLE • *See* Saccharin.

DIHYDROANETHOLE • *See* p-Propyl Anisole.

DIHYDROACARVYL ACETATE • Acetic Acid. A synthetic berry, fruit, mint, and spice flavoring agent for beverages, ice cream, ices, candy, baked goods, and alcoholic beverages. No known toxicity.

DIHYDROCARVEOL • A synthetic flavoring agent occurring naturally in black pepper. Used in liquor, mint, spice, and caraway flavorings for beverages, ice cream, ices, candy, baked goods, and alcoholic beverages. No known toxicity.

DIHYDROCHALCONES (DHC) • A new class of intensely sweet compounds—about fifteen hundred times sweeter than sugar—obtained by a simple chemical modification of naturally occurring bioflavonoids (*see*). Hydrogenation (*see*) of naringin and neohesperidin (the predominant bitter constituents in grapefruit and Seville orange rind) provides the intensely sweet dihydrochalcones. DHCs are seemingly safe. There have not been any reports, thus far, of side effects in either multigenerational feeding studies or in long-term feeding trials. The disadvantage is that they cannot be easily reproduced in the laboratory so supplies are dependent upon natural sources. A more serious problem is that the intense, pleasant sweetness of DHCs is slow in onset, with considerable lingering taste, which renders them unsuitable for many food uses. Approval to use DHCs in toothpaste and chewing gum is pending. Food scientists are now trying to find derivatives and analogs of DHCs to overcome the slow onset and lingering factor in the natural compounds.

DIHYDROCHOLESTEROL • *See* Cholesterol.

DIHYDROCHOLESTERYL OCTYLDECAOATE • *See* Cholesterol and Stearic Acid.

DIHYDROCOUMARIN • A synthetic flavoring agent occurring naturally in tonka bean, oil of lavender, and sweet clovers. Used in butter, caramel, coconut, floral, fruit, cherry, liquor, rum, nut, root beer, spice, cinnamon, vanilla, cream soda, and tonka flavorings for beverages, ice cream, ices, candy, baked goods, chewing gum, gelatin desserts, and puddings. Prolonged feeding has revealed a possible trend toward liver injury.

2, 3-DIKETOBUTANE • *See* Diacetyl.

DILAURYL CITRATE • *See* Fatty Alcohols and Citric Acid.

DILAURYL THIODIPROPIONATE • An antioxidant. White crystalline flakes with a sweet odor, in general food use to extend shelf life. In fats or oils up to 0.02 percent. The final report to the FDA of the Select Committee on GRAS Substances stated in 1980 that it there is no evidence in the available information that it is a hazard to the public when used as it is now and it should continue its GRAS status with no limitations other than good manufacturing practices.

DILINOLEATE • Dimer Acid. Widely used as an emulsifier, it is derived from Linoleic Acid (*see*).

DILINOLEIC ACID • *See* Linoleic Acid.

DILL • A natural flavoring agent from a European herb bearing a seedlike fruit. Used in sausage and spice flavorings for baked goods (4,800 ppm), meats, and pickles (8,200 ppm). Also used in medicine. Can cause sensitivity to light. The final report to the FDA of the Select Committee on GRAS Substances stated in 1980 that it should continue its GRAS status with no limitations other than good manufacturing practices.

DILL OIL • The volatile oil obtained from the crushed, dried seeds or fruits of the herb. Slightly yellow, with a caraway odor and flavor. Used in strawberry, fruit, sausage, and dill flavorings for beverages, ice cream, ices, baked goods, gelatin desserts, chewing gum, meat, liquors, pickles, and condiments. The final report to the FDA of the Select Committee on GRAS Substances stated in 1980 that it should continue its GRAS status with no limitations other than good manufacturing practices. *See* Dill for toxicity.

DILLSEED • Indian Dill. The volatile oil from a variety of dill herbs. Obtained by steam distillation. Light yellow, with a harsh carawaylike odor. Used in rye flavorings for baked goods, condiments, and meats. The final report to the FDA of the Select Committee on GRAS Substances stated in 1980 that it should continue its GRAS status with no limitations other than good manufacturing practices.

DILUENT • Any component of a color additive mixture that is not of itself a color additive and has been intentionally mixed in to facilitate the uses of the mixture in coloring cosmetics or in coloring the human body, food, and drugs. The diluent may serve another function in cosmetics, as, for example, an emulsifier or stabilizer. Ethylcellulose is an example.

DIMETHICONE • *See* Dimethyl Polysiloxane.

m-**DIMETHOXYBENZENE** • Resorcinol. A synthetic fruit, nut, and vanilla flavoring for beverages, ice cream, ices, candy, and baked goods. Used on the skin as a bactericidal and fungicidal ointment. Has the same toxicity as phenol (extremely toxic), but causes more severe convulsions.

p-**DIMETHOXYBENZENE** • A synthetic raspberry, fruit, nut, hazel nut, root beer, and vanilla flavoring agent for beverages, ice cream, ices, candy, and baked goods. *See* above for toxicity.

3, 4-DIMETHOXYBENZENECARBONAL • *See* Veratraldehyde.

DI-(2-METHOXYETHYL) PHTHALATE • Oily liquid with a moldy odor used as a plasticizer and solvent. Combustible.

DIMETHYL BENZYL CARBINOL • *See a,a*-Dimethylphenethyl alcohol.

DIMETHYL ETHERPROTOCATECHUALDEHYDE • *See* Veratraldehyde.

DIMETHYL ETHER RESORCINOL • A benzene derivative, originally obtained from certain resins but now usually synthesized. *See m-*Dimethoxybenzene.

2, 6-DIMETHYL-5-HEPTENAL • A synthetic fruit flavoring for beverages, ice cream, ices, candy, baked goods, gelatin desserts, and chewing gum. No known toxicity.

3, 7-DIMETHYL-7-HYDROXYOCTANAL • *See* Hydroxycitronellal.

DIMETHYL KETONE • *See* Diacetyl.

3, 7-DIMETHYL-1-OCTANOL • A synthetic flavoring, colorless, with a sweet roselike odor. Used in floral, rose, and fruit flavorings for beverages, ice cream, ices, candy, and baked goods. No known toxicity.

DIMETHYL POLYSILOXANE • Dimethicone. Antifoam A. An antifoaming agent for use in processing foods in "amounts reasonably required to inhibit foaming." Used as a chewing gum base, in molasses, soft drinks, sugar distillation, skimmed milk, wine fermentation, syrups, soups, rendered fats, and curing solutions. Not to exceed 10 ppm in nonalcoholic beverages. Zero tolerance in milk; 250 ppm in salt for cooking and 10 ppm in foods ready for consumption. Used to combat flatulence. Very low toxicity.

DIMETHYL RESORCINOL • *See m-*Dimethoxybenzene.

DIEMTHYL SUCCINATE • Succinic Acid. A synthetic fruit flavoring agent for beverages, ice cream, ices, candy, baked goods, and chewing gum. No known toxicity.

DIMETHYL SULFIDE • *See* Methyl Sulfide.

DIMETHYL SULFATE • Sulfuric Acid. Dimethyl Ester. Colorless, oily liquid used as a methylating agent (to add methyl) in the manufacture of cosmetic dyes, perfumes, and flavorings. Methyl salicylate is an example (*see*). Extremely hazardous, dimethyl sulfate has delayed lethal qualities. Liquid produces severe blistering, necrosis of the skin. Sufficient skin absorption can result in serious poisoning. Vapors hurt the eyes. Ingestion can cause paralysis, coma, prostration, kidney damage, and death.

a,a-DIMETHYLBENZYL ISOBUTYRATE • A synthetic fruit flavoring agent for beverages, ice cream, ices, candy, and baked goods. No known toxicity.

DIMETHYLGLYOXAL • *See* Diacetyl.

DIMETHYLKETOL • *See* Acetoin.

2, 4-DIMETHYLACETOPHENONE • A synthetic grape, vanilla, and cream soda flavoring agent for beverages, ice cream, ices, candy, baked goods, and liquor. No known toxicity.

DIMETHYLOL MELAMINE • A synthetic resin with formaldehyde (*see*), which is an indirect food additive from the packaging.

a,a-DIMETHYLPHENETHYL ACETATE. • Acetic Acid. A synthetic cherry and honey flavoring agent for beverages, ice cream, ices, candy, baked goods, and chewing gum. No known toxicity.

a,a-DIMETHYLPHENETHYL ALCOHOL • A synthetic fruit flavoring agent for beverages, ice cream, ices, candy, chewing gum, jellies, gelatin desserts, and baked goods. No known toxicity.

a,a-DIMETHYLPHENETHYL BUTYRATE • Butyric Acid. A synthetic fruit flavoring agent for beverages, ice cream, ices, candy, and baked goods. No known toxicity.

a,a-DIMETHYLPHENETHYL FORMATE • Formic Acid. A synthetic spice flavoring agent for beverages, ice cream, ices, and candy. No known toxicity.

2, 7-DINITROSO-1-NAPHTHOL • Used in the manufacture of dyes. *See* Coal Tar.

DINKUM OIL • *See* Eucalyptus Oil.

2,6-DINTRO-3-METHOXY-1-METHYL-4-TERT-BUTYL-BENZENE • *See* Musk.

DIOCTYL- • Containing two octyl groups. Octyl is obtained from octane, a liquid paraffin found in petroleum.

DIOCTYL ADIPATE • *See* Adipic Acid.

DIOCTYL DILINOLEATE • *See* Linoleic Acid.

DIOCYTL MALEATE • *See* Malic Acid.

DIOCYTL SODIUM SULFOSUCCINATE • Docustae Sodium. A waxlike solid that is very soluble in water it is used as a dispersing and solubilizing agent in foods, drugs, and cosmetics. In foods and beverages it is used as a dispersing and solubilizing agent for gums, cocoa, and various hard-to-wet materials. Also a wetting agent in the cleaning of fruits, vegetables, and leafy plant material. Used in nonalcoholic beverages and sherbets at a rate not to exceed 0.5 percent of the weight of such ingredients. Finished cocoa beverages can have 75 ppm in the finished products. It is a stool softener in laxatives. Eye irritation may result from use in eye preparations.

DIOXYMETHYLENE PROTOCATECHUICALDEHYDE • *See* Piperonal.

DIPENTINE • *See* Limonene.

DIPHENYL KETONE • *See* Benzophenones.

1,3-DIPHENYL-2-PROPANONE • A synthetic fruit, honey, and nut flavoring for beverages, ice cream, ices, candy, and baked goods. No known toxicity.

DIPOTASSIUM EDTA • *See* Ethylenediamine Tetraacetic Acid.

DIPOTASSIUM GLYCYRRHIZATE • The dipotassium salt of Glycyrrhizic Acid (*see*).

DIPOTASSIUM PHOSPHATE • A sequestrant. A white grain, very soluble in water. Used as a buffering agent to control the degree of acidity in solutions. It is used in the preparation of nondairy powdered coffee creams and in cheeses up to 3 percent by weight of cheese. It is used medicinally as a saline cathartic. No known toxicity. GRAS.

DIPROPYL DISULFIDE • A synthetic flavoring agent. Colorless, insoluble in water. Occurs naturally in onion. Used in imitation of onion flavoring for pickle products and in baked goods. No known toxicity.

DIPROPYL KETONE • See 4-Heptanone.

DISODIUM ADENOSINE TRIPHOSPHATE • A preservative derived from adenylic acid. See Adenosine Triphosphate.

DISODIUM CYANODITHIOMIDOCARBONATE • Bacteria-killing component in the processing of sugar cane. Any substance that releases the cyanide ion can cause poisoning. Sodium cyanide is one of the swiftest poisons known.

DISODIUM EDTA • White crystalline powder, soluble in water, used as a food preservative and sequestering agent. Promotes color retention in frozen white potatoes (100 ppm), canned potatoes (110 ppm), cooked chick peas (165 ppm), dried banana cereal (315 ppm), canned strawberry pie filling (500 ppm), gefilte fish (50 ppm), and salad dressing (75 ppm.) See Ethylenediamine Tetraacetic Acid (EDTA).

DISODIUM EDTA-COPPER • Copper Versenate. Used as a sequestering agent. See Ethylenediamine Tetraacetic Acid for toxicity.

DISODIUM GUANYLATE • A flavor intensifier believed to be more effective than sodium inosinate and sodium glutamate. It is the disodium salt of 5'-guanylic acid, widely distributed in nature as a precursor of RNA and DNA. Can be isolated from certain mushrooms and is used in canned vegetables. No known toxicity.

DISODIUM 5'-INOSINATE • Flavor potentiator (*see*), odorless and colorless, or white crystal or powder, with a characteristic taste. Used in canned vegetables. See Inosinate.

DISODIUM PHOSPHATE (DIBASIC) • A sequestering agent (*see*), used in evaporated milk up to 0.1 percent by weight of finished product; in macaroni and noodle products at not less than 0.5 percent nor more than 1 percent. It is used as an emulsifier up to 3 percent by weight in specified cheeses. Cleared by the U.S. Department of Agriculture's Meat Inspection department to prevent cooked-out juices in cured hams, pork shoulders, and loins, canned hams, chopped hams, and bacon (5 percent in the pickling and 5 percent injected into the product). Used as a buffer to adjust acidity in chocolate products, beverages, sauces, and toppings, and enriched farina. Incompatible with alkaloids. It is a mild saline cathartic and has been used in phosphorous deficiency treatment. It may cause mild irritation to the skin and mucous membranes, and can cause purging. GRAS.

DISODIUM PYROPHOSPHATE • Sodium Pyrophosphate. An emulsifier and texturizer used to decrease the loss of fluid from a compound. It is GRAS for use in foods as a sequestrant. *See* Sodium Pyrophosphate.

DISOYAMINE. • *See* Soybean oil.

DISPERSANT • A dispersing agent, such as polyphosphate, for promoting the formation and stabilization of a dispersion of one substance in another. An emulsion, for instance, would consist of a dispersed substance and the medium in which it is dispersed.

DISTARCH PHOSPHATE • A combination of starch and sodium metaphosphate. It is a water softener, sequestering agent, and texturizer. A modified starch once commonly used in baby foods. It is used in dandruff shampoos. The final report to the FDA of the Select Committee on GRAS Substances stated in 1980 that there is no evidence in the available information that it is a hazard to the public when used as it is now and it should continue its GRAS status with no limitations other than good manufacturing practices.

DISTARCH PROPANOL • A modified starch. The final report to the FDA of the Select Committee on GRAS Substances stated in 1980 that while there is no evidence in the available information to demonstrate a hazard to the public at current use levels, uncertainties exist, requiring that additional studies be conducted. The FDA allowed GRAS status to continue while tests were being completed and evaluated. Since 1980, however, nothing new has been reported.

DISTILLED • The result of evaporation and subsequent condensation of a liquid, as when water is boiled and steam is condensed.

DISTILLED ACETYLATED MONOGLYCERIDES • Food emulsifiers and binders in nutrient capsules and tablets to make them palatable; also food-coating agents. The FDA rules require that it is used "at level not in excess of the amount reasonably required to produce the intended effect." Cleared by the U.S.D.A. Meat Inspection Department as an emulsifier for shortening. No known toxicity.

DITTANY OF CRETE • A natural flavoring extracted from a small herb grown in Crete. Used in spice flavorings for beverages and baked goods. No known toxicity.

γ-DODECALACTONE • A synthetic flavoring, colorless, with a coconut odor that becomes butterlike in low concentrations. Used in butter, butterscotch, coconut, fruit, maple, and nut flavorings for beverages, ice cream, ices, candy, baked goods, gelatin desserts, puddings, and jellies. No known toxicity.

o-DODECALACTONE • A synthetic flavoring. Occurs naturally in butter, cream, and milk. Used in butter, fruit, and pear flavorings for candy, baked goods, oleomargarine, and toppings. Not to exceed 20 ppm in oleomargarine. No known toxicity.

DODECANOIC ACID • *See* Lauric Acid.

DODECYL GALLATE • An antioxidant. *See* Fatty Alcohols.

DOG GRASS EXTRACT • A natural flavoring extract used in maple flavoring for beverages, ice cream, ices, candy, and baked goods. Derives its name from the fact that it is eaten by sick dogs. No known toxicity. GRAS.

DRACO RUBIN EXTRACT • *See* Dragon's Blood Extract.

DRAGON'S BLOOD EXTRACT • The resinous secretion of the fruit of trees grown in Sumatra, Borneo, and India. Almost odorless and tasteless and available in the form of red sticks, pieces, or cakes. Makes a bright crimson powder. Used in bitters flavoring for beverages. Also used to color lacquers and varnishes. No known toxicity.

DRIED SORGHUM GRAIN SYRUP • A corn syrup substitute produced from the starch of sorghum grain. *See* Sorghum.

DRIED YEAST • A dietary source of folic acid. Used to enrich farina, corn meals, corn grits, and bakery products. Dried yeast is cleared for use in food provided the total folic acid content of the yeast does not exceed .04 milligrams per gram of yeast. Nontoxic.

DRY MILK, NONFAT • *See* Nonfat Dry Milk.

DRYING AGENTS • *See* Rosin.

DULCAMARA EXTRACT • Bitter Sweet Nightshade. Extract of the dried stems of *Solanum dulcamara*. Belonging to the family of the nightshades, it is used as a preservative. The ripe berries are used for pies and jams. The unripened berries are deadly. It is made into an ointment by herbalists to treat skin cancers and burns. It induces sweating.

DULSE • A natural flavoring extract from red seaweed. Used as a food condiment. No known toxicity. GRAS.

E

EARTH WAX • General name for Ozocerite, Ceresin, and Montan Waxes. *See* Waxes.

EDTA • *See* Etylenediamine Tetraacetic Acid.

EGG • Particularly associated with eczema in children. May also cause reactions ranging from hives to anaphylaxis. Eggs may also be found in root beer, soups, sausage, coffee, and in cosmetics.

EICOSAPENTAENOIC ACID (EPA) • Found in fish oil (*see*), it reduces production of thromboxane, a clotting agent, in the blood, thus making the platelets less "sticky."

ELAIDIC ACID • *See* Oleic Acid.

ELDER FLOWERS • A natural flavoring from the small white flowers of a shrub or small tree. Used in fruit, wine, and spice flavorings for beverages, ice cream, ices, candy, baked goods, and wine. The leaves and bark can cause nausea, vomiting, and diarrhea. GRAS.

ELDER TREE LEAVES • Flavoring for use in alcoholic beverages only. *See* Elder Flowers.

ELDERBERRY JUICE POWDER • Dried powder from the juice of the edible berry of a North American elder tree. Used for red coloring. Nontoxic.

ELECAMPANE RHIZOME AND ROOTS • Flavoring in alcoholic beverages only. From a large, coarse European herb having yellow ray flowers. No known toxicity.

ELEMI • A soft, yellowish, fragrant plastic resin from several Asiatic and Philippine trees. Slightly soluble in water but readily soluble in alcohol. An oily resin derived from the tropical trees. The gum is used in fruit flavoring for beverages, ice cream, ices, candy, and baked goods. The oil is used in citrus, fruit, vermouth, and spice flavorings for beverages, ice cream, ices, candy, baked goods, and soups. Used for gloss and adhesion in nail lacquer and to scent soaps and colognes. The resins are used industrially for making varnishes and inks. No known toxicity.

EMULSIFIERS • Widely used additives to stabilize a mixture and to ensure consistency. They make chocolate more mixable with milk and keep puddings from separating. One of the most widely used emulsifiers is lecithin (*see*) and another is polysorbate 60 (*see*). Di- and monoglycerides (*see* both) are also used in many products. Among common emulsifiers in cosmetics are stearic acid soaps such as potassium and sodium stearates.

EMULSIFYING OIL • Soluble Oil. An oil which, when mixed with water, produces a milky emulsion. Sodium sulfonate is an example.

EMULSIFYING WAX • Waxes that are treated so that they mix more easily.

EMULSION • What is formed when two or more nonmixable liquids are shaken so thoroughly together that the mixture continues to appear to be homogenized. Most oils form emulsions with water.

ENZYME • Any of a unique class of proteins which catalyze a broad spectrum of biochemical reactions. Enzymes are formed in living cells. One enzyme can cause a chemical process that no other enzyme can do. See Papain.

ENZYMATICALLY HYDROLYZED PROTEIN • Enzymes are used to break down the protein in solution. The final report to the FDA of the Select Committee on GRAS Substances stated in 1980 that it should continue its GRAS status with no limitations other than good manufacturing practices.

ENZYME-MODIFIED FATS • Enzymes such as lipase are used to break down fats and are used in the manufacture of cheese and similar foods and as a flavoring. No known toxicity.

EPICHLOROHYDRIN • A colorless liquid with an odor resembling chloroform. It is soluble in water but mixes readily with alcohol and ether. A modifier for food starches that the FDA permits to be used up to levels of 0.3 percent in starch. Used as a solvent for cosmetic resins and in the manufacture of varnishes, lacquers, and cements for celluloid articles. A strong skin irritant and sensitizer. Daily administration of 1 milligram per kilogram of body weight to skin killed all of a group of rats in four days, indicating a cumulative potential. Chronic exposure is known to cause kidney damage. A thirty-minute exposure to air concentrations of 8300 parts per million was lethal to mice. Poisoned animals showed cyanosis, muscular relaxation or paralysis, convulsions, and death. There may be 50,000 workers exposed to epichlorohydrin, according to OSHA. A two-year study of workers who had been exposed to the substance for six months or more before January 1966 showed an increase in the incidence of cancer. Chronic exposure is known to cause kidney damage in humans. Germany regulates it as a known carcinogen.

1,8-EPOXY-p-MENTHANE • *See* Eucalyptol.

EQUISETIC ACID • *See* Aconitic Acid.

ERGOCALCIFEROL • Vitamin D_2.

ERIGERON CANADENSIS • *See* Erigeron Oil.

ERIGERON OIL • Horseweed. Fleabane Oil. Derived from the leaves and tops of a plant grown in the northern and central United States. Use in fruit and spice flavorings for beverages, ice cream, ices, candy, baked goods, and sauces. No known toxicity.

ERIODICTYON CALIFORNIUM • *See* Yerba Santa Fluid Extract.

ERYTHROBIC ACID • Isoascorbic Acid. Antioxidant. White, slightly yellow crystals, which darken on exposure to light. Isoascorbic acid contains 1/20th the vitamin capacity of ascorbic acid (*see*). Antioxidant used in pickling brine at a rate of 7.5 ounces per 100 gallons; in meat products, at the rate of 0.75 ounces per hundred pounds; in beverages; baked goods; cured cuts and cured pulverized products to accelerate color fixing in curing, to 0.75 ounces per 100 pounds. Nontoxic. The final report to the FDA of the Select Committee on GRAS Substances stated in 1980 that it should continue its GRAS status with no limitations other than good manufacturing practices.

ERYTHROSINE • Sodium or potassium salt of tetraiodofluorescein, a coal-tar derivative. A brown powder that becomes red in solution. FD and C Red No. 3 is an example. *See* Coal Tar for toxicity.

ERYTHROXYLON COCA • *See* Coca Leaf Extract (Decocainized).

ESSENCE • An extract of a substance that retains its fundamental or most desirable properties in concentrated form, such as a flavoring or fragrance.

ESSENTIAL OIL • The oily liquid obtained from plants through a variety of processes. The essential oil usually has the taste and smell of the original plant. Essential oils are called volatile because most of them are easily vaporized. The only theories for calling such oils essential are (1) the oils were believed essential to life and (2) they were the "essence" of the plant. The use of essential oils as preservatives is ancient. A large number of oils have antiseptic, germicidal, and preservative action; however, they are primarily used for fragrances and flavorings. No known toxicity when used on the skin. A teaspoon may cause illness in an adult and less than an ounce may kill.

ESTER • A compound formed from an alcohol and an acid by elimination of water, as ethyl acetate (*see*). Usually fragrant liquids used for artificial fruit perfumes and flavors. Esterification of rosin, for example, reduces its allergy-causing properties. Toxicity depends on the ester.

ESTERASE-LIPASE • Derived from *Mucor Miehei*. An enzyme used as a flavor enhancer in cheese, fats, oils, and milk products. No known toxicity.

ESTRADIOL • Most potent of the natural estrogenic female hormones. *See* Hormone Creams and Lotions. Also used in perfumes.

ESTRADIOL BENZOATE • *See* Estradiol.

ESTRAGOLE • A colorless to light-yellow oily liquid occurring naturally in anise, anise star, basil, estragon oil, and pimento oil. Used as a synthetic fruit, licorice, anise, and spice flavoring for beverages, ice cream, ices, candy, baked goods, chewing gum, and condiments. No known toxicity. GRAS.

ESTRAGON • Tarragon. A flavoring agent from the oil of leaves of a plant native to Eurasia and used in fruit, licorice, liquor, root beer, and spice flavorings for beverages, ice cream, ices, candy, baked goods, meats, liquor, and condiments. GRAS.

ESTROGEN • A female hormone. *See* Hormones

ETHANAL • *See* Acetaldehyde; Heptanal.

ETHANOIC ACID • *See* Acetic Acid.

ETHANOL • Ethyl Alcohol. Rubbing Alcohol. Ordinary Alcohol. Used as a solvent in candy, candy glaze, beverages, ice cream, ices, baked goods, liquors, sauces, and gelatin desserts. An antibacterial used in mouthwashes, nail enamel, astringents, liquid lip rouge, and many other cosmetics products. Clear, colorless, and very flammable, it is made by the fermentation of starch, sugar, and other carbohydrates. Used medicinally as a topical antiseptic, sedative, and blood vessel dilator. Ingestion of large amounts may cause nausea, vomiting, impaired perception, stupor, coma, and death. When it is deliberately denatured (*see* Denaturant), it is poisonous. GRAS.

ETHANTHALDEHYDE • *See* Heptanal.

ETHANTHIC ALCOHOL • *See* Heptyl Alcohol.

ETHANTHYL ALCOHOL • *See* Heptyl Alcohol.

ETHANOLAMINE DITHIODIGLYCOATE • *See* Ethanolamines.

ETHANOLAMINE THIOGLYCOLATE • *See* Ethanolamines.

ETHANOLAMINES • Three compounds—monoethanolamine, diethanolamine, and triethanolamine—with low melting points, colorless and solid, which readily absorb water and form viscous liquids and are soluble both in water and alcohol. They have an ammonia smell and are strong bases. Used in cold permanent wave lotions as a preservative. Also form soaps with fatty acids (*see*) and are widely used as detergents and emulsifying agents. Very large quantities are required for a lethal oral dose in mice (2,140 milligrams per kilogram of body weight). They have been used medicinally as sclerosal agents for varicose veins. Can be irritating to skin if very alkaline.

ETHER • An organic compound. Acetic ether (*see* ethyl acetate) is used in nail polishes as a solvent. Water-insoluble, fat-insoluble liquid with a characteristic odor. It is obtained chiefly by the distillation of alcohol with sulfuric acid and is used chiefly as a solvent. A mild skin irritant. Inhalation or ingestion causes central nervous system depression.

ETHOVAN • *See* Ethyl Vanillin.

***p*-ETHOXYBENZALDEHYDE** • A synthetic fruit and vanilla flavoring for beverages, ice cream, ices, candy, and baked goods. No known toxicity.

ETHOXYLATE • Ethyl (from the gas ethane) and oxygen are mixed and added to an additive to make it less or more soluble in water, depending upon the mixture. Ethoxylate acts as an emulsifier.

ETHOXYLATED MONO- AND DIGLYCERIDES • Dough conditioners in bread used to increase the volume of the loaf (not to exceed 0.5

percent of flour used). Also used as an emulsifier in pan-release agents for yeast-leavened bakery products. *See* Glycerides.

ETHOXYQUIN • 1,2-dihydro-6-ethoxy-2,2,4-trimethylquinoline. An antioxidant (*see*) to preserve color in chili powder, paprika, and ground chili at levels not to exceed 100 ppm. The residues in or on edible products of animals are restricted to 5 ppm in or on the uncooked fat of meat from animals except poultry; 3 ppm in or on the uncooked liver and fat of poultry and 0.5 ppm in or on the uncooked muscle meat of animals. *See* Quinoline for toxicity.

ETHYL ACETATE • A colorless liquid with a pleasant fruit odor that occurs naturally in apples, bananas, grape juice, pineapples, raspberries, and strawberries. It is employed as a synthetic flavoring agent in blackberry, raspberry, strawberry, butter, lemon, apple, banana, cherry, grape, peach, pineapple, brandy, muscatel, rum, whiskey, mint, almond, and cream soda flavoring for beverages, ice cream, ices, candy, baked goods, chewing gum, gelatins, puddings, and liquor. A very useful solvent in nail enamels and nail polish remover. Also an artificial fruit essence for perfumes. It is a mild local irritant and central nervous system depressant. The vapors are irritating and prolonged inhalation may cause kidney and liver damage. Irritating to the skin. Its fat solvent action produces drying and cracking and sets the stage for secondary infections. GRAS.

ETHYL ACETOACETATE • Acetoacetic Ester. A synthetic flavoring that occurs naturally in strawberries. Pleasant odor. Used in loganberry, strawberry, apple, apricot, cherry, peach, liquor, and muscatel flavorings for beverages, ice cream, ices, candy, baked goods, chewing gum, and gelatin desserts. Moderately irritating to skin and mucous membranes.

ETHYL ACETONE • *See* 2-Pentanone.

ETHYL 2-ACETYL-3-PHENYLPROPIONATE • A synthetic fruit flavoring for beverages, ice cream, ices, candy, baked goods, chewing gum, and gelatin desserts. No known toxicity.

ETHYL ACONITATE • Aconitic Acid. A synthetic fruit, liquor, and rum flavoring for beverages, ice cream, ices, candy, baked goods, and gelatin desserts. No known toxicity.

ETHYL ACRYLATE • A synthetic flavoring agent that occurs naturally in pineapple and raspberries. Used in fruit, liquor, and rum flavorings for beverages, ice cream, ices, candy, baked goods, and chewing gum. Also used in the manufacture of water-resistant paint, paper coating, and leather finishes. Highly irritating to the eyes, skin, and mucous membranes and may cause lethargy and convulsions if concentrated vapor is inhaled. The final report to the FDA of the Select Committee on GRAS Substances stated in 1980 that it should continue its GRAS

status with no limitations other than good manufacturing practices.
ETHYL ALCOHOL • Contains ethanol (*see*), grain alcohol, and neutral spirits and is used as a solvent in candy glaze, beverages, ices, ice cream, candy, baked goods, liquors, sauces, gelatin desserts, and pizza crusts. It is rapidly absorbed through the gastric and intestinal mucosa. For ingestion within a few minutes, the fatal dose in adults is considered to be 1.5 to 2 pints of whiskey (40 to 55 percent ethyl alcohol). It was approved in 1976 for use in pizza crusts to extend handling and storage life.
ETHYL p-ANISATE • A synthetic flavoring agent, colorless to lightly yellow, liquid, with a light fruity smell. Used in berry, fruit, grape, licorice, anise, liquor, rum, and vanilla flavorings for beverages, ice cream, ices, candy, and baked goods. No known toxicity.
ETHYL ANTHRANILATE • Colorless liquid, fruit odor, soluble in alcohol and propylene glycol. A synthetic flavoring agent, clear, colorless to amber liquid with an odor of orange blossoms. Used in berry, mandarin, orange, floral, jasmine, neroli, fruit, grape, peach, and raisin flavorings for beverages, ice cream, ices, candy, baked goods, gelatin desserts, and chewing gum. Used in perfumery. No known toxicity.
ETHYL ASPARTATE • The ester of ethyl alcohol and aspartic acid (*see* both).
ETHYL BENZENECARBOXYLATE • *See* Ethyl Benzoate.
ETHYL BENZOATE • Essence de Niobe. Ethyl Benzenecarboxylate. An artificial fruit essence almost insoluble in water, with a pleasant odor. Used in currant, strawberry, fruit, cherry, grape, liquor, nut, walnut, vanilla, and raspberry flavorings for beverages, ice cream, ices, candy, baked goods, chewing gum, gelatin desserts, and liquors. No known toxicity.
ETHYL BENZOYLACETATE • A synthetic fruit flavoring agent for beverages, ice cream, ices, candy, and baked goods. It becomes yellow when exposed to light. Pleasant odor. No known toxicity.
ETHYL BENZYL ACETOACETATE • *See* Ethyl 2-Acetyl-3-Phenyl-propionate.
ETHYL BENZYL BUTYRATE • A synthetic fruit flavoring for beverages, ice cream, ices, candy, and baked goods. No known toxicity.
ETHYL BUTYL ACETATE • A synthetic fruit flavoring for beverages, ice cream, ices, candy. No known toxicity.
ETHYL BUTYRATE • Butyric Acid. Pineapple Oil. Colorless, with a pineapple odor. It occurs naturally in apples and strawberries. In alcoholic solution it is known as pineapple oil. Used in blueberry, raspberry, strawberry, butter, caramel, cream, orange, banana, cherry, grape, peach, pineapple, rum, walnut, and eggnog flavorings for

beverages, ice cream, ices, candy, baked goods, gelatins, puddings, and chewing gum (1,400 ppm). No known toxicity. GRAS.

ETHYL CAPRATE • *See* Cognac Oil.

ETHYL CAPROATE • Colorless to yellowish liquid, pleasant odor, soluble in alcohol and ether. Used in artificial fruit essences. *See* Cognac Oil.

ETHYL CAPRYLATE • *See* Cognac Oil.

ETHYL CARBONATE • Carbonic Acid Diethyl Ester. Pleasant odor. Practically insoluble in water. Solvent for nail enamels. No known toxicity.

ETHYL CARVACROL • *See* Carvacryl Ethyl Ether.

ETHYL CELLULOSE • Cellulose Ether. White granules prepared from wood pulp or chemical cotton and used as a binder and filler in dry vitamin preparations up to 35 percent; chewing gum up to 0.025 percent; and in confectionery up to 0.012 percent. Also used in the manufacture of plastics and lacquers. Binding, dispersing, and emulsifying agent used in cosmetics, particularly nail polishes and liquid lip rouge. Also used as a diluent (*see*). Not susceptible to bacterial or fungal decomposition. No known toxicity.

ETHYL CINNAMATE • Cinnamic Acid. An almost colorless, oily liquid with a faint cinnamon odor. Used as a synthetic flavoring in raspberry, strawberry, cherry, grape, peach, plum, spice, cinnamon, and vanilla flavorings for beverages, ice cream, ices, candy, baked goods, chewing gum, and gelatin desserts. Also used as a fixative for perfumes; also to scent heavy oriental and floral perfumes in soaps, toilet waters, face powders, and perfumes. Insoluble in water. No known toxicity for the skin.

ETHYL CITRATE • A bitter, oily sequestrant used in dried egg whites. No known toxicity. *See* Sequestering Agent.

ETHYL CYCLOHEXANEPROPIONATE • A synthetic pineapple flavoring agent for beverages, ice cream, ices, candy, and baked goods. No known toxicity.

ETHYL DECANOATE • Decanoic Acid. A synthetic flavoring occurring naturally in green and white cognac oils. Used in strawberry, cherry, grape, pineapple, liquor, brandy, cognac, and rum flavorings for beverages, ice cream, ices, candy, baked goods, gelatin desserts, and liquors. No known toxicity.

ETHYL DIISOPROPYLCINNAMATE • *See* Cinnamic Acid.

ETHYL DODECANOATE • *See* Ethyl Laurate.

ETHYL FORMATE • Formic Acid. A colorless, flammable liquid with a distinct odor occurring naturally in apples and coffee extract. Used as a yeast and mold inhibitor and as a fumigant for bulk and packaged raisins and dried currants; fungicide for cashew nuts, cereals, tobacco, and dried fruits. Also a synthetic flavoring agent for blueberry, raspberry, strawberry, butter, butterscotch, apple, apricot, banana, cherry, grape, peach, plum, pineapple, tutti-frutti, brandy, rum, sherry, and whiskey flavorings for beverages, ice cream, ices, candy, baked goods, liquor, gelatin and chewing gum. Irritating to the skin and mucous membranes, and in high concentrations it is narcotic. The final report to the FDA of the Select Committee on GRAS Substances stated in 1980 that it should continue its GRAS status with no limitations other than good manufacturing practices.

ETHYL 2-FURANPROPRIONATE • A synthetic raspberry, apple, cherry, and pineapple flavoring agent for beverages, ice cream, ices, candy, and baked goods. No known toxicity.

ETHYL FURYLPROPIONATE • *See* Ethyl 2-Furanpropionate.

ETHYL GLUTAMATE • The ester of ethyl alcohol and glutamic acid. *See* Glutamate.

4-ETHYL GUAIACOL • A synthetic coffee and fruit flavoring agent for beverages, ice cream, ices, and gelatin desserts. No known toxicity.

ETHYL HEPTANOATE • A synthetic flavoring agent, colorless, with a fruity, winelike odor and taste, and a burning aftertaste. Used in blueberry, strawberry, butter, butterscotch, coconut, apple, cherry, grape, melon, peach, pineapple, plum, vanilla, cheese, nut, rum brandy, and cognac flavorings for beverages, ice cream, ices, candy, baked goods, gelatin desserts, chewing gum, and liqueurs. No known toxicity.

2-ETHYL-2-HEPTENAL • A synthetic pineapple flavoring agent for beverages and candy. No known toxicity.

ETHYL HEXADECANOATE • *See* Ethyl Palmitate.

ETHYL 2,4-HEXADIENOATE • *See* Ethyl Sorbate.

ETHYL HEXANEDIOL • *See* Sorbic Acid.

ETHYL HEXANOATE • A synthetic flavoring agent that occurs naturally in apples, pineapples, and strawberries. Used in fruit, rum, nut, and cheese flavorings for beverages, ice cream, ices, candy, baked goods, chewing gum, gelatin desserts, and jelly. No known toxicity.

ETHYL 3-HYDROXYBUTRYATE • Used as a stabilizer and antioxidant. No known toxicity.

ETHYL HYDROXYMETHYL OLEYL OXAZOLINE • A synthetic wax. No known toxicity.

ETHYL a-HYDROXYPROPIONATE • *See* Ethyl Lactate.

ETHYL ISOBUTYRATE • Isobutyric Acid. A synthetic strawberry, fruit, cherry, and butter flavoring agent for beverages, ice cream, ices, candy, baked goods, gelatin desserts, and toppings. No known toxicity.

ETHYL ISOVALERATE • Colorless, oily liquid with a fruity odor derived from ethanol and valerate. A synthetic flavoring used in alcoholic solution for pineapple flavoring for beverages, ice cream, ices, candy, baked goods, chewing gum, and gelatin desserts. Used in essential oils, and perfumery. *See* Valeric Acid.

ETHYL LACTATE • Colorless liquid with a mild odor. Derived from lactic acid with ethanol. Used as a solvent for nitrocellulose, lacquers, resins, and enamels. Used in strawberry, butter, butterscotch, coconut, grape, rum, maple, cheese, and nut flavorings for beverages, ice cream, ices, candy, baked goods, chewing gum (3,100 ppm), gelatin desserts, syrup, and brandy (1,000 ppm). No known toxicity. *See* Lactic Acid.

ETHYL LAURATE • The ester of ethyl alcohol and lauric acid used as a synthetic flavoring agent. It is a colorless oil with a light, fruity odor. Insoluble in water, very soluble in alcohol. Used in berry, coconut, fruit, grape, liquor, cognac, rum, nut, spice, nutmeg, and cheese flavorings for beverages, ice cream, ices, candy, baked goods, chewing gum, and liqueurs. It is also used as a solvent. No known toxicity.

ETHYL LEVULINATE • 4-Oxopentanoic acid ethyl ester. Colorless liquid, soluble in water. Used as a solvent for cellulose acetate and starch and flavorings. A synthetic apple flavoring for beverages, ice cream, ices, candy, and baked goods. No known toxicity.

ETHYL LINOLEATE • 9,12-Octadecadienoic acid ethyl. The ester of ethyl alcohol and linoleic acid. Prepared from sunflower seed oil. Used in the vitamin industry. No known toxicity.

ETHYL MALATE • *See* Diethyl Malate.

ETHYL MALONATE • Colorless liquid, sweet ester odor. Insoluble in water. Used in certain pigments and flavoring. No known toxicity.

4-ETHYL-2-METHOXYPHENOL • *See* 4-Ethyl Guaiacol.

ETHYL TRANS-2-METHYL-2-BUTENOATE • *See* Ethyl Tiglate.

ETHYL 3-METHYLBUTYRATE • A synthetic fruit flavoring agent for beverages, ice cream, ices, and candy.

ETHYL METHYLPHENYLGLYCIDATE • Strawberry aldehyde. Colorless to yellowish liquid having a strong odor suggestive of strawberry. A synthetic berry, loganberry, raspberry, strawberry, coconut, fruit, cherry, grape, pineapple, liquor, and wine flavoring for beverages, ice cream, ices, candy, baked goods, gelatin, pudding, and chewing gum. Used in perfumery. Caused growth retardation in rats, particularly males, and testicular atrophy. Females showed paralysis of hindquarters and deterioration of muscles. GRAS.

ETHYL MYRISTATE • The ester of ethyl alcohol and myristic acid. (*See* both.) A synthetic coconut, fruit, honey, and cognac flavoring agent for beverages, ice cream, ices, candy, baked goods, and liqueurs. No known toxicity.

ETHYL NITRITE • Sweet Spirit of Niter. Spirit of Nitrous Ether. A synthetic flavoring agent, colorless or yellowish liquid with a characteristic odor and a burning, sweetish taste. Used in strawberry, cherry, pineapple, liquor, brandy, and rum flavorings for beverages, ice cream, ices, candy, baked goods, chewing gum, syrups, and icings. It may cause hemoglobinemia, in which oxygen is diminished in the red blood cells, low blood pressure, and, when it is in high concentration, narcosis.

ETHYL NONANOATE • Nonanoic Acid. A synthetic fruit and rum flavoring agent for beverages, ice cream, ices, candy, baked goods, gelatin desserts, chewing gum, icings, and liqueurs. No known toxicity.

ETHYL 2-NONYNOATE • A synthetic berry, fruit, and melon flavoring agent for beverages, ice cream, ices, candy, and baked goods. No known toxicity.

ETHYL OCTANOATE • Octanoic Acid. A synthetic flavoring agent that occurs naturally in both cognac green and cognac white oils. Used in strawberry, butter, citrus, apple, pineapple, rum, nut, and cheese flavorings for beverages, ice cream, ices, candy, baked goods, gelatin desserts, and chewing gum. No known toxicity.

ETHYL OCTYNE CARBONATE • *See* Ethyl 2-Nonynoate.

ETHYL OLEATE • Oleic Acid. A synthetic flavoring agent, yellowish, oily, insoluble in water. Used in butter and fruit flavorings for beverages, ice cream, ices, candy, baked goods, gelatin desserts, and puddings. An ingredient in nail polish remover. It is made from carbon, hydrogen, oxygen, and oleic acid (*see*). No known toxicity.

ETHYL 3-OXOBUTANOATE • *See* Ethyl Acetoacetate.

ETHYL OXYHYDRATE • *See* Rum Ether.

ETHYL PALMITATE • Ethyl Hexadecanoate. The ester of ethyl alcohol and palmitic acid (*see* both). A synthetic flavoring agent, colorless or nearly colorless liquid, with a pleasant odor. Used in butter, honey, apricot, and cherry flavorings for beverages, ice cream, ices, candy, and baked goods. No known toxicity.

ETHYL PERSATE • Persic Oil Acid, Ethyl Ester. The ethyl ester of the fatty acids derived from either apricot kernel oil or peach kernel oil. *See* Apricot and Peach-Kernel Oil.

ETHYL PHENYLACETATE • Phenylacetic Acid. A fixative for perfumes, colorless or nearly colorless liquid, with a sweet honey-rose odor. Also a synthetic flavoring agent in honey, butter, apricot, and cherry flavorings for beverages, ice cream, ices, candy, baked goods, and syrups. No known toxicity.

ETHYL PHENYLACRYLATE • *See* Ethyl Cinnamate.

ETHYL 3-PHENYLBUTYRATE • A synthetic berry, strawberry, fruit, and cherry flavoring agent for beverages, ice cream, ices, candy, baked goods, and gelatin desserts. No known toxicity.

ETHYL 4-PHENYLBUTYRATE • A synthetic fruit flavoring agent for beverages and candy. No known toxicity.

ETHYL 3-PHENYLPROPENOATE • *See* Ethyl Cinnamate.

ETHYL 3-PHENYLPROPIONATE • A synthetic fruit flavoring agent for beverages, ice cream, ices, candy, and baked goods. No known toxicity.

ETHYL 1-PROPENE-1,2,3-TRICARBOXYLATE • *See* Ethyl Aconitate.

ETHYL PROPIONATE • Propionic Acid. A synthetic flavoring agent, colorless, transparent liquid, with a fruit odor. Occurs naturally in apples. Used in butter, fruit, and rum flavorings for beverages, ice cream, gelatin desserts, baked goods, and chewing gum (1,100 ppm). No known toxicity.

ETHYL PYRUVATE • Pyruvic Acid. A synthetic chocolate, fruit, rum, maple, and spice flavoring agent for beverages, ice cream, ices, candy, and baked goods. No known toxicity.

ETHYL SALICYLATE • Salicylic Ether. Used in the manufacture of artificial perfumes. Occurs naturally in strawberries and has a pleasant odor. Used as a synthetic flavoring agent in fruit, root beer, sassafras, and wintergreen flavorings for beverages, ice cream, ices, candy, baked goods, chewing gum, gelatins, and puddings. At one time it was giving medically to rheumatics. May interact with harmful results with medications such as anticoagulants, antidepressants, and medications for cancer such as Methotrexate. May cause allergic reaction in persons allergic to salicylates (*see*).

ETHYL SEBACATE • *See* Diethyl Sebacate.

ETHYL SORBATE • A synthetic fruit flavoring agent for beverages, ice cream, ices, candy, and baked goods. No known toxicity.

ETHYL STEARATE • The ester of ethyl alcohol and stearic acid (*see* both).

ETHYL TETRADECANOATE • *See* Ethyl Myristate.

ETHYL TIGLATE • Tiglic Acid. A synthetic raspberry, strawberry, pineapple, and rum flavoring agent for beverages, ice cream, ices, candy, and liquor. No known toxicity.

ETHYL 10-UNDECENOATE • A synthetic coconut, fruit, cognac, and nut flavoring agent for beverages, ice cream, ices, candy, baked goods, and liquor. No known toxicity.

ETHYL VALERATE • Valeric Acid. A synthetic butter, apple, apricot, peach, and nut flavoring agent for beverages, ice cream, ices, candy, baked goods, gelatin desserts, and chewing gum. No known toxicity.

ETHYL VANILLIN • An ingredient in perfumes. Colorless flakes, with an odor and flavor stronger than vanilla. Used as a synthetic flavoring agent in raspberry, strawberry, butter, butterscotch, caramel, rum, butter, chocolate, cocoa, citrus, coconut, macaroon, cola, fruit, cherry, grape, honey, liquor, muscatel, rum, maple, nut, pecan, root beer, vanilla, and cream soda for beverages, ice cream, ices, candy, baked goods, gelatin desserts, puddings, chewing gum, imitation vanilla extract (28,000 ppm), liquor, icings, and toppings. Caused mild skin irritation in humans. In rats, it produced a reduction in growth rate and heart, kidney, liver, lung, spleen, and stomach injuries. GRAS.

ETHYLACETIC ACID • See Butyric Acid.

ETHYLENEBUTYRALDEHYDE • A synthetic chocolate flavoring agent for beverages, ice cream, ices, candy, and baked goods. No known toxicity.

2-ETHYLBUTRYIC ACID • A synthetic fruit, nut, and walnut flavoring agent for beverages, ice cream, ices, candy, and baked goods. No known toxicity.

ETHYLENE DICHLORIDE (EDC) • Dutch Liquid. 1,2-Dichlorethane. Ethylene Chloride. The halogenated aliphatic hydrocarbon derived from the action of chlorine on ethylene. It is used in the manufacture of vinyl chloride (*see*); as a solvent for fats, waxes, spices, and resins; as a lead scavenger in antiknock gasolines, in paint, varnish, and finish removers; as a wetting agent; as a penetrating agent; in organic synthesis; and in the making of polyvinyl chloride (PVC) (*see*). EDC is also used as an ingredient in cosmetics and as a food additive. It is one of the highest volume chemicals produced. It can be highly toxic whether taken into the body by ingestion, inhalation, or skin absorption. It is irritating to the mucous membranes. In cancer testing, the National Cancer Institute found this compound caused stomach cancer, vascularized cancers of multiple organs, and cancers beneath the skin in male rats. Female rats exposed to EDC developed mammary cancers—in some high-dose animals as early as the twentieth week of the study. The chemical also caused breast cancers as well as uterine cancers in female mice and respiratory tract cancers in both sexes. Deaths due to liver and kidney injury following ingestion of large amounts (30 to 70 grams) have been reported. Clouding of the eyes, hemorrhages, and destruction of the adrenal cortex have been reported in humans and dogs. Annual production in the United States is now estimated at about 10 billion pounds—the sixteenth largest of all chemicals. EDC has been found in human milk and in the exhaled breath of nursing mothers who were exposed to the chemical.

ETHYLENE DIOLEAMIDE • *See* Fatty Acids.

ETHYLENE DISTEARAMIDE • See Fatty Acids.

ETHYLENE OXIDE • A fumigant used on ground spices and other processed natural seasonings. A colorless gas, liquid at 12°C. Derived from the oxidation of ethylene in air or oxygen with silver catalyst. Irritant to the eyes and skin. A suspected human carcinogen.

ETHYLENE OXIDE–METHYL FORMATE MIXTURE • A mold and yeast control agent in dried and glacéed fruits. Ethylene oxide is highly irritating to the mucous membranes and eyes. High concentrations may cause pulmonary edema. Inhalation of methyl formate vapor produces nasal and eye irritation, retching, narcosis, and death from pulmonary irritation. Exposure to 1-percent vapor for 2½ hours or 5-percent vapor for ½ hour is lethal.

ETHYLENE OXIDE POLYMER • Used as a stabilizer in fermented malt beer (300 ppm by weight). *See* Ethylene Oxide and Polymer.

ETHYLENE UREA • *See* Urea.

ETHYLENEDIAMINE • Colorless, clear, thick, and strongly alkaline. A component of a bacteria-killing component in processing sugar cane. Also used as a solvent for casein, albumin, and shellac. Has been used as a urinary acidifier. It can cause sensitization leading to asthma and allergic skin rashes.

ETHYLENEDIAMINE TETRAACETIC ACID (EDTA) • Used as a sequestrant in carbonated beverages and as a metal deactivator in vegetable oils. EDTA salts are used in crab meat (cooked and canned) to retard struvite (crystal) formation and promote color retention. It is also used in nonstandardized dressings. It may be irritating to the skin and mucous membranes and cause allergies such as asthma and skin rashes. When ingested, it may cause errors in a number of laboratory tests, including those for calcium, carbon dioxide, nitrogen, and muscular activity. It is on the FDA list of food additives to be studied for toxicity. It can cause kidney damage. The trisodium salt of EDTA was fed to rats and mice for nearly two years. According to a summary of the report, ''Although a variety of tumors occurred among test and control animals of both species, the test did not indicate that any of the tumors observed in the test animals were attributed to EDTA.'' The tests were part of the National Cancer Institute's Carcinogenesis Bioassay Program.

trans-1,2-ETHYLENEDICARBOXYLIC ACID • *See* Fumaric Acid.

ETHYLFORMIC ACID • *See* Propionic Acid.

2-ETHYLHEXYL MERCAPTOACETATE • Preservative.

ETHYLPARABEN • *See* Propylparaben.

EUBATUS, RUBUS • *See* Blackberry Bark Extract.

EUCALYPTOL • Eucalyptus Oil. A chief constituent of eucalyptus and cajeput oils. Occurs naturally in allspice, star anise, bay, calamus, and peppermint oil. Eucalyptus oil is 70 to 80 percent active eucalyptol. Eucalyptol is used in mint flavorings for beverages, ice cream, ices, candy, baked goods, and chewing gum. An antiseptic, antispasmodic, and expectorant. Used to flavor toothpaste and mouthwash and to cover up maladors in depilatories. It is not used in hypoallergenic cosmetics. Fatalities followed ingestion of doses as small as 3 to 5 milliliters (about a teaspoon), and recovery has occurred after doses as large as 20 to 30 milliliters (about 4 to 5 teaspoons). Symptoms of poisoning are epigastric burning with nausea, weakness, water retention, and delirium.

EUCALYPTUS EXTRACT • *See* Eucalyptus Oil.

EUCALYPTUS GLOBULUS LEAVES • A flavoring. *See* Eucalyptus Oil.

EUCALYPTUS OIL • Dinkum Oil. The colorless to pale-yellow volatile liquid from the fresh leaves of the eucalyptus tree. It is 70 to 80 percent eucalyptol and has a spicy, cool taste and a characteristic aromatic, somewhat camphorlike odor. Used in fruit, mint, root beer, spice, and ginger ale flavorings for beverages, ice cream, ices, candy, baked goods, chewing gum, and liquor. Used as a local antiseptic. Has been used as an expectorant, vermifuge, and local antiseptic. Fatalities have followed doses as small as 3 to 5 milliliters (about equal to a teaspoon), and about one milliliter has caused coma. Symptoms include epigastric burning with nausea. Symptoms have been reported to occur as long as two hours after ingestion.

EUCHEUMA COTTONI EXTRACT • Eucheuma Spinosum Extract. A stabilizing and thickening agent in foods. Used in dairy products to suspend particles and for gelling. No known toxicity. *See* Hydrogenation and Carrageenan.

EUGENOL • An ingredient in perfumes and dentifrices obtained from clove oil. Occurs naturally in allspice, basil, bay leaves, calamus, pimento, and laurel leaves. It has a spicy, pungent taste. Used as a fixative in perfumes. Darkens and thickens upon exposure to air. Used as a defoamer in yeast production, in the manufacture of vanilla, and in perfumery. It is a synthetic fruit, nut, and spice flavoring for beverages, ice cream, ices, candy, baked goods, chewing gum, gelatin desserts, meats (2,000 ppm), and condiments. Eugenol also acts as a local antiseptic. When ingested, may cause vomiting and gastric irritation. Because of its potential as an allergen, it is left out of hypoallergenic cosmetics. Toxicity is similar to phenol, which is highly toxic. Death in laboratory animals given eugenol is due to vascular collapse. GRAS.

EUGENYL ACETATE • Acetic Acid. A synthetic berry, fruit, mint, spice, and vanilla flavoring agent for beverages, ice cream, ices, candy, baked goods, chewing gum, and condiments. No known toxicity.

EUGENYL BENZOATE • A synthetic fruit and spice flavoring agent for beverages, ice cream, ices, candy, and baked goods. No known toxicity.

EUGENYL FORMATE • Formic Acid. A synthetic spice flavoring agent used in condiments. *See* Formic Acid for toxicity.

EUGENYL METHYL ETHER • A synthetic raspberry, strawberry, fruit, spice, clove, and ginger flavoring agent for beverages, ice cream, ices, candy, baked goods, and jellies. No known toxicity.

EVERNIA FURFURACEA • *See* Oak Moss, Absolute.

EVERNIA PRUNASTIC • *See* Oak Moss, Absolute.

EXATOLIDE • *See* Pentadecalactone.

EXTRACT • The solution that results from passing alcohol or an alcohol-water mixture through a substance. Examples of extracts would be the alcohol-water mixture of vanillin, orange, or lemon extracts found among the spices and flavorings on the supermarket shelf. Extracts are not as strong as essential oils (*see*).

EYE ALLERGY • There are many forms of allergy of the eye. The mucous membranes of the eye may be involved in allergic rhinitis. Such allergic conjunctivitis may also occur by itself without irritation of the nose. Another form, Spring "pinkeye," is probably due to allergens in the air. Dust, mold spores, foods, and eye medications may all cause conjunctivitis. There is also a less severe, chronic form of allergic conjunctivitis. Symptoms include prolonged photophobia, itching, burning, and a feeling of dryness. There may be a watery discharge and finding the source of allergy is often difficult.

F

FARNESOL • A flavoring agent that occurs naturally in ambrette seed, star anise, cassia, linden flowers, oils of muskseed, citronella, rose, and balsam. Used in berry, apricot, banana, cherry, melon, peach, citrus, fruit, raspberry, and strawberry flavorings for beverages, ice cream, ices, candy, baked goods, and gelatin desserts. Used in perfumery to emphasize the odor of sweet floral perfumes such as lilac. No known toxicity.

FAT • The most concentrated source of food energy and very necessary to health. Fat deposits provide insulation and protection for body structure as well as a storehouse for energy. Food fats are carriers of fat-soluble vitamins and include certain essential unsaturated fatty acids (*see* Fatty Acids). Saturated fats contain only single-bond carbon linkages and are the least active chemically. They are usually solid at room temperature. Most animal fats are saturated. The common saturated fats are acetic, butyric, caproic, caprylic, capric, lauric, myristic, palmitic, stearic, arachidic, and behenic. Butterfat, coconut oil, palm oil and peanut oil are high in saturated fats. Unsaturated fats contain one or more double-bond carbon linkages and are usually liquid at room temperature. Vegetable oils and fish oils most frequently contain unsaturated fats. Among the unsaturated fats are caproleic, lauroleic, myristoleic, palmitoleic, oleic, petroselinic, vaccenic, linolenic, elaesosearic, gadoleic, arachdonic, and erucic.

FATIGUE • Everyone's nose becomes "fatigued" when smelling a certain odor. No matter how much you like a fragrance, you can only smell it for a short interval. It is nature's way of protecting humans from overstimulation of the olfactory sense.

FATTY ACID ESTERS • *See* Ester. The fatty acid esters of low molecular weight alcohols are widely used in hand products because they are oily but nongreasy when applied to the skin. They are emollients and emulsifiers. No known toxicity.

FATTY ACIDS • One of any mixture of liquid and solid acids, capric, caprylic, lauric, myristic, oleic, palmitic, and stearic. In combination with glycerin they form fat and are necessary for normal growth and healthy skin. Fatty acids are used in bubble baths and lipsticks, but chiefly for making soap and detergents. In foods they are used as emulsifiers, binders, and lubricants, and defoamer components in the processing of beat sugar and yeast. Polyglycerol esters of fatty acids are prepared from edible fats, oils, corn, cottonseed, palm, fruit, peanut, safflower, and soybean oils, lard, and tallow. Used as emulsifiers and defoaming agents in beet sugar and yeast production, and as lubricant binders and components in the manufacture of other food additives. Fatty acid salt (one or more of the aluminum, ammonium, calcium, magnesium, potassium, and sodium salts of all the above fatty acids) are used as emulsifiers, binders, and anticaking agents. A free fatty acid (FFA) is the uncombined fatty acid present in a fat. Some raw oils may contain as much as 3 percent FFA. These are removed in the refining process and refined fats and oils ready for use as foods usually have extremely low FFA content. *See* Stearic Acid. No known toxicity.

FATTY ALCOHOLS • Cetyl, Steryl, Lauryl, Myristyl. Solid alcohols made from acids and widely used in hand creams and lotions. Cetyl and stearyl alcohols form an occlusive film to keep skin moisture from evaporating and they impart a velvety feel to the skin. Lauryl and myristyl are used in detergents and creams. Very low toxicity. *See* above.

FD AND C COLORS • (Food Drug and Cosmetic Colors).   A color additive is a term to describe any dye, pigment, or other substance capable of coloring a food, drug, or cosmetic on any part of the human body. In 1900, there were more than 80 dyes used to color food. There were no regulations and the same dye used to color clothes could also be used to color candy. In 1906, the first comprehensive legislation for food colors was passed. There were only seven colors, which, when tested, were shown to be composed of known ingredients which demonstrated no harmful effects. Those colors were orange, erythrosine, ponceau 3R, amaranth, indigotine, naphthol yellow, and light green. A voluntary system of certification for batches of color dyes was set up. In 1938, new legislation was passed, superseding the 1906 act. The colors were given numbers instead of chemical names and every batch had to be certified. There were 15 food colors in use at the time. In 1950, children were made ill by certain coloring used in candy and popcorn. These incidents led to the delisting of FD and C Orange No. 1 and Orange No. 2 and FD and C Red No. 32. Since that time, because of experimental evidence of possible harm, Red 1 and Yellow 1, 2, 3, and 4 have also been delisted. Violet 1 was removed in 1973. In 1976, one of the most widely used of all colors, FD and C Red No. 2, was removed because it was found to cause tumors in rats. In 1976 Red No. 4 was banned for coloring maraschino cherries (its last use) and carbon black was also banned at the same time; both contain cancer-causing agents. Earlier, in 1960, scientific investigations were required by law to determine the suitability of all colors in use for permanent listing. Citrus Red No. 2 (limited to 2 ppm) for coloring orange skins has been permanently listed; Blue No. 1, Red No. 3, Yellow No. 5, and Red No. 40 are permanently listed but without any restrictions. In 1959, the Food and Drug Administration approved the use of "lakes," in which the dyes have been mixed with alumina hydrate to make them insoluble. See FD and C Lakes.

The other food coloring additives remained on the "temporary list." The provisional list permitted colors then in use to continue on a provisional, or interim, basis pending completion of studies to determine whether the colors should be permanently approved or terminated. FD and C Red No. 3 (Erythrosine) is permanently listed for use in food and ingested drugs and provisionally listed for cosmetics and externally applied drugs. It is used in foods such as gelatins, cake mixes, ice cream, fruit cocktail cherries, bakery goods, and sausage casings.

The FDA postponed the closing date for the provisionally listed color additives—FD and C Red No. 3, D & C Red No. 33, and D & C Red No. 36—to May 2, 1988, to allow additional time to study "complex scientific and legal questions about the colors before deciding to approve or terminate their use in food, drugs, and cosmetics." The agency asked for sixty days to consider the impact of the October 1987 U.S. Court of Appeals ruling that there is no exception to the Delaney Amendment (see) which says that cancer-causing agents may not be added to food. On July 13, 1988, the Public Citizens Health Research Group announced that the FDA agreed to revoke by July 15, 1988, the permanent listing of four color additives used in drugs and cosmetics—D & C Red No. 8, D & C Red No. 9, D & C Red No. 19, and D & C Orange No. 17. In a unanimous decision in October 1987, the U.S. Court of Appeals for the District of Columbia said the FDA lacked legal authority to approve two of the colors, D & C Orange No. 17 and D & C Red No. 19, since they had been found to induce cancer in laboratory animals. The Supreme Court ruled against an appeal on April 18, 1988. Meanwhile, Public Citizen also brought a similar suit, challenging the use of D & C Red No. 8 and D & C Red No. 9, which was before the U.S. Circuit Court of Appeals in Philadelphia. Under an agreement between the FDA and Public Citizen, the case was sent back to the FDA, and the agency delisted these colors as well as D & C Orange No. 17 and D & C Red No. 19. Other countries as well as the World Health Organization maintain there are inconsistencies in safety data and in the banning of some colors which, in turn, affects international commerce. As of this writing, there is still a great deal of confusion about the colors, with the FDA maintaining that the cancer risk is minimal—as low as one in a billion—for the colors, while groups such as Nader's Public Citizen maintain that *any* cancer risk for a food additive is unacceptable.

FD AND C BLUE NO. 1 • Brilliant Blue FD and C. A coal-tar derivative, triphenylmethane, it is used as a coloring in bottled soft drinks, gelatin desserts, ice cream, ices, dry drink powders, candy, confections, bakery products, cereals, and puddings. It is also used for hair colorings, face powders, and other cosmetics. May cause allergic reactions. On the FDA permanent list of color additives. Rated 1A, that is completely acceptable for nonfood use, by the World Health Organization. However, it produces malignant tumors at the site of injection and by ingestion in the rat. See FD and C Colors.

FD AND C BLUE NO. 2 • Indigotine. Indigo Carmine. A dark-blue powder, a coal-tar derivative, triphenylmethane, almost always contains sodium chloride or sulfate. Easily faded by light. Used in bottled soft drinks, bakery products, cereals, candy, confections, and dry drink powders. It is also used in mint-flavored jelly, frozen desserts, candy, confections, and rinses and as a dye in kidney tests and for testing milk. It is a sensitizer in the allergic. On the provisional list of approved color additives. Produces malignant tumors at the site of injection when introduced under the skin of rats. The World Health Organization gives it a toxicology rating of B—available data not entirely sufficient to meet requirements acceptable for food use. Permanently listed for foods and drugs in 1987. *See* FD and C Colors.

FD AND C CITRUS RED NO. 2 • Found in 1960 to damage internal organs and to be a weak cancer-causing agent. Used to color orange skins. The World Health Organization said the color has been shown to cause cancer and that toxicological data available were inadequate to allow the determination of a safe limit; they recommended that it not be used as a food color. The FDA ruled on October 28, 1971, that the results of several rodent studies and one dog study using both oral and injected Citrus Red No. 2 showed either no adverse effect or no adverse effect levels. No abnormalities in urinary bladders were reported. The FDA noted that a paper presented in 1965 by the University of Otega Medical School reported a significant level of urinary bladder cancers in rodents fed the dye for up to 24 months. The FDA said that since slides of the tissues in photographs were not yet available for examination, and since there has been no confirmation of the studies, the listing of Citrus Red No. 2 should remain unchanged until the Otega results can be confirmed by examination. *See* FD and C Colors.

FD AND C GREEN NO. 1 • Guinea Green B. A dull, dark-green powder used as a coloring in bottled soft drinks. The certified color industry did not apply for the extension of this color because of the small demand for its use, so it was automatically deleted from the list of color additives in 1966. Rated E by the World Health Organization, meaning it was found to be harmful and not to be used in food. *See* FD and C Colors.

FD AND C GREEN NO. 2 • Light Green S.F. Yellow. Coloring used in bottled soft drinks. Because of lack of demand for this color, the certified color industry did not petition for extension and it was automatically deleted in 1966. It produces tumors at the site of injection under the skin of rats. *See* FD and C Colors.

FD AND C GREEN NO. 3 • Fast Green. Permanently listed for use in food, drugs, and cosmetics except in the area of the eye by the FDA in 1983. Used as a coloring in mint-flavored jelly, frozen desserts, gelatin desserts, candy, confections, baking products, and cereals. Has been suspected of being a sensitizer in the allergic. On the FDA permanent list of approved color additives. Produces malignant tumors at the site of injection when introduced under the skin of rats. The World Health Organization gives it a toxicology rating of 1A, meaning that it is completely acceptable. *See* FD and C Colors.

FD AND C LAKES • Aluminum or Calcium Lakes. Lakes are pigments prepared by combining FD and C colors with a form of aluminum or calcium, which makes the colors insoluble. Aluminum and calcium lakes are used in confection and candy products and for dyeing egg shells and other products that are adversely affected by water. *See* FD and C Colors for toxicity.

FD AND C RED NO. 2 • Amaranth. Formerly one of the most widely used cosmetic and food colorings. A dark, reddish-brown powder that turns bright red when mixed with fluid. A monoazo color, it was used in lipsticks, rouges, and other cosmetics as well as in cereals, maraschino cherries, and desserts. The safety of this dye was questioned by American scientists for more than twenty years. Two Russian scientists found that FD and C Red No. 2 prevented some pregnancies and caused some stillbirths in rats. The FDA ordered manufacturers using the color to submit data on all food, drug, and cosmetic products containing it. Controversial tests at the FDA's National Center for Toxicological Research in Arkansas showed that in high doses, Red No. 2 caused a statistically significant increase in a variety of cancers in female rats. The dye was banned by the FDA in January 1976.

FD AND C RED NO. 3 • Erythrosine. Bluish Pink. A coal-tar derivative, a Xanthene color, used in toothpaste and in canned fruit cocktail, ice cream, cereals, puddings, fruit salad, sherbets, gelatin desserts, cherry pie mix (up to 0.01 percent), candy, confections, and mixes as maraschino cherries. Has been determined a carcinogen. It was reported in 1981 by NIH researchers that Red. No. 3 may interfere with transmission of nerve impulses in the brain. It contains iodine and has been shown to affect the thyroid glands of laboratory animals, but not of humans. Children who eat large amounts of artificially colored cherries, gelatin desserts, and other FD and C Red No. 3–colored products could be at risk. *See* FD and C Colors. The FDA was supposed to premanently list this color in 1988 but has postponed the ruling "to allow the agency additional time to study complex scientific and legal questions about the color before deciding to approve or terminate its use in food."

FD AND C RED NO. 3 ALUMINUM LAKE • The aluminum salt of certified FD and C Red No. 3 (*see*). *See* FD and C Colors and FD and C Lakes.

FD AND C RED NO. 4 • A monoazo color and coal tar. Used in mouthwashes, bath salts, and hair rinses. It was banned in food by the FDA in 1964 when it was shown to damage the adrenal glands and bladders of dogs. The agency relented and gave it provisional license for use in maraschino cherries. It was banned in all food in 1976 because it was shown to cause urinary bladder polyps and atrophy of the adrenal glands in animals. It was also banned in orally taken drugs but is still permitted in cosmetics for external use only. *See* FD and C Colors.

FD AND C RED NO. 20 • Permanently listed by the FDA in 1983 for general use in drugs and cosmetics (except in areas around the eye).

FD AND C RED NO. 22 • Permanently listed by the FDA in 1983 for general use in drugs and cosmetics (except in areas around the eyes).

FD AND C RED NO. 40 • Allura Red AC. Newest color. Used widely in the cosmetics industry. Approved in 1971, Allied Chemical has an exclusive patent on it. It is substituted for FD and C Red No. 4 in many cosmetics, food, and drug products. Permanently listed because unlike the producers of "temporary" colors, this producer supplied reproductive data. However, many American scientists feel that the safety of Red No. 40 is far from established, particularly because all of the tests were conducted by the manufacturer. Therefore, the dye should not have received a permanent safety rating. The National Cancer Institute reported that *p*-credine, a chemical used in preparation of Red No. 40, was carcinogenic in animals. The FDA permanently listed Red No. 40 for use in foods and ingested drugs but only temporarily listed it for cosmetics and externally applied drugs. *See* Azo Dyes and FD and C Colors.

FD AND C VIOLET NO. 1 • Used as a coloring matter in gelatin desserts, ice cream, sherbets, carbonated beverages, dry drink powders, candy, confections, bakery products, cereals, puddings, and as the dye used for the Department of Agriculture's meat stamp. A Canadian study in 1962 showed the dye caused cancer in 50 percent of the rats fed the dye in food. The FDA did not consider this valid evidence since the exact nature of the dye used could not be determined and all records and specimens were lost and not available for study. Furthermore, previous and subsequent studies have not confirmed evidence of Violet 1 causing cancer in rats. However, a two-year study with dogs did show noncancerous lesions on the dog's ears after being fed Violet 1. The FDA again felt the study was not adequate but that the ear lesions did not appear to be dye-related and that perhaps two years may be too short a period to determine their eventual outcome. The FDA ruled on October 28, 1971, that Violet 1 should remain provisionally listed pending the outcome of a new dog study to be started as soon as possible and to last seven years. The FDA finally banned the use of Violet 1 in 1973. In 1976, however, the U.S. Department of Agriculture found that Violet 1 was still being used as a "denaturant" on carcasses, meats, and food products. The USDA ruled that any such use of mixing Violet 1 with any substance intended for food use will cause the final product to be "adulterated." *See* FD and C Colors.

FD AND C YELLOW NO. 5 • Tartrazine. A coal-tar derivative, it is a pyrazole color used in prepared breakfast cereals, imitation strawberry jelly, bottled soft drinks, gelatin desserts, ice cream, sherbets, dry drink powders, candy, confections, bakery products, spaghetti, and puddings. Also used as a coloring in hair rinses, hair-waving fluids, and in bath salts. Causes allergic reactions in persons sensitive to aspirin. The certified color industry petitioned for permanent listing of this color in February 1966, with no limitation other than good manufacturing practice. However, in February 1966, the FDA proposed the listing of this color with a maximum rate of use of 300 parts per million in food. The color industry had objected to the limitations. Yellow No. 5 was thereafter permanently listed as a color additive without restrictions. Rated 1A by the World Health Organization—acceptable in food. It is estimated that half the aspirin-sensitive people, plus 47,000 to 94,000 others in the nation are sensitive to this dye. It is used in about 60 percent of both over-the-counter and prescription drugs. Efforts were made to ban this color in over-the-counter pain relievers, antihistamines, oral decongestants, and prescription anti-inflammatory drugs. Aspirin-sensitive patients have been reported to develop life-threatening asthmatic symptoms when ingesting Yellow No. 5. Since 1981, it is supposed to be listed on the label if it is used. *See* FD and C Colors.

FD AND C YELLOW NO. 5 ALUMINUM LAKE • *See* FD and C Yellow No. 5, FD and C Colors, and FD and C Lakes.

FD AND C YELLOW NO. 6 • Monoazo. Sunset Yellow FCF. A coal-tar monoazo color, used in carbonated beverages, bakery products, candy, confectionery products, gelatin desserts, and dry drink powders. It is also used in hair rinses as well as other cosmetics. It is not used in products that contain fats and oils. Since there is evidence that this causes allergic reactions, alcoholic beverages that contain it must list it on the label according to the Bureau of Alcohol. Rated 1A by the World Health Organization—acceptable in foods. Industry tests showed it causes tumors of the adrenal gland and kidney in animals. Permanently listed December 22, 1986. In 1989, a ruling went into effect that it had to be listed on the labels because of its ability to induce allergic reactions. *See* FD and C Colors.

FD AND C YELLOW NO. 6 ALUMINUM LAKE • *See* FD and C Yellow No. 6, FD and C Colors, and FD and C Lakes.

FECULOSE STARCH ACETATE • *See* Modified Starch.

FENCHOL • *See* Fenchyl Alcohol.

d-**FENCHONE** • A synthetic flavoring occurring naturally in common fennel (*see*). It is an oily liquid with a camphor smell and practically insoluble in water. Used in berry, liquor, and spice flavorings for beverages, ice cream, ices, candy, baked goods, and liquors. Used medically as a counterirritant.

FENCHYL ALCOHOL • A synthetic berry, lime, and spice flavoring agent for beverages, ice cream, ices, candy, and baked goods. No known toxicity.

FENNEL • Common. Sweet. One of the earliest known herbs from the tall beautiful shrub. The fennel flowers appear in June and are bright yellow, with a characteristic fennel taste. Common fennel is used as a sausage and spice flavoring for beverages, baked goods, meats, and condiments. Sweet fennel has the same function but includes ice cream, ices, and candy. Sweet fennel oil is used in raspberry, fruit, licorice, anise, rye, sausage, root beer, sarsaparilla, spice, wintergreen, and birch beer flavorings for beverages, ice cream, ices, candy, baked goods, gelatin desserts, condiments, meats, and liquors. Compresses of fennel tea are used by organic cosmeticians to soothe inflamed eyelids and watery eyes. May cause allergic reactions. GRAS.

FENUGREEK SEED • Greek Hay. An annual herb grown in southern Europe, North Africa, and India. The seeds are used in making curry. Fenugreek is a butter, butterscotch, maple, black walnut, and spice flavoring for beverages, ice cream, ices, candy, baked goods, syrups, meats, and condiments. The extract (*see*) is a butter, butterscotch, caramel, chocolate, coffee, fruit, maple, meat, black walnut, walnut, root beer, spice, and vanilla flavoring agent for beverages, ice cream, ices, pickles, liquors, and icings. The oleoresin (*see*) is a fruit, maple, and nut flavoring agent for beverages, ice cream, ices, candy, baked goods, puddings, and syrups. It is also used in hair tonic supposedly to prevent baldness; also added to powders, poultices, and ointments. No known toxicity. GRAS.

FERRIC CHOLINE CITRATE • *See* Iron Salts.

FERRIC ORTHOPHOSPHATE • *See* Iron Salts.

FERRIC PHOSPHATE • A nutrient supplement. The final report to the FDA of the Select Committee on GRAS Substances stated in 1980 that there is no evidence in the available information that it is a hazard to the public when used as it is now and it should continue its GRAS status with limitations on the amounts that can be added to food. *See* Iron Salts.

FERRIC PYROPHOSPHATE • *See* Iron Salts. GRAS.

FERRIC SODIUM PYROPHOSPHATE. • A nutrient supplement. The final report to the FDA of the Select Committee on GRAS Substances stated in 1980 that there is no evidence in the available information that it is a hazard to the public when used as it is now, and it should continue its GRAS status with limitations on the amounts that can be added to food. *See* Iron Salts.

FERROUS FUMARATE • Dietary Supplement. *See* Iron Salts.

FERROUS GLUCONATE • Gluconic Acid, Iron Salt. Iron Gluconate. Ferronicum. Used as a food coloring, it is a yellowish-gray. It is also used as a flavoring agent and to treat iron-deficiency anemia. It may cause gastrointestinal disturbances. When painted on mouse skin in 2,600-milligram doses per kilogram of body weight, it caused tumors. It is permanently listed as a coloring for ripe olives only. GRAS.

FERROUS LACTATE • Lactic Acid. Iron Salt. Iron Lactate. Greenish-white crystals that have a slightly peculiar odor. It is derived from the interaction of calcium lactate with ferrous sulfate, or the direct action of lactic acid on iron filings. It is used as a food additive and dietary supplement. Causes tumors when injected under the skin of mice. GRAS.

FERROUS SULFATE • Green or Iron Vitriol. Pale bluish-green, odorless crystals, efflorescent in dry air. An astringent and deodorant. Used in hair dyes. A source of iron used medicinally. *See* Iron Salts. GRAS.

FERULA ASSAFOETIDA • *See* Asafoetida Extract.

FIBER • Commonly termed "bulk"—the indigestible carbohydrates, including cellulose, hemicellulose, and gums. Fiber is added to food to reduce calorie content, as a thickening agent, and as a stabilizer. If an apple a day keeps the doctor away, it may be because of the fiber content. Scientists have suspected that the high intestinal cancer rate in the United States may be linked to the 80-percent decrease of consumption of fiber in the average diet during the past century. Essentially, there are three classes of fiber found in the fruit, leaves, stems, seeds, flowers, and roots of different plants. The first class is the insoluble cellulose found in the plant-cell wall. Some of the other polysaccharides constitute a second class and are also found in the cell wall (hemicellulose and pectic polyerms), in the endosperm of seeds (mucilages), or in the plant's surface (gums). The third class, the lignins, are noncarbohydrates that infiltrate and contribute to the death of the plant cell, which then becomes part of the woody reinforcing plant structure.

Enzymes from a number of the more than four hundred kinds of bacteria in the human colon are capable of digesting many components of plant fiber. Doctors have found that the water-holding capacity of some fibers may be helpful in treating colon disease. The fiber's bile absorption properties might be used in modifying cholesterol metabolism. Plant fibers are also capable of binding trace metals and bile acids. These properties modify the action of the gut contents. Fibers pass through the gut somewhat like a sponge, probably altering metabolism in the intestine. The fibers appear to protect intestinal cells by removing foreign substances, such as carcinogens produced by charbroiling. Increased fiber consumption has been recommended for relief of some symptoms of diverticular disease, irritable bowel syndrome, and constipation.

FICIN • An enzyme occurring in the latex of tropical trees. A buff-colored powder with an acrid odor. Absorbs water. Concentrated and used as a meat tenderizer. Ten to twenty times more powerful than papain tenderizers. Used to clot milk, as a protein digestant in the brewing industry, and as a chill-proofing agent in beer. Also used in cheese as a substitute for rennet in the coagulation of milk, and for removing casings from sausages. Can cause irritation to the skin, eyes, and mucous membranes and in large doses can cause purging.

FIELD POPPY EXTRACT • Extract of the petals of *Papaver rhoeas* used in coloring and as an odorant.

FILLED MILK • A combination of skim milk and vegetable oil to replace milk fat. Usually has the same amount of protein and calories as whole milk. Used as a milk substitute. It often contains the high-cholesterol fatty acids (*see*) of coconut oil. Nontoxic.

FINOCHIO • *See* Fennel.

FIR NEEDLE OIL • Fir Oil. Pine. Balsam. An essential oil obtained by the steam distillation of needles and twigs of several varieties of pine trees native to both Canada and Siberia. Used as a scent in perfumes and as a flavoring agent.

FISH GLYCERIDES • *See* Fish Oil and Glycerin.

FISH OIL • A fatty oil from fish or marine mammals used in soap manufacturing. Rich in Omega-3 fatty acids that were reported in the 1980s to reduce fats in the blood and thus are believed to reduce the risk of coronary artery disease. The final report to the FDA of the Select Committee on GRAS Substances stated in 1980 that it should continue its GRAS status for food packaging with no limitations other than good manufacturing practices.

FISH PROTEIN CONCENTRATE • Dietary Supplement. No known toxicity.

FIXATIVE • A chemical that reduces the tendency of an odor or flavor to vaporize, by making the odor or flavor last longer. An example is musk (*see*), which is used in perfume and undecyl aldehyde as a fixative for citrus flavors.

FLAVOR POTENTIATORS • One of the newest and fastest-growing categories of additives, potentiators enhance the total seasoning effect, generally without contributing any taste or odor of their own. They are effective in minute doses—in parts per million or even less. A potentiator produces no identifiable effect itself but exaggerates one's response. They alter the response of the sensory nerve endings on the tongue and in the nose. The first true potentiators in the United States were the 5'-nucleotides, which are derived from a natural seasoning long in use in Japan: small flakes of dry bonito (a tunalike fish) that are often added to modify and improve the flavor of soups, and from bonito a 5'-nucleotide, disodium 5'-inosinate (*see*), has been isolated and identified as a flavor potentiator. Another 5'-nucleotide is disodium guanylate (*see*), one of the newer additives on the market, which gives one a sensation of fullness and increased thickness of the food when eating. The product is advertised as being able to give diners a sense of "full-bodied flavor" when ingesting a food containing it.

FLAVORING COMPOUND • A flavoring composed of two or more substances. The substances may be natural or synthetic and they are usually closely guarded secrets. Normally, a flavoring compound is complete, that is, it is added to a food without any additional flavorings being necessary. A strawberry flavoring compound, for example, may contain 28 separate ingredients before it is complete.

FLAVORINGS • There are more than two thousand flavorings added to foods, of which approximately five-hundred are natural and the rest synthetic. This is the largest category of additive. Lemon and orange are examples of natural flavorings, while benzaldehyde and methyl salicylates (*see* both) are examples from the laboratory.

FLAXSEED • The seed of the flax plant may be "hidden" in cereals and milk of cows fed flaxseed. It is also in flaxseed tea and the laxative Flaxolyn. It is a frequent allergen when ingested, inhaled, or in direct contact. Flaxseeds are the source of linseed oil. Among other hidden sources are: dog food, wave-setting preparations, shampoos, hair tonics, depilatories, patent leather, insulating materials, rugs and some cloths, Roman meal, cough remedies, and muffins.

FLEABANE OIL • Oil of Canada Fleabane. Erigeron Oil. The pale-yellow, volatile oil from a fresh flowering herb. It takes its name from its supposed ability to drive away fleas. Used in fruit and spice flavorings for beverages, ice cream, ices, candy, baked goods, and sauce. No known toxicity.

FLUORIDE • An acid salt used in toothpaste to prevent tooth decay. *See* Fluorine Sources.

FLUORINE SOURCES • Calcium Fluoride; Hydrofluorosillic Acid; Potassium Fluoride; Sodium Fluoride; and Sodium Silicofluoride. All have been used in the fluoridation of water. Fluorides cross the placental barrier and the effects on the fetus are unknown. New clinical evidence shows that kidney disturbance sometimes is due to the amount of fluoride it contributes to the blood. No longer permitted as a dietary supplement but may be in the water used in processing.

FOAM INHIBITOR • An antifoaming agent such as dimethyl polysiloxane (*see*) used in chewing gum bases, soft drinks, and fruit juices to keep them from foaming. *See* Defoamer.

FOAMING AGENT • Used to help whipped topping peak when it is being whipped with cold milk. A commonly added foaming agent is sodium caseinate (*see*).

FOAM STABILIZERS • Used in soft drinks and brewing. *See* Vegetable Gums.

FOLIC ACID • A yellowish-orange compound and member of the Vitamin B Complex, used as a nutrient. Used in cosmetic emollients. Occurs naturally in liver, kidney, mushrooms, and green leaves. Aids in cell formation, especially red blood cells. No known toxicity.

FOOD RED 6 • Formerly Ext. FD and C Red No. 15, FD and C Red No. 1, and Ponceau 3 R. One of the first approved certified coal-tar colors. Food Red 6 was delisted as a food additive as possibly harmful. Dark red powder, it changes to cherry red in solution. *See* FD and C Colors.

FORMALDEHYDE • Paraformaldehyde. Preservative in defoaming agents and in animal feeds. A colorless gas obtained by the oxidation of methyl alcohol and generally used in watery solution. Formaldehyde generally is known as a disinfectant, germicide, fungicide, defoamer, and preservative, and is used in embalming fluid. One ounce taken by mouth causes death within two hours. Skin reaction after exposure. It is a highly reactive chemical that is damaging to the hereditary substances in the cells of several species. It causes lung cancer in rats and has a number of other harmful biological consequences. Researchers from the Division of Cancer Cause and Prevention of the National Cancer Institute recommended in April 1983 that since formaldehyde is involved in DNA damage and inhibits its repair, and potentiates the toxicity of X rays in human lung cells, and since it may act in concert with other chemical agents to produce mutagenic and carcinogenic effects, it should be "further investigated." The question is whether we ingest any formaldehyde when we ingest the animals that ate the feed and the products that had undergone "defoaming" by formaldehyde.

FORMALIN • Fungicide in water of salmon, trout, largemouth bass, catfish, and blue gills. *See* Formaldehyde.

FORMIC ACID • Colorless, pungent, highly corrosive, it occurs naturally in apples and other fruits. It is used as a synthetic fruit flavoring. Also used as a decalcifier and for dehairing hides. Chronic absorption is known to cause albuminuria—protein in the urine. It caused cancer when administered orally in rats, mice, and hamsters in doses from 31 to 49 milligrams per kilogram of body weight

FORMIC ETHER • See Ethyl Formate.

FORTIFIED • Fortification of food refers to the addition of nutrients such as Vitamin C to breakfast drinks and Vitamin D to milk. It actually increases the nutritional values of the original food.

FRANKINCENSE • Aromatic gum resin obtained from African and Asian trees and used chiefly as incense. For food use, *see* Olibanum Extract.

FRUCTOSE • A sugar occurring naturally in large numbers of fruits and honey. It is the sweetest of the foodstuffs. It is also used as a medicine, preservative, common sugar, and to prevent sandiness in ice cream. Researchers at the General Clinical Research Center at the University of Colorado School of Medicine in Denver report that fructose is absorbed in the gastrointestinal tract more slowly than sugars like sucrose, which contain glucose. As a result, even though the body converts some fructose to glucose, 80 to 90 percent of the sugar is absorbed intact, and there is only a slight increase in blood glucose levels immediately after consumption. Fructose can be up to two times sweeter than sucrose. Recent advances in enzyme technology have made it possible to produce fructose on a commercial scale. It caused tumors in mice when injected under the skin in 5,000-milligram doses per kilogram of body weight.

FRUIT JUICE • Used to color foods consistent with good manufacturing practices. Permanently listed. No known toxicity.

FUMARIC ACID • White, odorless, derived from many plants and essential to vegetable and animal tissue respiration; prepared industrially. An acidulant used as a leavening agent and a dry acid for dessert powders and confections (up to 3 percent). Also an apple, peach, and vanilla flavoring agent for beverages, baked goods (1,300 ppm), and gelatin desserts (3,600 ppm). Used in baked goods as an antioxidant and as a substitute for tartaric acid (*see*). No known toxicity. GRAS.

2-FURALDEHYDE • *See* Furfural.

2-FURANACROLEIN • *See* Furyl Acrolein.

FURCELLERAN • Sodium, Calcium, Potassium, and Ammonium. Extracted from red seaweed grown in Northern European waters. The processed gum is a white, odorless powder soluble in water as an emulsifier, stabilizer, and thickener in foods. It is a natural colloid and gelling agent. Also used in puddings, ice cream, and jams, in products for diabetics, as a carrier for food preservatives, and in bactericides. It is also used in over-the-counter drugs for weight reducing and toothpastes. On the FDA list of additives to be studied for mutagenic, teratogenic, subacute, and reproductive effects since 1980. As of this writing, nothing new has been reported by the FDA.

FURFURAL • Artificial Ant Oil. A colorless liquid with a peculiar odor. Occurs naturally in angelica root, apples, coffee, peaches, skim milk. Used as a solvent, insecticide, fungicide, to decolor resins, and as a synthetic flavoring in butterscotch, butter, caramel, coffee, fruit, brandy, rum, rye, molasses, nut, and cassia flavorings for beverages, ice cream, ices, candy, gelatin, desserts, syrups (the biggest user; up to 30 ppm), and spirits. Darkens when exposed to air. It irritates mucous membranes and acts on the central nervous system. Causes tearing and inflammation of the eyes and throat. Ingestion or absorption of 0.06 grams produces persistent headache. Used continually, it leads to nervous disturbances and eye disorders (including photosensitivity).

FURFURYL ACETATE • Acetic Acid. A synthetic raspberry, fruit, and ginger ale flavorings for beverages, ice cream, ices, candy, baked goods, and chewing gum. No known toxicity.

FURFURYL ALCOHOL • A synthetic flavoring obtained mainly from corncobs and roasted coffee beans. Has a faint burning odor and a bitter taste. Used in butter, butterscotch, caramel, coffee, fruit, and brandy flavorings for beverages, ice cream, ices, candy, baked goods, gelatin desserts, and icings. It is poisonous.

FURFURYL MERCAPTAN • A synthetic fruit, liquor, rum, nut, chocolate, and spice flavoring agent that occurs naturally in coffee and is used for beverages, ice cream, ices, candy, and baked goods. No known toxicity.

2-FURFURYLIDENE BUTYRALDEHYDE • A synthetic fruit, liquor, rum, nut, and spice flavoring agent for beverages, ice cream, ices, candy, and baked goods. No known toxicity.

FURYL ACETONE • *See* (2-Furyl)-2-Propanone.

FURYL ACROLEIN • A synthetic coffee, fruit, cassia, and cinnamon flavoring agent for beverages, ice cream, ices, candy, baked goods, gelatin desserts, and puddings. No known toxicity.

4-(2-FURYL)-3-BUTEN-2-ONE • A synthetic nut, almond, and spice flavoring agent for beverages, ice cream, ices, candy, baked goods, and gelatin desserts. No known toxicity.

(2-FURYL)-2-PROPANONE • A synthetic fruit flavoring agent for ice cream, ices, candy, and baked goods. No known toxicity.

FUSEL OIL (REFINED) • A synthetic flavoring that occurs naturally in cognac oil. It is also a product of carbohydrate fermentation to produce ethyl alcohol (*see*) and varies widely in composition. Used in grape, brandy, cordial, rum, rye, Scotch, whiskey, and wine flavorings for beverages, ice cream, ices, candy, baked goods, chewing gum, gelatin desserts, puddings, and liquor. Commercial amyl alcohol (*see*), its major ingredient, is more toxic than ethyl alcohol and as little as 30 milligrams has caused death. Smaller amounts have caused methemoglobinuria (blood cells in the urine) and kidney damage.

G

GALANGAL ROOT • East Indian Root. Chinese Ginger. The pungent aromatic oil of the galangal root is a bitters, vermouth, spice, and ginger ale flavoring agent for beverages. The extract is a bitters, fruit, liquor, spice, and ginger ale flavoring agent for beverages, ice cream, ices, candy, baked goods, bitters, and liquors. Related to true ginger, it was formerly used in cooking and in medicine to treat colic. No known toxicity. GRAS.

GALBANUM OIL • A yellowish to green or brown aromatic bitter gum resin from an Asiatic plant used as incense. The oil is a fruit, nut, and spice flavoring for beverages, ice cream, ices, candy, baked goods, and condiments. Has been used medicinally to break up intestinal gas and as an expectorant. No known toxicity.

GALLIC ACID • *See* Propyl Gallate.

GALLOTANNIC ACID • *See* Tannic Acid.

GAMBIR CATECHU • *See* Catechu Extract.

GAMBIR GUM • *See* Catechu Extract.

GARDEN ROSEMARY OIL • *See* Rosemary Extract.

GARDENOL • *See* a-Methylbenzyl Acetate.

GARLIC EXTRACT • An extract from *Allium sativum,* a yellowish liquid with a strong odor used in fruit and garlic flavorings. Is being tested as an antibiotic and has been used to counteract intestinal worms.

GARLIC OIL • Yellow liquid with a strong odor, obtained from the crushed bulbs or cloves of the plant. Used in fruit and garlic flavorings for beverages, ice cream, ices, candy, baked goods, chewing gum, and condiments. Has been used medicinally to combat intestinal worms. Reevaluated and found to be GRAS by the FDA's committee of experts in 1976.

GAS • A combustion product from the controlled combustion in air of butane, propane, or natural gas. It is used for removing or displacing oxygen in the processing, storage, or packaging of citrus products, vegetable fats, vegetable oils, coffee, and wine. No known toxicity when using in packaging.

GEL • A semisolid, apparently homogenous substance that may be elastic and jellylike (gelatin) or more or less rigid (silica gel) and that is formed in various ways such as by coagulation or evaporation.

GELATIN • Gelatin is a protein obtained by boiling skin, tendons, ligaments, or bones with water. It is colorless or slightly yellow, tasteless, and absorbs 5 to 10 times its weight of cold water. Used as a food thickener and stabilizer and a base for fruit gelatins and puddings. Employed medicinally to treat malnutrition and brittle fingernails. Used in protein shampoos because it sticks to the hair and gives it "more body," in peelable face masks, and as a fingernail strengthener. No known toxicity.

GENET, ABSOLUTE • A natural flavoring from flowers used in fruit and honey flavorings for beverages, ice cream, ices, candy, baked goods, and chewing gum. The extract is a raspberry and fruit flavoring for beverages. No known toxicity.

GENTIAN ROOT EXTRACT • The yellow or pale bitter root of Central and Southern European plants used in angostura, chocolate, cola, fruit, vermouth, maple, root beer, and vanilla flavorings for beverages, ice cream, ices, candy, and liquors. It has been used as a bitter tonic. No known toxicity.

GERANIAL • *See* Citral.

GERANIALDEHYDE • *See* Citral.

GERANIOL • Used in perfumery to compound artificial attar of roses and artificial orange blossom oil. Also used in depilatories to mask odors. Oily sweet, with a rose odor, it occurs naturally in apples, bay leaves, cherries, grapefruit, ginger, lavender, and a number of other essential oils. A synthetic flavoring agent that occurs naturally in apples, bay leaves, cherries, coriander, grapefruit, oranges, tea, ginger, mace oil, and the oils of lavender, lavandin, lemon, lime, mandarin, and petitgrain. A berry, lemon, rose, apple, cherry, peach, honey, root beer, cassia, cinnamon, ginger ale, and nutmeg flavoring for beverages, ice cream, ices, candy, baked goods, chewing gum, and toppings. Geraniol is omitted from hypoallergenic cosmetics. Can cause allergic reactions. Whereas no specific toxicity information is available, deaths have been reported from ingestion of unknown amounts of citronella oil (*see*) which is 93 percent geraniol; the gastric mucosa was found to be severely damaged. GRAS.

GERANIUM • An essential oil used as flavoring. *See* Geranium Rose Oil. GRAS.

GERANIUM ROSE OIL • A synthetic flavoring agent that occurs naturally in geranium herbs and rose petals added. Used in strawberry, lemon, cola, geranium, rose, violet, cherry, honey, rum, brandy, cognac, nut, vanilla, spice, and ginger ale flavorings for beverages, ice cream, ices, candy, baked goods, gelatin desserts, chewing gum, and jelly. A geranium root derivative has been used as an astringent and to treat chronic diarrhea in dogs. A teaspoon may cause illness in an adult and less than an ounce may kill. May affect those allergic to geraniums.

GERANYL ACETATE • Geraniol Acetate. Clear, colorless liquid with the odor of lavender, it is a constituent of several essential oils. Used in berry, lemon, orange, floral, apple, grape, peach, pear, honey, spice, and ginger ale flavorings for beverages, ice cream, ices, candy, baked goods, gelatin desserts, chewing gum, and syrup. No known toxicity but it is obtained from geraniol (*see*). GRAS.

GERANYL ACETOACETATE • A synthetic fruit flavoring agent for beverages, ice cream, ices, candy, and baked goods. *See* Geranyl Acetate for toxicity.

GERANYL BENZOATE • Benzoic Acid. A synthetic flavoring agent, slight yellowish liquid, with a floral odor. Used in floral and fruit flavorings for beverages, ice cream, ices, candy, baked goods, and candy. *See* Geraniol for toxicity.

GERANYL BUTYRATE • Geraniol Butyrate. Colorless liquid which occurs in several essential oils, it is used in perfumes. It is used in berry, citrus, fruit, apple, cherry, pear, and pineapple flavorings for beverages, ice cream, ices, candy, baked goods, chewing gum, and gelatin desserts. Used as a synthetic attar of rose. *See* Geraniol.

GERANYL FORMATE • Geraniol Formate. Colorless liquid with a roselike odor, insoluble in alcohol, it occurs in several essential oils. Used in perfumes and soaps as a synthetic neroli bigarade oil (*see*). A fresh, leafy, rose odor, it is used in berry, citrus, apple, apricot, and peach flavorings for beverages, ice cream, ices, candy, baked goods, gelatins, chewing gum, and puddings. *See* Geraniol.

GERANYL HEXANOATE • Hexanoic Acid. A synthetic citrus and pineapple flavoring agent for beverages, ice cream, ices, candy, and baked goods. *See* Geraniol for toxicity.

GERANYL ISOBUTYRIC ACID • Isobutryic Acid. A synthetic floral, rose, apple, pear, and pineapple flavoring agent for beverages, ice cream, ices, candy, baked goods, chewing gum, gelatin desserts, and puddings. *See* Gerianol for toxicity.

GERANYL ISOVALERATE • A synthetic berry, lime, apple, peach, and pineapple flavoring agent for beverages, ice cream, ices, candy, and baked goods. *See* Geraniol for toxicity.

GERANYL PHENYLACETATE • Phenylacetic Acid. A synthetic flavoring, yellow liquid with a honey-rose odor. Used in fruit flavorings for beverages, ice cream, ices, candy, baked goods, and chewing gum. *See* Geraniol for toxicity.

GERANYL PROPIONATE • Geraniol Propionate. Colorless liquid with a roselike odor, it is soluble in most oils and is used in perfumery. A synthetic flavoring used in berry, geranium, apple, pear, pineapple, and honey flavorings for beverages, ice cream, ices, candy, baked goods, chewing gum, and gelatin desserts. *See* Geraniol for toxicity.

GERMANDER • Flavoring in alcoholic beverages only. An American plant. *See* Sage.

GHATTI GUM • Indian Gum. The gummy exudate from the stems of a plant abundant in India and Ceylon. Used as an emulsifier and in butter, butterscotch, and fruit flavorings for beverages. Has caused an occasional allergy but when ingested in large amounts, it has not caused obvious distress. The FDA's reevaluation in 1976 found the gum was GRAS if used at the rate of 0.2 percent for alcoholic beverages and 0.1 percent for all other food categories. In pharmaceutical preparations one part ghatti usually replaces two parts acacia (*see*). The final report to the FDA of the Select Committee on GRAS Substances stated in 1980 that there is no evidence in the available information that it is a hazard to the public when used as it is now and it should continue its GRAS status with limitations on the amount that can be added to food.

GIBBERELLIC ACID AND ITS SALTS • Used for malt beverages and distilled spirits. A plant growth-promoting hormone synthesized in 1978. No known toxicity.

GIGARTINA EXTRACTS • A stabilizer from red algae of the sea. *See* Algae, Red.

GINGER • Derived from the rootlike stem of plants cultivated in all tropical countries, it is used in apple, plum, sausage, eggnog, pumpkin, ginger, ginger ale, and ginger beer flavorings for beverages, ice cream, ices, baked goods (2,500 ppm), and meats. The extract is used for cola, sausage, root beer, ginger, ginger ale, and ginger beer flavorings for beverages, ice cream, ices, candy, baked goods, chewing gum, meats, and condiments. The oleoresin, which is a ginger flavoring, is used in root beer and ginger ale for the same products. Ginger has been used to break up intestinal gas and colic. No known toxicity. GRAS.

GINGER OIL • Obtained from the dried rhizomes of *Zingiber officinale,* it is used in flavorings for beverages, ice cream, ices, candy, baked goods, chewing gum, meats, and condiments. It is also used in perfumes. Employed medicinally to break up intestinal gas. No known toxicity.

GINSENG • Root of the ginseng plant grown in China, Korea, and the United States. It produces a resin, a sugar starch, glue, and volatile oil. Ginseng is used as a flavoring and has a sweetish, licoricelike taste and is widely used in Oriental medicines as an aromatic bitter. It is used in American cosmetics as a demulcent (*see*). No known toxicity.

GLUCAMINE • An organic compound that is prepared from glucose (*see*).

GLUCOAMYLASE • An enzyme used to break down sugars in food processing. No known toxicity.

GLUCOMANNAN • A powder extracted from the roots of the konjac plant. The promoters claim that the powder, taken in a capsule before meals, absorbs liquid and swells in the stomach to form a gel and reduces hunger. The FDA was asked to approve it as GRAS but refused to do so unless scientific data were submitted.

GLUCONATE • Calcium and Sodium. A sequestering agent (*see*) derived from glucose, a sugar. Odorless, tasteless. Used as a buffer for confections and a firming agent for tomatoes and apple slices. Sodium gluconate is also used as a nutrient and dietary supplement. The final report to the FDA of the Select Committee on GRAS Substances stated in 1980 that it should continue its GRAS status with no limitations other than good manufacturing practices.

GLUCONIC ACID • A light, amber liquid with the faint odor of vinegar, produced from corn. It is water soluble and used as a dietary supplement and as a sequestering agent (*see*). The magnesium salt of gluconic acid has been used as an antispasmodic. No known toxicity. GRAS.

GLUCONO-DELTA-LACTONE • An acid with a sweet taste; fine, white, odorless. it is used as a leavening agent in jelly powders and soft drink powders where dry food acid is desired. Used in the dairy industry to prevent milk stone, and by breweries to prevent beer stone, and is also a component of many cleaning compounds. Cleared by the U.S. Department of Agriculture's Meat Inspection Division for use at 8 ounces for each 100 pounds of cured, pulverized meat or meat food products to speed up the color-fixing process and to reduce the time required for smoking. No specific data on toxicity.

GLUCOSE • Occurs naturally in blood, grape, and corn sugars. A source of energy for plants and animals. Sweeter than sucrose (*see*), glucose syrup is used to flavor sausage, hamburger, meat loaf, luncheon meat, and chopped or pressed ham. It is also used as an extender in maple syrup. It is used medicinally for nutritional purposes and in the treatment of diabetic coma. Used to soothe the skin, and as a filler in cosmetics. No known toxicity in cosmetics but confectioners frequently suffer erosions and fissures around their nails, and the nails loosen and sometimes fall off.

GLUCOSE GLUTAMATE • Used as a humectant in hand creams and lotions, it occurs naturally in animal blood, grape, and corn sugars, and is a source of energy for plants and animals. It is sweeter than sucrose. Glucose syrup is used to flavor sausage, hamburger, and other processed meats. Also used as an extender in maple syrup and medicinally as a nutrient. Glutamate is the salt of glutamic acid and is used to enhance natural food flavors. The FDA asked for further studies as to its potential mutagenic, teratogenic, subacute, and reproductive effects in 1980. Since then, the FDA has not reported any action.

D-GLUCOSE ISOMERASE • High-fructose corn syrup (*see*).

D-GLUCOSE OXIDASE • An enzyme that adds flavor and color preservation in eggs and juices. No known toxicity.

GLUCURONIC ACID • A carbohydrate that is widely distributed in the animal kingdom.

GLUTAMATE • Ammonium and monopotassium salt of glutamic acid (*see*). Used to impart meat flavor to foods and to enhance other natural food flavors and to improve the taste of tobacco. It is used as an antioxidant in cosmetics to prevent spoilage. It is being studied by the FDA for mutagenic, teratogenic, subacute, and reproductive effects. The final report to the FDA of the Select Committee on GRAS Substances stated in 1980 that there is no evidence in the available information that it is a hazard to the public when used as it is now and it should continue its GRAS status with limitations on the amount that can be added to food.

GLUTAMIC ACID • A white, practically odorless, free-flowing crystalline powder, a nonessential amino acid (*see*) usually manufactured from vegetable protein. A salt substitute, it has been used to treat epilepsy and to correct stomach acids. It is used to enhance food flavors and to add meat flavor to foods. Glutamic acid with hydrochloride (*see* Hydrochloric Acid) is used to improve the taste of beer. It is also employed as an antioxidant in cosmetics and as a softener in permanent wave solutions to help protect against hair damage. It is being studied by the FDA for mutagenic, teratogenic, subacute, and reproductive effects. The final report to the FDA of the Select Committee on GRAS Substances stated in 1980 that there is no evidence in the available information that it is a hazard to the public when used as it is now and it should continue its GRAS status with limitations on the amount that can be added to food.

GLUTAMINE • A nonessential amino acid (*see*) used as a medicine and as a culture medium. Nontoxic.

GLUTARAL • Glutaraldehyde. An amino acid (*see*) that occurs in green sugar beets. It is used as a flavor enhancer in foods and in cosmetic creams and emollients. It has a faint agreeable odor. *See* Glutaric Acid.

GLUTARIC ACID • Pentanedioic Acid. A crystalline fatty acid that occurs in green sugar beets, meat, and in crude wood. Very soluble in alcohol and ether. Widely used in Oriental medicine as an aromatic bitter. It is used in American cosmetics as a demulcent (*see*). No known toxicity.

GLUTEN • A mixture of proteins from wheat flour, obtained as an extremely sticky, yellowish-gray mass by making a dough and then washing out the starch. It consists almost entirely of two proteins, gliadin and glutelin, the exact proportions of which depend upon the variety of wheat. Contributes to the porous and spongy structure of bread. No known toxicity.

GLY- • The abbreviation for glycine (*see*).

(MONO)GLYCERIDE CITRATE • Aids the action of and helps dissolve antioxidant formulations for oils and fats, such as shortenings for cooking. No known toxicity.

GLYCERIDES • Monoglycerides, Diglycerides, and Monosodium Glycerides of Edible Fats and Oils. Any of a large class of compounds that are esters (*see*) of the sweet alcohol glycerin. They are also made synthetically. Emulsifying and defoaming agents. Used in bakery products to maintain "softness," in beverages, ice cream, ices, ice milk, milk, chewing gum base, shortening, lard, oleomargarine, confections, sweet chocolate, chocolate, rendered animal fat, and whipped toppings. The diglycerides are on the FDA list of food additives to be studied for possible mutagenic, teratogenic, subacute, and reproductive effects. The glycerides are also used in cosmetic creams as texturizers, emulsifiers, and emollients. The final report to the FDA of the Select Committee on GRAS Substances stated in 1980 that it should continue its GRAS status with no limitations other than good manufacturing practices.

GLYCERIN • Glycerol. Any by-product of soap manufacture, it is a warm-tasting, oily fluid obtained by adding alkalies (*see*) to fats and fixed oils. A sweet (about 0.6 times as sweet as cane sugar) substance. Used as a humectant in tobacco and in marshmallows, pastilles, and jellylike candies; as a solvent for colors and flavors; as a bodying agent in combination with gelatins and edible gums; as a plasticizer in edible coatings for meat and cheese. It is used, too, in beverages, confectionery, baked goods, chewing gum, gelatin desserts, meat products, soda-fountain fudge. Also used in perfumery. A solvent, humectant, and emollient in many cosmetics, it absorbs moisture from the air and therefore helps keep moisture in creams and other products, even if the consumer leaves the cap off the container. Also helps the products to spread better. Among the many products containing glycerin are cream rouge, face packs and masks, freckle lotions, hand creams and lotions, hair lacquer, liquid face powder, mouthwashes, protective creams, skin fresheners, and toothpastes. In concentrated solutions it is irritating to the mucous membranes, but as used, nontoxic, nonirritating, nonallergenic. Contact with strong oxidizing agents such as chromium trioxide, potassium chlorate, or potassium permanganate (*see*) may produce an explosion. The final report to the FDA of the Select Committee on GRAS Substances stated in 1980 that it should continue its GRAS status with no limitations other than good manufacturing practices.

GLYCEROL • *See* Glycerin.

GLYCEROL ESTER OF WOOD ROSIN • Made from refined, pale, yellow-colored wood rosin and food-grade glycerin (*see*). A hard, pale, amber-colored resin, it is used as a chewing gum base and as a beverage stabilizer. No known toxicity.

GLYCERYL ABIETATE • A density adjuster for citrus oil used in the preparation of alcoholic beverages and still and carbonated fruit drinks. Also cleared as a plasticizing material in chewing gum base. No known toxicity.

GLYCERYL BEHENATE • Used to form tablets. GRAS. *See* Behenic Acid.

GLYCERYL CAPRATE • The monoester of glycerin and caprylic acid (*see* both).

GLYCERYL CAPRYLATE • *See* Glycerin and Caprylic Acid.

GLYCERYL CAPRYLATE/CAPRATE. • A mixture of caprylic acid and capric acid (*see* both).

GLYCERYL COCONATE. • *See* Glycerin and Coconut Oil.

GLYCERYL DILAURATE • *See* Glycerin and Lauric Acid.

GLYCERYL DIOLEATE • The diester of glyceric and oleic acid (*see* both).

GLYCERYL DISTEARATE • The diester of glycerin and stearic acid (*see* both).

GLYCERYL HYDROSTEARATE • *See* Glyceryl Monostearate.

GLYCERYL HYDROXYSTEARATE • The monoester of glycerin and hydroxystearic acid (*see* both).

GLYCERYL ISOSTEARATE • *See* Glyceryl Monostearate.

GLYCERYL LACTOOLEATE AND LACTOPALMITATE OF FATTY ACIDS • Food emulsifiers used in shortening where free and combined lactic acid does not exceed 1.75 percent of shortening plus additive. They add calories but are considered nontoxic. The final report to the FDA of the Select Committee on GRAS Substances stated in 1980 that it should continue its GRAS status with no limitations other than good manufacturing practices.

GLYCERYL LANOLATE • The monoester of glycerin and lanolin (*see* both).

GLYCERYL LINOLEATE • The monoester of glycerin and linoleic acid (*see* both).

GLYCERYL MONO- AND DIESTERS • Manufactured by reacting edible glycerides with ethylene oxide. These are used as defoamers in yeast production. No known toxicity. The final report to the FDA of the Select Committee on GRAS Substances stated in 1980 that it should continue its GRAS status with no limitations other than good manufacturing practices.

GLYCERYL MONOSTEARATE • An emulsifying and dispersing agent used in oleomargarine, shortenings, and other food products as well as in baby creams, face masks, foundation cake makeup, liquid powders, hair conditioners, hand lotions, mascara, and nail whiteners. It is a mixture of two glyceryls, a white waxlike solid or beads, and is soluble in hot organic solvents such as alcohol. Lethal when injected in large doses into mice. No known toxicity.

GLYCERYL MYRISTATE • *See* Glycerin and Myristic Acid.

GLYCERYL OLEATE • *See* Glycerin and Oleic Acid.

GLYCERYL PABA • The ester of glycine and para-aminobenzoic acid (*see* both).

GLYCERYL PALMITATE LACTATE • The lactic acid ester (*see*) of glyceryl palmitate.

GLYCERYL RICINOLEATE • *See* Glycerin.

GLYCERYL SESQUIOLEATE • *See* Glycerin.

GLYCERYL STARCH • *See* Starch and Glycerols.

GLYCERYL STEARATE • An emulsifier. *See* Glycerin.

GLYCERYL STEARATE SE • *See* Glyceryl Monostearate.

GLYCERYL TRIACETATE • *See* Triacetin. GRAS.

GLYCERYL TRIBUTYRATE • *See* Tributyrin.

GLYCERYL TRIMYRISTATE • *See* Glycerin and Myristic Acid.

GLYCINE • Used as a texturizer in cosmetics. An amino acid (*see*) classified as nonessential. Made up of sweet-tasting crystals, it is used as a dietary supplement and as a gastic antacid. No known toxicity.

GLYCOFUROL • The ethoxylated ether of tetrahydrofurfuryl alcohol. *See* Furfural.

GLYCOGEN • Distributed throughout cell protoplasm, it is an animal starch found especially in liver and muscle. Used as a violet dye and in biochemical research. No known toxicity.

GLYCOHOLIC ACID • A product of mixing cholic acid and glycine, it is the chief ingredient of bile in vegetarian animals. It is used as an emulsifying agent for dried eggs whites up to 0.1 percent. No known toxicity. The final report to the FDA of the Select Committee on GRAS Substances stated in 1980 that it should continue its GRAS status with no limitations other than good manufacturing practices.

GLYCOLIC ACID • Contained in sugar cane juice, it is an odorless, slightly water-absorbing acid used to control the acid-alkali balance in cosmetics and whenever a cheap organic acid is needed. It is also used in copper brightening, decontamination procedures, and in dyeing. It is a mild irritant to the skin and mucous membranes. The final report to the FDA of the Select Committee on GRAS Substances stated in 1980 that it should continue its GRAS status with no limitations other than good manufacturing practices.

GLYCOL DISTEARATE • Alcohol from glycol. *See* Glycols.

GLYCOL STEARATE SE • An emulsifier. *See* Glycols and Stearic Acid.

GLYCOLS • Propylene Glycol. Glycerin, Ethylene Glycol, Carbitol. Diethylene Glycol. Glycol literally means "glycerin" plus "alcohol." A group of syrupy alcohols derived from hydrocarbons (*see*) and used in foods as emulsifiers and in chewing gum bases and in cosmetics as humectants. The FDA cautions manufacturers that glycols may cause adverse reactions in users. Propylene glycol and glycerin (*see* both) are considered safe. Other glycols in low concentrations may be harmless for external application but ethylene glycol, carbitol, and diethylene glycol are hazardous in concentrations exceeding 5 percent even in preparations for use on small areas of the body. Therefore, in sunscreen lotions and protective creams where the area of application is extensive, they should not be used at all. Wetting agents (*see*) increase the absorption of glycols and therefore their toxicity.

GLYCYRRHETINIC ACID • Used as a flavoring, to soothe skin, and as a carrier. Prepared from licorice root, it is soluble in chloroform, alcohol, and acetic acid (*see*). It has been used medicinally to treat a disease of the adrenal gland. No known toxicity when used in cosmetics.

GLYCYRRHETINYL STEARATE • The stearic acid ester of glycyrrhetinic acid (*see*).

GLYCYRRHIZA AND GLYCYRRHIZA EXTRACT • GRAS. *See* Glycyrrhizin, Ammoniated.

GLYCYRRHIZIC ACID • Used as a flavoring, coloring, and to soothe the skin in cosmetics. Extracted from licorice, the crystalline material is soluble in hot water and alcohol. *See* Glycyrrhetinic Acid.

GLYCYRRHIZIN, AMMONIATED • Licorice. Product of dried root from the Mediterranean region used in licorice, anise, root beer, wintergreen, and birch beer flavorings for beverages, ice cream, ices, candy, and baked goods. Also used as a demulcent and expectorant and as a drug vehicle. The final report to the FDA of the Select Committee on GRAS Substances stated in 1980 that it should continue its GRAS status with no limitations on amounts that can be added to food. Cases have been reported of avid licorice eaters who develop high blood pressure. *See* Licorice.

GLYOXYLIC ACID • Used as a coloring. Syrup or crystals that occur in unripe fruit, young leaves, and baby sugar beets. Malodorous and strong corrosive. Forms a thick syrup, very soluble in water, sparingly soluble in alcohol. It absorbs water from the air and condenses with urea to form allantoin, a natural metabolic compound in humans. It gives a nice blue color with sulfuric acid. It is a skin irritant and corrosive.

GRAINS OF PARADISE • Pungent aromatic seeds of a tropical African plant of the ginger family. It is a natural flavoring used in fruit, ginger, ginger ale, and pepper flavorings for beverages, ice cream, ices, and candy. No known toxicity. GRAS.

GRAMINIS • *See* Dog Grass Extract.

GRAPE COLOR EXTRACT • The extract of the pulp of *Vitis vinifera* used as a coloring. Permanently listed since 1981. No known toxicity.

GRAPE JUICE • The liquid expressed from fresh grapes used as a coloring.

GRAPE LEAF EXTRACT • The extract of the seeds of the grapefruit, *Citrus paradisi*.

GRAPE POMACE • Source of natural red and blue colorings. *See* Anthocyanins

GRAPE SKIN EXTRACT • Enocianina. Used in still and carbonated drinks and ades, beverage bases, and alcoholic beverages. Permanently listed since 1966. No known toxicity.

GRAPEFRUIT OIL • The yellow, sometimes reddish liquid is an ingredient in fragrances obtained by expression from the fresh peel of the grapefruit. Used in grapefuit, lemon, lime, orange, and peach flavorings for beverages, ice cream, ices, candy, baked goods, gelatin desserts, chewing gum (1,500 ppm), and toppings. No known toxicity. GRAS.

GRAPE-SEED OIL • An ingredient in fragrances obtained by expression from the fresh peel of the grapefruit. The yellow, sometimes reddish liquid is also used in fruit flavorings. No known toxicity.

GRAPESKIN EXTRACT • Enocianina. A purple-red liquid extracted from the residue of grapes pressed for use in grape juice and wine. Used for coloring in still and carbonated drinks and ales, beverage bases, and alcoholic beverages. Regarding the sprayng of grapes, specifications by the FDA restrict pesticide residues to not more than 10 ppm lead and not more than 1 ppm arsenic.

GRAS • The Generally Recognized as Safe list was established in 1958 by Congress. Those substances that were being added to food over a long time, which under conditions of their intended use were generally recognized as safe by qualified scientists, would be exempt from premarket clearance. Congress had acted on a very marginal response—on the basis of returns from those scientists sent questionnaires. Approximately 355 out of 900 responded, and only about 100 of those responses had substantive comments. Three items were removed from the originally published list. Since then, developments in the scientific fields and in consumer awareness have brought to light the inadequacies of the testing of food additives and, ironically, the complete lack of testing of the Generally Recognized as Safe list. President Nixon directed the FDA to reevaluate items on the GRAS list. The reevaluation was completed and a number of items were moved from the list. Although there were a number of others on the list, some of them top priority, to be studied in 1980, nothing has been reported by the FDA on their status since then.

GREEN • *See* FD and C Green (Nos. 1, 2, 3).

GREEN BEAN EXTRACT • The extract of the unripe beans of domesticated species of *Phaseolus*.

GROUND LIMESTONE • Used as a flavoring. GRAS.

GROUNDSEL EXTRACT • Extract of *Senecio vulgaris,* a North American maritime shrub or tree.

GROWTH HORMONES • *See* Hormones.

GUAIAC WOOD OIL • Yellow to amber semisolid mass with a floral odor. Soluble in alcohol. Derived from steam distillation of guaiac wood, from a Mexican tree. A gum resin used in fruit and rum flavorings for beverages, ice cream, ices, candy, and baked goods. The oil is a raspberry, strawberry, rose, fruit, honey, ginger, and ginger ale flavoring for beverages, ice cream, candy, baked goods, gelatin desserts, and chewing gum. Formerly used to treat rheumatism. Used as a perfume fixative and modifier, soap odorant, and in fragrances. No known toxicity.

GUAIACYL ACETATE • A synthetic berry flavoring for beverages, ice cream, ices, candy, gelatin, chewing gum, and baked goods. No known toxicity.

GUAIARETIC ACID • A synthetic flavoring. *See* Guaiac Wood Oil.

GUAIYL ACETATE • Guaiac Wood Acetate. A synthetic tobacco and fruit flavoring for beverages, ice cream, ices, candy, gelatin, chewing gum, and baked goods. No known toxicity.

GUAIYL PHENYLACETATE • A synthetic berry, coffee, honey, tobacco, and smoke flavoring agent flavoring for beverages, ice cream, ices, candy, baked goods, and toppings. No known toxicity.

GUANIDOETHYL CELLULOSE • *See* Guaiac Wood Oil.

GUAR GUM • Guar Flour. From ground nutritive seed tissue of plants cultivated in India, it has five to eight times the thickening power of starch. A free-flowing powder, it is used as a stabilizer for frozen fruit, icings, glazes, and fruit drinks and as a thickener for hot and cold drinks. Also a binder for meats, confections, baked goods, cheese spreads, cream cheese, ice cream, ices, French dressing, and salad dressing. Keeps tablet formulations from disintegrating, and is used in cosmetic emulsions, toothpastes, lotions, and creams. Employed also as a bulk laxative, appetite suppressant, and to treat peptic ulcers. The FDA's reevaluation in 1976 found guar gum to be GRAS if used as a stabilizer, thickener, and firming agent at 0.35 percent in baked goods, 1.2 percent in breakfast cereals; 2.0 percent in fats and oils, 1.2 percent in gravies; 1.0 percent in sweet sauces, toppings, and syrups; and 2.0 percent in processed vegetables and vegetable juices. In large amounts, it may cause nausea, flatulence, or abdominal cramps. The final report to the FDA of the Select Committee on GRAS Substances stated in 1980 that there is no evidence in the available information that it is a hazard to the public when used as it is now and it should continue its GRAS status with limitations on amounts that can be added to food.

GUARANA GUM • The dried paste consisting mainly of crushed seed from a plant grown in Brazil. Contains about 4 percent caffeine. Used in cola flavorings for beverages and candy. *See* Caffeine for toxicity.

GUARANINE • *See* Caffeine.

GUAVA • Extracted from the fruit of a small shrubby American tree widely cultivated in warm regions. The fruit is sweet, sometimes acid, globular, and yellow. It is used to flavor jelly. No known toxicity. GRAS.

GUINEA GREEN B • *See* FD and C Green No. 1.

GUM • True plant gums are the dried exudates from various plants obtained when the bark is cut or other injury is suffered. Gums are soluble in hot or cold water, and sticky. Today the term gum, both for natural and synthetic sources, usually refers to resins. Gums are also used as emulsifiers, stabilizers, and suspending agents. No known toxicity.

GUM ACACIA • *See* Acacia.

GUM ARABIC • Acacia Gum. The exudate from acacia trees grown in the Sudan used in face masks, hair sprays, setting lotions, rouge, and powders for compacts. Serves as an emulsifier, stabilizer, and gelling agent. It may cause allergic reactions such as hay fever, dermatitis, gastrointestinal distress, and asthma. GRAS.

GUM BENJAMIN • *See* Benzoin.

GUM BENZOIN • Used as a preservative in creams and ointments and as a skin protective. It is the balsamic resin from benzoin grown in Thailand, Cambodia, Sumatra, and Cochin China. Also used to glaze confections. No known toxicity.

GUM DAMMAR • A semitransparent exudate from a plant grown in the East Indies and Philippines. Used in varnishes, lacquers, and paper. May cause allergic reactions.

GUM GHATTI • *See* Ghatti Gum.

GUM GUAIAC • Resin from the wood of the guaiacum used widely as an antioxidant in edible fats or oils, beverages, rendered animal fat, or a combination of such fats and vegetable fats. It is also used in cosmetic creams and lotions. Brown or greenish-brown. Formerly used in treatment of rheumatism. No known toxicity. The final report to the FDA of the Select Committee on GRAS Substances stated in 1980 that it should continue its GRAS status with no limitations other than good manufacturing practices.

GUM KARAYA • Sterculia Gum Used in hair sprays, beauty masks, setting lotions, depilatories, rouge, powder for compacts, shaving creams, denture adhesive powder, hand lotions, and tooth-pastes. It is the dried exudate of a tree native to India. Karaya came into wide use during World War I as a cheaper substitute for gum tragacanth (*see*). Karaya swells in water and alcohol, but does not dissolve. It is used in finger wave lotions, which dry quickly and are not sticky. Because of its high viscosity at low concentrations, its ability to produce highly stable emulsions, and its resistance to acids, it is widely used in frozen food products. In 1971, however, the FDA put this additive on the list of chemicals to be studied for teratogenic, mutagenic, subacute, and reproductive effects. It can cause allergic reactions such as hay fever, dermatitis, gastrointestinal diseases, and asthma. It is omitted from hypoallergenic cosmetics. GRAS.

GUM ROSIN • *See* Rosins.

GUM SUMATRA • *See* Gum Benzoin.

GUM TRAGACANTH • The dried gummy exudate from plants found in Iran, Asia Minor, and Syria. A thickener and stabilizer, odorless, and with a gluelike taste. Used in fruit jelly, ornamental icings, fruit, sherbets, water ices, salad dressing, French dressing, confections, and candy. An emulsifier used in brilliantines, shaving creams, tooth-pastes, face packs, foundation creams, hair sprays, mascara, depila-tories, compact powder, rouge, dentifrices, setting lotions, eye makeup, and hand lotions. Also employed in compounding drugs and pastes. One of the oldest known natural emulsifiers, its history predates the Christian era by hundreds of years; it has been recognized in the U.S. Pharmacopoeia since 1829. It has a long shelf life and is resistant to acids. Aside from occasional allergic reactions, it can be ingested in large amounts with little harm except for diarrhea, gas, or constipation. When reevaluated it was found to be GRAS in the following percentages: 0.2 percent for baked goods; 0.7 percent in condiments and relishes; 1.3 percent in fats and oils; 0.8 percent in gravies and sauces; 0.2 percent in meat products; 0.2 percent in processed fruits; and 0.1 percent in all other categories. GRAS.

H

HAW BARK • Black Extract. Extract of the fruit of a hawthorn shrub or tree. Used in butter, caramel, cola, maple, and walnut flavorings for beverages, ice cream, ices, candy, and baked goods. Has been used as a uterine antispasmodic. No known toxicity.

HAZEL NUT OIL • The oil obtained from the various species of the hazel nut tree, *genus Corylus.*

HCL • The abbreviation for Hydrochloride.

HEATHER EXTRACT • An extract of *Calluna vulgaris,* also called Ling Extract.

HECTORITE • An emulsifier and extender. A clay consisting of silicate of magnesium and lithium, it is used in the chill-proofing of beer. The dust can be irritating to the lungs. No known toxicity of the skin.

HEDEONA OIL • *See* Pennyroyal Oil.

HELIOTROPINE • *See* Heliotropin.

HELIOTROPIN • Piperonal. Used in cherry and vanilla flavors. A purple diazo dye used in perfumery and soaps. Consists of colorless, lustrous crystals that have a helioptrope odor. Usually made from oxidation of piperic acid. Ingestion of large amounts may cause central nervous system depression. Applications to the skin may cause allergic reactions and skin irritations. Not recommended for use in cosmetics or perfumes.

HELIOTROPYL ACETATE • *See* Piperonyl Acetate.

HELIUM • This colorless, odorless, tasteless gas is used as propellant for foods packed in pressurized containers. No known toxicity. The final report to the FDA of the Select Committee on GRAS Substances stated in 1980 that it should continue its GRAS status with no limitations other than good manufacturing practices.

HEMLOCK OIL • Spruce Oil   A natural flavoring extract from North American or Asian nonpoisonous hemlock. Used in fruit, root beer, and spice flavorings for beverages, ice cream, ices, candy, baked goods, gelatin desserts, puddings, and chewing gum. No known toxicity.

HENDECANAL • *See* Undecanal.

HENDECEN-9-OL • *See* 9-Undecanal.

10-HENDECENYL ACETATE • *See* 10-Undecen-1-yl Acetate.

y-HEPTALACTONE • A synthetic coconut, nut, and vanilla flavorings for beverages, ice cream, ices, candy, and baked goods. No known toxicity.

HEPTALDEHYDE • *See* Heptanal.

HEPTAL PARABEN • A preservative in beer and non-carbonated soft drinks, it is an ester of *p*-hydroxybenzoic acid (*see*).

HEPTANAL • Heptaldehyde.   Oily, colorless liquid with a penetrating fruit odor made from castor oil. A sythetic flavoring agent used in citrus, apple, melon, cognac, rum, and almond flavorings for beverages, ice cream, ices, candy, baked goods, and liqueurs. Used in perfumery. No known toxicity.

HEPTANAL DEMETHYL ACETAL • A synthetic fruit, melon, and mushroom flavoring agent for beverages, ice cream, ices, candy, baked goods, chewing gum, and condiments. No known toxicity.

HEPTANAL GLYCERYL ACETAL • A synthetic mushroom flavoring for beverages, ice cream, ices, candy, and baked goods. No known toxicity.

2, 3-HEPTANEDIONE • A synthetic raspberry, strawberry, butter, fruit, rum, nut, and cheese flavoring agent for beverages, ice cream, ices, candy, baked goods, and chewing gum. No known toxicity.

HEPTANOIC ACID • Enanthic Acid.   Found in various fusel oils and in rancid oils, it has the faint odor of tallow. It is made from grapes and is a fatty acid used chiefly in making esters (*see*) for flavoring materials. No known toxicity.

1-HEPTANOL • A synthetic flavoring agent, liquid, and miscible with alcohol and ether. *See* Heptyl Alcohol for use.

2-HEPTANONE • A synthetic flavoring agent, liquid, with a penetrating odor, used to give a ''peppery'' smell to such cheeses as Roquefort. Found in oil of cloves and in cinnamon bark oil. Used in berry, butter, fruit, and cheese flavorings for beverages, ice cream, ices, candy, baked goods, chewing gum, and condiments (25 ppm). Used also in perfumery as a constituent of artificial carnation oils. Found naturally in oil of cloves and in cinnamon bark oil. The lethal concentration in air for rats is 4,000 ppm. In high doses it is narcotic, and a suspected irritant to human mucous membranes.

3-HEPTANONE • A synthetic melon flavoring agent for beverages, ice cream, ices, candy, and baked goods. *See* 2-Heptanone, which is a similar compound.

4-HEPTANONE • A synthetic strawberry and fruit flavoring agent for beverages, ice cream, ices, candy, baked goods, and gelatin desserts. *See* 2-Heptanone, which is a similar compound.

1-HEPTYL ACETATE • A synthetic berry, banana, melon, pear, and pineapple flavoring agent for beverages, ice cream, ices, candy, and baked goods. No known toxicity. *See* 2-Heptanone.

HEPTYL ALCOHOL • 1-Heptanol. Colorless, fragrant liquid miscible with alcohol. A synthetic flavoring agent with a fatty, citrus odor, used in fruit flavorings for beverages, ice cream, ices, candy, and baked goods. No known toxicity. Used in perfumery. *See* 2-Heptanone.

HEPTYL ALDEHYDE • *See* Heptanal.

HEPTYL BUTYRATE • Butyric Acid. A synthetic raspberry, floral, violet, apricot, melon, and plum flavoring agent for beverages, ice cream, ices, candy, baked goods. No known toxicity.

***y*-HEPTYL BUTYROLACTONE** • *See y*-Undecalactone.

HEPTYL FORMATE • Used in artificial fruit essences. *See* 2-Heptanone.

HEPTYL HEPTANOATE • Colorless liquid with fruity odor used in artificial fruit essences. *See* 2-Heptanone.

HEPTYL ISOBUTYRATE • A synthetic coconut, apricot, peach, pineapple, and plum flavoring agent for beverages, ice cream, ices, candy, and baked goods. No known toxicity.

***n*-HEPTYLIC ACID** • *See* Heptanoic Acid.

HEPTYLPARABEN • A preservative. *See* Parabens.

HEPTYL PELARGONATE • Liquid with pleasant odor used in flavors and perfumes. *See* 2-Heptanone.

HERB ROBERT EXTRACT • Extract of the entire plant, *Geranium robertianum*. *See* Geranium Oil.

1-HEXADECANOIC ACID • *See* Palmitic Acid.

1-HEXADECANOL • Cetyl Alcohol. A synthetic chocolate flavoring agent for ice cream, ices, and candy. No known toxicity.

***w*-6-HEXADECENLACTONE** • Ambrettolide. 6-Hexadecenolide. A synthetic fruit flavoring agent for beverages, ice cream, ices, candy, baked goods, gelatin desserts, and chewing gum. No known toxicity.

6-HEXADECENOLIDE • *See w*-6-Hexadecenlactone.

HEXADECYLIC ACID • *See* Palmitic Acid.

2,4-HEXADIENOATE • *See* Allyl Sorbate.

HEXAHYDROPYRIDENE • *See* Piperidine.

HEXAHYDROTHYMOL • *See* Menthol.

γ-HEXALACTONE • A synthetic butter, fruit, honey, and vanilla flavoring for beverages, ice cream, ices, candy, baked goods, chewing gum, and gelatin desserts. No known toxicity.

HEXALDEHYDE • *See* Hexanal.

HEXANAL • Hexaldehyde. Hexoic Aldehyde. A synthetic flavoring agent occurring naturally in apples, coffee, cooked chicken, strawberries, tea, and tobacco leaves (oils). Used in butter, fruit, honey, and rum flavorings for beverages, ice cream, ices, candy, baked goods, chewing gum, and gelatin desserts. No known toxicity.

1-HEXANAL • *See* Hexyl Alcohol.

2,3-HEXANDIONE • A synthetic strawberry, butter, citrus, banana, pineapple, rum, and cheese flavoring agent for beverages, ice cream, ices, candy, and baked goods. No known toxicity.

HEXANE • A colorless volatile liquid derived from distillation of petroleum and used as a solvent for spice oleoresins (*see*). Also used in low-temperature thermometers instead of mercury, usually with a blue or red dye. It is a mild central nervous system depressant which may be irritating to the respiratory tract.

HEXANEDIOIC ACID • *See* Adipic Acid.

1,2,6-HEXANETRIOL • An alcohol used as a solvent. No known skin toxicity.

HEXANOIC ACID • A synthetic flavoring agent that occurs naturally in apples, butter acids, cocoa, grapes, oil of lavender, oil of lavandin, raspberries, strawberries, and tea. Used in butter, butterscotch, chocolate, berries, strawberries, and tea. Used in butter, butterscotch, chocolate, berries, fruit, rum, pecan, and cheese flavorings for beverages, ice cream, ices, candy, baked goods, chewing gum, and condiments. No known toxicity.

HEXANOL • Hexyl Alcohol. Used as an antiseptic and preservative in cosmetics, it occurs as the acetate (*see*) in seeds and fruits of *Heracleum sphondylium* and *Umbelliferae*. Colorless liquid slightly soluble in water, it is miscible with alcohol. No known toxicity.

2-HEXEN-1-OL • A synthetic flavoring that occurs naturally in grapes; similar in compound to 3-Hexen-1-ol (*see*). Used in fruit and mint flavorings for beverages, ice cream, ices, candy, and baked goods. No known toxicity.

3-HEXEN-1-OL • Leaf Alcohol. Blatteralkohol. A synthetic flavoring that occurs naturally in leaves of odoriferous plants and grapefruit, raspberries, and tea. Strong odor. Used in fruit and mint flavorings for beverages, ice cream, ices, candy, and baked goods. No known toxicity.

2-HEXEN-1-YL ACETATE • A synthetic fruit flavoring agent for beverages, ice cream, ices, candy, and baked goods. No known toxicity.

2-HEXENAL • A synthetic berry and fruit flavoring agent that occurs naturally in apples and strawberries and is used for beverages, ice cream, ices, candy, and baked goods. No known toxicity.

cis-3-HEXENAL • A synthetic fruit flavoring agent for beverages, ice cream, ices, and candy. No known toxicity.

2-HEXENOIC ACID • *See* Methyl Hexenoate.

HEXOIC ACID • *See* Methyl Hexenoate.

HEXOIC ALDEHYDE • A synthetic berry, apple, pear, and pineapple flavoring agent for beverages, ice cream, ices, candy, baked goods, and chewing gum.

HEXYL ACETATE • Acetic Acid. Hexyl Ester. A synthetic berry, apple, pear, and pineapple flavoring agent for beverages, ice cream, ices, candy, baked goods, and chewing gum. No known toxicity.

2-HEXYL-4-ACETOXYTETRAHYDROFURAN • A synthetic fruit flavoring agent for beverages, ice cream, ices, candy, and baked goods. No known toxicity.

HEXYL ALCOHOL • 1-Hexanol. A synthetic flavoring agent that occurs naturally in apples, oil of lavender, strawberries, and tea. Used in berry, coconut, and fruit flavorings for beverages, ice cream, ices, candy, baked goods, chewing gum, and gelatin desserts. Also used in antiseptics and in perfumery. *See* Hexanol.

HEXYL ESTER • *See* Hexyl Acetate.

HEXYL FORMATE • Formic Acid. A synthetic raspberry and fruit flavoring agent for beverages, ice cream, ices, candy, and baked goods. *See* Formic Acid for toxicity.

HEXYL 2-FUROATE • A synthetic coffee, maple, and mushroom flavoring agent for candy and condiments. No known toxicity.

HEXYL HEXANOATE • Hexanoic Acid. A synthetic fruit flavoring agent for beverages, ice cream, ices, candy, and baked goods. No known toxicity.

2-HEXYL-5(OR 6)-KETO-1, 4-DIOXANE • A synthetic cream flavoring agent for beverages, ice cream, ices, candy, and baked goods. No known toxicity.

HEXYL LAURATE • *See* Lauric Acid.

HEXYL OCTANOATE • Octanoic Acid. A synthetic fruit flavoring agent for beverages and puddings. No known toxicity.

HEXYL PROPIONATE • Propionic Acid. A synthetic fruit flavoring agent for beverages, ice cream, ices, candy, and baked goods. No known toxicity.

***a*-HEXYLCINNAMALDEHYDE** • A synthetic flavoring, pale-yellow liquid with a jasminelike odor. Used in berry, fruit, and honey flavorings for beverages, ice cream, ices, candy, baked goods, and gelatin desserts. No known toxicity.

HEXYLENE GLYCOL DIACETATE • *See* 1,3-Nonanediol Acetate.

2-HEXYLIDENE CYCLOPENTANONE • A synthetic fruit flavoring agent for beverages, ice cream, ices, candy, and baked goods. No known toxicity.

HICKORY BARK EXTRACT • A natural flavoring extract from the hickory nut tree and used in butter, caramel, rum, maple, nut, spice, tobacco, and smoke flavorings for beverages, ice cream, ices, candy, baked goods, condiments, and liquors. No known toxicity. GRAS.

HIGH-AMYLOSE CORNSTARCH • Cornstarch that has been treated with enzymes to make it sweeter.

HIGH-FRUCTOSE CORN SYRUP • Corn syrup (*see*) that has been treated with enzymes to make it sweeter.

HINOKITIOL • The organic compound distilled from the leaves of *Arbor Vitae,* it is a pale-yellow oil with a camphor smell and is used in perfumery and flavoring. Low toxicity.

HIPBERRY EXTRACT • *See* Rose Hips Extract.

HISTAMINE • A chemical released by most cells and considered responsible for much of the swelling and itching characteristics of hay fever and other allergies.

HISTIDINE • L and DL forms. A basic essential amino acid (*see*) used as a nutrient. It is a building block of protein, used as a nutrient. Soluble in water. (L-Histidine is the natural form.) It is used in cosmetic creams. Histidine has been on the FDA list of additives that need further study since 1980. Nothing new has been reported by the FDA since then. GRAS.

HONEY • Used as a coloring, flavoring, and emollient in cosmetics. Formerly used in hair bleaches. The common, sweet, viscous material taken from the nectar of flowers and manufactured in the sacs of various kinds of bees. The flavor and color depend upon the plants from which it was taken.

HONEYDEW MELON JUICE • Liquid expressed from fresh honeydew.

HONEYSUCKLE • The common fragrant tubular flowers, filled with honey, which are used in perfumes. No known toxicity.

HOPS • Used in beer brewing and in fruit and root beer flavorings for beverages. Derived from the carefully dried pineconelike fruit of the hop plant grown in Europe, Asia, and North America. Light-yellow or greenish, it is an oily liquid with a bitter taste and aromatic odor. A solid extract is used in bitters, fruit, and root beer flavorings for beverages, ice cream, ices, candy, and baked goods. Hops oil is used in raspberry, grape, whiskey, and spice flavorings for beverages, ice cream, ices, candy, baked goods, chewing gum, and condiments. Hops at one time were thought to be a sedative. No known toxicity.

HOPS OIL • *See* Hops.

HOREHOUND EXTRACT • Hoarhound. A flavoring extracted from a mintlike plant cultivated in Europe, Asia, and the United States. It has a very bitter taste and is used in maple, nut, and root beer flavorings for beverages, ice cream, ices, candy, and baked goods. It is also a bitter tonic and expectorant. No known toxicity. GRAS.

HORMONES • A hormone is a chemical produced by a gland and secreted into the bloodstream, affecting the function of distant cells or organs. United States beef producers have been using growth hormones, a very powerful chemical from the pituitary gland at the base of the brain, to increase the cattle's weight from 10 to 20 percent for the same amount of feed. Diethylstilbestrol, another hormone, an estrogen, was used by beef and poultry producers to increase the weight of meat for which they are paid by the pound. The FDA has tried to ban diethylstilbestrol for that purpose because it has been shown to be carcinogenic, but spot checks have shown that it is still present in some meat and poultry products. In 1988, the 12 nation European Community put a ban on American beef because of the use of growth hormones. The Community adopted a law in December 1985 prohibiting the use of any hormones in raising cattle for meat. The American position is that the growth hormones approved for cattle by the Department of Agriculture are not harmful to humans. Environmentalists who testified in favor of the European legislators have maintained that such hormones create tumors and genital deformities in children.

HORSE CHESTNUT • The seeds of *Aeschylus hippocastanum*. A tonic, natural astringent for skin, and fever-reducing substance that contains tannic acid (*see*). No known toxicity.

HORSEMINT LEAVES EXTRACT • A flavoring extract from any of several coarse, aromatic plants, grown from New York to Florida and from Texas to Wisconsin. Used in fruit flavorings for beverages (600 ppm). Formerly used as an aromatic stimulant and to break up intestinal gas. No known toxicity. GRAS.

HORSERADISH EXTRACT • Scurvy Grass. A condiment ingredient utilizing the grated root from the tall, coarse, white-flowered herb native to Europe. Often combined with vinegar or other ingredients. Contains ascorbic acid (*see*) and acts as an antiseptic in cosmetics. No known toxicity. GRAS.

HOUSELEEK EXTRACT • Extract of the common houseleek *Sempervivum tectorum*. Old herbal remedy for soothing the skin.

HPP • Hydrolyzed Plant Protein. *See* Hydrolyzed Vegetable Protein.

HUMECTANT • A substance used to preserve the moisture content of materials, used to preserve moisture in confections and tobacco. Glycerin, propylene, glycol, and sorbitol (*see* all) are widely used humectants. *See* individual substances for toxicity.

HUMULUS • A hop plant, a herbaceous vine with palmate leaves and pistillate flowers. No known toxicity.

HVP • *See* Hydrolyzed Vegetable Protein.

HYACINTH, ABSOLUTE • It is the extract of the very common fragrant flower. It is used as a flavoring for chewing gum and in perfumes and soaps. Dark green liquid with a penetrating ordor, a juice of hyacinth is very irritating to the skin and can cause allergic reactions. The bulb can cause severe gastrointestinal symptoms.

HYACINTHIN • *See* Phenylacetaldehyde.

HYBRID SAFFLOWER OIL • The oil derived from the seeds of a genetic strain which contains mostly oleic acid tryglyceride as distinct from safflower oil.

HYDRATED • Combined with water.

HYDRATED ALUMINA • *See* Alumium Hydroxide.

HYDRATED SILICA • An Aerogel anticaking agent to keep loose powders free-flowing. *See* Silica and Hydrated.

HYDRATROPALDEHYDE • *See* 2-Phenylpropionaldehyde.

HYDRATROPALDEHYDE DIMETHYL ACETAL • *See* 2-Phenylpropionaldehyde Dimethyl Acetal.

HYDRAZINE HYDRATE • Colorless, fuming liquid used as a solvent and catalyst for inorganic materials. Strong irritant to skin and eyes.

HYDROCARBONS • A large class of organic compounds containing only carbon and hydrogen. Petroleum, natural gas, coal, and bitumens are common hydrocarbon products. Hydrocarbons also include mineral oils, paraffin wax, and ozokerite (*see* all).

HYDROCHLORIC ACID • An acid used as a modifier for food starch, in the manufacture of sodium glutamate (*see*) and gelatin, for the conversion of cornstarch to syrup (0.012 percent), and to adjust the pH (acid-alkalinity balance) in the brewing industry (0.02 percent). Also used as a solvent. A clear, colorless or slightly yellowish, corrosive liquid, it is a water solution of hydrogen chloride of varying concentrations. Used in hair bleaches to speed up oxidation in rinses and to remove color. Inhalation of the fumes causes choking and inflammation of the respiratory tract. Ingestion may corrode the mucous membranes, esophagus, and stomach, and cause diarrhea. Circulatory collapse and death can occur. GRAS. Though safer than many propellant gases, their use has diminished because of suspected effects on stratospheric ozone.

HYDROGEN PEROXIDE • A bleaching and oxidizing agent, a detergent, and an antiseptic. Used in skin bleaches, hair bleaches, cold creams, mouthwashes, toothpastes, and in cold permanent waves. An unstable compound readily broken down into water and oxygen. It is made from barium peroxide and diluted phosphoric acid. Generally recognized as safe as a preservative and germ killer in milk and cheese as well as in cosmetics. Bleaches tripe and butter; used in the treatment of eggs before drying and in cheddar and Swiss cheeses. A 3-percent solution is used medicinally as an antiseptic and germicide. A strong oxidizer, undiluted it can cause burns of the skin and mucous membranes. In 1980, the Japanese notified the World Health Organization that hydrogen peroxide was a suspect as a cancer-causing agent. It was widely used in Japanese fish cakes. The noodles were dipped in dilute hydrogen peroxide for disinfections. The fish meat and raw flour were also mixed with hydrogen peroxide. In laboratory rats, it was discovered that in the sixty-fifth week, the lining of the duodenum was thickened but no cancers occurred. The Japanese Welfare Ministry decided that hydrogen peroxide is safe for food when it is entirely decomposed and that the food should not contain any residual.

HYDROGENATED HONEY • Controlled hydrogenation (*see*) of honey.

HYDROGENATED OIL • Oil that is partially converted from naturally polyunsaturated fats to saturated. Makes liquid oils partially solid. May adversely affect the levels of fat in the blood and has been linked to colon cancer in some reports. *See* Hydrogenation.

HYDROGENATED PEANUT OIL • *See* Peanut Oil and Hydrogenation.

HYDROGENATED SOYBEAN OIL • *See* Soybean Oil and Hydrogenation.

HYDROGENATED SOY GLYCERIDE • *See* Soybean Oil and Hyprogenation.

HYDROGENATED STARCH HYDROSYLATE • The end product of the hydrogenation of corn syrup. *See* Corn Syrup and Hydrogenation.

HYDROGENATED TALLOW • A component used in the production of beet sugar and yeast in amounts to inhibit foaming. *See* Hydrogenation. No known toxicity. The final report to the FDA of the Select Committee on GRAS Substances stated in 1980 that it should continue its GRAS status with no limitations other than good manufacturing practices.

HYDROGENATED TALLOW ACID • *See* Hydrogenated Tallow.

HYDROGENATED TALLOW ALCOHOL • *See* Hydrogenated Tallow, which has the same uses. The final report to the FDA of the Select Committee on GRAS Substances stated in 1980 that it should continue its GRAS status with no limitations other than good manufacturing practices.

HYDROGENATED TALLOW BETAINE • *See* Hydrogenated Tallow and Betaine.

HYDROGENATED TALLOW GLYCERIDE • *See* Hydrogenated Tallow and Glycerides.

HYDROGENATED TALLOWTRIMONIUM CHLORIDE • *See* Quaternary Ammonium Compounds.

HYDROGENATION • The process of adding hydrogen gas under high pressure to liquid oils. It is the most widely used chemical process in the edible fats industry. Used in the manufacture of petrol from coal, and in the manufacture of margarine and shortening. Used primarily in the cosmetics and food industries to convert liquid oils to semisolid fats at room temperature. Reduces the amount of acid in the compound and improves color. Usually, the higher the amount of hydrogenation, the lower the unsaturation in the fat and the less possibility of flavor degradation or spoilage due to oxidation. Hydrogenated oils still contain some unsaturated components that are susceptible to rancidity. Therefore, the addition of antioxidants is still necessary. In the food industry, primary use is to convert liquid oils to semisolid fats— Crisco, for example, at room temperature.

HYDROLYZED • Subject to hydrolysis or turned partly into water. Hydrolysis is derived from the Greek *hydro,* meaning "water," and *lysis,* meaning "a setting free." It occurs as a chemical process in which the decomposition of a compound is brought about by water, resolving into a simpler compound. Hydrolysis also occurs in the digestion of foods. The proteins in the stomach react with water in an enzyme reaction to form peptones and amino acids (*see*).

HYDROLYZED CASEIN • *See* Casein and Hydrolyzed.

HYDROLYZED SOY PROTEIN • *See* Soybean and Hydrolyzed.

HYDROLYZED VEGETABLE PROTEIN • HPP. HVP. The hydrolysate (liquefied product) of vegetable protein derived by acid, enzyme, or other method of hydrolysis. A flavor enhancer used in soup, beef, and stew. High salt and glutamate content with low-quality protein. On the GRAS list, but the Select Committee of the Federation of American Societies for Experimental Biology (FASEB) advised the FDA that hydrolyzed vegetable protein contains dicarboxylic amino acid (a building block of the protein that affects growth, when used at present levels in strained and junior baby foods). They said that the effects of this substance on children should be studied further, the effects on adults of vegetable and animal protein hydrolysates demonstrate "no current hazard," but the FASEB voiced uncertainties about future consumption levels for those products and recommended further studies.

HYDROLYZED YEAST • The hydrolysate of yeast (liquefication) derived by acid, enzyme, or other method of hydrolysis.
HYDROLYZED YEAST PROTEIN • *See* Hydrolyzed Yeast.
HYDROQUINONE • Used only in polyurethane resins for foods, it is a white crystalline phenol that occurs naturally but is usually manufactured in the laboratory. Hydroquinone combines with oxygen very rapidly and becomes brown when exposed to air. Death has occurred from the ingestion of as little as 5 grams. Ingestion of as little as one gram (1/30th of an ounce) has caused nausea, vomiting, ringing in the ears, delirium, a sense of suffocation, and collapse. Industrial workers exposed to the chemical have suffered clouding of the eye lens. Application to the skin may cause allergic reactions. It can cause depigmentation in a 2-percent solution. When injected into the abdomen of mice in 28-milligram doses per kilogram of body weight, it caused bladder cancers but other studies in which animals were fed the chemical did not show it to induce cancer. However, it did cause atrophy of the liver and aplastic anemia.
HYDROQUINONE DIMETHYL ETHER • White flakes with sweet clover odor used as a fixative in foods, perfumes, dyes, cosmetics and especially in suntan preparations. *See* Hydroquinone.
_p_-HYDROXYANISOLE • *See* Guaiacol.
HYDROXYANTHROQUINONEAMINOPROPYL METHYL MORPHO-LIUMIUN METHOSULFATE • A solvent for resins and waxes; an antioxidant and plasticizer. May be irritating to the skin.
_p_-HYDROXYBENZOATE • *See* Propylparaben.
_o_-HYDROXYBENZOIC ACID • *See* Salicylic Acid.
_p_-HYDROXYBENZOIC ACID • Prepared from p-bromophenol. Used as a preservative and fungicide. *See* Benzoic Acid for toxicity.
3-HYDROXY-2-BUTANONE • *See* Acetoin.
2-HYDROXY-_p_-CYMENE • *See* Carvacrol.
5-HYDROXY-4-OCTANONE • A synthetic butter, butterscotch, fruit, cheese, and nut flavoring agent for beverages, ice cream, ices, candy, and baked goods. No known toxicity.
HYDROXY PROPYLMETHYL CELLULOSE CARBONATE • Prepared from wood pulp or cotton by treatment with methyl chloride. Used as a substitute for water-soluble gums, to render paper greaseproof, and as a thickener. The final report to the FDA of the Select Committee on GRAS Substances stated in 1980 that it should continue its GRAS status with limitations on amounts that can be added to food.
_o_-HYDROXYBENZALDEHYDE • *See* Salicylaldehyde.
_p_-HYDROXYBENZYL ACETONE • *See* 4-(*p*-Hydroxyphenyl)-2-Butanone.

***p*-HYDROXYBENZYL ISOTHIOCYANATE** • A derivative of mustard oil used in flavoring. The final report to the FDA of the Select Committee on GRAS Substances stated in 1980 that it should continue its GRAS status with no limitations other than good manufacturing practices.

2-HYDROXYCAMPHANE • *See* Borneol.

HYDROXYCITRONELLAL • Colorless liquid obtained by the addition of citronellol. Used as a fixative and a fragrance in perfumery for its sweet lily-like odor. It can cause allergic reactions.

HYDROXYCITRONELLAL DIETHYL ACETAL • A synthetic citrus and fruit flavoring agent for beverages, ice cream, ices, candy, and baked goods. No known toxicity.

HYDROXYCITRONELLAL DIMETHYL ACETAL • A synthetic flavoring agent, colorless liquid, with a light floral odor. Used in fruit and cherry flavorings for beverages, ice cream, ices, candy, and baked goods. No known toxicity.

HYDROXYCITRONELLOL • A synthetic lemon, floral, and cherry flavoring agent for beverages, ice cream, ices, candy, baked goods, gelatin desserts, and chewing gum. No known toxicity.

HYDROXYLAMINE HCL • In the body is reportedly decomposed to sodium nitrite. An antioxidant for fatty acids and soaps, sodium nitrite (*see* Nitrite) may be slightly irritating to skin, eyes, and mucous membranes, and may cause depletion of oxygen in the blood when ingested.

HYDROXYLATE • The process in which an atom of hydrogen and an atom of oxygen are introduced into a compound to make the compound more soluble.

HYDROXYLATED LECITHIN • An emulsifier and antioxidant used in baked goods, ice cream, and margarine. According to the Food and Agricultural Organization/World Health Organization Expert Committee on Food Additives, the safety of hydroxylated lecithin (*see* Lecithin) has not been adequately established. It has been cleared by the FDA for use as a food emulsifier.

HYDROXYLATION • The process in which an atom of hydrogen and an atom of oxygen are introduced into a compound to make that compound more soluble.

HYDROXYMETHYLCELLULOSE • Thickener and bodying agent derived from plants. Used to thicken cosmetics and as a setting aid in hair products. *See* Carboxymethyl Cellulose.

4-HYDROXYMETHYL-2,6-di-*tert*-butylphenol • An antioxidant added to food and not to exceed 0.02 percent of the oil or fat content of the food. *See* Quinoline for toxicity.

HYDROXYOCTACOSANYL HYDROXYSTEARATE • *See* Stearic Acid and Hydroxylation.

4-(*p*-HYDROXYPHENYL)-2-BUTANONE • A synthetic fruit flavoring for beverages, ice cream, ices, candy, baked goods, gelatin desserts, and chewing gum. No known toxicity.

HYDROXYPHENYL GLYCINAMIDE • Derived from the nonessential amino acid glycine (*see*) used as a buffering agent and as a violet scent.

HYDROXYPROLINE • L-Proline. The hydroxylated (*see*) amino acid used to add "protein" to cosmetics.

HYDROXYPROPYL CELLULOSE • A thickener. See Hydroxymethylcellulose and Cellulose Gums.

HYDROXYPROPYL GUAR • Guar Gum, 2-Hydroxypropyl Ether. *See* Guar Gum.

HYDROXYPROPYL METHYLCELLULOSE • An emulsifier used in foods such as salad dressings and frozen desserts. See Cellulose Gums.

HYDROXYPROPYLAMINE NITRITE • *See* Isopropanolamine.

HYDROXYPROPYL STARCH, HYDROXYPROPYL STARCH OXIDIZED, AND HYDROXYPROPYL DISTARCHPHOSPHATE • These are all modified starches. The final report to the FDA of the Select Committee on GRAS Substances stated in 1980 that while no evidence in the available information on these starches demonstrates a hazard to the public when they are used at levels that are now current and in the manner now practiced, uncertainties exist requiring that additional studies should be conducted. In 1980, the FDA said GRAS status would continue while tests were being completed and evaluated. Nothing new has been reported by the FDA since then.

HYDROXYQUINOLINE • Was used in cottage cheese but was banned by the FDA in the 1980s.

HYDROXYSTEARIC ACID • *See* Stearic Acid.

HYDROXYSTEARMIDE MEA • A mixture of ethanolamide of Hydroxystearic Acid. See Stearic Acid.

HYDROXYSTEARYL METHYLGLUCAMINE • An amino sugar. *See* Glucose.

HYPNONE • *See* Acetophenone.

HYPERICUM • Hypericin. Blue-black needles obtained from pyridine (*see*). The solutions are red or green with a red cast. Small amounts seem to be a tranquilizer and have been used as an antidepressant in medicine. It can produce a sensitivity to light.

HYPERSENSITIVITY • The condition in persons previously exposed to an antigen in which tissue damage results from an immune reaction to a further dose of the antigen. Classically, four types of hypersensitivity are recognized, but the term is often used to mean the type of allergy associated with hay fever and asthma.

HYPO • Prefix from the Greek, meaning "under" or "below," as in hypoacidity—acidity in a lesser degree than is usual or normal.

HYPOPHOSOPHORIC ACID • Crystals used in baking powder, sodium salt. No known toxicity.

HYSSOP EXTRACT • Extract of *Hyssopus Officinalis.* A Synthetic flavoring from the aromatic herb. Used in bitters. The extract is a liquor flavoring for beverages, ice cream, and ice. The oil is liquor and spice flavoring. No known toxicity. GRAS.

I

ICELAND MOSS EXTRACT • The extract of *Lichen islandicus.* A water-soluble gum which gels on cooling. Used to flavor alcoholic beverages, as a food additive and in comedic gels. No known toxicity.

IMITATION • A flavor containing any portion of nonnatural materials. For instance, unless a strawberry flavoring is made entirely from strawberries, it must be called imitation. When a processor fails to use all the standard ingredients in mayonnaise, he must call it salad dressing. Imitation means that the product contains fewer vitamins, minerals, or the other nutrients than the food it resembles. With reference to a fragrance, containing all or some portion of nonnatural materials. For instance, unless a strawberry flavoring used in gelatin is made entirely from strawberries, it must be called imitation.

IMITATION MILK • Contains no milk derivative. Usually contains water, sugar, and vegetable fat. A source of protein (such as soybean) with various additive flavorings. Imitation milk contains 1 percent protein compared to 3.5 percent in whole cow's milk.

IMMORTELLE EXTRACT • A natural flavoring extract from a red flowered tropical tree. The name derives from the French *immortel—* "immortal" or "everlasting." Used in raspberry, fruit, and liquor flavoring for beverages, ice cream, ices, baked goods, candy, gelatin desserts, and chewing gum. GRAS.

IMPERARATA • A flavoring from a tropical grass used in malt beer. No known toxicity.

INDIAN GUM • *See* Ghatti Gum.

INDIAN TRAGACANTH • *See* Karaya Gum.

INDIGO CARMINE • *See* FD and C Blue No. 2.

INDOLE • A white, lustrous, flaky substance with an unpleasant odor, occurring naturally in jasmine oil and orange flowers and used as a synthetic flavoring agent in raspberry, strawberry, bitters, chocolate, orange, coffee, violet, fruit, nut, and cheese flavorings for beverages, ice cream, ices, candy, baked goods, and gelatin desserts. Also used in perfumes. It can be extracted from coal tar and feces; in highly diluted solutions, the odor is pleasant. The lethal dose in dogs is 60 milligrams per kilogram of body weight. No known toxicity on the skin.

INOSINATE • A salt of inosinic acid used to intensify flavor, as with sodium glutamate (*see*). Inosinic acid is prepared from meat extract; also from dried sardines. No known toxicity.

INOSITOL • A dietary supplement of the Vitamin B family used in emollients. Found in plant and animal tissues. Isolated commercially from corn. A fine, white, crystalline powder, it is odorless with sweet taste. Stable in air. No known toxicity. The final report to the FDA of the Select Committee on GRAS Substances stated in 1980 that it should continue its GRAS status with no limitations other than good manufacturing practices.

INTERMEDIATE • A chemical substance found as part of a necessary step between one organic compound and other, as in the production of dyes, pharmaceuticals, or other artificial products that develop properties only upon oxidation. Used frequently for artificial colors.

INVERT SUGAR • Inversol. Nulomoline. Colorose. A mixture of 50 percent glucose and 50 percent fructose. It is sweeter than sucrose. Commercially produced by "inversion" of sucrose. Honey is mostly invert sugar. Invert sugar is used in confectionery and in brewing. Like glycerin (*see*) it holds in moisture and prevents drying out. Used medicinally in intravenous solutions. No known toxicity. The final report to the FDA of the Select Committee on GRAS Substances stated in 1980 that there is no evidence in the available information that it is a hazard to the public when used as it is now and it should continue its GRAS status with limitations on amounts that can be added to food.

IODINE SOURCES • Calcium Iodate, Cuprous Iodide, Potassium Iodate, and Potassium Iodide. Discovered in 1811 and classed among the rarer earth elements, it is found in the earth's crust as bluish-black scales. Nearly two hundred products contain this chemical. They are prescription and over-the-counter medications. Iodine is an integral part of the thyroid hormones which have important metabolic roles, and is an essential nutrient for humans. Iodine deficiency leads to thyroid enlargement or goiter. Nutritionists have found that the most efficient way to add iodine to the diet is through the use of iodized salt. The FDA has ordered all table salts to specify whether the product contains iodide. However, many commercially prepared food items do not contain iodized salt. Iodized salt contains up to 0.01 percent; dietary supplements contain 0.16 percent. Cuprous and potassium iodides are used in table salts; potassium iodide is in some drinking water; and potassium iodate is used in animal feeds. Dietary iodine is absorbed from the intestinal tract, and the main human sources are from food and water. Seafoods are good sources, and dairy products may be good sources if the cows eat enriched grain. Adult daily iodine requirement is believed to be 110 to 150 milligrams. Growing children and pregnant or lactating women may need more. Iodine compounds are used in expectorants and thinners, particularly in the treatment of asthma and in contrast media for X rays and fluoroscopy. They can produce a diffuse red pimply rash, hives, asthma, and sometimes anaphylactic shock. Iodine is also used as an antiseptic and germicide in cosmetics.

IONONE • Used as a scent in perfumery and as a flavoring agent in foods, it occurs naturally in *Boronia,* an Australian shrub. Colorless to pale yellow with an odor reminiscent of cedarwood or violets. It may cause allergic reactions.

IRIS FLORENTINA • *See* Orris.

IRISH MOSS • Emulsifier for frozen desserts, dressings, fruits, jelly, and preserves. *See* Carrageenan.

***a*-IRISONE** ® • *See* Ionone.

***b*-IRISONE** ® • *See* Ionone.

IRON • It is an essential mineral element and occurs widely in foods, especially organ meats such as liver, red meats, poultry, and leafy vegetables. The principal foods to which iron or iron salts are added are enriched cereals and some beverages, including milk, poultry stuffing, cornmeal, corn grits, and bread. Iron ammonium citrate is an anticaking agent in salt. Iron-choline citrate is cleared for use as a source of iron in foods for special dietary use. Iron peptonate, a combination of oxide and peptone, is made soluble by the presence of sodium citrate and is used in the treatment of iron-deficiency anemia. The recommended daily allowances for children and adults is from 0.2 milligrams to 1.0 milligram and 18 milligrams per day for pregnant women. Iron is potentially toxic in all forms.

IRON CAPRYLATE, IRON LINOLEATE, IRON NAPHTHENATE, AND IRON TALLATE • All are used in packaging. Iron naphthenate was said by the Select Committee on GRAS Substances to have so little known about it that there was nothing upon which to base an evaluation of it when it is used as a food ingredient. As for the others, the final report to the FDA of the Select Committee on GRAS Substances stated in 1980 that they should continue their GRAS status with no limitations other than good manufacturing practices.

IRON-CHOLINE CITRATE COMPLEX • *See* Iron and Citrate Salts.

IRON OXIDE • Any of several natural or synthetic oxides of iron (iron combined with oxygen) varying in color from red-brown or black-orange to yellow. Used for dyeing eggshells and for pet food. *See* Iron for toxicity.

IRON SALTS • Iron Sources: Ferric, Choline Citrate, Ferric Ortho-phosphate; Ferric Phosphate; Ferric Sodium Pyrophosphate; Ferrous Fumarate; Ferrous Gluconate; Ferrous Lactate; and Ferrous Sulfate. Widely used as enrichment for foods, ferric phosphate is used as a food supplement, particularly in enriched bread. Ferric pyrophosphate is a grayish-blue powder used in ceramics. Ferric sodium pyrophosphate is used in prepared breakfast cereals, poultry stuffing, enriched flours, self-rising flours, farina, cornmeal, corn grits, bread, and rolls. The final report to the FDA of the Select Committee on GRAS Substances stated in 1980 that there is no evidence in the available information that it is a hazard to the public when used as it is now and should continue as GRAS with limitations on amounts that can be added to food. It may cause gastrointestinal disturbances. Ferrous lactate is greenish-white with a sweet iron taste. It is affected by air and light. It is also used to treat anemia. The final report to the FDA of the Select Committee on GRAS Substances stated in 1980 that there is no evidence that ferrous lactate is hazardous and therefore it should continue as GRAS with limitations. Ferrous sulfate is blue-green and odorless and oxidized in air and is used as a wood preservative, weed killer, and treatment for anemia. Large quantities can cause gastrointestinal disturbances. For ferric choline citrate, *see* Choline Chloride. Among other irons used are ferrous gluconate, ferrous fumarate, sodium ferric EDTA; sodium ferricitropyrophosphate; and ferrous citrate and ferrous ascorbate. Iron salts are used in cosmetics mainly as colorings and astringents.

a-IRONE • A synthetic flavoring derived from the violet family and usually isolated from irises and orris oil. A light-yellow, viscous liquid, it gives off the delicate fragrance of violets when put in alcohol. It is also used in perfumery and in dentifrices for flavoring. *See* Orris for toxicity.

IRRADIATED ERGOSTEROL • *See* Vitamin D_2.

ISO • Greek for "equal." In chemistry, it is a prefix added to the name of one compound to denote another composed of the same kinds and numbers of atoms but different from each other in structural arrangement.

ISOAMYL ACETATE • A synthetic flavoring agent that occurs natu-rally in bananas and pears. Colorless, with a pearlike odor and taste, it is used in raspberry, strawberry, butter, caramel, coconut, cola, apple, banana, cherry, grape, peach, pea, pineapple, rum, cream soda, and vanilla flavorings for beverages, ice cream, ices, candy, baked goods, chewing gum (2,700 ppm), and gelatin desserts. Also used in perfuming shoe polish among other industrial uses. Exposure to 950 ppm for one hour has caused headache, fatigue, shoulder pain, and irritation of the mucous membranes.

ISOAMYL ACETOACETATE • A synthetic fruit and apple flavoring for beverages, ice cream, ices, candy, and baked goods. No known toxicity.

ISOAMYL ALCOHOL • A synthetic flavoring agent that occurs naturally in apples, cognac, lemons, peppermint, raspberry, strawberry, and tea. Used in chocolate, apple, banana, brandy, and rum flavorings for beverages, ice cream, ices, candy, baked goods, gelatin desserts, chewing gum, and brandy. A central nervous system depressant. Vapor exposures have caused marked irritation of the eyes, nose, and throat, and headache. Amyl alcohols are highly toxic, and ingestion has caused human deaths from respiratory failure. Isoamyl alcohol may cause heart, lung, and kidney damage.

ISOAMYL BENZOATE • A synthetic berry, apple, cherry, plum, prune, liquor, rum, and maple flavoring agent for beverages, ice cream, ices, candy, gelatin desserts, baked goods, and chewing gum. Also used in perfumery and cosmetics. No known toxicity.

ISOAMYL CINNAMATE • A synthetic strawberry, butter, caramel, chocolate, cocoa, fruit, peach, pineapple, and honey flavoring agent for beverages, ice cream, candy, and baked goods. No known toxicity.

ISOAMYL FORMATE • Formic Acid. A synthetic flavoring agent, colorless, liquid, with a fruity smell. Used in strawberry, apple, apricot, banana, peach, and pineapple flavorings for beverages, ice cream, candy, baked goods, gelatin desserts, and chewing gum. *See* Formic Acid for toxicity.

ISOAMYL 2-FURANBUTYRATE • A synthetic chocolate, coffee, fruit, and whiskey flavoring agent for beverages, ice cream, ices, candy, baked goods, and gelatin. No known toxicity.

ISOAMYL 2-FURANPROPIONATE • A synthetic chocolate, coffee, fruit, and whiskey flavoring agents for beverages, ice cream, ices, candy, and baked goods. No known toxicity.

a-**ISOAMYL FURFURYLACETATE** • *See* Isoamyl 2-Furanpropionate.

a-**ISOAMYL FURFURYLPROPIONATE** • *See* Isoamyl 2-Furanbutyrate.

ISOAMYL ISOBUTYRATE • A synthetic fruit and banana flavoring agent for beverages, ice cream, ices, candy, baked goods, gelatin desserts, puddings, and chewing gum (2,000 ppm). Used in manufacture of artificial rum and fruit essences. No known toxicity.

ISOAMYL ISOVALERATE • A synthetic flavoring agent, clear, colorless, liquid, with an apple odor. Occurs naturally in bananas and peaches. Used in raspberry, strawberry, apple, apricot, banana, cherry, peach, pineapple, honey, rum, walnut, vanilla, and cream soda flavoring for beverages, ice cream, ices, candy, baked goods, gelatin desserts, puddings, jellies, liqueurs, and chewing gum. No known toxicity.

ISOAMYL LAURATE • The ester of isoamyl alcohol and lauric acid (*see* both) used as a synthetic fruit flavoring for beverages, ice cream, ices, candy, and baked goods. No known toxicity.

ISOAMYL NONANOATE • A synthetic chocolate, fruit, and liquor flavoring agent for beverages, ice cream, ices, candy, baked goods, and gelatin desserts. No known toxicity.

ISOAMYL OCTANOATE • A synthetic chocolate, fruit, and liquor flavoring agent for beverages, ice cream, ices, candy, baked goods, and gelatin desserts. No known toxicity.

ISOAMYL PHENYLACETATE • A synthetic butter, chocolate, cocoa, peach, honey, licorice, and anise flavoring agent for beverages, ice cream, ices, candy, baked goods, toppings, and gelatin desserts. No known toxicity.

ISOAMYL PYRUVATE • A synthetic flavoring agent, colorless, liquid, with a pleasant odor. Used in root beer and fruit flavorings for beverages, ice cream, ices, candy, and baked goods. Also used in perfumery and soaps. *See* Salicylic Acid for toxicity.

ISOBORNEOL • A synthetic fruit and spice flavoring agent for beverages, ice cream, ices, candy, baked goods, and chewing gum. *See* Borneol for toxicity.

ISOBORNYL ACETATE • A synthetic pine odor in bath preparations. Also used as a synthetic fruit flavoring for beverages, ice cream, ices, candy, baked goods, and gelatin. No known toxicity.

ISOBUTYL ACETATE • The ester of isobutyl alcohol and acetic acid used as a synthetic flavoring agent. A clear, liquid with a fruity odor. Used in raspberry, strawberry, butter, banana, and grape flavorings for beverages, ice cream, ices, candy, baked goods, gelatin desserts, chewing gum, and icings. It may be mildly irritating to mucous membranes and in high concentrations, it is narcotic.

ISOBUTANE • A propellant. GRAS. *See* Butane.

ISOBUTYL ACETOACETATE • A synthetic berry and fruit flavoring agent for beverages, ice cream, ices, candy, and baked goods. *See* Isobutyl Acetate for toxicity.

ISOBUTYL ANTHRANILATE • A synthetic mandarin, cherry, and grape flavoring agent for beverages, ice cream, ices, candy, baked goods, and chewing gum (1,700 ppm). No known toxicity.

ISOBUTYL BENZOATE • A synthetic berry, cherry, plum, and pineapple flavoring agent for beverages, ice cream, ices, candy, and baked goods. No known toxicity.

ISOBUTYL BUTYRATE • A synthetic berry, apple, banana, pineapple, liquor, and rum flavoring agent for beverages, ice cream, ices, candy, puddings, liquors, and baked goods. No known toxicity.

ISOBUTYL 2-FURANPROPIONATE • A synthetic berry and pineapple flavoring agent for beverages, ice cream, ices, gelatin desserts, chewing gum, and ices. No known toxicity.

ISOBUTYL HEXANOATE • A synthetic apple and pineapple flavoring agent for beverages, ice cream, ices, chewing gum, and baked goods. No known toxicity.

ISOBUTYL ISOBUTYRATE • A synthetic strawberry, butter, fruit, banana, and liquor flavoring agent for beverages, ice cream, ices, candy, gelatin desserts, puddings, liquors, and baked goods. No known toxicity.

ISOBUTYL PABA • *See* Propylparaben.

ISOBUTYL PALMITATE • *See* Palmitic Acid.

ISOBUTYL PARABEN • *See* Parabens.

ISOBUTYL PELARGONATE • The ester of isobutyl alcohol and pelargonic acid (*see* both).

ISOBUTYL PHENYLACETATE • A synthetic butter, caramel, chocolate, fruit, honey, and nut flavoring agent for beverages, ice cream, ices, candy, puddings, maraschino cherries, and baked goods. No known toxicity.

ISOBUTYL PROPIONATE • A synthetic strawberry, butter, peach, and rum flavoring agent for beverages, ice cream, candy, and baked goods. Used in the manufacture of fruit essences. No known toxicity.

ISOBUTYL SALICYLATE • A synthetic flavoring agent, colorless liquid, with an orchid odor. Used in fruit and root beer flavorings for beverages, ice cream, ices, candy, and baked goods. *See* Salicylic Acid for toxicity.

ISOBUTYL STEARATE • The ester of isobutyl alcohol and stearic acid. *See* Fatty Alcohols. Used in waterproof coatings, polishes, face creams, rouges, ointments, soaps, dyes, and lubricants. No known toxicity.

ISOBUTYLENE/ISOPYRENE COPOLYMER • A copolymer of isobutylene and isopyrene monomers derived from petroleum and used as resins. A chewing gum base. Isobutylene is used to produce antioxidants for foods, food supplements, and packaging. Vapors may cause asphyxiation.

ISOBUTYLENE/MALEIC ANHYDRIDE COPOLYMER • A copolymer of isobutylene and maleic anhydride monomers derived from petroleum and used as a resin. Strong irritant.

***a*-ISOBUTYLPHENETHYL ALCOHOL** • A synthetic butter, caramel, chocolate, fruit, and spice flavoring agent for beverages, ice cream, ices, candy, baked goods, liqueurs, and chocolate. *See* Isoamyl Alcohol for toxicity.

ISOBUTRYALDEHYDE • A synthetic flavoring agent which occurs naturally in soy sauce, tea, tobacco, and coffee. It has a pungent odor. Used in berry, butter, caramel, fruit, liquor, and wine flavorings for beverages, ice cream, ices, candy, baked goods, and liquor. No known toxicity.

ISOBUTYRIC ACID • A synthetic flavoring agent which occurs naturally in bay, bay leaves, parsley, and strawberries. It has a pungent odor. Used in butter, butterscotch, fruit, liquor, rum, cheese, nut, vanilla, and cream soda flavorings for beverages, ice cream, ices, candy, baked goods, chewing gum, and margarine. It is a mild irritant. A pungent liquid that smells like butyric acid (*see*).

ISOCETYL ALCOHOL • *See* Cetyl Alcohol.

ISOCETYL ISODECANOATE • *See* Cetyl Alcohol.

ISOCETYL PALMITATE • *See* Cetyl Alcohol and Palmiric Acid.

ISOCETYL STEARATE • *See* Cetyl Alcohol and Stearic Acid.

ISOCETYL STEAROYL STEARATE • The ester of isocetyl alcohol, stearic alcohol and stearic acid. *See* Fatty Acids.

ISOEUGENOL • An aromatic liquid phenol oil obtained from eugenol (*see*) by mixing with an alkali. A synthetic flavoring agent, pale yellow, viscous, with a floral odor. Occurs naturally in mace oil. Used in mint, fruit, spice, cinnamon, and clove flavorings for beverages, ice cream, ices, baked goods, chewing gum (1,000 ppm), and condiments. Used in the manufacture of vanillin (*see*). No known toxicity. Also used in hand creams. Strong irritant. Not recommended.

ISOEUGENYL ACETATE • A synthetic berry, fruit, and spice flavoring agent for beverages, ice cream, ices, candy, baked goods, and chewing gum. No known toxicity.

ISOEUGENYL ETHYL ETHER • A synthetic flavoring agent, white, crystalline, with a spicy, clovelike odor. Used in fruit and vanilla flavorings for beverages, ice cream, ices, candy, and baked goods. No known toxicity.

ISOEUGENYL FORMATE • A synthetic spice flavoring agent used in condiments. *See* Formic Acid for toxicity.

ISOEUGENYL METHYL ETHER • A synthetic raspberry, strawberry, cherry, and clove flavoring agent for beverages, ices, ice cream, candy, baked goods, gelatin desserts and chewing gum. No known toxicity.

ISOEUGENYL PHENYLACETATE • A synthetic fruit, honey, and spice flavoring agent for beverages, ice cream, ices, candy, and baked goods. No known toxicity.

ISOLEUCINE • L and D Forms. An essential amino acid not synthesized within the human body. Isolated commercially from beet sugar, it is a building block of protein. The FDA asked for further study of this nutrient in 1980. Since then, nothing new has been reported. GRAS.

ISONONYL ISONONANOATE • The ester (*see*) produced by the reaction of nonyl alcohol with nonanoic acid. Used in fruit flavorings for lipsticks and mouth washes. Occurs in cocoa, oil of lavender. No known toxicity.

ISOPROPANOL • *See* Isopropyl Alcohol.

ISOPROPYL ALCOHOL • Isopropanol. An antibacterial, solvent, and denaturant (*see*). Solvent for spice oleoresins. Used in hair color rinses, body rubs, hand lotions, after-shave lotions, and many other cosmetics. It is prepared from propylene, which is obtained in the cracking of petroleum. Also used in antifreeze compositions and as a solvent for gums, shellac, and essential oils. Ingestion or inhalation of large quantities of the vapor may cause flushing, headache, dizziness, mental depression, nausea, vomiting, narcosis, anesthesia, and coma. The fatal ingested dose is around a fluid ounce. No known toxicity to the skin.

ISOPROPYL CITRATE • A sequestrant and antioxidant agent used in oleomargarine and salad oils. *See* Citrate Salts for toxicity. The final report to the FDA of the Select Committee on GRAS Substances stated in 1980 that it should continue its GRAS status with no limitations other than good manufacturing practices.

ISOPROPYL FORMATE • Formic Acid. A synthetic berry and melon flavoring agent for beverages, ice cream, candy, and baked goods. *See* Formic Acid for toxicity.

ISOPROPYL HEXANOATE • A synthetic pineapple flavoring agent for beverages, ice cream, ices, candy, and baked goods. No known toxicity.

ISOPROPYL ISOBUTYRATE • A synthetic pineapple flavoring agent for beverages, ice cream, ices, candy, and baked goods. No known toxicity.

ISOPROPYL ISOVALERATE • A synthetic pineapple and nut flavoring agent for beverages, ice cream, ices, candy, and baked goods. No known toxicity.

ISOPROPYL PHENYLACETATE • A synthetic butter, caramel, and honey flavoring agent for beverages, ice cream, ices, candy, and baked goods. No known toxicity.

ISOPROPYL ISOSTEARATE • *See* Stearic Acid and Propylene Glycol.

ISOSTEARIC ACID • A fatty acid (*see*) similar to stearic acid (*see*).

ISOVALERIC ACID • Occurs in valerian, hop oil, tobacco, and other plants. Colorless liquid with a disagreeable taste and odor used in flavors and perfumes. *See* Valeric Acid.

ISOVINYL FORMATE • Formic Acid. A synthetic fruit flavoring agent for beverages, ice cream, ices, candy, and baked goods. *See* Formic Acid for toxicity.

ISOVINYL PROPIONATE • *See* Isovinyl Formate.

IVA • A flavoring for alcoholic beverages from a small American ground pine that smells like skin. No known toxicity.

J

JAGUAR GUM • *See* Guar Gum.

JAPAN WAX • Japan Tallow. Sumac Wax. Vegetable Wax. Japan Tallow. A fat squeezed from the fruit of a tree grown in Japan and China. Pale yellow flat cakes, disks, or squares, with a fatlike rancid odor and taste. Used as a substitute for beeswax in cosmetics and in food packaging; also floor waxes and polishes. It is related to poison ivy and may cause allergic contact dermatitis. The final report to the FDA of the Select Committee on GRAS Substances stated in 1980 that there were insufficient relevant biological and other studies upon which to base an evaluation of it when it is used as a food ingredient. It remains GRAS for packaging.

JASMINE • Oil and Spiritus (alcoholic solution). The oil is extracted from a tropical shrub with extremely fragrant white flowers and is used in raspberry, strawberry, floral, and cherry flavorings for beverages, ice cream, ices, candy, baked goods, gelatin desserts, chewing gum, and jelly. The spiritus is used in blackberry, strawberry, and fruit flavoring for beverages, ice cream, ices, candy, baked goods, gelatin, and cherries. Used in perfumes. May cause allergic reactions. GRAS.

JASMINE ABSOLUTE • Oil of jasmine obtained by extraction with volatile or nonvolatile solvents. Sometimes called the "natural perfume" because the oil is not subjected to heat and distilled oils. *See* Absolute. May cause allergic reactions.

JASMONYL • *See* 1,3-Nonanediol Acetate.

JUNIPER • Extract, Oil, and Berries. A flavoring from the dried ripe fruit of trees grown in Northern Europe, Asia, and North America. The greenish yellow extract is used in liquor, root beer, sarsaparilla, wintergreen, and birch beer flavorings for beverages, ice cream, ices, candy, and baked goods. The oil is used in berry, cola, pineapple, gin, rum, whiskey, root beer, ginger, and meat flavorings for beverages, ice cream, ices, candy, baked goods, gelatin desserts, chewing gum, meats, and liquors. The berries are used in gin flavoring for condiments and liquors. Juniper is used also in fumigating and was formerly a diuretic for reducing body water. No known toxicity. GRAS.

K

KADAYA • *See* Karaya Gum.

KAOLIN • China Clay. Used as an anticaking agent in food. Aids in the covering ability of face powder and in absorbing oil secreted by the skin. Used in baby powder, bath powder, face masks, foundation cake makeup, liquid powder, face powder, dry rouge, and emollients. Originally obtained from Kaoling Hill in Kiangsi Province in Southeast China. Essentially a hydrated aluminum silicate (*see*). It is a white or yellowish-white mass or powder, insoluble in water and absorbent. Used medicinally to treat intestinal disorders, but in large doses it may cause obstructions, perforations, or granuloma (tumor) formation. It is also used in the manufacture of porcelain, pottery, bricks, and color lakes (*see* FD and C Lakes). No known toxicity for the skin. The final report to the FDA of the Select Committee on GRAS Substances stated in 1980 that it should continue its GRAS status with no limitations other than good manufacturing practices. *See* also Clays.

KARAYA GUM • Kaday. Katilo. Kullo. Kuterra. Sterculia. Indian Tragacanth. Mucara. The exudate of a tree found in India. The finely ground white powder is used in gelatins and in gumdrops, prepared ices, and ice cream, and as a filler for lemon custard. Also a citrus and spice flavoring agent for beverages, ice cream, ices (1,300 ppm), candy, meats, baked goods, toppings (3,500 ppm), and emulsions (18,000 ppm). Used instead of the more expensive gum tragacanth (*see*) and in bulk laxatives. Reevaluated by the FDA in 1976 and found to be GRAS in the following percentages: 0.3 percent for frozen dairy desserts and mixes; 0.02 percent for milk products; 0.9 percent for soft candy; and 0.002 for all other food categories.

KATILO • *See* Karaya Gum.

KAUTSCHIN • *See* Limonene.

KELP • Recovered from the giant Pacific marine plant *Macrocystis pyriferae*. Used as seasonings or flavoring and to provide iodine when used in dietary foods. It has many minerals that are associated with sea water and, as a result, is very high in sodium. The Japanese report that kelp reduced normal thyroid function, probably because of its iodine content. The FDA has also reported that high levels of arsenic have been found in people who eat a lot of kelp as a vegetable. The final report to the FDA of the Select Committee on GRAS Substances stated in 1980 that it should continue its GRAS status with no limitations other than good manufacturing practices.

KETONAROME • *See* Methylcyclopentenolone.

KETONE C-7 • *See* 2-Heptanone.

2-KETOPROPIONALDEHYDE • *See* Pyruvaldehyde.

a-KETOPROPIONALDEHYDE • *See* Pyruvic Acid.

KIDNEY BEAN EXTRACT • Extract of *Phaseolus Vulgaris,* the beans were used as a nutrient and a laxative by the American Indians. No known toxicity.

KOLA NUT EXTRACT • Guru Nut. A natural extract from the brownish seed, about the size of a chestnut, produced by trees in Africa, West Indies, and Brazil. Contains caffeine (*see*). Used in butter, caramel, chocolate, cocoa, coffee, cola, walnut, and root beer flavorings for beverages, ice cream, ices, candy, and baked goods. Has been used to treat epilepsy. GRAS.

KRAMERIA EXTRACT • Rhatany Extract. A synthetic flavoring derived from the dried root of either of two American shrubs. Used in raspberry, bitters, fruit, and rum flavorings. Used in cosmetics as an astringent. Low oral toxicity. Large doses may produce gastric distress. Can cause tumors and death after injection, but not after ingestion.

KULLO • *See* Karaya Gum.

KUTEERAL • *See* Karaya Gum.

L

LABDANUM • Absolute, Oil, and Oleoresin. A synthetic musk flavoring agent. It is a volatile oil obtained by steam distillation from gum extracted from various rockrose shrubs. Golden yellow, viscous, with a strong balsamic odor and a bitter taste. The absolute is used in raspberry, fruit, and vanilla flavorings for beverages, ice cream, ices, candy, baked goods, gelatin desserts, and chewing gum. The oil is used in fruit and spice flavorings for beverages, ice cream, ices, candy, and baked goods. The oleoresin (*see*) is used in fruit and vanilla flavorings for beverages, ice cream, ices, candy, and baked goods. Also used in perfumes, especially as a fixative. No known toxicity.

LABRADOR TEA EXTRACT • Hudson's Bay Tea. Marsh Tea. The extract of the dried flowering plant or young shoots of *Ledum palustre* or *Ledum groelandicum,* a tall, resinous evergreen shrub found in bogs and swamps and moist meadows. Brewed like tea, it has a pleasing odor and is stimulating. It was used by the Indians and settlers as a tonic supposed to purify blood. It was also employed to treat wounds. The *Ledum palustre* contains, among other things, tannin and valeric acid (*see* both). No known toxicity.

LACTASE ENZYME PREPARATION FROM *KLYVEROMYCES LAC-TIS* • An enzyme that breaks down lactose (*see*). No known toxicity. GRAS.

LACTIC ACID • Butyl Lactate. Ethyl Lactate. Odorless, colorless, usually a syrupy product normally present in blood and muscle tissue as a product of the metabolism of glucose and glycogen. Present in sour milk, beer, sauerkraut, pickles, and other food products made by bacterial fermentation. Also an acidulant. It is produced commercially by fermentation of whey, cornstarch, potatoes, and molasses. Used as an acidulant in beverages, candy, olives, dried egg whites, cottage cheese, confections, bread, rolls, buns, cheese products, frozen desserts, sherbets, ices, fruit jelly, butter, preserves, jams (sufficient amounts may be added to compensate for the deficiency of fruit acidity), and in the brewing industry. Also used in infant-feeding formulas. Used in blackberry, butter, butterscotch, lime, chocolate, fruit, walnut, spice, and cheese flavorings for beverages, ice cream, ices, candy, baked goods, gelatins, puddings, chewing gum, toppings, pickles, and olives (24,000 ppm). Also used in skin fresheners. It is caustic in concentrated solutions when taken internally or applied to the skin. In cosmetic products, it may cause stinging in sensitive people, particularly in fair-skinned women. The final report to the FDA of the Select Committee on GRAS Substances stated in 1980 that it should continue its GRAS status with no limitations other than good manufacturing practices.

LACTIC YEASTS • Obtained from milk. *See* Lactic Acid.

LACTOFLAVIN • *See* Riboflavin.

LACTOSE • Milk Sugar. Saccharum Lactin. D-Lactose. A slightly sweet-tasting, colorless sugar present in the milk of mammals (humans have 6.7 percent and cows 4.3 percent). Occurs as a white powder or crystalline mass as a by-product of the cheese industry. Produced from whey (*see* Whey Protein). It is inexpensive and is widely used in the food industry as a culture medium, such as in souring milk, and as a humectant (*see*) and nutrient in infants' or debilitated patients' formulae. Also used as a medical diuretic and laxative. Used widely as a base in eye lotions. Stable in air but readily absorbs odors. It is generally nontoxic. However, it was found to cause tumors when injected under the skin of mice in 50-milligram doses per kilogram of body weight.

LACTYLIC ESTERS OF FATTY ACIDS • Emulsifiers used in food products. *See* Esters and Fatty Acids.

LACTYLIC STEARATE • Salt of stearic acid (*see*) used as a dough conditioner to add volume to keep baked products soft; it makes bread less sticky. *See* Stearic Acid for toxicity.

LADY'S MANTLE EXTRACT • From the dried leaves and flowering shoots of *Achemilla Vulgaris*. A common European herb covered with spreading hairs, it has been used for centuries by herbalists to concoct love potions.

LAKES, COLOR • A lake is an organic pigment prepared by precipitating a soluble color with a form of aluminum, calcium, barium potassium, strontium, or zirconium, which then makes the colors insoluble. Not all colors are suitable for making lakes.

LAMINARIA • Seaweed from which algin is extracted. *See* Alginates. GRAS.

LANOLIN • Wool Fat. Wool Wax. A product of the oil glands of sheep. Used as a chewing gum base component. Used in lipstick, liquid powder, mascara, nail polish remover, protective oil, rouge, eye shadow, foundation creams, foundation cake makeup, hair conditioners, eye creams, cold creams, brilliantine hairdressings, ointment bases, and emollients. A water-absorbing base material and a natural emulsifier, it absorbs and holds water to the skin. Chemically a wax instead of a fat. Contains about 25 to 30 percent water. Advertisers have found that the words "contains lanolin" help to sell a product and have promoted it as being able to "penetrate the skin better than other oils," although there is little scientific proof of this. Lanolin has been found to be a common skin sensitizer causing allergic contact skin rashes. It will not prevent or cure wrinkles and will not stop hair loss. It is not used in pure form today because of its allergy-causing potential. Products derived from it are less likely to cause allergic reactions.

LANTANA • *See* Oregano.

LARCH GUM • Larch Turpentine. Venice Turpentine. Oleoresin (*see*) from *Larix decidua Mill.*, grown in middle and southern Europe. A yellow, sometimes greenish, tenacious, thick liquid with a pleasant, aromatic odor, it has a hot, somewhat bitter taste. It becomes hard and brittle on prolonged exposure. It is used as a stabilizer, thickener, and texturizer. No known toxicity.

LARD AND LARD OILS • Pork Fat and Oils. It is the purified internal fat from the abdomen of the hog. It is a soft, white, unctuous mass, with a slight characteristic odor and a bland taste. It is used in packaging and in chewing gum bases. Easily absorbed by the skin, it is used as a lubricant, emollient, and base in shaving creams, soaps, and various cosmetic creams. Insoluble in water. When lard was fed to laboratory animals in doses of from 2 to 25 percent of the diet, the male mice had a shortened life span and increased osteoarthritis. This was thought to be due to the large amounts of fat and not specifically to lard. The final report to the FDA of the Select Committee on GRAS Substances stated in 1980 that it should continue its GRAS status with no limitations other than good manufacturing practices.

LARD GLYCERIDE • *See* Lard.

LARIXINIC ACID • *See* Malitol.

LAUREL • The fresh berries and leaf extract of the laurel tree. The berries are used as a flavoring for beverages and the leaf extract is a spice flavoring for vegetables. No known toxicity. GRAS.

LAURIC ACID • *n*-Dodcanoic Acid. A common constituent of vegetable fats, especially coconut oil and laurel oil. A white, glossy powder, insoluble in water, and used in the manufacture of miscellaneous flavors for beverages, ice cream, candy, baked goods, gelatins, and puddings. Its derivatives are widely used as a base in the manufacture of soaps, detergents, and lauryl alcohol (*see* Fatty Alcohols) because of their foaming properties. Has a slight odor of bay and makes large copious bubbles when in soap. A mild irritant but not a sensitizer.

LAURIC ALDEHYDE • *See* Lauric Acid.

LAUROSTEARIC ACID • *See* Lauric Acid.

LAURYL ALCOHOL, SYNTHETIC • *See* Fatty Alcohols.

LAVANDIN OIL • A flavoring from a hybrid related to the lavender plant, pale-yellow liquid with a camphor-lavender smell. Used in berry and citrus flavorings for beverages, ice cream, ices, candy, baked goods, and chewing gum. Used in soaps and perfumes. No known toxicity. GRAS.

LAVENDER OIL • The colorless liquid extracted from the fresh, flowery tops of the plant. Smells like lavender, and used in ginger ale flavoring for beverages. *Lavender absolute* is a fruit flavoring for beverages, ice cream, ices, candy, and baked goods. *Lavender concrete* is also a fruit flavoring for beverages, ice cream, ices, candy, and baked goods. Lavender was once used to break up stomach gas. Used in skin fresheners, powders, shaving preparations, mouthwashes, dentifrices, and perfumes. It can cause allergic reactions and has been found to cause adverse skin reactions when the skin is exposed to sunlight. GRAS.

LEAF ALCOHOL • *See* 3-Hexen-1-ol.

LEAVENING • From the Latin *levare,* "to raise." It is a substance, such as yeast, acting to produce fermentation in dough or liquid. Leavening serves to lighten or enliven, such as baking soda when it produces a gas that lightens dough or batter.

LECITHIN • From the Greek, meaning "egg yolk." A natural antioxidant and emollient composed of units of choline, phosphoric acid, fatty acids, and glycerin (*see* all). Commercially isolated from eggs, soybeans, corn, and egg yolk and used as an antioxidant in prepared breakfast cereal, candy, sweet chocolate, bread, rolls, buns, and oleomargarine. Egg yolk is 8 to 9 percent lecithin. Hydroxylated lecithin is a defoaming component in yeast and beet sugar production. Lecithin with or without phosphatides (components of fat) is an emulsifier for sweet chocolate, milk chocolate, bakery products, frozen desserts, oleomargarine, rendered animal fat, or a combination of vegetable-animal fats. Also used in eye creams, lipsticks, liquid powders, hand creams and lotions, soaps, and many other cosmetics. Also a natural emulsifier and spreading agent. Nontoxic. The final report to the FDA of the Select Committee on GRAS Substances stated in 1980 that it should continue its GRAS status with no limitations other than good manufacturing practices.

LEMON • Extract and Oil.   The common fresh fruit. The extract is used in lemon flavorings for beverages, ice cream, ices, candy, baked goods, and icings. Lemon oil is a blueberry, loganberry, strawberry, butter, grapefruit, lemon, lime, orange, cola, coconut, honey, wine, rum, root beer, and ginger ale flavoring for beverages, ice cream, ices, candy, baked goods, gelatin desserts, chewing gum (1,900 ppm), condiments, meats, syrups, icings, and cereals. Lemon oil is suspected of being a cancer-causing agent. GRAS.

LEMON BALM • Sweet Balm. Garden Balm.   Used in perfumes and as a soothing facial treatment. An Old World mint cultivated for its lemon-flavored, fragrant leaves. Often considered a weed, it has been used by herbalists as a medicine and to flavor foods and medicines. It reputedly imparts long life. Also used to treat earache and toothache. Nontoxic.

LEMON EXTRACT • *See* Lemon Oil.

LEMON JUICE • *See* Lemon.

LEMON OIL • Cedro Oil.   Used in perfumes and food flavorings, it is the volatile oil expressed from the fresh peel. A pale yellow to deep yellow, it has a characteristic odor and taste of the outer part of fresh lemon peel. It can cause an allergic reaction and has been suspected of being a cancer-causing co-agent.

LEMONGRASS OIL • Indian Oil of Verbena.   Used in perfumes, especially those added to soap. It is the volatile oil distilled from the leaves of lemon grasses. A yellowish or reddish brown liquid, it has a strong odor of verbena. Also used in insect repellent. Used in lemon, and fruit flavorings for beverages, ice cream, ices, candy, baked goods, gelatin desserts, and chewing gum. Death reported when taken internally, and autopsy showed lining of the intestines was severely damaged. Skin toxicity unknown.

LEMON OIL, TERPENELESS • A lemon fruit, ginger, and ginger ale flavoring agent for beverages, ice cream, ices, candy, baked goods, gelatin desserts, chewing gum, and toppings. Terpene, which is removed to improve flavor, is a class of unsaturated hydrocarbons. *See* Lemon for toxicity.

LEMON PEEL • From the outer rind, the extract is used as a flavor in medicines and in beverages, confectionery, and cooking. *See* Lemon for toxicity.

LEMON VERBENA EXTRACT • Extract of *Lippia Citriodoral. See* Lemongrass Oil.

LEUCINE • L and DL forms. An essential amino acid (*see*) for human nutrition not manufactured in the body. It is isolated commercially from gluten, casein, skin, and hair. It has a sweet taste. The FDA says it needs further study. GRAS.

LICORICE • Liquorice. Glycyrrhizin. Monoammonium Glycrrhizinate. Ammoniated Glyceryrrhizin. Extract, Extract Powder, and Root. A black substance derived from a plant, *Glycyrrhiza glabra,* "sweet root" belonging to the *Leguminosae* and cultured from Southern Europe to Central Asia. It is used in fruit, licorice, anise, maple, and root beer flavorings for beverages, ice cream, ices, candy (29,000 ppm), baked goods, gelatin, chewing gum, and syrups. Licorice root is used in licorice and root beer flavorings for beverages, candy, baked goods, chewing gum (3,200 ppm), tobacco, and medicines. Some people known to have eaten licorice candy regularly and generously had raised blood pressure, headaches, and muscle weakness. It can cause asthma, intestinal upsets and contact dermatitis. No known skin toxicity. Tentatively affirmed as GRAS in 1983.

LIGHT GREEN • *See* FD and C Green No. 2.

LIME OIL • A natural flavoring extracted from the fruit of a tropical tree. Colorless to greenish. Used in grapefruit, lemon, lemon-lime, lime, orange, cola, fruit, rum, nut, and ginger flavorings for beverages, ice cream, ices, candy, baked goods, gelatin desserts, chewing gum (3,100 ppm), and condiments. Terpeneless (*see* Lemon Oil), lime oil is used in lemon, lime, lemon-lime, cola, pineapple, ginger, and ginger ale flavorings for beverages, ice cream, ices, candy, baked goods, gelatin desserts, chewing gum, and syrups. Also used in perfumery and as an antiseptic. A source of Vitamin C. Can cause an adverse reaction when skin applied with lime oil is exposed to sunlight.

LIMONENE • D, L, and DL forms. A synthetic flavoring agent that occurs naturally in star anise, buchu leaves, caraway, celery, oranges, coriander, cumin, cardamon, sweet fennel, common fennel, mace, marigold, oil of lavandin, oil of lemon, oil of mandarin, peppermint, petigrain oil, pimento oil, orange leaf (absolute), orange peel (sweet oil), origanum oil, black pepper, peels of citrus, macrocarpa bunge, and hops oil. Used in lime, fruit, and spice flavorings for beverages, ice cream, ices, candy, baked goods, gelatin desserts, and chewing gum. A skin irritant and sensitizer. GRAS.

LINALOE WOOD OIL • Bois de Rose Oil. A natural flavoring agent that is the colorless to yellow volatile essential oil distilled from a Mexican tree. It has a pleasant flowery scent and is soluble in most fixed oils. Used in berry, citrus, fruit, liquor, and ginger flavorings for beverages, ice cream, ices, candy, baked goods, and liquors. Also used in perfumes. May cause allergic reactions.

LINALOOL • Linalol. A synthetic flavoring that occurs naturally in basil, bois de rose oil, cassia, coriander, cocoa, grapefruit, grapefruit oil, oranges, peaches, tea, bay and bay-leaf extract, ginger, lavender, laurel leaves, and other oils. Used in flavorings such as blueberry, chocolate, and lemon. Used in perfumes and soaps instead of bergamot or French lavender. It is a fragrant, colorless liquid. May cause allergic reactions.

LINALYL ACETATE • A colorless, fragrant liquid, slightly soluble in water, it is the most valuable constituent of bergamot and lavender oils, which are used in perfumery. It occurs naturally in basil, jasmine oil, lavandin oil, lavender oil, and lemon oil. It has a strong floral scent. Colorless, it is used in berry, citrus, peach, pear, and ginger flavorings for beverages, ice cream, ices, candy, baked goods, gelatin desserts, and chewing gum. No known toxicity. GRAS.

LINALYL ANTHRANILATE • A synthetic berry, citrus, fruit, and grape flavoring agent for beverages, ice cream, ices, candy, and baked goods. No known toxicity.

LINALYL BENZOATE • A synthetic flavoring, brownish yellow, with a roselike odor. Used in berry, citrus, fruit, and peach flavorings agent for beverages, ice cream, ices, candy, gelatin desserts, and baked goods. No known toxicity.

LINALYL CINNAMATE • A synthetic loganberry, floral, rose, fruit, grape, and honey flavoring agent for beverages, ice cream, ices, candy, and baked goods. No known toxicity.

LINALYL FORMATE • Formic Acid. A synthetic flavoring agent that occurs naturally in oil of lavandin. Used in berry, apple, apricot, peach, and pineapple flavorings for beverages, ice cream, ices, candy, and baked goods. *See* Formic Acid for toxicity.

LINALYL HEXANOATE • A synthetic fruit flavoring agent for beverages, ice cream, ices, candy, and baked goods. No known toxicity.

LINALYL ISOBUTRYATE • A synthetic flavoring, colorless to slightly yellow, with a fruity odor. Used in berry, citrus, fruit, banana, black currant, cherry, pear, pineapple, plum, nut, and spice flavorings for beverages, ice cream, ices, candy, and baked goods. No known toxicity.

LINALYL ISOVALERATE • A synthetic flavoring, colorless to slightly yellow, with a fruity odor. Used in loganberry, apple, apricot, peach, pear, and plum flavorings for beverages, ice cream, ices, candy, gelatin desserts, and baked goods. No known toxicity.

LINALYL OCTANOATE • A synthetic citrus, rose and apple, pineapple, and honey flavoring agent for beverages, ice cream, ices, candy, gelatin desserts, and baked goods. No known toxicity.

LINALYL PROPIONATE • A synthetic currant, orange, banana, pear, and pineapple flavoring agent for beverages, ice cream, ices, candy, and baked goods. No known toxicity.

LINDEN FLOWERS • A natural flavoring extract from the flowers of the tree grown in Europe and the United States. Used in raspberry and vermouth flavorings for beverages (2,000 ppm). Also used in fragrances. No known toxicity. GRAS.

LINOLEIC ACID • An essential fatty acid (*see*) prepared from edible fats and oils. Component of Vitamin F and a major constituent of many vegetable oils, for example, cottonseed and soybean. Used in emulsifiers and vitamins. Large doses can cause nausea and vomiting. When given in large doses to rats, weight loss and progressive secondary anemia developed. No known skin toxicity and, in fact, may have emollient properties. The final report to the FDA of the Select Committee on GRAS Substances stated in 1980 that it should continue its GRAS status with no limitations other than good manufacturing practices.

LINSEED OIL • Golden-amber or brown oil with a peculiar odor and gland taste. Used in paints, varnishes, as a film, in printing inks, and for its protein. *See* Flaxseed.

LIPASE • Any class of enzymes that break down fat to glycerol and fatty acids (*see* both). It is used in the manufacture of cheeses. No known toxicity.

LOCUST BEAN GUM • St. John's Bread. Carob Bean Gum. A thickener and stabilizer in cosmetics and foods. Also used in depilatories. A natural flavor extract from the seed of the carob tree cultivated in the Mediterranean area. The history of the carob tree dates back more than two thousand years when the ancient Egyptians used locust bean gum as an adhesive in mummy binding. It is alleged that the ''locust'' (through confusion of the locusts with carob) and wild honey, which sustained John the Baptist in the wilderness, was from this plant, thus the name St. John's Bread. The carob pods are used as feed for stock today because of their high protein content. They are also eaten by some health food enthusiasts for the same purpose. They are also used as a thickener and stabilizer (*see* Gum). Carob bean extract is used in raspberry, bitters, butter, butterscotch, caramel, chocolate, cherry, brandy, wine, maple, root beer, spice, vanilla, cream soda, and grape flavorings for beverages, ice cream, ices, candy, baked goods, gelatin desserts (600 ppm), icings, and toppings (1,000 ppm). A University of Minnesota pediatric cardiologist reported in 1981 that locust bean may lower blood cholesterol levels. Dr. James Zavoral and associates found that 28 adults and children with histories of familial hypercholesterolemia were fed food products rich in locust bean gum. Some of those included breads, cookies, cracker, and "Tater Tots." After four weeks on the special diets their cholesterol dropped 10 percent and after six weeks, 20 percent. The final report to the FDA of the Select Committee on GRAS Substances stated in 1980 that it should continue its GRAS status with limitations on amounts that can be added to food.

LOVAGE • Smallage. Flavoring obtained from the root of an aromatic herb native to southern Europe and grown in monastery gardens centuries ago for medicine and food flavoring. It has a hot, sharp, biting taste. The yellow-brown oil is extracted from the root or other parts of the herb. It has a reputation for improving health and inciting love; Czechoslovakian girls reportedly wear it in a bag around their necks when dating boys. It supposedly has deodorant properties when added to bath water. Used in bitters, maple, and walnut flavorings for beverages, ice cream, ices, candy, baked goods, chewing gum, and table syrups. The extract is used in berry, butter, butterscotch, caramel, coffee, fruit, maple, meat, black walnut, and spice flavorings for the same foods as above, plus condiments and icings. The oil, yellowish-brown and aromatic, is used in butter, butterscotch, caramel, coffee, fruit, licorice, liquor, maple, nut, walnut, and spice flavorings for the same foods as the extract. No known toxicity.

LUPULIN EXTRACT • Lupine. Hops. Extract of *Lupinus alba*. The seed has been used as a food since earliest times. A natural flavoring agent from a plant (*Humulus lupulis*) grown in Europe, Asia, and North America. Used in beer brewing. Formerly used as aromatic bitters and as a sedative. At one time veterinary usage was recommended for treatment of nymphomania. It produces a light blue dye. No known toxicity. GRAS.

LUTEIN • *See* Xanthophyll.

LYCOPENE • Red crystals, insoluble in water. The main pigment of tomato, paprika, and rose hips. No known toxicity.

LYSINE • L Form. An essential amino acid (*see*) isolated from casein, fibrin, or blood. It is used for food enrichment for wheat-based foods. Lysine improves their protein quality and results in improved growth and tissue synthesis. Employed in the fortification of specialty bread and cereal mixes up to 0.25 percent to 0.5 percent of the weight of flour. On the FDA list for further study since 1980. GRAS.

L-LYSINE • *See* Lysine.

M

MACE • Oil and Oleoresin. Obtained by steam distillation from the ripe, dried seed of the nutmeg. Colorless to pale yellow, with the taste and odor of nutmeg. Used in bitters, meat, and spice flavorings for beverages, ice cream, ices, candy, baked goods, condiments, and meats (2,000 ppm). The oil is used in chocolate, cocoa, coconut, cola, fruit, nut, spice, and ginger ale flavorings for beverages, ice cream, ices, candy, baked goods, chewing gum, condiments, and meats. The oleoresin (*see*) is used in sausage and spice flavorings for baked goods, condiments, meats, and pickles. *See* Nutmeg for toxicity. The final report to the FDA of the Select Committee on GRAS Substances stated in 1980 that while no evidence in the available information on it demonstrates a hazard to the public at current use levels, uncertainties exist, requiring that additional studies be conducted. The FDA continued the GRAS status while tests were being completed evaluated in 1980. Nothing new has been reported by the FDA since then.

MAGNESIUM • Magnesium Acetate. Magnesium Phosphate, Magnesium Sulfate, Magnesium Oxide, Magnesium Silicate, Magnesium Chloride, Magnesium Carbonate, Magnesium Cyclamate, Magnesium Stearate, and Magnesium Hydroxide. A silver-white, light, malleable metal that occurs abundantly in nature and is widely used in combination with various chemicals as a powder. *Magnesium acetate* is used as a buffer and neutralizer in nonalcoholic beverages. GRAS. *Magnesium phosphate,* a white, odorless powder, and *magnesium sulfate,* are used as mineral supplements for food. Recommended Daily Allowances, according to the National Academy of Sciences, are 40 milligrams for infants; 100 to 300 milligrams for children; and 350 milligrams for adult males and females. *Magnesium sulfate* is used also as a corrective in the brewing industry and for fertilizers. *Magnesium oxide,* a white, bulky powder, is an alkali used as a neutralizer in frozen dairy products, butter, cacao products, and canned peas. *Magnesium silicate,* a fine, white, odorless and tasteless powder, is used in table salt and vanilla powder as an anticaking agent. In table salt it is limited to 2 percent. *Magnesium chloride* is used for color retention and as a firming agent in canned peas. *Magnesium carbonate* is used as an alkali for sour cream, butter, ice cream, cacao products, and canned peas. It is also used as a drying agent and an anticaking agent. *Magnesium carbonate* is also used as a perfume carrier and coloring agent. Used in baby powder, bath powder, tooth powders, face masks, liquid powders, face powders, dry rouge. It is a silver-white, very crystalline salt that occurs in nature as magnetite or dolomite. Can be prepared artificially and is also used in paint, printing ink, table salt, and as an antacid. Nontoxic to the intact skin but may cause irritation when applied to abraded skin. *Magnesium chloride* is used as a buffer and neutralizer in nonalcoholic beverages and is used for color retention and as a firming agent. GRAS. *Magnesium citrate* is a buffer and neutralizer in nonalcoholic beverages. *Magnesium cyclamate* was banned in 1969 as an artificial sweetener. *Magnesium hydroxide* is used as an alkali in dentifrices and skin creams, in canned peas, and as a drying agent and color-retention agent for improved gelling in the manufacture of cheese. Slightly alkaline crystalline compound obtained by hydration of magnesium or precipitation of seawater by lime. Toxic when inhaled. Harmless to skin and in fact soothes it. *Magnesium stearate,* a soft, white powder, tasteless, odorless, and insoluble in water, is used as a dietary supplement, in food packaging, and as an emulsifying agent in cosmetics. Magnesium was reevaluated by the FDA in 1976 as not harmful in presently used current levels. However the World Health Organization Food Committee recommends further study of magnesium silicate because kidney damage in dogs has been reported upon ingestion. Magnesium carbonate, chloride, sulfate, stearate, phosphate, and silicate are all GRAS according to the final report to the FDA of the Select Committee on GRAS Substances and they should continue their GRAS status with no limitations other than good manufacturing practices.

MAGNESIUM GLUCONATE • A buffering agent in soda water. *See* Magnesium.

MAGNESIUM LACTATE • Buffering and neutralizing agent in cacao products and in canned peas. *See* Magnesium.

MAIDENHAIR FERN • Venus Hair. Extract of the leaves of the fern *Adiantum capillus-veneris*. Used as a flavoring in alcoholic beverages only and to soothe irritated skin in herbal creams.

MALEIC HYDRAZIDE • Regulates the growth of unwanted "suckers" on about 90 percent of the United States tobacco crop. It is also applied to 10 to 15 percent of domestic potatoes and onions to prevent sprouting after harvest. It is highly toxic to humans and has produced central nervous system disturbances and liver damage in experimental animals. It has led to liver and other tumors in some mice. However, other studies, including one done for the National Cancer Institute and published in 1969, show no carcinogenic effects from it. It has produced genetic damage in plant and animal systems, a fact that often signals a cancer-causing effect.

MALIC ACID • A colorless, crystalline compound with a strong acid taste that occurs naturally in a wide variety of fruits, including apples and cherries. A flavoring agent and aid in aging wine. It has a strong acid taste. Used as an alkali in frozen dairy products, beverages, baked goods, confections, fruit, butter, and jelly and jam preserves "in amount sufficient to compensate for the deficiency of fruit in artificially sweetened fruit." An alkali and antioxidant in cosmetics and ingredient of hair lacquer. Irritating to the skin and can cause allergic reaction when used in hair lacquers. The final report to the FDA of the Select Committee on GRAS Substances stated in 1980 that it should continue its GRAS status with no limitations other than good manufacturing practices.

MALLOW EXTRACT • From the herb family. A moderate purplish-red that is paler than magenta rose. Used in coloring and also a a source of pectin (*see*). No known toxicity.

MALT EXTRACT • Extracted from barley that has been allowed to germinate, then heated to destroy vitality, and dried. It contains sugars, proteins, and salts from barley. The extract is mixed with water and allowed to solidify. It is used as a nutrient and in cosmetics as a texturizer. it is also widely used in the brewing industry. No known toxicity. GRAS.

MALTITOL • Obtained by the hydrogenate from maltose (*see*).

MALTODEXTRIN • The sugar obtained by hydrolysis of starch. A combination of maltol (*see*) and dextrin (*see*) used as a texturizer and flavor enhancer in candies, particularly chocolate. No known toxicity. The final report to the FDA of the Select Committee on GRAS Substances stated in 1980 that it should continue its GRAS status with no limitations other than good manufacturing practices.

MALTOL • A white, crystalline powder with a butterscotch odor, found in the bark of young larch trees, pine seeds, chicory, wood tars, and in the roasted malt. It imparts a "freshly baked" odor and flavor to bread and cakes. Used as a synthetic chocolate, coffee, fruit, maple, nut, and vanilla flavoring agent for beverages, ice cream, ices, candy, baked goods, gelatin desserts, chewing gum, and jelly. No known toxicity.

MALTOSE • Malt Sugar. Colorless crystals derived from malt extract and used as a nutrient, sweetener, culture medium and stabilizer. It is soluble in water and is used as a sweetener for diabetics. It is also used in brewing and as a stabilizer. It is nontoxic, but it has been reported to cause tumors when injected under the skin of mice in doses of 500 milligrams per kilogram of body weight.

MANDARIN OIL • Obtained by expression of the peel of a ripe mandarin orange. Clear, dark orange to reddish yellow, with a pleasant orangelike odor. It is an orange, tangerine, cherry, and grape flavoring for beverages, ice cream, ices, candy, baked goods, chewing gum, and gelatin desserts.

MANGANESE SOURCES: • Manganese Acetate, Manganese Carbonate, Manganese Chloride, Manganese Citrate, Manganese Gluconate, Manganese Sulfate, Manganese Glycerophosphate, Manganese Hypophophite, and Manganese Oxide. A mineral supplement first isolated in 1774, it occurs in minerals and in minute quantities in animals, plants, and in water. Many forms are used in dyeing. Manganous salts are activators of enzymes and are necessary to the development of strong bones. They are used as nutrients and as dairy substitutes. Toxicity occurs by inhalation. Symptoms include languor, sleepiness, wakefulness, emotional disturbances, and Parkinsonlike symptoms. *Manganese chloride, citrate, glycerophosphate,* and *hypophosphite* are all considered GRAS according to the final report of the Select Committee on GRAS Substances and should continue their GRAS status as nutrients with no limitations other than good manufacturing practices. However, the Select Committee has conceded that there is not enough known about *manganese oxide* upon which to base an evaluation when it is used as a food ingredient.

MANGANOUS OXIDE • A dietary supplement derived by reduction of the dioxide in hydrogen or by heating the carbonate without air. It is also used in ceramics, paints, animal feeds, fertilizers and the bleaching of tallows. GRAS.

MANNITOL • Widespread in plants but mostly prepared from seaweed, it is white, crystalline solid, odorless, and sweet tasting. It's used as a texturizer in chewing gum and candy, up to 5 percent. It has been used as a sweetener in ''sugar-free'' products but has calories and carbohydrates. It's also used as a dusting or antisticking agent in a number of food products, a humectant in hand creams and lotions, and as an emulsifier and antioxidant in hair-grooming products. It is under study by the FDA because it can cause gastrointestinal disturbances and may worsen kidney disease. It is considered permitted on an interim basis. In 1982, the FDA reported that mannitol does not cause cancer in rats. GRAS.

MANNOSE • A carbohydrate occurring in some plants. It has a sweet taste.

MAPLE, MOUNTAIN • Flavoring. No known toxicity.

MARGARINE • Oleomargarine. A butter substitute made from animal or vegetable fats or oils. If oils are used they are ''hardened'' into fats by the process of hydrogenation (*see*). Skimmed milk, water, salt, coloring matter (*see* carotene), artificial flavors, lecithin (*see*), and small amounts of vitamins are usually added. By federal regulations, margarine contains at least 80 percent fat. No known toxicity.

MARIGOLD, POT • A natural plant extract. The oil is used in various flavorings for beverages, ice cream, ices, candy, and baked goods. No known toxicity. *See* Tagetes. GRAS.

MARJORAM, POT • Sweet Marjoram. The natural extract of the flowers and leaves of two varieties of the fragrant marjoram plant. The *oleoresin* (*see*) is used in sausage and spice flavorings for condiments and meats. The *seed* is used in sausage and spice flavorings for meats (3,500 ppm) and condiments. Sweet marjoram is used in sausage and spice flavorings for beverages, baked goods (2,000 ppm), condiments, meats, and soups. The *sweet oil* is used in vermouth, wine, and spice flavorings for beverages, ice creams, ices, candy, baked goods, and condiments. Also used in hair preparations, perfumes, and soaps. Can irritate the skin. The redness, itching, and warmth experienced when marjoram is applied to the skin are caused by local dilation of the blood vessels or by contraction of smooth muscles in the skin. May produce allergic reactions. Essential oils such as marjoram are believed to penetrate the skin easily and produce systemic effects. GRAS.

MARSHMALLOW ROOT • *See* Althea Root.

MATE EXTRACT • Paraguay Tea Extract. St. Bartholomew's Tea. Jesuit's Tea. A natural flavoring extract from small gourds grown in South America where mate is a stimulant beverage. Among its constituents are caffeine, purines, and tannins. *See* Caffeine and Tannic Acid for toxicity. GRAS.

MATRICARIA EXTRACT • Wild Chamomile Extract. Extract of the flower heads of *Matricaria chamomilla*. Used as a soothing tea and tonic internally and externally as a soothing medication for contusions and other inflammation. *See* Tannic Acid. GRAS.

MATRICARIA OIL • Camomile Oil. Wild Chamomile Extract. The volatile oil distilled from the dried flower heads of *Matricaria chamomilla*. Used internally as a tonic and soothing tea and externally as a soothing medication for contusions and other inflammation. *See* Matricaria Extract.

MATURING AGENTS • *See* Bleaching Agents.

MAYONNAISE • The common salad dressing. Semisolid, made with eggs, vegetable oil, and vinegar or lemon juice.

MELISSA • *See* Balm Oil. GRAS.

MELONAL • *See* 2,6-Dimethyl-5-Heptenal.

MENADIONE • Vitamin K_3. Used as a dietary supplement and as a preservative in emollients. A synthetic with properties of Vitamin K. Bright-yellow crystals which are insoluble in water. They are used medically to prevent blood clotting and in food to prevent souring of milk products. Can be irritating to mucous membranes, respiratory passages, and the skin.

***p*-MENTHA-1,8-DIEN-7-OL** • A synthetic citrus, fruit, mint, and vanilla flavoring agent for beverages, ice cream, ices, candy, and baked goods. It is found naturally in caraway. Can cause skin irritation.

MENTHOL • A flavoring agent that can be obtained naturally from peppermint or other mint oils and can be made synthetically by hydrogenation (*see*) of thymol (*see*). Used in butter, caramel, fruit, peppermint, and spearmint flavorings for beverages, ice cream, ices, candy, baked goods, chewing gum (1,100 ppm), and liquor. Also used in perfumes, emollient creams, hair tonics, mouthwashes, shaving creams, preshave lotions, after-shave lotions, body rubs, liniments, and skin fresheners. it gives that ''cool'' feeling to the skin after use. It is a local anesthetic. It is nontoxic in low doses, but in concentrations of 3 percent or more it exerts an irritant action that can, if continued long, induce changes in all layers of the mucous membranes. It can also cause severe abdominal pain, nausea, vomiting, vertigo, and coma when ingested in its concentrated form. The lethal dose in rats is 2.0 grams per kilogram of body weight. GRAS.

(d)-NEO-MENTHOL • A flavoring agent that occurs naturally in Japanese mint oil. Used in mint flavorings for beverages, ice cream, candy, and baked goods. *See* Menthol for toxicity.

MENTHONE • A synthetic flavoring agent that occurs naturally in raspberries and peppermint oil. Bitter, with a slight peppermint taste. Used in fruit and mint flavorings for beverages, ice cream, ices, candy, baked goods, and chewing gum. May cause gastric distress.

MENTHYL ACETATE • A natural flavoring agent that occurs naturally in peppermint oil. Colorless, with a mint odor. Used in fruit, mint, and spice flavorings for beverages, ice cream, ices, candy, baked goods, and chewing gum; also in perfumes and toilet waters No known toxicity. GRAS.

METHANETHIOL • Methyl Mercaptan. A pesticide and fungicide isolated from the roots of a plant. Occurs in the ''sour'' gas of West Texas, in coal tar, and in petroleum. Produced in the intestinal tract by action of bacteria. Found in urine after ingestion of asparagus. Its odors may cause nausea and it may be narcotic in high concentrations.

METHIONINE • An essential amino acid (*see*) that occurs in protein. Used as a dietary substance. It is attracted to fat and Rutgers University researchers patented a process to impregnate a carrier material with methionine for use in deep-fried cooking oil to impart a ''fresh'' potato or potato chip flavor to snack foods, soups, or salad dressings. Used as a texturizer in cosmetic creams. On the FDA list of additives requiring further study since 1980. GRAS.

p-METHOXY BENZYLACETATE • *See* Anisyl Acetate.

p-METHOXY BENZYL ALCOHOL • *See* Anisyl Alcohol.

2-METHOXY-4-METHYLPHENOL • Creosol. A synthetic flavoring that occurs naturally in cassien and is used in fruit, rum, nut, and clove flavorings for beverages, ice cream, ices, candy, baked goods, and liqueurs. About the same toxicity as phenol, a highly caustic, poisonous compound derived from benzene.

1-METHOXY-4-PROPENYLBENZENE • *See* Anethole.

2-METHOXY-4-PROPENYLPHENOL • *See* Isoeugenol.

***p*-METHOXYACETOPHENONE** • *p*-Acetanisole. Crystalline solid with a pleasant odor. Soluble in alcohol and fixed oils and derived from the interaction of anisole and acetyl chloride with aluminum chloride and carbon disulfide. Used in flavoring and in perfumery for a synthetic floral odor.

METHOXYBENZENE • *See* Anisole.

***o*-METHOXYBENZALDEHYDE** • A synthetic flavoring agent that occurs naturally in cassia oil and is used in spice and cinnamon flavorings for beverages, baked goods, and chewing gum. No known toxicity.

***p*-METHOXYBENZALDEHYDE** • Anisaldehyde. A synthetic flavoring agent that occurs naturally in hawthorn, fennel, oil of anise, star, anise, and Tahiti vanilla beans. Used in raspberry, strawberry, butter, caramel, chocolate, apricot, cherry, peach, licorice, anise, nut, black, walnut, walnut, spice, and vanilla flavorings for beverages, ice cream, ices, candy, baked goods, gelatin desserts, and chewing gum. No known toxicity.

***p*-METHOXYBENZYL FORMATE** • *See* Anisyl Formate.

METHOXYETHANOL • *See* Ethanol.

4-METHOXYTOLUENE-2,5-DIAMINE HCL • A colorless liquid used in perfumery and flavorings. *See* Tolualdehydes.

METHYL ACETAMIDE • *See* Methyl Acetate.

METHYL ACETATE • Acetic Acid. Colorless liquid that occurs naturally in coffee, with a pleasant apple odor. Used in perfume to emphasize floral notes (*see*), especially that of rose, and in toilet waters having a lavender odor. Also naturally occurs in peppermint oil. A flavoring used in fruit, rum, and nut flavorings for beverages, ice cream, ices, candy, baked goods, gelatin desserts, puddings, and liquor. Used as a solvent for many resins and oils. May be irritating to the respiratory tract and, in high concentrations, may be narcotic. Since it has an effective fat-solvent drying effect on skin, it may cause skin problems such as chafing and cracking.

METHYL ACRYLATE • 2-Propanoic Acid, Methyl Ester. Derived from ethylene chlorohydrin, it is transparent and elastic. Used to coat paper and plastic film. Can be highly irritating to the eyes, skin, and mucous membranes. Convulsions occur if vapors are inhaled in high concentrations. GRAS for packaging. The final report to the FDA of the Select Committee on GRAS Substances stated in 1980 that there were insufficient relevant biological and other studies upon which to base an evaluation of it when used as a food ingredient.

METHYL ALCOHOL • Solvent for spice oleoresins and in hops extract for beer. Clear, colorless liquid derived from carbon monoxide and hydrogen under pressure. Toxic by ingestion. Can cause blindness. Used in the manufacture of formaldehyde, acetic acid, and other compounds. Used to denature (*see*) alcohol.

METHYL AMYL KETONE • *See* 2-Heptanone.

METHYL ANISATE • Anisic Acid. A synthetic fruit, melon, liquor, root beer, and spice flavoring agent for beverages, ice cream, ices, candy, and baked goods. No known toxicity.

METHYL ANTHRANILATE • Occurs naturally in neroli, ylang-ylang, bergamot, jasmine, and other essential oils. Colorless to pale-yellow liquid with a bluish fluorescence and a grapelike odor. It is made synthetically from coal tar (*see*). Used in loganberry, strawberry, orange, floral, rose, violet, cherry, grape, melon, liquor, wine, and honey flavorings for beverages, ice cream, ices, candy, baked goods, chewing gum (2,200 ppm), and liquors. Used as an "orange" scent for ointments, in the manufacture of synthetic perfumes, and in suntan lotions. Can irritate the skin. GRAS.

METHYL BENZOATE • Essence of oil of Niobe. Made from methanol (wood alcohol) and benzoic acid (*see*). Colorless, transparent liquid with a pleasant, fruity odor. Used in fruit, rum, liquor, nut, spice, and vanilla flavorings for beverages, ice cream, ices, candy, and baked goods. Also used in perfumes. No known toxicity.

METHYL BUTYRATE • A synthetic flavoring agent that occurs naturally in apples. Colorless. Used in fruit and rum flavorings for beverages, ice cream, candy, and baked goods. No known toxicity.

METHYL p-tert-BUTYPHENYLACETATE • A synthetic chocolate, fruit, and honey flavorings for beverages, ice cream, ices, candy, and baked goods. No known toxicity.

METHYL CINNAMATE • White crystals, strawberrylike odor, and soluble in alcohol. Derived by heating methanol, cinnamic acid and sulfuric acid. A synthetic strawberry, butter, cream, cherry, grape, peach, plum, and vanilla flavoring agent for beverages, ice cream, ices, candy, baked goods, chewing gum, and condiments. Used also in perfumes. *See* Cinnamic Acid.

METHYL DISULFIDE • A synthetic onion flavoring agent for baked goods, condiments, and pickle products. No known toxicity.

METHYL ESTER OF ROSIN-PARTIALLY HYDROGENATED • Used as a constituent of chewing gum base. *See* Rosin and Hydrogenated.

METHYL ESTER OF FATTY ACIDS • Produced from edible fats and oils. Used in dehydrating grapes to produce raisins. *See* Esters and Fatty Acids.

METHYL ETHYL CELLULOSE • A foaming, aerating, and emulsifying agent prepared from wood pulp or chemical cotton. Used in vegetable-fat whipped topping as an emulsifying agent. Used as a bulk laxative but absorbed from the bowel. For toxicity *see* Sodium Carboxymethyl Cellulose.

METHYLGLUCOSIDE OF FATTY ACIDS OF EDIBLE COCONUT OIL • Used in the manufacture of beet sugar and as an aid in crystallization of sucrose and dextrose. No known toxicity except that coconut is thought to contribute to cholesterol clogging of the arteries.

METHYL HEPTANOATE • A synthetic berry, grape, peach, and pineapple flavoring agent for beverages, ice cream, ices, candy, and baked goods. No known toxicity.

6-METHYL-5-HEPTEN-2-ONE • A synthetic flavoring agent that occurs naturally in oil of lavender and oil of lemon. Used in berry, citrus, banana, melon, pear, peach, and pineapple flavorings for beverages, ice cream, ices, candy, baked goods, and gelatin desserts. No known toxicity.

METHYL HEXANOATE • A synthetic pineapple flavoring agent for beverages, ice cream, ices, candy, and baked goods. No known toxicity.

METHYL HYDROGEN SILOXANE • *See* Silicones.

METHYL-*p*-HYDROXY-BENZOATE • Methylparaben. A preservative in beverages, baked goods, candy, and artificially sweetened jellies and preserves. Methylparaben may cause allergic skin reaction. On the FDA list of additives requiring further study. GRAS.

METHYL ISOBUTYL KETONE • A synthetic fruit flavoring agent for beverages, ice cream, ices, candy, and baked goods. Used as solvent for cellulose and lacquer. Similar in toxicity to methyl ethyl ketone, which is irritating to the eyes and mucous membranes, but likely more toxic. Causes intestinal upsets and central nervous system depression.

METHYL ISOBUTYRATE • A synthetic fruit flavoring agent for beverages, ice cream, ices, candy, and baked goods. *See* Methyl Isobutyl Ketone.

METHYL LAURATE • The ester of methyl alcohol and lauric acid. Derived from coconut oil. A synthetic flavoring agent for beverages, ice cream, ices, candy, and baked goods. It is also used in detergents, emulsifiers, wetting agents, stabilizers, resins, lubricants, and plasticizers. No known toxicity.

METHYL LINOLEATE • The ester of methyl alcohol and linoleic acid, it is a colorless oil derived from safflower oil and used in detergents, emulsifiers, wetting agents, stabilizers, resins, lubricants, and plasticizers. No known toxicity.

METHYL MERCAPTAN • A synthetic flavoring agent that occurs naturally in caseinate, cheese, skim milk, coffee, and cooked beef. Used in coffee flavorings for beverages, ice cream, ices, candy, and baked goods. *See* Methanethiol for toxicity.

METHYL b-NAPHTHYL KETONE • Oranger Crystals. 2′ Acetonaphtone. A synthetic flavoring agent used in berry, strawberry, citrus, fruit, grape, and vanilla flavorings for beverages, ice cream, ices, candy, baked goods, gelatin desserts, and chewing gum. *See* Methyl Isobutyl Ketone for toxicity.

METHYL NONANOATE • A synthetic berry, citrus, pineapple, honey, and cognac flavoring agent for beverages, ice cream, ices, candy, and baked goods. No known toxicity.

METHYL 2-NONENOATE • A synthetic berry and melon flavoring agent for beverages, ice cream, ices, candy, and baked goods. No known toxicity.

METHYL 2-NONYNOATE • A synthetic berry, floral, violet, fruit, and banana flavoring agent for beverages, ice cream, ices, candy, gelatin desserts, baked goods, and condiments. No known toxicity.

METHYL MYRISTATE • *See* Myristic Acid.

METHYL OCTANOATE • A synthetic flavoring agent that occurs naturally in pineapple. Used in pineapple and berry flavorings for beverages, ice cream, ices, candy, and baked goods. No known toxicity.

METHYL 2-OCTYNOATE • A synthetic flavoring agent used in berry, raspberry, strawberry, floral, violet, fruit, peach, liquor, and muscatel flavorings for beverages, ice cream, ices, candy, baked goods, gelatin desserts, chewing gum, and jellies. No known toxicity.

METHYL PELARGONATE • Nonanoic Acid, Methyl Ester. The ester of ethyl alcohol and pelargonic acid used in perfume and flavorings. No known toxicity.

4-METHYL-2-PENTANONE • A synthetic fruit flavoring for beverages, ice cream, ices, candy, and baked goods. No known toxicity.

2-METHYL-4-PHENYL-2-BUTYL ACETATE • A synthetic fruit and tea flavoring agent for beverages, ice cream, ices, candy, and baked goods. No known toxicity.

METHYL PHENYLACETATE • Colorless liquid with a honeylike odor used in strawberry, chocolate, peach, and honey flavorings for beverages, ice cream, ices, baked goods, candy, gelatin desserts, chewing gum, and syrup. Also used in perfumery. *See* Phenyl Acetate.

2-METHYL-4-PHENYLBUTYRALDEHYDE • A synthetic nut flavoring agent for beverages, ice cream, ices, candy, and baked goods. No known toxicity.

3-METHYL-2-PHENYLBUTYRATE • A synthetic fruit flavoring for beverages, ice cream, ices, and candy. No known toxicity.

METHYL 4-PHENYLBUTYRATE • A synthetic strawberry, fruit, and honey flavoring agent for beverages, ice cream, ices, candy, and baked goods. No known toxicity.

METHYL PIPERAZINE • Colorless liquid that absorbs water. Used as a surfactant (*see*).

METHYL SALICYLATE • Salicylic Acid. Oil of Wintergreen. Found naturally in sweet birch, cassien, and wintergreen. Used in strawberry, grape, mint, walnut, root beer, sarsaparilla, spice, wintergreen, birch beer, and vanilla flavorings for beverages, ice cream, ices, candy, baked goods, chewing gum (8,400 ppm), and syrup. The volatile oil is obtained by maceration. Used in perfumery and as a counterirritant, local anesthetic, and disinfectant in cosmetics and in sunburn lotions as a ultraviolet absorber. Toxic by ingestion. Use in foods restricted by the FDA. Lethal dose is 30 cc in adults, 10 milliliters in children. The FDA proposed that liniments and other liquid preparations containing more than 5 percent methyl salicylate be marketed in special child-resistant containers.

METHYL SILICONE • Prepared by hydrolyzing (*see* Hydrolyzed) dimethyldichlorosilane or its esters, it is used to help compounds resist oxidation. No known toxicity. *See* Silicones.

METHYL SULFIDE • A synthetic flavoring agent that occurs naturally in caseinate, cheese, coffee, coffee extract, and skim milk. Disagreeable odor. Used in chocolate, cocoa, fruit, and molasses flavorings for beverages, ice cream, ices, candy, baked goods, gelatin desserts, and syrups. Used also as a solvent for minerals. No known toxicity.

METHYL 9-UNDECENOATE • A synthetic citrus and honey flavoring agent for beverages, ice cream, ices, candy, and baked goods. No known toxicity.

METHYL 2-UNDECYNOATE • A synthetic floral and violet flavoring agent for beverages, ice cream, ices, candy, and baked goods. No known toxicity.

METHYL VALERATE • A synthetic flavoring agent that occurs naturally in pineapple. Used in fruit flavorings for beverages, ice cream, ices, candy, and baked goods. No known toxicity.

2-METHYL VALERIC ACID • A synthetic chocolate flavoring agent for candy. No known toxicity.

METHYLACETALDEHYDE • *See* Propionaldehyde.

METHYLACETIC ACID • *See* Propionic Acid.

2-METHYLALLYL BUTYRATE • A synthetic pineapple flavoring for beverages, ice cream, ices, candy, and baked goods. No known toxicity.

METHYLBENZYL ACETATE • A synthetic flavoring agent, colorless, with a gardenia odor. Used in cherry and fruit flavorings for beverages, ice cream, ices, candy, baked goods, gelatin desserts, and chewing gum. *See* Methyl Acetate for toxicity.

a-**METHYLBENZYL ACETATE** • Acetic Acid. A synthetic berry and fruit flavoring agent for beverages, ice cream, ices, candy, baked goods, chewing gum, and toppings. *See* Methyl Acetate for toxicity.

a-**METHYLBENZYL ALCOHOL** • A synthetic flavoring agent, colorless, with a hyacinth odor. Used in strawberry, rose, fruit, and honey flavorings for beverages, ice cream, ices, candy, baked goods, gelatin desserts, and chewing gum. Methyl alcohol is wood alcohol, a widely used solvent in paints, varnishes, and paint removers. Readily absorbed from the gastrointestinal tract; as little as two teaspoonfuls is considered toxic if ingested. The fatal dose lies between 2 and 8 ounces.

a-**METHYLBENZYL BUTYRATE** • A synthetic berry and fruit flavoring agent for beverages, ice cream, ices, candy, and baked goods. No known toxicity.

a-**METHYLBENZYL ISOBUTYRATE** • A synthetic fruit flavoring agent for beverages, ice cream, ices, candy, and baked goods. No known toxicity.

a-**METHYLBENZYL FORMATE** • Formic Acid. A synthetic fruit and berry flavoring agent for beverages, ice cream, ices, candy, and baked goods. *See* Formic Acid for toxicity.

2-METHYLBUTYALDEHYDE • A synthetic flavoring agent that occurs naturally in coffee and tea. Used in chocolate and fruit flavoring for beverages, ice cream, ices, candy, and baked goods. No known toxicity.

3-METHYLBUTYRALDEHYDE • A synthetic flavoring agent that occurs naturally in coffee extract, oil of lavender, and peppermint oil. Used in butter, chocolate, cocoa, fruit, and nut flavorings for beverages, ice cream, ices, candy, baked goods, and gelatin desserts. No known toxicity.

2-METHYLBUTYRIC ACID • A synthetic fruit flavoring agent for beverages, ice cream, ices, and candy. No known toxicity.

METHYLCELLULOSE • Cellulose, Methyl Ether. A binder, thickener, dispersing and emulsifying agent, it is prepared from wood pulp or chemical cotton by treatment with alcohol. Swells in water. Soluble in cold water and insoluble in hot. The commercial product has a methoxyl content of 29 percent. It is used as a bodying agent for beverages and canned fruits sweetened with artificial sweeteners; a thickener for kosher food products; a bulking agent for low-calorie crackers; a binder in nonwheat baked goods for nonallergic diets; a beer foam stabilizer; a condiment carrier; in food products for diabetics and low-calorie dietetic products; an edible film for food products; a leavening agent for prepared mixes; a clarifier for vinegar and beverages; in imitation jellies and jams, processed cheese, confectionery, and toppings. It is also used in wave-setting lotions, foam stabilizers, bath oils, and other cosmetic products. It is a bulk laxative. Ingestion of large doses may cause flatulence, distention of the abdomen, or intestinal obstruction, and may also affect the absorption of minerals or other drugs. A dose injected into the abdomen of rats causes cancer. Nontoxic on the skin. The final report to the FDA of the Select Committee on GRAS Substances stated in 1980 that there is no evidence in the available information that it is a hazard to the public when used as it is now and it should continue its GRAS status with limitations in the amounts that can be added to foods. *See* also Carboxymethyl Cellulose. GRAS.

6-METHYLCOUMARIN • A synthetic flavoring agent used in butter, caramel, coconut, fruit, nut, root beer, and vanilla flavorings for beverages, ice cream, ices, candy, baked goods, gelatin desserts, puddings, and chewing gum. Unlike methylcoumarin, which is listed as GRAS by the Flavor Extract Manufacturers Association, coumarin, once widely used in foods, is banned. Prolonged feeding of coumarin causes liver injury.

METHYLCYCLOPENTENOLONE • A synthetic flavoring agent used in berry, butter, butterscotch, caramel, maple, hazelnut, pecan, walnut, fruit, and vanilla flavorings for beverages, ice cream, ices, candy, baked goods, gelatin desserts, and syrups. No known toxicity.

5-METHYLFURFURAL • A synthetic honey, maple, and meat flavoring for beverages, ice cream, ices, candy, and baked goods. No known toxicity.

o-**METHYLANISOLE** • A synthetic fruit and nut flavoring for beverages, ice cream, ices, candy, and baked goods. No known toxicity.

p-**METHYLANISOLE** • A synthetic berry, maple, black walnut, walnut, and spice flavoring agent for beverages, ice cream, ices, candy, baked goods, gelatin desserts, puddings, condiments, and syrups. No known toxicity.

METHYLENE CHLORIDE • A colorless gas that compresses into a colorless liquid of pleasant odor and sweet taste. A solvent in the microencapsulation of thiamine (*see* Thiamine Hydrochloride) intended for use in both dry beverage and dry gelatin mixes. One of the most commonly used solvents, it is used to remove caffeine from coffee and tea. The FDA estimates, based on coffee industry tests, that about 0.10 ppm remain in most brands decaffeinating this way. Once absorbed into the body, methylene chloride generates carbon monoxide, affecting the blood's ability to pick up oxygen. Because of public concern about methylene chloride, some brands are now using other methods of decaffeinating. Methylene chloride is also used as a solvent for nail enamels and for cleansing creams. Used as an anesthetic in medicine. High concentrations are narcotic. Damage to the liver, kidney, and central nervous system can occur, and persistent postrecovery symptoms after inhalation include headache, nervousness, insomnia, and tremor. Can be absorbed through the skin and is then converted to carbon monoxide which, in turn, can cause stress in the cardiovascular system. It is also a skin irritant.

2-METHYLOCTANAL • A synthetic citrus flavoring agent for beverages, ice cream, ices, candy, and baked goods. No known toxicity.

METHYLPARABEN • Methyl p-Hydroxybenzoate. Preservative in jelly and preserves. Used in bubble baths, cold creams, eyeliners, and liquid makeup. It is an antimicrobial and preservative made of small, odorless, colorless crystals that have a burning taste. Nontoxic in small amounts but can cause allergic skin reactions. See Methyl p-Hydroxy-Benzoate.

2-METHYLPENTANOIC ACID • See 2-Methyl Valeric Acid.

b-METHYLPHENETHYL ALCOHOL • A synthetic berry, rose, melon, and honey flavoring agent for beverages, ice cream, ices, and candy, baked goods. No known toxicity.

METHYLPHENYL ETHER • See Anisole.

METHYLPROTOCATECHUIC ALDEHYDE • See Vanillin.

4-METHYLQUINOLINE • A synthetic butter, caramel, fruit, honey, and nut flavoring agent for beverages, ice cream, ices, candy, and baked goods. No known toxicity.

METHYLTHEOBROMINE • See Caffeine.

2-METHYLUNDECANAL • A synthetic flavoring agent, colorless, with a fatty odor. Used in a variety of foods. No known toxicity.

4(p-METHOXYPHENYL)-2-BUTANONE • A synthetic fruit, licorice, and anise flavoring agent for beverages, ice cream, ices, candy, baked goods, chewing gum, and gelatin desserts. No known toxicity.

1-(p-METHOXYPHENYL)-1-PENTEN-3-ONE • A synthetic butter, cream, fruit, maple, nut, and vanilla flavoring agent for beverages, ice cream, ices, candy, and baked goods. No known toxicity.

1-(p-METHOXYPHENYL)-2-PROPANONE • A synthetic flavoring agent that occurs naturally in star anise. Used in fruit and vanilla flavorings for beverages, ice cream, ices, candy, and baked goods. No known toxicity.

p-METHOXYTOLUENE • See p-Methylanisole.

MEXICAN SAGE • See Oregano.

MICROCAPSULES • Microcapsules are now used to encapsulate flavoring substances and probably will be used to encapsulate high-fat or high-calorie substances to keep them from being digested. They are made from gelatin, arabinoglactan and silicon dioxide. Toxicity depends upon components, but generally they are nontoxic.

MILFOIL • *See* Yarrow.

MILK • Milk may be a hidden ingredient in cream of rice, macaroni, filled candy bars, Ovaltine, Junket, prepared flours, frankfurters, and other sausages. Some people are allergic to milk. *See* also Nonfat Dry Milk.

MILK-CLOTTING ENZYME • An enzyme derived from fermentation, the additive is used in cheese production. The generating organism that causes the fermentation is removed. No known toxicity.

MILO STARCH • *See* Modified Starch. The final report to the FDA of the Select Committee on GRAS Substances stated in 1980 that it should continue its GRAS status with no limitations other than good manufacturing practices.

MIMOSA, ABSOLUTE • Reddish-yellow solid with a long-lasting, pleasant odor resembling ylang-ylang, used in perfumes. Derived from trees, shrubs, and herbs native to tropical and warm regions. Mimosa droops and closes its leaves when touched. A natural flavoring agent used in raspberry and fruit flavorings for beverages, ice cream, ices, candy, and baked goods. Also used in tanning. May produce allergic skin reactions.

MINERAL OIL • White Oil. It is a mixture of refined liquid hydrocarbons (*see*) derived from petroleum. Colorless, transparent, odorless, and tasteless. It is used as a defoaming component in the processing of beet sugar and yeast; as a coating for fresh fruits and vegetables; a lubricant and binder for capsules and tablets supplying small amounts of flavor, spice condiments, and vitamins. Also employed as a lubricant in food-processing equipment; a dough-divider oil; pan oil; and a lubricant in meat-packing plants. It is also used in confectionery as a sealant. It is also employed in baby creams, baby lotions, bay oil, brilliantine hairdressings, cleansing creams, cold creams, emollients, moisturizing creams, eye creams, foundation creams and makeup, hair conditioners, hand lotions, lipsticks, mascaras, rouge, shaving creams, compact powders, makeup removers, suntan creams, oils, and ointments. Also a cosmetic lubricant, protective agent, and binder. When heated, it smells like petroleum. It stays on top of the skin and leaves a shiny protective surface. May inhibit absorption of digestive fats and it has a mild laxative effect.

MINT • *See* Spearmint, Peppermint Oil, and Wintergreen Oil.

MIXED CARBOHYDRASE AND PROTASE ENZYME PRODUCTS • Enzymes. GRAS. *See* Enzymes.

MODIFIED SEA SALT • Salts derived from sea water with a reduced sodium chloride content.

MODIFIED STARCH • Ordinary starch that has been altered chemically to modify such properties as thickening or jelling. Babies have difficulty in digesting starch in its original form. Modified starch is used in baby food on the theory that it is easier to digest. Questions about safety have arisen because babies do not have the resistance to chemicals as do adults. Among chemicals used to modify starch are propylene oxide, succinic anhydride, 1-octenyl succinic anhydride, aluminum sulfate, and sodium hydroxide (*see* all). On the FDA top-priority list for reevaluation since 1980. Nothing new reported by the FDA since.

MOLASSES EXTRACT • Extract of sugar cane, a thick, brown, viscid syrup. Separated from raw sugar in the successive processes of sugar manufacture and graded according to its quality. It is a natural flavoring agent for candy, baked goods, ice cream, and medicines. No known toxicity.

MOLYBDATE ORANGE • A solution of lead chromate, lead molybdate, and lead sulfate. Used in printing inks. Toxic by ingestion.

MOLYBDENUM • A dietary supplement. The dark-gray, powdered mineral is a trace element in animal and plant metabolism. Resembles chromium and tungsten in many of its properties. Low order of toxicity.

MOLYBDIC ACID • White or slightly yellow powder, used in ceramic glazes and as a clarifying agent. No known toxicity.

MONARDA SPECIES • *See* Horsemint Leaves Extract.

4-MONOAMINOPHOSPHATIDE • *See* Lecithin.

4-MONOAMMONIUM GLUTAMATE • GRAS. *See* Glutamate.

MONOAZO COLOR • A dye made from diazonium and phenol, both coal-tar derivatives (*see* Coal Tar).

MONOCALCIUM PHOSPHATE • Buffer and neutralizing agent in self-rising cereal flours or meals. GRAS. *See* Calcium Phosphate.

MONO- AND DIGLYCERIDES OF FATS OR OILS • Mono- and diglycerides of edible fat-forming acids, used as emulsifiers in oleomargarine. GRAS. *See* Glycerides.

MONOGLYCERIDES OF FATTY ACIDS • Stabilizers in shortenings. *See* Fatty Acids. No known toxicity.

MONOGLYCERIDE CITRATE • Helps dissolve antioxidant formulations which retard rancidity in oils and fats. *See* Citrate Salts for toxicity. The final report to the FDA of the Select Committee on GRAS Substances stated in 1980 that there were insufficient relevant biological and other studies upon which to base an evaluation of it when it is used as a food ingredient.

MONOGLYCEROL CITRATE • A preservative. *See* Glycerin.

MONOISOPROPYL CITRATE • A sequestrant. GRAS. *See* Isopropyl Citrate.

MONOMER • A molecule that by repetition in long chain builds up a large structure or polymer (*see*). Ethylene, the gas, for instance, is the monomer of polyethylene (*see*).

MONOPOTASSIUM GLUTAMATE • *See* Glutamate.

MONOSODIUM GLUTAMATE (MSG) • The monosodium salt of glutamic acid (*see*), one of the amino acids. Occurs naturally in seaweed, sea tangles, soybeans, and sugar beets. Used to intensify meat and spice flavorings in meats, condiments, pickles, soups, candy, and baked goods. Believed responsible for the so-called "Chinese Restaurant Syndrome" in which diners suffer from chest pain, headache, and numbness after eating a Chinese meal. Causes brain damage in young rodents and brain damage effects in rats, rabbits, chicks, and monkeys. Baby-food processors removed MSG from baby-food products. Depression, irritability, and other mood changes have been reported. On the FDA list of additives needing further study for mutagenic, teratogenic, subacute, and reproductive effects. Studies have shown that MSG administered to animals during the neonatal period resulted in reproductive dysfunction when both males and females became adults. Females treated with MSG had fewer pregnancies and smaller litters, while males showed reduced fertility. The final report to the FDA of the Select Committee on GRAS Substances stated in 1980 that, while no evidence in the available information on it demonstrates a hazard to the public at current use levels, uncertainties exist requiring that additional studies be conducted. GRAS status has continued since 1980 while tests were being completed and evaluated. Nothing has been reported by the FDA since.

MONOPOTASSIUM PHOSPHATE • A derivative of edible fat. Used as an emulsifying agent in food products and as a buffer in prepared cereal. Cleared by the USDA's Meat Inspection Department to decrease the amounts of cooked-out juices in canned hams, pork shoulders, pork loins, chopped hams, and bacon. Monosodium phosphate is a urinary acidifier but has no known toxicity. The final report to the FDA of the Select Committee on GRAS Substances stated in 1980 that it should continue its GRAS status with no limitations other than good manufacturing practices.

MONOSACCHARIDE LACTATE CONDENSATE • The condensation product of sodium lactate and the sugars glucose, fructose, ribose, glucosamine, and deoxyribose.

MONOSODIUM PHOSPHATE DERIVATIVES OF DIGLYCERIDES • Derived from edible fats or oils or edible fat-forming fatty acids and used as emulsifiers. GRAS.

MONOSTARCH PHOSPHATE • A modified starch (*see*). The final report to the FDA of the Select Committee on GRAS Substances stated in 1980 that there is no evidence in the available information that it is a hazard to the public when used it is now and it should continue its GRAS status with limitations on amounts that can be added to food.

MONOUNSATURATED FATS • The saturation of fat refers to the chemical structure of its fatty acids. Saturated fats, which are hard at room temperature—lard, suet and butter fat are examples—consist primarily of fatty acids that contain a full load of hydrogen atoms. Monounsaturated fatty acids, however, can accept two additional hydrogen atoms. Fats that contain primarily monounsaturated fatty acids are liquid at room temperature but may become thickened when refrigerated. Polyunsaturated fats, which are liquid at room temperature, remain so even in the refrigerator, and consist mainly of fatty acids that can hold four or more additional hydrogen atoms. Examples of polyunsaturated fats are safflower and corn oil. Examples of monounsaturated fats are olive oil, rapeseed oil, cashews, and avocados. Once thought to be neutral, monounsaturated fats may be beneficial for blood cholesterol levels. This concept evolved from epidemiological studies of populations who have diets high in monounsaturates and lower arterial disease rates than populations with high saturated fat diets. Some even suggest that monounsaturates may be even better than polyunsaturates in preventing heart disease. Monounsaturates are manufactured normally by the body and are believed to be less likely to have some of the side effects thought to occur with polyunsaturates.

MORELLONE • *See* 3-Benzyl-4-Heptanone.

MORPHOLINE • Salt Fatty Acid. Coating on fresh fruits and vegetables. Broad industrial uses. Used as a surfactant (*see*) and an emulsifier in cosmetics. Prepared by taking the water out of diethanolamine, a crystalline alcohol. A mobile, water-absorbing liquid that mixes with water. It has a strong ammonia odor. A cheap solvent for resins, waxes, and dyes. Also used as a corrosion inhibitor, antioxidant, plasticizer, viscosity improver, insecticide, fungicide, local anesthetic, and antiseptic. Irritating to the eyes, skin, and mucous membranes. It may cause kidney and liver injury and can produce sloughing of the skin. A strong alkali.

MORPHOLINE STEARATE • A coating and preservative. *See* Morpholine.

MOSCHUS MOSCHIFERUS • *See* Musk.

MOUNTAIN ASH EXTRACT • The extract from the berries of the European tree or shrub *Sorbus aucuparia*. High in Vitamin C, the berries have been used by herbalists to cure and prevent scurvy and to treat nausea. Used in cosmetics as an antioxidant. No known toxicity.

MOUNTAIN MAPLE EXTRACT • Extract from a tall shrub or bushy tree found in the eastern United States. Used in chocolate, malt, and maple flavoring for beverages, ice cream, ices, candy, and baked goods. No known toxicity.

MSG • *See* Monosodium Glutamate.

MUCOUS MEMBRANES • The thin layers of tissues that line the respiratory and intestinal tracts and are kept moist by a sticky substance called mucus. These membranes line the nose and other parts of the respiratory tract, and are found in other parts of the body that have communication with air.

MUGWORT • The extract of the flowering herb *Artemisia absinthium*. *See* Wormwood and Sesquiterpene Lactones.

MUIRA PUAMA EXTRACT • A wood extract used as an aromatic resin and fat. No known toxicity.

MULBERRY EXTRACT • An extract of the dried leaves of various species of *Morus* which produces a purplish-black dye.

MULLEIN FLOWERS • The flowers from Common Mullein, *Verbascum thapsis*. Used as a flavoring in alcoholic beverages only and in henna hair coloring.

MUSHROOM EXTRACT • The extract of various species of mushrooms used as an oil and plasticizer.

MUSK • It is the dried secretion from preputial follicles of the northern Asian small hornless deer, which has musk in its glands. Musk is a brown, unctuous, smelly substance associated with attracting the opposite sex and which is promoted by stores for such purposes. As *musk ambrette* it is used in fruit, cherry, maple, mint, nut, black walnut, pecan, spice, and vanilla flavorings for beverages, ice cream, ices, candy, baked goods, gelatin desserts, pudding, and chewing gum. Musk ambrette, as a synthetic fixative, is widely used as a fragrance agent in perfumes, soaps, detergents, creams, lotions, and dentifrices in the United States at an estimated 100,000 pounds per year. It reportedly damages the myelin, the covering of nerve fibers. It can cause photosensitivity (*see*) and contact dermatitis. The problem is mostly with after-shave lotions. (Musk tetralin, in use for twenty years as a fragrance ingredient, was identified as a neurotoxin and removed from the market in 1978.) Musk ambrette has been generally recognized as safe as a food additive by the FDA. As *musk tonquin* it is used in fruit, maple, and molasses flavorings for beverages, ice cream, ices, candy, baked goods, and syrups. As *musk ketone* it is used in chewing gum and candy. Musk, of course, is also used in perfumery. At one time was a stimulant and nerve sedative in medicine. Can cause allergic reactions. GRAS.

MUSTARD • Black, Brown, and Red. Pulverized, dried, ripe seeds of the mustard plant (*Brassica nigra*) grown in Europe and Asia and naturalized in the U.S. Used in mustard and spice flavorings for condiments (5,200 ppm) and meats (2,300 ppm). Used as an emetic. Has been used as a counterirritant on the skin. Used in soaps, liniments, and lubricants. It has an intensely pungent odor that can be irritating. It is a strong skin blisterer and is used diluted as a counterirritant and to stimulate the scalp. Can cause allergic reactions. May cause a sensitivity to light. On the FDA list of products to be studied for possible mutagenic, teratogenic, subacute, and reproductive effects. The final report to the FDA of the Select Committee on GRAS Substances stated in 1980 that it should continue its GRAS status with no limitations other than good manufacturing practices.

MUSTARD • Yellow and White. The pulverized, dried, ripe seeds of the mustard plant (*Brassica alba*) grown in Europe and Asia and naturalized in the U.S. Used in sausage and spice flavoring for beverages, baked goods, condiments (8,200 ppm), meats, and pickles (3,800 ppm). Used as an emetic. The final report to the FDA of the Select Committee on GRAS Substances stated in 1980 that it should continue its GRAS status with no limitations other than good manufacturing practices. *See* Mustard, Black, for toxicity.

MUSTARD OIL • *See* Allyl Isothiocyanate.

MUTAGENIC • Having the power to cause mutations. A mutation is a sudden change in the character of a gene that is perpetuated in subsequent divisions of the cells in which it occurs. It can be induced by the application of such stimuli as radiation, certain food chemicals, or pesticides. Certain food additives such as caffeine have been found to "break" chromosomes.

MYRCENE • A synthetic flavoring agent that occurs naturally in galbanum oil, pimenta oil, orange peel, palma rosa oil, and hop oil. Pleasant aroma. Used in fruit, root beer, and coriander flavorings for beverages, ice cream, ices, candy, and baked goods. No known toxicity.

MYRISTALDEHYDE • A synthetic citrus and fruit flavoring agent for beverages, ice cream, ices, candy, baked goods, and gelatin desserts. *See* Nutmeg for toxicity.

MYRISTIC ACID • Used in shampoos, shaving soaps, and creams. A solid organic acid that occurs naturally in butter acids (such as nutmeg, which is 80 percent butter), oil of lovage, coconut oil, mace oil, cire d'abeille in palm seed fats, and in most animal and vegetable fats. Used in butter, butterscotch, chocolate, cocoa, and fruit flavorings for beverages, ice cream, ices, candy, baked goods, and gelatin desserts. No known toxicity.

MYRISTIC FRAGRANS HOUTT • *See* Mace and Nutmeg.

MYRISTYL ALCOHOL • *See* Fatty Alcohols.

MYROXYLON • *See* Balsam Peru.

MYRRH • Used in perfumes, dentifrices, and skin topics. One of the gifts of the Magi, it is a yellowish to reddish-brown aromatic bitter gum resin that is obtained from various trees, especially from East Africa and Arabia. Used by the ancients as an ingredient of incense and perfumes and as a remedy for localized skin problems. The gum is used in fruit, liquor, tobacco, and smoke flavorings for beverages, baked goods, ice cream, ices, candy, chewing gum, and soups. The oil is used in honey and liquor flavorings for beverages, ice cream, ices, candy, and baked goods. The gum resin has been used to break up intestinal gas and as a topical stimulant. No known toxicity.

MYRTLE LEAVES • The extract of the leaves of *Myrtus communis,* a European shrub used in alcoholic beverages only.

MYRTRIMONIUM BROMIDE • *See* Quaternary Ammonium Compounds.

N

NAPHTHYL ANTHRANILATE • A synthetic fruit and grape flavoring agent for beverages, ice cream, ices, baked goods, and candy. No known toxicity.

b-**NAPHTHYL ETHYL ETHER** • White crystals with an orange-blossom odor, it is used in perfumes, soaps, and flavoring. See Nerol.

b-**NAPHTHYL METHYL ETHER** • White crystals with a menthol odor. Used to perfume soaps. A synthetic berry, fruit, honey, and nut flavoring agent for beverages, ice cream, ices, chewing gum, candy, and baked goods. No known toxicity.

NARINGIN EXTRACT • Naringin is in the flowers, fruit, and rind of the grapefruit tree. Most abundant in immature fruit. Extracted from grapefruit peel. Used in bitters, grapefruit, and pineapple flavorings for beverages, ice cream, ices, and liquors. No known toxicity. GRAS.

NASTURTIUM EXTRACT • The extract of the leaves and stems of *Tropaaeolum majus.* A member of the mustard family, it has pungent and tasty leaves. It is very rich in Vitamin A and C as well as containing Vitamins B and B_2. It is soothing to the skin and supposedly has blood thinning factors and increases the flow of urine. No known toxicity.

NATAMYCIN • Pimaricin. An antifungal produced from *Strepto-*

myces natalensis from soil near Pietermaritzburg, South Africa, applied to the surface of cuts and slices of cheese to inhibit mold spoilage at the rate of 200 to 300 ppm. As with any antibiotic added to the food we eat, a resistance to other antibiotics given for illness may occur after a period of time. Allergic reactions to these hidden antibiotics may also be manifested.

NATURAL • To be advertised as "natural," the Federal Trade Commission requires that food may not contain synthetic or artificial ingredients and may not be more than minimally processed. For example, minimal processing includes such actions as washing or peeling fruits or vegetables; homogenizing milk; canning, bottling, and freezing food; baking bread; aging and roasting meats; and grinding nuts. It does not include processes that, in general, cannot be done in a home kitchen and involve certain types of chemicals or sophisticated technology; for example, chemically bleached foods will not qualify as minimally processed.

N-BUTANE • *See* Butane.

NDGA • *See* Nordihydroguaiaretic Acid..

NEO-DHC • *See* Dihydrochalcones.

NEOFOLINONE • Occurs naturally in oil of lavender, orange leaf (absolute), palma rosa oil, rose, neroli, and oil of pettigrain. Used in citrus, honey, and neroli flavorings for beverages, ice cream, ices, candy, baked goods, chewing gums, gelatin desserts, and puddings. No known toxicity.

NEOHESPERIDINE DIHYDROCHALCONE • *See* Dihydrochalcones.

NEROL • A primary alcohol used in perfumes, especially in rose and orange-blossom scents. Occurs naturally in oil of lavender, orange leaf, palma rosa oil, rose, neroli, and oil of pettigrain. It is colorless, with the odor of rose. Used in citrus, neroli, and honey flavorings for beverages, ice cream, ices, candy, baked goods, gelatin desserts, puddings, and chewing gum. Similar to turpentine in toxicity.

NEROLI BIGARADE OIL • Used chiefly in cologne and in perfumes. Named for the putative discoverer, Anna Maria de la Tremoille, princess of Nerole (1670). A fragrant, pale-yellow essential oil obtained from the flowers of the sour orange tree, it darkens upon standing. Used in berry, orange, cola, cherry, spice, and ginger ale flavorings for beverages, ice cream, ices, candy, baked goods, and chewing gum. No known toxicity. GRAS.

NEROLIDOL • A sesquiterpene alcohol. A straw-colored liquid with an odor similar to rose and apple. Occurs naturally in Peru Balsam and oils of orange flower, neroli, sweet orange, and ylang-ylang. Also made synthetically. Used in perfumery and flavoring. *See* Nerol.

NEROSOL • *See* Nerol.

NERYL ACETTE • A synthetic citrus, fruit, and neroli flavoring for beverages, ice cream, ices, candy, and baked goods. No known toxicity.

NERYL BUTYRATE • A synthetic berry, chocolate, cocoa, citrus, and fruit flavoring agent for beverages, ice cream, ices, candy, and baked goods. No known toxicity.

NERYL FORMATE • Formic Acid. A synthetic berry, citrus, apple, peach, and pineapple flavoring agent for beverages, ice cream, ices, candy, and baked goods. *See* Formic Acid for toxicity.

NERYL ISOBUTYRATE • A synthetic citrus and fruit flavoring agent for beverages, ice cream, ices, candy, and baked goods. No known toxicity.

NERYL ISOVALERATE • A synthetic berry, rose, and nut flavoring agent for beverages, ice cream, ices, candy, and baked goods. No known toxicity.

NERYL PROPIONATE • A synthetic berry and fruit flavoring agent for beverages, ice cream, ices, candy, and baked goods. No known toxicity.

NETTLES • Used in hair tonics and shampoos. It is obtained from a troublesome weed with stingers. It has a long history and was used in folk medicine. Its flesh is rich in minerals and plant hormones, and it supposedly stimulates hair growth and shines and softens hair. Also used to make tomatoes resistant to spoilage, to encourage the growth of strawberries, and to stimulate the fermentation of humus. No known toxicity.

NEUTRALIZING AGENT • A substance, such as ammonium bicarbonate or tartaric acid (*see* both), used to adjust the acidity or alkalinity of certain foods. *See* pH.

NGDA • *See* Nordehydroguaiaretic Acid.

NIACIN • Nicotinic Acid. Nicotinamide. White or yellow crystalline powder, it is an essential nutrient that participates in many energy-yielding reactions and aids in the maintenance of a normal nervous system. It is a component of the Vitamin B complex. Added to prepared breakfast cereals, peanut butter, baby cereals, enriched flours, macaroni, noodles, breads, rolls, cornmeal, corn grits, and farina. Niacin is distributed in significant amounts in liver, yeast, meat, legumes, and whole cereals. Recommended daily intake is 18 to 19 milligrams for males and 13 to 15 milligrams for females. The final report to the FDA of the Select Committee on GRAS Substances stated in 1980 that it should continue its GRAS status with no limitations other than good manufacturing practices.

NIACINAMIDE • Nicotinamide. Vitamin B. Used as a skin stimulant. A white or yellow, crystalline, odorless powder used to treat pellagra, a vitamin deficiency disease, and in the assay of enzymes for substrates. No known skin toxicity. The final report to the FDA of the Select Committee on GRAS Substances stated in 1980 that it should continue its GRAS status with no limitations other than good manufacturing practices.

NIACINAMIDE ASCORBATE • A complex of ascorbic acid (*see*) and niacinamide (*see*). Occurs as a yellow powder which is practically odorless but which may gradually darken on exposure to air. Used as a dietary supplement. *See* Niacin.

NICKEL • Metal that occurs in the earth. Lustrous, white, hard metal which is used as a catalyst for the hydrogenation (*see*) of fat. Nickel may cause dermatitis in sensitive individuals and ingestion of large amounts of the soluble salts may cause nausea, vomiting, diarrhea. The final report to the FDA of the Select Committee on GRAS Substances stated in 1980 that it should continue its GRAS status with no limitations other than good manufacturing practices.

NICKEL SULFATE • Occurs in the earth's crust as a salt of nickel. Obtained as green or blue crystals and is used chiefly in nickel plating. Used in hair dyes and astringents. It has a sweet astringent taste. Used as a mineral supplement up to 1 milligram per day. It acts as an irritant and causes vomiting when swallowed. Its systemic effects include blood vessel, brain, and kidney damage, and nervous depression. Frequently causes skin rash when used in cosmetics. The lethal dose varies widely. The dose in guinea pigs is 62 milligrams per kilogram of body weight.

NICOTINAMIDE • *See* Niacin.

NICOTINIC ACID • *See* Niacin.

NISIN • An antibiotic allowed in pasteurized cheese in 1989. It does not have to be listed on the label. Also used as a preservative in canned fruit and vegetables.

NITER • *See* Nitrate.

NIOSH • National Institute of Occupational Safety and Health.

NITRATE • Potassium and Sodium. *Potassium nitrate,* also known as saltpeter and niter, is used as a color fixative in cured meats. *Sodium nitrate,* also called Chile saltpeter, is used as a color fixative in cured meats. Both nitrates are used in matches and to improve the burning properties of tobacco. They combine with natural stomach saliva and food substances (secondary amines) to create nitrosamines, powerful cancer-causing agents. Nitrosamines have also been found in fish treated with nitrates. Researchers at Michael Reese Medical Center's Department of Pathology in Chicago induced cancer in mice by giving single doses of one three-thousandth of a gram (0.3 microgram) of nitrosamine for each gram of the animal's weight. This is in contrast to the way other researchers have induced cancer in laboratory animals with nitrosamines by using repeated small doses or single large doses. The tumors that developed were analogous to human liver tumors. Nitrosamines caused pancreatic cancer in hamsters, similar to human pancreatic cancers. Nitrates have caused deaths from methemoglobinemia (it cuts off oxygen to the brain). Because nitrates are difficult to control in processing, they are being used less often. However, they are still employed in long-curing processes, such as country hams, as well as dried, cured, and fermented sausages. In the early seventies, baby-food manufacturers voluntarily removed nitrates from their products. The U.S. Department of Agriculture, which has jurisdiction over meats, and the FDA, which has jurisdiction over processed poultry, have asked manufacturers to show that the use of nitrates is safe. Efforts to ban nitrates have failed because manufacturers claim there is no good substitute for them.

Nitrates change into nitrites on exposure to air. Our major intake of nitrates in foodstuffs comes primarily from vegetables or water supplies that are high in nitrate content, or from nitrates used as additives in the meat-curing process. Nitrates are natural constituents of plants. They occur in very small amounts in fruits but are high in certain vegetables—spinach, beets, radishes, eggplant, celery, lettuce, collards, and turnip greens—as high as more than 3,000 parts per million. The two most important factors responsible for large accumulations of nitrates in vegetables are the high levels of fertilization with nitrate fertilizers and the tendency of the species to accumulate nitrate.

NITRITE • Potassium and Sodium. *Potassium nitrite* is used as a color fixative in the more than $125-billion-a-year cured-meat business. *Sodium nitrite* has the peculiar ability to react chemically with the myoglobin molecule and impart red-bloodiness to processed meats, to convey tanginess to the palate, and to resist the growth of *Clostridium botulinum* spores. It is used as a color fixative in cured meats, bacon, bologna, frankfurters, deviled ham, meat spread, potted meats, spiced ham, Vienna sausages, smoke-cured tuna fish products, and in smoke-cured shad and salmon. Nitrite combines with natural stomach and food chemicals (secondary amines) to create nitrosamines, powerful cancer-causing agents. The U.S. Department of Agriculture, which has jurisdiction over processed meats, and the FDA, which has jurisdiction over processed poultry, asked manufacturers to show that the use of nitrites was safe and that nitrosamines were not formed in the products as preliminary tests showed in bacon. Processors claimed there was no alternate chemical substitute for nitrites. They said alternate processing methods could be used but the products would not look or taste the same. Baby-food manufacturers voluntarily removed nitrites from baby foods in the early seventies. The FDA found that adding Vitamin C to processed meats prevents or at least retards the formation of nitrosamines. In May 1978, the USDA announced plans to require bacon manufacturers to reduce their use of nitrite from 150 to 120 parts per million and to use preservatives that retard nitrosamine formation. Processors would have been required to keep nitrosamine levels to 10 ppm under the interim plan.

But in August 1978 a new concern about nitrite was raised. The USDA and the FDA issued a joint announcement that the substance has been directly linked to cancer by a Massachusetts Institute of Technology study. That work was later disputed. In 1982, amyl and butyl nitrites used by homosexual men were linked to Kaposi's Syndrome and other abnormalities of the immune system.

Researchers at Michael Reese Hospital linked infinitesimal amounts of nitrite to cancer in young laboratory mice, especially in the liver and lungs. Dr. Koshlya Rijhsinghani and her colleagues gave single doses of one three-thousandths of a gram (0.3 microgram) of nitrosamine for each gram of the animal's weight. This method differs from the way other researchers have induced cancer in mice with nitrosamines: repeated small doses or single large doses. Nitrosamines also produce cancer in hamsters similar to pancreatic cancers in humans.

In 1980, the FDA revoked its proposed phase-out because manufacturers said there was no adequate substitute for nitrites. In 1977 Germany banned nitrites and nitrates except in certain species of fish. However, a Committee on Nitrites and Alternative Curing Agents in Food, formed by the National Research Council in the United States, concluded that there was no single agent or process that could replace nitrites completely: "Several chemical and physical treatments appear to be comparable in inhibiting outgrowth of *Clostridium botulinum* spores in types of meat products but none confers the color and flavor that consumers have come to expect in nitrite-cured meats." Until the all-purpose agent comes along or until consumer preference changes, the best compromise probably will be continued use of nitrites in conventional amounts with Vitamins C and E added to block formation of nitrosamines, or the use of smaller amounts of nitrites in combination with biological acidification, irradiation, or the chemicals potassium sorbate, sodium hypophosphite, or fumarate esters, the Committee said.

To reduce nitrosamines in bacon, the U.S. Department of Agriculture requires meat packers to add sodium ascorbate or sodium erythorbate (Vitamin Cs) to the curing brine. This offers only a partial barrier because ascorbate is soluble in water and its activity in fat is limited. Vitamin E, however, inhibits nitrosation in fatty tissues. The committee suggested that both C and E be added to provide more complete protection.

If you must eat nitrite-laced meats, include a food or drink high in Vitamin C at the same time—for example, orange juice, grapefruit juice, cranberry juice, or lettuce.

NITRO • A prefix denoting one atom of nitrogen and two of oxygen. Nitro also denotes a class of dyes derived from coal tars. Nitro dyes can be absorbed through the skin. When absorbed or ingested they can cause a lack of oxygen in the blood. Chronic exposure may cause liver damage. *See* FD and C Colors.

NITROGEN • A gas that is 78 percent of the atmosphere by volume and essential to all living things. Odorless. Used as a preservative for cosmetics, in which it is nontoxic. In high concentrations, it can asphyxiate. Toxic concentration in humans is 90 ppm; in mice, 250 ppm. GRAS.

NITROGEN OXIDES • Nitrous Oxide (*see* below), Nitric Oxide, Nitrogen Dioxide, Nitrogen Trioxide, Nitrogen Pentoxide. Bleaching agent for cereal flour, *nitrogen dioxide* is a deadly poison gas. Short exposure may cause little pain or discomfort but several days later, fluid retention and inflammation of the lungs can cause death. About 200 ppm can be fatal.

NITROSYL CHLORIDE • Nonexplosive, very corrosive reddish-yellow gas, intensely irritating to the eyes, skin, and mucosa. Used as a bleaching agent for cereal flour. Inhalation may cause pulmonary edema and hemorrhage.

NITROUS OXIDE • Laughing Gas. A whipping agent for whipped cosmetic creams and a propellant in pressurized cosmetic containers. Slightly sweetish odor and taste. Colorless. Used in rocket fuel. Less irritating than other nitrogen oxides but narcotic in high concentrations and it can asphyxiate. GRAS.

g-**NONALACTONE** • Aldehyde C-18. Prunolide. Coconut Aldehyde. A synthetic berry, coconut, fruit, and nut flavoring agent for beverages, ice cream, ices, candy, baked goods, gelatin desserts, chewing gum, and icings. No known toxicity.

NONALOL • *See* Nonyl Alcohol.

NONANAL • Pelargonic Aldehyde. Colorless liquid with an orange-rose odor. A synthetic flavoring that occurs naturally in lemon oil, rose, sweet orange oil, mandarin, lime, orris, and ginger. Used in lemon and fruit flavorings for beverages, ice cream, ices, candy, baked goods, chewing gum, and gelatin desserts. Used also in perfumery. No known toxicity. *See* Aldehyde.

1,3-NONANEDIOL ACETATE • Colorless to slightly yellow mixture of isomers used in synthetic berry and fruit flavoring for beverages, ice cream, ices, candy, and baked goods. No known toxicity. *See* Nonanoic Acid and Acetic Acid.

NONANOIC ACID • Pelargonic Acid. Nonoic acid. Nonglic Acid. A colorless, oily liquid that is insoluble in water, it occurs in the oil of pelargonium plants such as the geranium. Used in berry, fruit, nut, and spice flavorings for beverages, ice cream, ices, candy, baked goods, and shortenings. It is practically insoluble in water and is used in producing salts and in the manufacture of lacquers. Can be very irritating to the skin.

1-NONANOL • *See* Nonyl Alcohol.

NONANOL ISOVALERATE • See Nonyl Isovalerate.

3-NONANON-1-YL-ACETATE • A synthetic berry, rose, fruit, and cheese flavoring agent for beverages, ice cream, ices, candy, and baked goods. No known toxicity.

NONANNOYL 4-HYDROXY-3-METHOXYBENZYLAMIDE • Perlargonyl Vanillylamide. A synthetic spice flavoring agent for candy, baked goods, and condiments. No known toxicity.

NONATE • *See* Isoamyl Nonanoate.

NONFAT DRY MILK • The solid residue produced by removing the water from defatted cow's milk. The following are comparisons between whole and dry milk: 100 grams fluid whole milk contains 68 calories; 87 grams of water; 3.5 grams of protein; 3.9 grams of fat; 0.7 grams of ash; 4.9 grams of carbohydrates; 118 milligrams of calcium; 93 milligrams of phosphorous; 0.1 milligrams of iron; 50 milligrams of sodium; 140 milligrams of potassium; 160 international units of Vitamin A; 0.04 milligrams of Vitamin B_1; 0.17 milligrams of B_2; 0.1 milligrams of nicotinic acid; and 1 milligram of Vitamin C. Total calories for one cup of milk is 166. Nonfat dry milk has 362 calories per 100 grams; 3.5 grams of water; 35.6 grams of protein; 1 gram of fat; 7.9 grams of ash; total carbohydrates, 52 grams; 1,300 milligrams of calcium; 1,030 milligrams of phosphorus; 0.6 milligrams of iron; 77 milligrams of sodium; 1,130 milligrams of potassium; 40 international units of Vitamin A; 0.35 milligrams of Vitamin B_1; 196 milligrams of Vitamin B_2; 1.1 milligrams of nicotinic acid; and 7 milligrams of Vitamin C. The total calories for a tablespoon of nonfat dry milk is 28. *See* Milk.

NONNUTRITIVE SWEETENERS • Sugar substitutes that contain no calories. Saccharin and cyclamates (*see* both) are examples.

NONYLCARBINOL • *See* 1-Decanol.

NONYL ACETATE • An ester produced by the reaction of nonyl alcohol and acetic acid (*see*). Pungent odor, suggestive of mushrooms but when diluted it resembles the odor of gardenias. Insoluble in water. Used for beverages, ice cream, ices, candy, and baked goods. No known toxicity.

NONYL ALCOHOL • Nonalol. A synthetic flavoring, colorless to yellow with a citronella oil odor. Occurs in oil of orange. Used in butter, citrus, peach, and pineapple flavorings for beverages, ice cream, ices, candy, and chewing gum. Also used in the manufacture of artificial lemon oil. In experimental animals it has caused central nervous system and liver damage.

NONYL ISOVALERATE • A synthetic fruit and hazel nut flavoring agent for beverages, ice cream, ices, candy, and baked goods. No known toxicity.

y-NONYL LACTONE • Yellowish to almost colorless liquid with a coconutlike odor. Used in perfumery and flavors. See Nonyl Alcohol.

NONYL NONANOATE • Nonyl Pelargonate. Liquid with a floral odor used in flavors, perfumes, and organic synthesis. See Nonyl Alcohol.

NOPINENE • See B-Pinene.

NORBIXIN • From the seeds of *Bixa zorellana* used in a suspension of vegetable oil for coloring food. See Annatto.

NORDIHYDROGUAIARETIC ACID • NGDA. An antioxidant used in brilliantines and other fat-based cosmetics. Occurs in resinous exudates of many plants. White or grayish-white crystals. Lard containing 0.01 percent NGDA stored at room temperature for 19 months in diffuse daylight showed no appreciable rancidity or color change. Used as an antioxidant in prepared pie crust mix, candy, lard, butter, ice cream, and pressure-dispensed whipped cream. Canada banned the additive in food in 1967 after it was shown to cause cysts and kidney damage in a large percentage of rats tested. The FDA removed it from the Generally Recognized as Safe list of food additives in 1968 and prohibited its use in products over which it has control. However, the U.S. Department of Agriculture, which controls antioxidants in lard and animal shortenings, banned it in 1971.

NOVATONE • See Acetanisole.

NORVALINE • A protein amino acid (*see*), soluble in hot water and insoluble in alcohol. See Valeric Acid.

NOTE • A distinct odor or flavor. "Top" note is the first note normally perceived when a flavor is smelled or tasted; usually volatile and gives "identity." "Middle" or "main" note is the substance of the flavor, the main characteristic. "Bottom" note is what is left when top and middle notes disappear. It is the residue when the aroma of flavoring evaporates.

NUTMEG • A natural flavoring extracted from the dried, ripe seed. Used in cola, vermouth, sausage, eggnog, and nutmeg flavorings for beverages, ice cream, ices, baked goods (2,000 ppm), condiments, meats, and pickles. The oil is used in loganberry, chocolate, lemon, cola, apple, grape, muscatel, rum, sausage, eggnog, pistachio, root beer, cinnamon, dill, ginger, mace, nutmeg, and vanilla flavorings for beverages, ice cream, ices, candy, baked goods, chewing gum, condiments, meats, syrups, and icings. In common household use since the Middle Ages, nutmeg is still a potentially toxic substance. Ingestion of as little as 3 whole seeds or 5 to 15 grams of grated spice can cause flushing of the skin, irregular heart rhythm, absence of salivation, and central nervous system excitation, including euphoria and hallucinations. GRAS.

NUTRA-SWEET® • *See* Aspartame.

O

OAK BARK EXTRACT • Oak Chip Extract. The extract from the white oak used in bitters and whiskey flavorings for beverages, ice cream, ices, candy, whiskey (1,000 ppm), and baked goods. Contains tannic acid (*see*) and is exceedingly astringent. In a wash, the Indians used it for sore eyes and as a tonic. Used in astringents in herbal cosmetics. No known toxicity.

OAK MOSS, ABSOLUTE • Any one of several lichens that grow on oak trees and yield a resin for used as a fixative (*see*) in perfumery. Stable green liquid with a long-lasting characteristic odor. Soluble in alcohol. Used in fruit, honey, and spice flavorings for beverages, ice cream, ices, candy, baked goods, gelatin desserts, condiments, and soups. No known toxicity but a common allergen in after-shave lotions

OAT BRAN • The broken coat of oats, *Avena sativa*. *See* Oat Flour.

OAT EXTRACT • The extract of the seeds of oats, *Avena sativa*. *See* Oat Flour.

OAT FLOUR • Flour from the cereal grain that is an important crop grown in the temperate regions. Light yellowish or brown to weak greenish or yellow powder. Slight odor; starchy taste. Makes a bland ointment for cosmetic treatments, including soothing baths. No known toxicity.

OAT GUM • A plant extract used as a thickener and stabilizer in foods and cosmetics. Also an antioxidant in butter, creams, and candy up to 1.5 percent. It is used as a thickener and stabilizer in pasteurized cheese spreads and cream cheese. In foods, it can cause an allergic reaction, including diarrhea and intestinal gas. No known toxicity. GRAS.

OATMEAL • Meal obtained by grinding of oats from which the husks have been removed.

OCIMUM BASILICUM • *See* Basil.

OCOTEA CYMBARUM OIL • An oil obtained by steam distillation from the wood of a Brazilian tree. Used chiefly as a source of safrole (*see*), a natural oil, and as a substitute for sassafras oil (*see* Sassafras Bark Extract). No known toxicity.

9-OCTADECENOIC ACID • *See* Oleic Acid.

OCTAFLUOROCYCLOBUTANE • A nonflammable gas. A refrigerant and propellant and aerating agent in foamed or sprayed food products. Used alone or in combination with carbon dioxide or nitrous oxide (*see* both). Nontoxic when used alone.

2-OCTANONE • A synthetic fruit and cheese flavoring agent for beverages, ice cream, ices, candy, and baked goods. No known toxicity.

3-OCTANONE • A synthetic flavoring that occurs naturally in oil of lavender. Used in citrus, coffee, peach, cheese, and spice flavorings for beverages, ice cream, ices, candy, and baked goods. No known toxicity.

1-OCTEN-3-OL • A synthetic fruit and spice flavoring agent for beverages, ice cream, ices, candy, baked goods, condiments and soups. No known toxicity.

1-OCTENYL SUCCINIC ANHYDRIDE • A starch modifier incorporating up to 3 percent of the weight of the product. Limited to 2 percent in combination with aluminum sulfate (*see*). No known toxicity.

OCTODECANOIC ACID • *See* Stearic Acid.

OCTYL ALCOHOL • Caprylic Alcohol. Colorless, viscous liquid soluble in water and insoluble in oil. Used in the manufacture of perfumes and of food additives. Occurs naturally in the oils of lavender, lemon, lime, lovage, orange peel, and coconut. It has a penetrating aromatic scent. No known toxicity.

OCTYL BUTYRATE • Butyric Acid. A synthetic strawberry, butter, citrus, fruit, cherry, melon, peach, pineapple, pumpkin, and liquor flavoring agent for beverages, ice cream, ices, candy, and baked goods. No known toxicity.

OCTYL FORMATE • Formic Acid. A synthetic flavoring, colorless with a fruity odor. Used in citrus and fruit flavorings for beverages, ice cream, ices, candy, and baked goods. *See* Formic Acid for toxicity.

OCTYL HEPTANOATE • A synthetic citrus, coconut, and fruit flavorings for beverages, ice cream, ices, candy, and baked goods. No known toxicity.

OCTYL ISOBUTYRATE • Isobutyrate Acid. A synthetic citrus, fruit, melon, peach, liquor, and wine flavoring agent for beverages, ice cream, ices, candy, and baked goods. No known toxicity.

OCTYL ISOVALERATE • Isovaleric Acid. A synthetic berry, butter, citrus, apple, cherry, grape, honey, and nut flavoring agent for beverages, ice cream, ices, candy, and baked goods. No known toxicity.

OCTYL OCTANOATE • Octanoic Acid. A synthetic citrus, grape, and pineapple flavoring agent for beverages, ice cream, ices, candy, and baked goods. No known toxicity.

OCTYL PHENYLACETATE • Phenylacetic Acid. A synthetic berry, apple, banana, grape, peach, pear, and honey flavoring agent for beverages, ice cream, ices, candy, and baked goods. No known toxicity.

OCTYL PROPIONATE • Propionic Acid. A synthetic berry, citrus, and melon flavoring agent for beverages, ice cream, ices, candy, and baked goods. No known toxicity.

1-OCTYL SUCCINIC ANHYDRIDE • Modifier for food starch. *See* Modified Starch.

OIL OF NIOBE • *See* Methyl Benzoate.

OIL OF SASSAFRAS, SAFROL FREE • Used as a flavoring agent. *See* Sassafras Bark Extract.

OLEIC ACID • Obtained from various animal and vegetable fats and oils. Colorless. On exposure to air, it turns a yellow to brown color and develops a rancid odor. Used as a defoaming agent; as a synthetic butter, cheese, and spice flavoring agent for beverages, ice cream, ices, candy, and baked goods, and condiments; as a lubricant and binder in various foods; and as a component in the manufacture of food additives. Used in soft soap, permanent wave solutions, vanishing creams, brushless shave creams, cold creams, brilliantines, nail polish, toilet soaps, and lipsticks. Possesses better skin penetrating properties than vegetable oils. Also employed in liquid makeup, liquid lip rouge, shampoos, and preshave lotions. Low oral toxicity but is mildly irritating to the skin. It caused tumors when injected under the skin of rabbits in 3,120-milligram doses per kilogram of body weight and when painted on the skin of mice in 62-milligram doses per kilogram of body weight. The final report to the FDA of the Select Committee on GRAS Substances stated in 1980 that it should continue its GRAS status with no limitations other than good manufacturing practices. The final report of the select committee also said that oleic acid should continue its GRAS status for packaging with no limitations other than good manufacturing practices.

OLEINIC ACID • *See* Oleic Acid.

OLEORESIN • A natural plant product consisting of essential oil and resin extracted from a substance, such as ginger, by means of alcohol, ether, or acetone. The solvent, alcohol, for example, is percolated through the ginger. Although the oleoresin is very similar to the spice from which it is derived, it is not identical because not all the substances in the spice are extracted. Oleoresins are usually more uniform and more potent than the original product. The normal use range of an oleoresin is from one fifth to one twentieth the corresponding amount for the crude spice. Certain spices are extracted as oleoresins for color rather than for flavor. Examples of color-intensifying oleoresins are those from paprika and turmeric (*see* both.)

OLESTRA • Sucrose Polyester. A fat substitute, developed by Procter and Gamble, that cannot be digested. It has no calories. It supposedly can replace conventional fats in French fries and baked desserts. However, it reportedly causes tumor and liver changes in animals.

OLIBANUM EXTRACT • Frankincense Extract. The extract of *Boswellia carterri* of various species. The volatile, distilled oil from the gum resin of a plant found in Ethiopia, Egypt, and Arabia. It was one of the gifts of the Magi. It is used in cola, fruit, and spice flavorings for beverages, ice cream, ices, candy, and baked goods. No known toxicity.

OLIVE OIL • A monounsaturated fat (*see*). Superior to mineral oils in penetrating power. Used in brilliantine hair dressings, emollients, eyelash oils, lipstick, nail polish removers, shampoos, soaps, face powders, and hair colorings. Antiwrinkle and massage oils. It is a pale yellow or greenish fixed oil obtained from ripe olives grown around the Mediterranean Sea. May cause allergic reactions. Has been reported to be beneficial to blood cholesterol.

OMEGA-3 FATTY ACIDS • Found in fish oils, reported to lower fats in the blood and thus reduce the risk of coronary artery disease. *See* Fish Oil.

ONION EXTRACT • Extract of the bulbs of onion, *Allium cepa,* discovered in Asia. Used in meat, onion, and spice flavorings for beverages, ice cream, ices, baked goods, condiments, meats, and pickles. No known toxicity. GRAS.

ORANGE BLOSSOMS • Orange blossoms, absolute, is a natural flavoring derived from the fruit of the bitter plant species. Used in citrus and fruit flavorings for beverages, ice cream, ices, candy, baked goods, and chewing gum. The flowers provide a natural flavoring extract for citrus and cola flavorings for beverages (2,000 ppm). The orange leaf extract is used as a natural fruit flavoring for beverages, ice cream, ices, and baked goods. Orange peel bitter oil is expressed from the fresh fruit and is used in orange and fruit flavorings for beverages, ice cream, ices, candy, gelatin desserts, chewing gum, and liquors. No known toxicity. GRAS.

ORANGE CRYSTALS • *See* Methyl B-Naphthyl Ketone.

ORANGE FLOWER, BITTER OIL • *See* Nerol.

ORANGE LEAF • *See* Orange Blossoms.

ORANGE B • Coal-tar dye. Coloring for casing of frankfurters and sausages. The color additive was limited to not more than 150 ppm by weight of finished food. In 1978, the FDA said use could result in exposure of consumers to beta-naphthylamine, a known cancer-causing agent. Although it was permanently listed by the FDA, the only manufacturer of it stopped making it.

ORANGE OIL • Sweet Orange Oil. Yellow to deep-orange, highly volatile, unstable liquid with a characteristic orange taste and odor expressed from the fresh peel of the ripe fruit of the sweet orange plant species. Once used as an expectorant, it is now employed in perfumery, soaps, and flavorings. Used in orange and fruit flavorings for beverages, ice cream, ices, candy, baked goods, gelatin desserts, and chewing gum. Inhalation or frequent contact with oil of orange may cause severe symptoms such as headache, dizziness, and shortness of breath. Perfumes, colognes, and toilet water containing oil of orange may cause allergic reaction in the hypersensitive. Omitted from hypoallergenic cosmetics.

ORANGE PEEL, BITTER OIL • *See* Orange Blossoms.

ORANGE PEEL, SWEET EXTRACT • From the fresh rind of the fruit. Sweetish, fragrant odor; slightly bitter taste. Used in orange and ginger ale flavorings for beverages, ice cream, ices, candy, and baked goods. No known toxicity.

ORANGE PEEL, SWEET OIL (TERPENELESS) • From the fresh rind of the fruit. Sweetish, fragrant odor; slightly bitter taste. Used in orange and fruit flavoring for beverages, ice cream, ices, candy, baked goods, gelatin desserts, and puddings. No known toxicity.

OREGANO • Mexican Oregano. Mexican Sage. Origanum. The wild marjoram (*see*) plant, but spicier, ordinarily found in Eurasia. Used in loganberry, cherry, sausage, root beer, and spice flavorings for beverages, baked goods, condiments (2,800 ppm), and meats. *See* Origanum Oil for toxicity. GRAS.

ORGANIC • There are no federal standards for the term, but it usually means produce grown without pesticides, herbicides, or synthetic fertilizers on land that has been free of such chemicals for one to seven years.

ORIGAN • *See* Oregano.

ORIGANOL • *See* 4-Carvomenthenol.

ORIGANUM OIL • The volatile oil is obtained by steam distillation from a flowering herb. Yellowish red to dark brown, with a pungent odor. Used in vermouth, sausage, root beer, and spice flavorings for beverages, ice cream, ices, candy, baked goods, condiments, and meats. A teaspoonful can cause illness and less than an ounce has killed adults. GRAS.

ORIZANOL • The ester of ferulic acid and terpene alcohol widely found in plants used in flavorings and perfumes. *See* Cinnamic Acid.

ORRIS • Orris Root Oil. White Flag. Love Root. Made from the roots of the plant. Yellowish, semisolid, and fragrant oil. Distilled for use in raspberry, blackberry, strawberry, violet, cherry, nut, and spice flavorings for beverages, ice cream, ices, candy, baked goods, gelatin desserts, chewing gum, and icings. It is also used in dusting powders, perfumes, dry shampoos, toothpaste, and sachets. Discontinued in the United States because of the frequent allergic reactions to orris, including infantile eczema, hay fever, stuffy nose, red eyes, and asthma. *See* Orris Root Extract.

ORRIS ROOT EXTRACT • Obtained from dried orris root. Has an intense odor and is used in perfumery. Used in chocolate, fruit, nut, vanilla, and cream soda flavorings for beverages, ice cream, ices, candy, baked goods, gelatin desserts, and chewing gum. Causes frequent allergic reactions.

OURICURY WAX • The wax exuded from the leaves of the Brazilian palm tree. The hard brown wax has the same properties and uses as carnauba wax (*see*).

OXAZOLINE • A series of synthetic waxes that are versatile and miscible with most natural waxes and can be applied to the same uses.

OX BILE • Oxgall. Emulsifier from the fresh bile of male castrated bovines. Brownish green or dark green; viscous. Characteristic odor. Bitter, disagreeable taste. Used in dried egg whites up to 0.1 percent. No known toxicity. The final report to the FDA of the Select Committee on GRAS Substances stated in 1980 that it should continue its GRAS status with no limitations other than good manufacturing practices.

OXIDIZED POLYETHYLENE • The resin produced by exposing polyethylene (*see*) to air. It is used as a protective coating or component of protective coatings for fresh avocados, bananas, beets, coconuts, eggplant, garlic, grapefruit, lemons, limes, mangos, muskmelons, onions, oranges, papaya, peas (in pods), pineapple, plantain, pumpkin, rutabaga, squash (acorn), sweet potatoes, tangerines, turnips, watermelon, Brazil nuts, chestnuts, filberts, hazelnuts, pecans, and walnuts (all nuts in shells).

OXIDIZED TALLOW • A defoaming component used in yeast and beet sugar production in reasonable amounts required to inhibit foaming. *See* Tallow Flakes.

OXIDIZER • A substance that causes oxygen to combine with another substance. Oxygen and hydrogen peroxide are examples of oxidizers.

OXYSTEARIN • A mixture of the glycerides (*see*) of partially oxidized stearic acids (*see*) and other fatty acids (*see*). Occurs in animal fat and used chiefly in manufacture of soaps, candles, cosmetics, suppositories, pill coatings. Tan, waxy. Used as a crystallization inhibitor in cottonseed and soybean cooking. In salad oils up to 0.125 percent. Also used as a defoamer in the production of beet sugar and yeast. The Select Committee of the Federation of American Societies for Experimental Biology advising on food additives recommended further study of this additive. The final report to the FDA of the Select Committee on GRAS Substances stated in 1980 that while no evidence in the available information on it demonstrates a hazard to the public at current use levels, uncertainties exist, requiring that additional studies be conducted. GRAS status has continued since 1980 while tests were being completed and evaluated. Nothing new has been reported by the FDA since.

OXYTETRACYCLINE • An antibiotic substance used in feed to increase growth and found in edible tissue of chickens and turkeys. Permitted in birds up to 0.0007 percent. Because it is an antimicrobial, it may cause sensitivity to light, nausea, inflammation of the mucous membranes of the mouth, and diarrhea.

P

PABA • *See* (Para)-Aminobenzoic Acid.

PALATONE • *See* Maltol.

PALE CATECHU • *See* Catechu Extract.

PALM OIL • Palm Butter. Palm Tallow. Yellow-brown, buttery, edible solid at room temperature. Oil palms are native to Central Africa and Malaysia. A reddish yellow to dark dirty red. A fatty mass with a faint violet odor. Used as a shortening and as a substitute for tallow. It is also used in making soaps and ointments. No known toxicity.

PALM OIL GLYCERIDE • *See* Palm Oil.

PALMA ROSA OIL • Geranium Oil. The volatile oil obtained by steam distillation from a variety of partially dried grass grown in East India and Java. Used in rose, fruit, and spice flavorings for beverages, ice cream, ices, candy, and baked goods. Believed as toxic as other essential oils, causing illness after ingestion of a teaspoonful and death after ingestion of an ounce. GRAS.

PALAMIDE MEA • A mixture of ethanolamides of the fatty acids derived from palm oil (*see*).

PALMITIC ACID • A mixture of solid organic acids obtained from fats consisting chiefly of palmitic acid with varying amounts of stearic acid (*see*). It is white or faintly yellow and has a fatty odor and taste. Palmitic acid occurs naturally in allspice, anise, calamus oil, cascarilla bark, celery seed, butter acids, coffee, tea, and many animal fats and plant oils. It forms 40 percent of cow's milk. Obtained from palm oil, Japan wax, or Chinese vegetable tallow. No known toxicity to skin and hair, provided no salts of oleic or lauric acids (*see* both) are present. Used in butter and cheese flavorings for seasoning preparations. Used as a texturizer in shampoos, shaving creams, and soaps. No known toxicity.

PALMITOYL HYDROLYZED MILK PROTEIN • The condensation product of palmitic acid chloride and hydrolyzed milk protein. *See* Hydrolyzed and Milk.

PANSY EXTRACT • The extract obtained from *Viola tricolor*. Flavoring in alcoholic beverages only. Also used as a coloring in cosmetics. No known toxicity.

PANTOTHENIC ACID • Vitamin B_5. A necessity in human diets. It is involved in the metabolism of fats and proteins. Nontoxic.

PANTHENOL • Dexpanthenol. Vitamin B Complex Factor. A viscous, slightly bitter liquid used as a medicinal supplement in foods to aid digestion and in liquid vitamins. Used in hair products and in emollients. Employed medically to aid digestion. It is good for human tissues. No known toxicity.

d-**PANTOTHENAMIDE** • Vitamin B Complex. Vitamin B_5. Made synthetically from the jelly of the queen bee, yeast, and molasses. Cleared for used as a source of pantothenic acid in foods for special dietary use. Pantothenic acid (common sources are liver, rice bran, molasses) is essential for metabolism of carbohydrates, fats, and other important substances. Nerve damage has been observed in patients with low pantothenic acid. It is involved with the release of energy from carbohydrates in the breakdown of fats. Children and adults need from 5 to 10 milligrams per day. *See* Calcium Pantothenate.

d-**PANTOTHENYL ALCOHOL** • The final report to the FDA of the Select Committee on GRAS Substances stated in 1980 that it should continue its GRAS status with no limitations other than good manufacturing practices. *See* Calcium Pantothenate.

PANTOTHENYL ETHYL ETHER • The ethyl ether of the B vitamin pantothenol (*see*).

PANTOTHENYL ETHYL ETHERACETATE • The ester of acetic acid and the ethyl ether of the B vitamin panthenol (*see*).

PAPAIN • A proteinase enzyme for meat tenderizing. Prepared from papaya, a fruit grown in tropical countries. Used for clearing beverages. Added to enriched farina to reduce cooking time. Used medically to prevent adhesions. It is deactivated by cooking, but because of its protein-digesting ability it can dissolve necrotic material with disastrous results. The usual grade used in food digests about 35 times its weight of lean meat. It may cause allergic reactions. The final report to the FDA of the Select Committee on GRAS Substances stated in 1980 that it should continue its GRAS status with no limitations other than good manufacturing practices.

PAPAYA • A fruit grown in tropical countries. It contains an enzyme, papain, used as a meat tenderizer and, medicinally, to prevent adhesions. It is deactivated by cooking. Because of its protein-digesting ability, it can dissolve necrotic (dead) material. It may cause allergic reactions. *See* Papain.

PAPRIKA • The finely ground pods of dried, ripe, sweet pepper. The strong, reddish-orange powder is used in sausage and spice flavorings for baked goods (1,900 ppm), condiments, meats (7,400 ppm), and soups (7,500 ppm). The *oleoresin* (*see*) is used in fruit, meat, and spice flavorings for beverages, ice cream, ices, candy, baked goods, condiments, and meats. Both paprika and paprika oleoresins are used as red coloring. No known toxicity. Permanently listed since 1966 for use in foods consistent with good manufacturing practices.

PARABENS • Butylparaben. Heptylparaben. Methylparaben. Propylparapen. Parahydroxybenzoate. The parabens are the most commonly used preservatives in the United States. The parabens have a broad spectrum of antimicrobial activity, are safe to use—relatively nonirritating, nonsensitizing, and nonpoisonous—are stable over the pH (*see*) range in cosmetics, and are sufficiently soluble in water to be effective in liquids. The typical paraben preservative system contains 0.2 percent methyl- and 0.1 percent propylparaben. Methyl and propylparaben are esters of parahydroxybenzoic acid. Neither occurs in nature. In foods parabens function as preservatives that prevent the growth of molds and yeasts. They are used in baked goods, in sugar substitutes, and in artificially sweetened jams, mince meats, milk preparations, soft drinks, packaged fish, meat, poultry, jellies, fats, and oils, and in frozen dairy desserts and many milk products. Methyl- and propylparabens are used in the amount of 1,000 ppm in tomato pulp, puree, catsup, pickles, and relishes. The only adverse effect of parabens reported was that methylparaben caused birth defects in offspring of mice and rats fed 550 milligrams per kilogram of body weight daily during pregnancy, and in hamsters fed 300 milligrams under the same conditions.

PARAFFIN WAX • A colorless, somewhat translucent, odorless mass with a greasy feel. Used as a defoaming component in yeast and beet sugar production. Not digested or absorbed in the intestines. Used to cover food products. Used in solid brilliantines, cold creams, wax depilatories, eyelash creams, and oils, eyebrow pencils, lipsticks, liquefying creams, protective creams, and mascaras; also used for extracting perfumes from flowers. Obtained from the distillate of wood, coal, petroleum, or shale oil. Easily melts over boiling water. Cleared for use as a synthetic masticatory substance in chewing gum. Pure paraffin is harmless to the skin but the presence of impurities may give rise to irritations and eczema.

PARAFORMALDEHYDE • Preservative used to control fungus in maple tree tap holes (2 ppm of formaldehyde in maple syrup).

PARSLEY • The aromatic leaves of the annual herb cultivated everywhere. Used in spice flavorings for beverages, meats, soups, baked goods, and condiments. Parsley *oil* is obtained by steam distillation of the ripe seeds of the herb. The *oleoresin* (*see*) is used in spice flavorings for condiments. Used as a preservative, perfume, and flavoring in cosmetics, it is obtained by steam distillation of the ripe seeds of the herb. Yellow to light brown, with a harsh odor. Parsley may cause skin to break out with a rash, redden, and swell when exposed to light. It may also cause an allergic reaction in the sensitive. GRAS.

PARSLEY SEED OIL • *See* Parsley.

PARTIALLY DELACTOSED WHEY (PDW) • Used increasingly as a substitute for nonfat dry milk, which is more expensive. PDW is used in processed cheese foods and spreads. It is the result of the partial removal of lactose (*see*) from the milk ingredient whey (*see*).

PARTIALLY DEMINERALIZED AND DELACTOSED WHEY • Removal of some minerals as well as lactose (*see*). *See* Partially Delactosed Whey.

PASSION FLOWER • Extract of the various species of *Passiflora carnata*. Indians used passion flower for reducing swellings, relieving sore eyes, and inducing vomiting. It is used as a flavoring. It has been shown that an extract of the plant depresses the motor nerves of the spinal cord.

PATCHOULI OIL • Patchouly Oil. It is the essential oil obtained from the leaves of an East Indian shrubby mint. Yellowish to greenish-brown liquid, with the pleasant fragrance of summer flowers. Used in cola, fruit, nut, and spice flavorings for beverages, ice cream, ices, candy, baked goods, and chewing gum. Used in perfume formulations to impart a long-lasting Oriental aroma in soaps and cosmetics. May produce allergic reactions.

PEACH ALDEHYDE • *See* y-Undecalactone.

PEACH EXTRACT • *See* Peach Juice Extract.

PEACH JUICE EXTRACT • The liquid obtained from the pulp of the peach, *Prunus persica*. It is used as a natural flavoring and as an emollient. Nontoxic.

PEACH-KERNEL OIL • Persic Oil. It is a light yellow liquid expressed from a seed. Smells like almonds. Used as a natural flavoring in conjunction with other natural flavorings. Used as an oil base in emollients, eyelash creams, and brilliantines. No known toxicity. GRAS.

PEACH LEAVES • Flavoring for alcoholic beverages only. *See* Peach Juice Extract.

PEANUT OIL • Arachis Oil. Greenish yellow, with a pleasant odor. Prepared by pressing shelled and skinned seeds of the peanut. A solvent used in salad oil, shortening, mayonnaise, and confections. Also used in conjunction with natural flavorings. Peanut butter is about 50 percent peanut oil suspended in peanut fibers. Used in the manufacture of soaps, baby preparations, hair-grooming aids, nail driers, shampoos, and as a solvent for ointments and liniments; also in night creams and emollients. It is used as a substitute for almond and olive oils in cosmetic creams, brilliantines, antiwrinkle oils, and sunburn preparations. Has been reported to be a mild irritant in soap, but considered harmless to the skin. The oil acts as a mild cathartic and as a protectant for the gastrointestinal tract when corrosive poisons have been swallowed. The final report to the FDA of the Select Committee on GRAS Substances stated in 1980 that it should continue its GRAS status with no limitations other than good manufacturing practices.

PEANUTAMIDE MEA • Loramine Wax. *See* Peanut Oil.

PEANUTAMIDE MIPA • A mixture of isopropanolamides of the fatty acids derived from peanut oil (*see*).

PEANUT STEARINE • *See* Peanut Oil. GRAS.

PECAN SHELL POWDER • A coloring agent used in cosmetics. Employed medicinally by the American Indians. It is the nut from a hickory tree of the southern central United States with a rough bark and hard but brittle wood. Edible. No known toxicity.

PECTIN • Pectin is found in roots, stems, and fruits of plants and forms an integral part of such structures. It is a coarse or fine powder, practically odorless, with a gluey taste. Richest source of pectin is lemon or orange rind, which contains about 30 percent of this polysaccharide. Used as a stabilizer, thickener, and bodying agent for artificially sweetened beverages, syrups for frozen products, ice cream, ice milk, confections, fruit sherbets, water ices, French dressing, fruit jelly, preserves, and jams to compensate for a deficiency in natural pectin. Used in foods as a "cementing agent." Used in cosmetics as a gelling and thickening agent. Emulsifying agent used in place of various gums in toothpastes, hair-setting lotions, and protective creams. It is soothing and mildly acidic. Also used as an antidiarrheal medicine. No known toxicity. The final report to the FDA of the Select Committee on GRAS Substances stated in 1980 that it should continue its GRAS status with no limitations other than good manufacturing practices.

PECTINASE • An enzyme used as a clarifying agent (*see*) in wine and juice. No known toxicity.

PEGU CATECHU EXTRACT • *See* Catechu Extract.

PELARGONALDEHYDE • *See* Nonanal.

PELARGONIC ACID • Nonanoic Acid. A synthetic flavoring agent that occurs naturally in cocoa and oil of lavender. Used in berry, fruit, nut, and spice flavorings. A strong irritant.

PELARGONIC ALDEHYDE • *See* Pelargonic Acid.

PELARGONIC VANILLYLAMIDE • *See* Pelargonic Acid.

PENNYROYAL OIL • Squaw Mint. Hedeoma. An extract of the flowering herb *Mentha pulegium*. Used since ancient days as a medicine, scent, flavoring, and food. Obtained from the dried flower tops and leaves, it contains tannin which is soothing to the skin. Used in mint flavorings for beverages, ice cream, ices, candy, and baked goods. Formerly used as an aromatic perspirant; to stimulate menstrual flow; for flatulence; as an abortion inducer; and a counteractant for painful menstruation. Brain damage has been reported following doses of less than 1 teaspoon. Nausea, vomiting, bleeding, circulatory collapse, confusion, restlessness, and delirium have been reported.

PENTADECALACTONE • Angelica Lactone. Exaltolide. It is obtained from the fruit and root of a plant grown in Europe and Asia. A synthetic berry, fruit, liquor, wine, nut, and vanilla flavoring agent for beverages, ice cream, ices, candy, baked goods, gelatin desserts, and alcoholic beverages. Used as a cosmetic fragrance. No known toxicity.

PENTADECANOLIDE • *See* Pentadecalactone.

PENTAERYTHRITOL ESTER OF MALEIC ANHYDRIDE MODIFIED WOOL ROSIN • Coating on citrus fruit. Pentaerythritol is a resin made by treating acetaldehyde (*see*) with formaldehyde (*see*) in a solution of calcium hydroxide.

PENTADESMA BUTTER • Kanya Butter. The vegetable fat extracted from the nut of the *Pentadesma butyracea. See* Shea Butter.

PENTANAL • *See* Valeraldehyde.

PENTANE • The aliphatic hydrocarbon derived from petroleum. Used as a solvent. Narcotic in high doses.

PENTANOIC ACID • *See* Valeric Acid.

1-PENTANOL • Pentyl Alcohol. *n*-Amyl Alcohol. Liquid, with a mild, pleasant odor, slightly soluble in water. Used as a solvent. Irritating to the eyes and respiratory passages, and absorption may cause a lack of oxygen in the blood.

2-PENTANONE • A synthetic flavoring that occurs naturally in apples. Used in fruit flavorings for beverages, ice cream, ices, candy, and baked goods. No known toxicity.

4-PENTENOIC ACID • A synthetic butter and fruit flavoring agent for beverages, ice cream, ices, candy, baked goods, and margarine. No known toxicity.

PENTYL ALCOHOL • *See* Amyl Alcohol.

PENTYL BUTYRATE • *See* Amyl Butyrate.

PEPPER, BLACK • A pungent product obtained from the dried, unripe berries of the East Indian pepper plant, *Piper nigrum*. Used in sausage and spice flavorings for beverages, baked goods, condiments, meats, soups, and pickles. Black pepper *oil* is used in meat and spice flavorings for beverages, ice cream, ices, candy, baked goods, condiments, and meats. Black pepper *oleoresin* (*see*) is used in sausage and pepper flavorings for beverages, ice cream, ices, candy, baked goods, condiments and meats. Pepper was formerly used as a carmtinative to break up intestinal gas, to cause sweating, and as a gastric agent to promote gastric secretion. No known toxicity.

PEPPER, RED • *See* Cayenne Pepper.

PEPPER, WHITE • The pungent product obtained from the undecorticated (with the outer covering intact) ripe berries of the pepper plant. Used in sausage and spice flavorings for beverages, baked goods, condiments, meats, and soups. White pepper *oil* is used in spice flavorings for baked goods. White pepper *oleoresin* (*see*) is used in spice flavorings for meats. *See* Pepper, Black for toxicity.

PEPPER TREE OIL • *See* Schinus Molle Oil.

PEPPERMINT EXTRACT • *See* Peppermint Oil.

PEPPERMINT LEAVES • *See* Peppermint Oil.

PEPPERMINT OIL • It is the oil made from the dried leaves and tops of a plant common to Asian, European, and American gardens. Used in chocolate, fruit, cordial, creme de menthe, peppermint, nut, and spice flavorings for beverages, ice cream, ices, candy (1,200 ppm), baked goods, gelatin desserts, chewing gum (8,300 ppm), meats, liquors, icings, and toppings. Peppermint has been used as a carminative to break up intestinal gas and as an antiseptic. Used in toothpaste and tooth powders, eye lotions, shaving lotions, and toilet waters. It can cause allergic reactions such as hay fever and skin rash. Two patients who consumed large quantities of peppermint candy over a long period of time developed irregular heart rhythms. GRAS.

PEPSIN • A digestive enzyme found in gastric juice that helps break down protein. The product used to aid digestion is obtained from the glandular layer of the fresh stomach of a hog. Slightly acid taste and a mild odor. No known toxicity.

PEPTONES • Secondary protein derivatives formed during the process of digestion—the result of the action of the gastric and pancreatic juices upon protein. Peptones are used as a foam stabilizer for beer and as a processing aid in baked goods, confections, and frostings. No known toxicity. Determined to be GRAS in 1982.

PERACETIC ACID • Peroxyacetic Acid. A starch modifier prepared from acetaldehyde (*see*). It is 40 percent acetic acid and highly corrosive. Acrid odor; explodes violently on heating to 110 degrees.

PERLITE • A filtering aid that the final report to the FDA of the Select Committee on GRAS Substances stated in 1980 should continue its GRAS status with no limitations other than good manufacturing practices.

PEROXIDE • Benzoyl, Calcium, and Hydrogen. *Benzoyl peroxide* is a compound used as a bleaching agent for flours, oils, and cheese. Has been used as a paste for treating poison ivy and for burns. May explode when heated. *Calcium peroxide or dioxide* is odorless, almost tasteless. Used as a dough conditioner and oxidizing agent for bread, rolls, and buns. Formerly as an antiseptic. *Hydrogen peroxide or dioxide* is a compound used as a bleaching and oxidizing agent, a modifier for food starch, and a preservative and bactericide for milk and cheese. Bitter taste. May decompose violently if traces of impurities are present. A strong oxidant that can injure skin and eyes. Chemists are cautioned to wear rubber gloves and goggles when handling it. Used in hair bleaches. May cause hair breakage and is an irritant. On the FDA list of additives to be studied for mutagenic, teratogenic, subacute, and reproductive effects.

PERSIC OIL • *See* Apricot and Peach-Kernel Oil.

PERUVIAN BALSAM • *See* Balsam Peru. GRAS.

PETROLATUM • Crude or Mineral Oil. Vaseline. Petroleum Jelly. Paraffin Jelly. It is a purified mixture of semisolid hydrocarbons from petroleum. Yellowish to light amber or white, semisolid, unctuous mass, practically odorless and tasteless, almost insoluble in water. A releasing agent and sealant for confections. A coating for fruits, vegetables, and cheese. A defoaming agent in yeast and beet sugar production. Used in baking products, as a lubricant in meat-packing plants, and in dried-egg albumin. Used in cold creams, emollient creams, conditioning creams, wax depilatories, eyebrow pencils, eyeshadows, liquefying creams, liquid powders, nail whites, lipsticks, protective creams, baby creams, and rouge. As a lubricant in lipsticks, it gives them a shine and in creams it makes them smoother. Helps to soften and smooth the skin in the same way as any other emollient and is less expensive. The oily film helps prevent evaporation of moisture from the skin and protects the skin from irritation. However, petrolatum does cause allergic skin reactions in the hypersensitive. When ingested, it produces a mild laxative effect. Not absorbed but may inhibit digestion. It is generally nontoxic.

PETROLEUM • Waxes. A defoaming agent in processing beet sugar and yeast and as a coating on cheese, raw fruits, and vegetables. Formerly used for bronchitis, tapeworms, and externally for arthritis and skin problems. No known toxicity.

PETROLEUM NAPHTHA • Derived from petroleum, primarily a mixture of hydrocarbons, paraffin and naphthalene (*see* all) it is permitted as a component of protective coatings for fresh avocados, bananas, beets, coconuts, eggplant, garlic, grapefruit, lemons, limes, mango, muskmelons, onions, oranges, papaya, peas (in pods), pineapple, plantain, pumpkin, rutabaga, squash (acorn), sweet potatoes, tangerines, turnips, watermelon, Brazil nuts, chestnuts, filberts, hazelnuts, pecans, and walnuts (all nuts in shells). *See* Coal Tar.

PETTIGRAIN OIL • Used extensively in perfumes. It is the volatile oil obtained from the leaves and twigs and unripe fruit of the bitter orange tree. Brownish to yellow with a bittersweet odor. Used in loganberry, violet, apple, banana, berry, grape, peach, pear, honey, muscatel, nut, ginger, and ginger ale flavorings for beverages, ice cream, ices, candy, baked goods, gelatin desserts, chewing gum, and condiments. Supposedly dissolves in sweat, and under the influence of sunlight becomes an irritant. May cause allergic skin reactions. GRAS.

PETTIGRAIN OIL (LEMON) • A fragrant, essential oil from a variety of citrus trees. Used in citrus and fruit flavorings for beverages, ice cream, ices, candy, and baked goods. No known toxicity. GRAS.

PETTIGRAIN OIL (MANDARIN) • The fragrant, essential oil from a variety of citrus tree. Used in orange, tangerine, and grape flavorings for beverages, ice cream, ices, candy, baked goods, and gelatin desserts. No known toxicity. GRAS.

pH • The scale used to measure acidity and alkalinity. pH is the hydrogen (H) ion concentration of a solution. The *p* stands for the power of hydrogen ion. The pH of a solution is measured on a scale of 14. A truly neutral solution, neither acidic nor alkaline, such as water, is 7. Acid is less than 7. Alkaline is more than 7. The pH of blood is 7.3; vinegar is 2.3; lemon juice is 2.3; and lye is 13. Skin and hair are naturally acidic. Soap and detergents are alkaline.

A-PHELLANDRENE • A synthetic flavoring agent that occurs naturally in allspice, star anise, angelica root, bay, dill, sweet fennel, black pepper, peppermint oil, and pimenta. Isolated from the essential oils of the eucalyptus plant. Used in citrus and spice flavorings for beverages, ice cream, ices, candy, and baked goods. Can be irritating to, and is absorbed through, the skin. Ingestion can cause vomiting and diarrhea.

PHENETHYL ALCOHOL • 2-Phenethyanol.   It occurs naturally in oranges, raspberries, and tea. A synthetic fruit flavoring agent that is used in strawberry, butter, caramel, floral, fruit, and honey flavorings for beverages, ice cream, ices, candy, baked goods, chewing gum, and gelatin desserts. Practically all rose perfumes contain it. It is also used as a preservative in cosmetics. It is a sensitizer. It is a strong local anesthetic and has caused central nervous system injury in mice.

PHENETHYL ANTHRANILATES • A synthetic butter, caramel, fruit, honey, and grape flavoring agent for beverages, ice cream, ices, candy, and baked goods. *See* Coal Tar.

PHENETHYL BENZOATE • A synthetic fruit and honey flavoring agent for beverages, ice cream, ices, candy, chewing gum, and baked goods. *See* Coal Tar.

PHENETHYL BUTYRATE • A synthetic butter, strawberry, caramel, floral, apple, peach, pineapple, and honey flavoring agent for beverages, ice cream, ices, candy, and baked goods. *See* Coal Tar.

PHENETHYL CINNAMATE • A synthetic fruit flavoring agent for beverages, ice cream, ices, candy, puddings, and baked goods. *See* Coal Tar.

PHENETHYL FORMATE • Formic Acid.   A synthetic berry, apple, apricot, banana, cherry, peach, pear, plum, and honey flavoring agent for beverages, ice cream, ices, candy, and baked goods. *See* Coal Tar.

PHENETHYL ISOBUTYRATE • A synthetic flavoring agent, slightly yellow, with a rose odor. Used in strawberry, floral, rose, apple, peach, pineapple, honey, and cheese flavorings for beverages, ice cream, ices, candy, and baked goods. *See* Coal Tar.

PHENETHYL ISOVALERATE • A synthetic apple, apricot, peach, pear, and pineapple flavoring agent for beverages, ice cream, ices, candy, baked goods, and chewing gum. *See* Coal Tar.

PHENETHYL PHENYLACETATE • A synthetic fruit and honey flavoring agent for beverages, ice cream, ices, candy, maraschino cherries, and baked goods. *See* Coal Tar.

PHENETHYL PROPIONATE • A synthetic fruit and honey flavoring agent for beverages, ice cream, ices, candy, and baked goods. *See* Coal Tar.

PHENETHYL SALICYLATE • A synthetic apricot and peach flavoring agent for beverages, ice cream, ices, candy, and baked goods. *See* Coal Tar.

PHENETHYL SENECIOATE • A synthetic liquor and wine flavoring agent for beverages, ice cream, ices, candy, and alcoholic beverages. *See* Coal Tar.

PHENETHYL TIGLATE • A synthetic fruit and nut flavoring agent for beverages, ice cream, ices, candy, and baked goods. *See* Coal Tar.

PHENOL • Obtained from coal tar (*see*), it is used in the manufacture of many food additives and processing aids. Ingestion of even small amounts of phenol may cause nausea, vomiting, circulatory collapse, paralysis, convulsions, coma, respiratory failure, and cardiac arrest. It is an antiseptic and general disinfectant.

PHENOXYACETIC ACID • A synthetic fruit and honey flavoring agent for beverages, ice cream, ices, candy, and baked goods. Used as a fungicide to soften calluses and corns and other hard surfaces. A mild irritant.

2-PHENOXYETHYL ISOBUTYRATE • A synthetic fruit flavoring, colorless, with a roselike odor. Used in beverages, ice cream, ices, candy, and baked goods. No known toxicity.

PHENYL ACETATE • A synthetic flavoring agent prepared from phenol and acetic chloride. Used in berry, butter, caramel, floral, rose, fruit, honey, and vanilla flavorings for beverages, ice cream, ices, candy, and baked goods. Phenol is highly toxic. Death from 1.5 grams has been reported.

4-PHENYL-2-BUTANOL • A synthetic fruit flavoring for beverages, ice cream, ices, candy, and baked goods. No known toxicity.

4-PHENYL-3-BUTEN-2-OL • A synthetic fruit flavoring for beverages, ice cream, ices, candy, and baked goods. No known toxicity.

4-PHENYL-3-BUTEN-2-ONE • A synthetic chocolate, cocoa, fruit, cherry, nut, and vanilla flavoring agent for beverages, ice cream, ices, candy, baked goods, gelatin desserts, and shortenings. No known toxicity.

4-PHENYL-2-BUTYL ACETATE • A synthetic fruit and peach flavoring agent for beverages, ice cream, ices, candy, and baked goods. *See* Acetic Acid for toxicity.

PHENYL DIMETHYL CARBONYL ISOBUTYRATE • *See* a-a-Dimethylbenzyl Isobutyrate.

PHENYL 2-FUROATE • A synthetic chocolate and mushroom flavoring agent for beverages, candy, and gelatin desserts. No known toxicity.

1-PHENYL-3-METHYL-3-PENTANOL • A synthetic fruit flavoring agent for beverages, candy, and gelatin desserts. No known toxicity.

PHENYL PELARGONATE • Liquid, insoluble in water. Used in flavorings, perfumes, bactericides, and fungicides.

1-PHENYL-1-PROPANOL • A synthetic fruit and honey flavoring agent for beverages, ice cream, ices, candy, and baked goods. No known toxicity.

3-PHENYL-1-PROPANOL • A synthetic flavoring that occurs naturally in tea. Used in strawberry, apricot, peach, plum, hazelnut, pistachio, cinnamon, and walnut flavorings for beverages, ice cream, ices, candy, baked goods, liqueurs and chewing gum. No known toxicity.

3-PHENYL PROPYL ISOBUTYRATE • A synthetic apple, apricot, peach, pear, pineapple, and plum flavoring agent for beverages, ice cream, ices, candy, and baked goods. No known toxicity.

PHENYLACETALDEHYDE • An oily colorless liquid with a harsh odor. Upon dilution, emits the fragrance of lilacs and hyacinths. Derived from phenethyl alcohol. A synthetic raspberry, strawberry, apricot, cherry, peach, honey, and spice flavoring for beverages, ice cream, ices, candy, baked goods, and chewing gum. Used also in perfumes. Less irritating than formaldehyde (*see*), but a stronger central nervous system depressant. In addition, it sometimes produces fluid in the lungs upon ingestion. Because it is considered an irritant, it is not used in baby-cosmetics preparations.

PHENYLACETALDEHYDE 2,3-BUTYLENE GLYCOL ACETAL • A synthetic floral and fruit flavoring agent for candy. *See* Phenylacetaldehyde for toxicity.

PHENYLACETALDEHYDE DIMETHYL ACETAL • A synthetic fruit, apricot, cherry, honey, and spice flavoring agent for beverages, ice cream, ices, candy, baked goods, and chewing gum. *See* Phenylacetaldehyde and Acetic Acid for toxicity.

PHENYLACETALDEHYDE GLYCERYL ACETAL • A synthetic floral and fruit flavoring agent for beverages, candy, ice cream, and ices. *See* Phenylacetaldehyde and Acetic Acid for toxicity.

PHENYLACETIC ACID • A synthetic flavoring agent that occurs naturally in Japanese mint, oil of neroli, and black pepper. A glistening, white solid with a persistent, honeylike odor. Used in butter, chocolate, rose, honey, and vanilla flavorings for beverages, ice cream, ices, candy, baked goods, gelatin desserts, chewing gum, liquors, and syrups. Used as a starting material in the manufacture of perfumes and soaps. Also used in the manufacture of penicillin. No known toxicity.

PHENYLALANINE • (L form only). An essential amino acid (*see*) considered essential for growth in normal human beings and not synthesized by the body. It is associated with phenylketonuria (PKU), an affliction that, if not detected soon after birth, leads to mental deterioration in children. Restricting phenylalanine in diets results in improvement. Whole egg contains 5.4 percent and skim milk 5.1 percent. Used to improve penetration of emollients. In 1980 the FDA asked for further study of this amino acid as a food additive. Nothing new has been reported by the FDA since.

2-PHENYLETHYL ISOVALERATE • *See* Phenethyl Isovalerate.

PHENYLETHYLACETATE • A colorless liquid with a floral odor, insoluble in most oils. Used as a flavoring agent. No known toxicity.

2-PHENYLPROPIONALDEHYDE • A synthetic berry, rose, apricot, cherry, peach, plum, and almond flavoring agent for beverages, ice cream, ices, candy, and baked goods. No known toxicity.

3-PHENYLPROPIONALDEHYDE • A synthetic flavoring agent, slightly yellow, with a strong, floral odor. Used in berry, rose, apricot, cherry, peach, plum, and almond flavorings for beverages, ice cream, ices, candy, and baked goods. No known toxicity.

2-PHENYLPROPIONALDEHYDE DIMETHYL ACETAL • A synthetic berry, floral, rose, fruit, honey, mushroom, nut and spice flavoring agent for beverages, ice cream, ices, candy, baked goods, chewing gum, and condiments. *See* Acetic Acid for toxicity.

3-PHENYLPROPYL ACETATE • A synthetic flavoring, colorless, with a spicy floral odor. Used in berry, fruit, and spice flavorings for beverages, ice cream, ices, candy, baked goods, chewing gum, and condiments. Propyl acetate may be irritating to skin and mucous membranes and narcotic in high concentrations.

2-PHENYLPROPYL BUTYRATE • A synthetic flavoring used in beverages, ice cream, ices, candy, and baked goods. No specific flavorings listed. No known toxicity.

3-PHENYLPROPYL CINNAMATE • A synthetic butter, caramel, chocolate, cocoa, coconut, grape, and spice flavoring agent for beverages, ice cream, ices, candy, and baked goods. No known toxicity.

3-PHENYLPROPYL FORMATE • Formic Acid. A synthetic currant, raspberry, butter, caramel, apricot, peach, and honey flavoring agent for beverages, ice cream, ices, candy, and baked goods. *See* Formic Acid for toxicity.

3-PHENYLPROPYL HEXANOATE • A synthetic fruit flavoring for beverages, ice cream, ices, candy, and baked goods. No known toxicity.

2-PHENYLPROPYL ISOBUTYRATE • A synthetic fruit flavoring for beverages, ice cream, ices, and candy. No known toxicity.

3-PHENYLPROPYL ISOVALERATE • A synthetic butter, caramel, apple, pear, and nut flavoring agent for beverages, ice cream, ices, candy, and baked goods. No known toxicity.

3-PHENYLPROPYL PROPIONATE • A synthetic apricot flavoring for beverages, ice cream, ices, candy, and baked goods. No known toxicity.

2-3 (3-PHENYLPROPYL) TETRAHYDROFURAN • A synthetic fruit, honey, and maple flavoring agent for beverages, ice cream, ices, candy, gelatin, puddings, and chewing gum. No known toxicity.

PHOSPHATE • A salt of ester of phosphoric acid (*see*). Used as an emulsifier and texturizer and sequestering agent (*see*) in foods. Sodium phosphate is used in evaporated milk up to 0.1 percent of weight. A carbonated beverage contains phosphoric acid. Without sufficient phosphate there is abnormal parathyroid (gland) function, bone metabolism, intestinal absorption, malnutrition, and kidney malfunction. Chemicals that interfere with phosphate action include detergents, mannitol (an alcohol used as a dietary supplement, the basis of dietetic sweets), Vitamin D, and aluminum hydroxide (*see*), a leavening agent. Ingestion of large amounts of phosphates can cause kidney damage and may adversely affect the absorption and other mineral imbalances.

PHOSPHATE AMMONIUM • Dibasic and Monobasic. *See* Ammonium Phosphate.

PHOSPHATE, CALCIUM HEXAMETA- • *See* Calcium Hexametaphosphate.

PHOSPHATE, CALCIUM, MONOBASIC AND TRIBASIC. • *See* Calcium Phosphate.

PHOSPHATE, POTASSIUM • Monobasic and Dibasic. *See* Potassium Phosphate.

PHOSPHATED DISTARCH PHOSPHATE • The final report to the FDA of the Select Committee on GRAS Substances stated in 1980 that there is no evidence in the available information that it is a hazard to the public when used as it is now and it should continue its GRAS status with limitations on amounts that can be added to food. *See* Modified Starches.

PHOSPHOLIPIDS • Phosphatides. Complex fat substances found in all living cells. Lecithin is an example. It is used in hand creams and lotions. Phospholipids contain phosphoric acid and nitrogen and are soluble in the usual fat solvents, with the exception of acetone (*see*). They are used in moisturizers because they bind water and hold it in place. No known toxicity.

PHOSPHORIC ACID • A colorless, odorless solution made from phosphate rock. Mixes with water and alcohol. An acid sequestering agent (*see*) for rendered animal fat or a combination of such fat with vegetable fat. Also used as an acidulant and flavoring in soft drink beverages, jellies, frozen dairy products, bakery products, candy, cheese products, and in the brewing industry. It is also used as a sequestrant and antioxidant in hair tonics, nail polishes, and skin fresheners. Concentrated solutions are irritating to the skin and mucous membranes. The final report to the FDA of the Select Committee on GRAS Substances stated in 1980 that it should continue its GRAS status with no limitations other than good manufacturing practices.

PHOSPHOROUS CHLORIDE • Phosphate derivative used as a starch modifier and a chlorinating agent. Intensely irritating to the skin, eyes, mucous membranes. Inhalation may cause fluid in the lungs.

PHOSPHOROUS OXYCHLORIDE • Phosphoryl Chloride. Colorless, clear, strongly fuming vapors, used as a starch modifier and as a solvent and chlorinating agent. Inhalation may cause pulmonary edema.

PHOSPHOROUS SOURCES: • Calcium Phosphate, Magnesium Phosphate, Potassium Glycerophosphate, and Sodium Phosphate. Mineral supplements for cereal products, particularly breakfast foods such as farina. They are also used in incendiary bombs and tracer bullets. Phosphorus was formerly used to treat rickets and degenerative disorders. *See* Phosphate.

PHOTOSENSITIVITY • A condition in which the application or ingestion of certain chemicals, such as propylparaben (*see*), causes skin problems—including rash, hyperpigmentation, and swelling—when the skin is exposed to sunlight.

PICRAMIC ACID • 4,6-Dinitro-2-Aminophenol. A red crystalline acid obtained from phenol and used chiefly in making azo dyes (*see*). Highly toxic material. Readily absorbed through intact skin. Vapors absorbed through respiratory tract. Produces marked increase in metabolism and temperature, profuse sweating, collapse, and death. May cause skin rash, cataracts, and weight loss.

PILEWORT EXTRACT • An extract of *Ranunculs ficuria,* the coarse hairy perennial figwort of eastern and central United States. It was once used to treat tuberculosis. No known toxicity.

PIMENTA LEAF OIL • Jamaica Pepper. Allspice. Derived from the dried ripe fruit of the evergreen shrub grown in the West Indies and Central and South America. Used in raspberry, fruit, nut, and spice flavorings for beverages, ice cream, ices, candy, baked goods, gelatin desserts, chewing gum, condiments, and meat products. No known toxicity. GRAS.

PINE MOUNTAIN OIL • *See* Pine Needle Oil and Pine Needle Dwarf Oil.

PINE NEEDLE DWARF OIL • Pine Mountain Oil. The volatile oil obtained by steam distillation from a variety of pine trees. Colorless with a pleasant pine smell. Used in citrus, pineapple, and liquor flavorings for beverages, ice cream, ices, candy, and baked goods.

PINE NEEDLE OIL • Pine Mountain Oil. An extract of various species of *Pinus* as a natural flavoring in pineapple, citrus, and spice flavorings. Also used to scent bath products. Ingestion of large amounts can cause intestinal hemorrhages.

PINE SCOTCH OIL • Volatile oil obtained by steam distillation from the needles of a pine tree. Colorless or yellowish, with an odor of turpentine. Used in various flavorings for beverages, candy, and baked goods. *See* Turpentine for toxicity.

PINE TAR • A product obtained by distillation of pine wood. A blackish-brown, viscous liquid, slightly soluble in water. Used as an antiseptic in skin diseases. May be irritating to the skin.

PINE TAR OIL • The extract from a variety of pine trees. A synthetic flavoring obtained from a species of pine wood. Used in licorice flavorings for ice cream, ices, and candy. Also used as a solvent, disinfectant, and deodorant. As a pine tar it is used in hair tonics; also a solvent, disinfectant, and deodorant. As an oil from twigs and needles, it is used in pine bath oil emulsions, bath salts, and perfumery. Irritating to the skin and mucous membranes. Bornyl acetate, a substance obtained from various pine needles, has a strong pine odor and is used in bath oils. It can cause nausea, vomiting, convulsions, and dizziness if ingested. In general, pine oil in concentrated form is an irritant to human skin and may cause allergic reactions. In small amounts it is nontoxic.

PINEAPPLE EXTRACT • *See* Pineapple Juice

PINEAPPLE JUICE • The common juice from the tropical plant. Contains a protein-digesting and milk-clotting enzyme, bromelin (*see*). An antiinflammatory enzyme, it is used in cosmetic treatment creams. It is also used as a texturizer. No known toxicity.

a-**PINENE** • A synthetic flavoring agent that occurs naturally in angelica root oil, anise, star anise, asafoetida oil, coriander, cumin, fennel, grapefruit, juniper berries, oils of lavender and lime, mandarin orange leaf, black pepper, peppermint, pimenta, and yarrow. It is the principal ingredient of turpentine (*see*). Used chiefly in the manufacture of camphor. Used in lemon and nutmeg flavorings for beverages, ice cream, ices, candy, baked goods, and condiments. Also used as a chewing gum base. Readily absorbed from the gastrointestinal tract, the skin, and respiratory tract. It is a local irritant, central nervous system depressant, and an irritant to the bladder and kidney. Has caused benign skin tumors from chronic contact. The fatal dose is estimated at 180 grams orally as turpentine.

2-PINENE • *See a*-Pinene.

B-PINENE • A synthetic flavoring that occurs naturally in black currant buds, coriander, cumin, black pepper, and yarrow herb. Used in citrus flavorings for beverages, ice cream, ices, candy (600 ppm), and baked goods (600 ppm). Also cleared for use in chewing gum base. *See a*-Pinene for toxicity.

PINUS PUMILIO OIL • *See* Pine Needle Dwarf Oil.

PIPERIDINE • A synthetic flavoring that occurs naturally in black pepper. Used in beverages, candy, baked goods, meats, soups, and condiments. Soapy texture. Has been proposed for use as a tranquilizer and muscle relaxant. No known toxicity.

PIPERINE • Celery Soda. A synthetic flavoring agent that occurs naturally in black pepper, it is used as a pungent brandy flavoring. It is also used as a nontoxic insecticide. Believed to be more toxic than the commercial pyrethrins.

PIPERITONE • A synthetic flavoring agent that occurs naturally in Japanese mint. Used in beverages, ice cream, ices, candy, and baked goods. Used to give dentifrices a minty flavor and to give perfumes their peppermint scent. No known toxicity.

PIPERONAL. HELIOTROPIN • A synthetic flavoring and perfume agent that occurs naturally in vanilla and black pepper. White crystalline powder, with a sweet floral odor. Used in strawberry, cola, cherry, rum, maple, nut, and vanilla flavorings in beverages, ice cream, ices, baked goods, gelatin puddings, and chewing gum. Used chiefly in perfumery. Ingestion of large amounts may cause central nervous system depression. Has been reported to cause skin rash. In lipsticks, said to produce marking of the skin. Not recommended by some cosmetic chemists because of its ability to produce skin irritation.

PIPERONYL ACETATE • A synthetic fruit flavoring agent for beverages, ice cream, ices, candy, and baked goods. *See* Piperonal for toxicity.

PIPERONYL ALDEHYDE • *See* Peperonal.

PIPERONYL ISOBUTYRATE • A synthetic fruit and cheese flavoring for beverages, ice cream, ices, candy, and baked goods. *See* Piperonal for toxicity.

PIPERONYLPIPERIDINE • *See* Piperine.

PIPSISSEWA LEAVES EXTRACT. LOVE-IN-WINTER. PRINCE'S PINE • Extracted from the leaves of an evergreen shrub. Used in root beer, sarsaparilla, wintergreen, and birch beer flavorings for beverages and candy. Its leaves have been used as an astringent, diuretic, and tonic. The Cree name means "to break up"—bladder stones, that is. GRAS.

PLANTAIN EXTRACT • The extract of various species of plantain. The starchy fruit is a staple item of diet throughout the tropics and is used for bladder infections by herbalists. It is a natural astringent and antiseptic with soothing and cooling effects on blemishes and burns.

PLANTAROME • *See* Yucca Extract.

PLUM EXTRACT • The extract of the fruit of the plum tree, *Prunus domestica*. The Indians boiled the wild plum and gargled with it to cure mouth sores.

POLYACRYLAMIDE • The polymer of acrylamide monomers, it is a white solid, water soluble, that is used as a thickening agent, suspending agent, and as an additive to adhesives. *See* Acrylic resins. Used as a film former in the imprinting of soft-shell gelatin capsules. Used in washing fruits and vegetables. Used in the manufacture of plastics used in nail polishes. Highly toxic and irritating to the skin. Causes central nervous system paralysis. Can be absorbed through unbroken skin.

POLYACRYLIC ACID • *See* Acrylic Resins.

POLYAMINO SUGAR CONDENSATE • The condensation product of the sugars fructose, galactose, glucose, lactose, maltose, mannose, rhamnose, ribose, or xylose, with a minute amount of amino acids such as alanine, arginine, aspartic acid, glutamic acid, glycine, histidine, hydroxyproline, isoleucine, leucine, lysine, methionine, phenylalanine, proline, pyroglutamic acid, serine, threonine, tyrosine, or valine. *See* Amino Acid.

POLYDEXTROSE • A reduced-calorie bulking agent developed by Pfizer, Inc., and approved for use in foods by the FDA in June 1981. The FDA says it is not a substitute for saccharin (*see*) nor a general sweetener but that it can replace sucrose (*see*) as a bulking agent in frozen desserts, cakes, and candies, and reduce calories in some products by as much as 50 percent. According to Pfizer, it is a one-calorie-per-gram bulking agent capable of replacing higher-calorie—four to nine calories per gram—ingredients such as sucrose, carbohydrates, and fats in many food products.

POLYETHOXYLATED ALKYLPHENOL • Dodecyl, Nonyl, and Octyl. Components of a commercial detergent for raw foods, followed by water rinsing. The only symptoms shown in animals poisoned with this substance is gastrointestinal irritation.

POLYETHYLENE • A polymer (*see*) of ethylene; a product of petro-leum gas or dehydration of alcohol. One of a group of lightweight thermoplastics that have a good resistance to chemicals, low moisture absorption, and good insulating properties. Used as a chewing gum base ingredient and as a film former and sheets for packaging. Used in hand lotions. No known skin toxicity, but implants of large amounts in rats caused cancer. Ingestion of large oral doses has produced kidney and liver damage.

POLYETHYLENE GLYCOL • 400–2,000 molecular weight. PEG. Defoaming agent in processed beet sugar and yeast. Used in hair straighteners, antiperspirants, baby products, fragrances, polish re-movers, hair tonics, lipsticks, and protective creams. It is a binder, plasticizing agent, solvent, and softener widely used for cosmetic cream bases and pharmaceutical ointments. Improves resistance to moisture and oxidation. No known toxicity.

POLYETHYLENE GLYCOL (600) DIOLEATE • Polyethylene glycol esters of mixed fatty acids from tall oil; Polyethylene Glycol (400–6,000). An agent in nonnutritive artificial sweeteners; a component of coatings and binders in tablet food; improves resistance to oxidation and moisture. *See* Polyols.

POLYGYLCERATE 60 • *See* Glycerides.

POLYGLYCEROL • Prepared from edible fats, oils, and esters of fatty acids. Derived from corn, cottonseed, palm, peanut, safflower, sesame, and soybean oils, lard, and tallow. Used as an emulsifier in cosmetics. No known toxicity.

POLYGLYCEROL ESTER • One of several partial or complete esters of saturated and unsaturated fatty acids with a variety of derivatives of polyglycerols ranging from diglycerol to triacontaglycerol. Prepared from edible fats, oils, and fatty acids, hydrogenated or nonhydrogenated (*see* Hydrogenation). Derived from corn, cottonseed, palm, peanut, safflower, sesame, and soybean oils, lard, and tallow. Used as lubricants, plasticizers, gelling agents, humectants, surface-active agents, dispersants, and emulsifiers in food and cosmetics preparations.

POLYGLYCERYL-4 COCOATE • *See* Coconut Oil and Polyglycerol.

POLYGLYCERYL-10 DECALINOLEATE • *See* Polyglycerol and Linoleic Acid.

POLYGLYCERYL-10 DECAOLEATE • *See* Oleic Acid and Polyglycerol.

POLYGLYCERYL-2 DIISOSTEATE • *See* Isostearic Acid and Polyglycerol.

POLYGLYCERYL-6 DIOLEATE • *See* Oleic Acid and Glycerin.

POLYGLYCERYL-6 DISTEARATE • *See* Stearic Acid and Glycerin.

POLYGLYCERYL-3 HYDROXYLAURYL ETHER • *See* Fatty Alcohols and Glycerin.

POLYGLYCERYL-4 ISOSTEARATE • *See* Isostearic Acid and Glycerin.

POLYGLYCERYL-3 OR -4 OR -8 OLEATE • An ester of oleic acid and glycerin (*see* both).

POLYGLYCERYL-3 OR -4 OLEATE • Oily liquid prepared by adding alcohol to coconut oil or other triglycerides with a polyglyceryl. Used in foods, drugs, and cosmetics as fat emulsifiers in conjunction with other emulsifiers to prepare creams, lotions, and other emulsion products. In addition, they may also be used as lubricants, plasticizers, gelling agents, and dispersants. No known toxicity.

POLYGLYCERYL-3-PEG-2 COCOAMIDE • *See* Coconut Oil and Glycerin.

POLYGLYCERYL-2-SESQUIISOSTEARATE • A mixture of esters of isostearic acid and glycerin (*see* both).

POLYGLYCERYL-2-SESQUILOLEATE • A mixture of ester of oleic acid and glycerin (*see* both).

POLYGLYCERYL SORBITOL • A condensation product of glycerin and sorbitol (*see* both).

POLYGLYCERYL-3, -4, OR -8 STEARATE • An ester of stearic acid and glycerin (*see* both).

POLYGLYCERYL-10 TETRAOLEATE • An ester of oleic acid and glycerin (*see* both).

POLYGLYCERYL-2 TETRASTEARATE • *See* Stearic Acid and Glycerin.

POLYISOBUTYLENE • *See* Resin, Isobutylene.

POLYLIMONENE • A general fixative derived from citrus oils. It is used in candy (4,500 ppm), chewing gum, and baked goods (1,000 ppm). It can be skin irritant and sensitizer. *See* Limonene.

POLYMER • A substance or product formed by combining many small molecules (monomers). The result is essentially recurring long-chain structural units that have tensile strength, elasticity, and hardness. Examples of polymers (literally, "having many parts") are plastics, fibers, rubber, and human tissue.

POLYMIXIN B$_4$ • A generic term for antibiotics obtained from fermentations of various media by strains of *Bacillus polymyxa*. Used as a bactericide in yeast culture for beer. May cause symptoms of renal irritation and damage.

POLYOLS • Alcohol compounds that absorb moisture. They have a low molecular weight: polyols with a molecular weight above 1,000 are solids and less toxic than those with a weight of 600 or below. The latter are liquid and although higher in toxicity, very large doses are required to kill animals. Such deaths in animals have been found to have occurred because of kidney damage. *See* Propylene Glycol and Polyethylene Glycol as examples.

POLYOXYALKALENE GLYCOL • Defoaming agent in beet sugar production. No known toxicity.

POLYOXYETHYLENE COMPOUNDS • The nonionic emulsifiers used in hand creams and lotions. Usually oily or waxy liquids. No known toxicity.

POLYOXYETHYLENE GLYCOL • Ester of edible cottonseed oil and fatty acids. Solubilizing agent in pickles. No known toxicity.

POLYOXYETHYLENE GLYCOL (600) MONORICINOLEATE • Defoaming component used in processing beet sugar and yeast. No known toxicity.

POLYOXYETHYLENE (140) MONOSTEARATE • Defoaming agent in processed foods; emulsifier for frozen desserts. Application to the skin of mice has been shown to cause skin tumors. The compound has been fed to animals and does not appear to produce tumors on its own but there is a suggestion that it allows cancer-causing agents to penetrate more quickly. On the FDA list for further study for long- and short-term effects since 1980.

POLYOXYETHYLENE (20) SORBITAN MONOSTEARATE • Polysorbate 60. An emulsifier and flavor-dispersing agent in shortening and edible oils. Used in whipped vegetable oil toppings, cake, and cake mixes; caking icing or filling; sugar-type confection coatings; coconut spread; beverage mixes; confectionery; chicken bases; gelatin desserts; dressings made without egg yolks; solid-state, edible vegetable fat–water emulsions used in substitutes for milk or cream; dietary vitamin supplements; foaming agents in nonalcoholic beverage mixes to be added to alcoholic beverages; and a wetting and dispersing agent for powdered processed foods. The FDA asked for further study of this additive in 1980.

POLYOXYETHYLENE (20) SORBITAN MONOOLEATE • Emulsifier and defoamer in the production of beet sugar; a dietary vitamin and mineral supplement. Used in dill oil in spiced green beans, icing, frozen custard, iced milk, fruit, and sherbet. The FDA asked for short-term, mutagenic, teratogenic, subacute, and reproductive effects in 1980 and has not reported any findings since.

POLYOXYETHYLENE (20) SORBITAN MONOPALMITATE • An emulsifier, flavor-dispersing agent, and defoaming agent. Used in whipped cream, beverages, confectionery, and soup. The FDA asked for further study of the safety of this additive in 1980 and has reported nothing about it since.

POLYOXYETHYLENE (20) SORBITAN TRISTEARATE • An emulsifier, defoaming agent, and flavor-dispersing agent. Used in cakes and cake mixes, including doughnuts, whipped mixes, whipped vegetable oil toppings, cake icings and fillings, ice cream, frozen custard, ice milk, fruit sherbet, and nonstandardized frozen desserts; solid-state edible vegetable fat–water emulsions used as substitutes for milk or cream in coffee; and as a wetting and dispersing agent in processed powdered food. No known toxicity.

POLYOXYETHYLENE STEARATE • A mixture of stearate (*see* Stearic Acid) and ethylene oxide, it is a waxy solid added to bread to make it "feel fresh." It was fed to rats as one-fourth of their diets and resulted in the formulation of bladder stones, and subsequently a number of tumors. Banned in 1952.

POLYOXYPROPYLENE GLYCOL • Defoaming agent for yeast and beet sugar. No known toxicity.

PROPYLENE GLYCOL • Defoaming agent in processed beet sugar and yeast. No known toxicity.

POLYSORBATES • 1 through 85. These are widely used emulsifiers and stabilizers. For example *polysorbate 20* is a viscous, oily liquid derived from lauric acid. It is an emulsifier used in cosmetic creams and lotions and a stabilizer of essential oils in water. It is used as a nonionic surfactant (*see*).

POLYSORBATE 60 AND POLYSORBATE 80 • Both are emulsifiers that have been associated with the contaminant 1,4 dioxane, known to cause cancer in animals. The 60 is a condensate of sorbitol with stearic acid and the 80 a condensate of sorbitol and oleic acid (*see* all). The 60 is waxy, is soluble in solvents, and is used as an emulsifier, stabilizer, wetting and dispersing agent for powdered processed foods, and a foaming agent for beverage mixes. It is added to chocolate coatings to prevent cocoa butter substitutes from tasting greasy. It is found in frozen and gelatin desserts, cakes, cake mixes, doughnuts, and artificial chocolate coatings, nondairy whipped cream and creamers, powdered convenience foods, salad dressings made without egg yolks, and vitamin supplements. The 80 is a viscous liquid with a faint caramel odor and is used as an emulsifier, stabilizer, and humectant. It prevents oil separating from nondairy whipped cream and helps nondairy coffee whiteners to dissolve. It is found in baked goods, nondairy whipped cream, coffee whiteners, ice cream, frozen custard, shortenings, and in vitamin and mineral supplements. Polysorbate 80 is also widely used in baby lotions, cold creams, cream deodorants, antiperspirants, suntan lotions, and in bath oil products. Polysorbate 40 is also widely used as an emulsifier in cosmetic creams and lotions and as a stabilizer of essential oils in water. No known toxicity for the polysorbates.

POLYSTYRENE • Used in the manufacture of cosmetic resins. Reported to be an unintentional additive when tea and coffee are drunk from polystyrene cups. Colorless to yellowish oily liquid with a penetrating odor. Obtained from ethylbenzene by removing the hydrogen or by chlorination. Sparingly soluble in water; soluble in alcohol. May be irritating to the eyes, mucous membranes, and, in high concentrations, may be narcotic.

POLYUNSATURATED FATS • The saturation of fat refers to the chemical structure of its constituent fatty acids. Polyunsaturates are liquid at room temperature and consist mainly of fatty acids that can hold four or more additional hydrogen atoms. *See* Monounsaturated Fats.

POLYVINYL ACETATE • Used in chewing gum base. No known toxicity. *See* Polyvinyl Alcohol.

POLYVINYL ALCOHOL • Synthetic resins used in lipstick, setting lotions, various creams. A polymer is prepared from polyvinyl acetates by replacement of the acetate groups with the hydroxyl groups. Dry, unplasticized polyvinyl alcohol powders are white to cream colored and have different viscosities. Solvent in hot and cold water but certain ones require alcohol-water mixtures. No known toxicity.

POLYVINYL BUTYRAL • The condensation of polyvinyl alcohol and butyraldehyde (*see* both), it is a synthetic flavoring found in coffee and strawberry and is used in the manufacture of rubber and synthetic resins and plasticizers. May be an irritant and narcotic.

POLYVINYL CHLORIDE. PVC. • Chloroethylene Polymer. Derived from vinyl chloride (*see*), it consists of a white powder or colorless granules that are resistant to weather, moisture, acids, fats, petroleum products, and fungus. It is widely used for everything from plumbing to raincoats. The use of PVC as a plastic wrap for food, including meats, and for human blood, has alarmed some scientists. Human and animal blood can extract potentially harmful chemicals from the plastic. The chemicals are added to polyvinyl chloride to make it flexible, and they migrate from the plastic into the blood and into the meats in amounts directly proportional to the length of time of storage. The result can be contamination of the blood, causing lung shock, a condition in which the patient's blood circulation to lungs is impeded. PVC is also used in cosmetics and toiletries in containers, nail enamels, and creams. PVC has caused tumors when injected under the skin of rats in doses of 100 milligrams per kilogram of body weight.

POLYVINYL ETHYL ETHER • *See* Polyvinyl Alcohol.

POLYVINYL IMIDAZOLINIUM ACETATE • The polymer of vinyl imidazolinium aceta. *See* Polyvinylpyrrolidone.

POLYVINYL METHYL ETHER • *See* Polyvinyl Alcohol.

POLYVINYLPOLYPYRROLIDONE • Used in dietary products up to 40 milligrams per day. Also a clarifying agent in vinegar. *See* Polyvinylpyrrolidone for toxicity.

POLYVINYLPYRROLIDONE. PVP • A faintly yellow solid plastic resin resembling albumin. Clarifying agent in vinegar and used as a plasma expander in medicine. In vinegar, up to 0.004 milligrams. It is used to give a softer set in shampoos, hair sprays, and lacquers; also a carrier in emollient creams, liquid lip rouge, and face rouge; also a clarifier in vinegar and a plasma expander in medicine. Ingestion may produce gas and fecal impaction or damage to lungs and kidneys. It may last in the system several months to a year. Strong circumstantial evidence indicates thesaurosis—foreign bodies in the lung—may be produced in susceptible individuals from concentrated exposure to PVP in hair sprays. Modest intravenous doses in rats caused them to develop tumors.

POMEGRANATE BARK EXTRACT • A flavoring from dried bark, stem, or root of trees in the Mediterranean region and elsewhere. Contains about 20 percent tannic acid (*see*); rind of fruit contains 30 percent. Formerly used to expel tapeworms. Overdose can cause nausea, vomiting, and diarrhea. GRAS.

POPPY SEED • The seed of the poppy. Used as a natural spice for flavoring for baked goods (8,600 ppm). Also used in the manufacture of paints, varnishes, and soaps. No known toxicity. GRAS.

POPLAR EXTRACT • Balm of Gilead. Extract of the leaves and twigs of *Populus nigra*. In ancient times, the buds were mashed to make a soothing salve that was spread on sunburned areas, scalds, scratches, inflamed skin, and wounds. They were also simmered in lard for use as an ointment and for antiseptic purposes. The leaves and bark were steeped by American colonists to make a soothing tea. It supposedly helped allergies and soothed reddened eyes. No known toxicity.

POT MARIGOLD • *See* Marigold, Pot. GRAS.

POT MARJORAM • *See* Marjoram, Pot. GRAS.

POTASSIUM ACETATE • Colorless, water-absorbing crystals or powder, odorless or with a faint acetic aroma and a salty taste. Used as a buffer, antimicrobial preservative. Very soluble in water. Also used medicinally to treat irregular heartbeat and as a diuretic. No known toxicity.

POTASSIUM ACID TARTRATE • The salt of tartaric acid. Colorless with a pleasant odor. An acid and buffer, it is the acid constituent of some baking powders. Used in effervescent beverages. It is also used in some confectionery products. Formerly a cathartic. No known toxicity.

POTASSIUM ALGINATE • *See* Alginates.

POTASSIUM ALUM • *See* Alum.

POTASSIUM ASPARTAME • *See* Aspartame.

POTASSIUM ASPARTATE • The potassium salt of aspartic acid (*see*).

POTASSIUM BICARBONATE • Carbonic Acid, Monopotassium Salt. Colorless, odorless, transparent crystals or powder, slightly alkaline, salty taste. Considered a miscellaneous general-purpose food additive, it is present in fluids and tissues of the body as a product of normal metabolic processes. Soluble in water. It is used in baking, soft drinks, and in low-pH liquid detergents. The final report to the FDA of the Select Committee on GRAS Substances stated in 1980 that it should continue its GRAS status with no limitations other than good manufacturing practices.

POTASSIUM BISULFITE • Same uses as for sodium sulfite (*see*) in ale, beer, fruit-pie mix. The final report to the FDA of the Select

Committee on GRAS Substances stated in 1980 that there is no evidence in the available information that it is a hazard to the public when used as it is now and it should continue its GRAS status with limitations on the amounts that can be added to food.

POTASSIUM BROMATE • The compound is added as an improving agent in bread. The expected result is to obtain a fine spongelike quality with the action of oxygen. This method is used in Great Britain, the United States, and Japan. Legal allowance of potassium bromate is below 50 ppm. Antiseptic and astringent in toothpaste, mouthwashes, and gargles as 3- to 5-percent solution. Colorless or white crystals. Very toxic when taken internally. Burns and skin irritation have been reported from its industrial uses. In toothpaste it has been reported to have caused inflammation and bleeding of gums. In 1980, the Ames Test (*see*) found it to be a mutagen.

POTASSIUM BROMIDE • A preservative used in washing fruits and vegetables. Used medicinally as a sedative and antileptic. In large doses it can cause central nervous system depression. Prolonged intake may cause bromism. Bromism's main symptoms are headache, mental inertia, slow heart beat, gastric distress, skin rash, acne, muscular weakness, and occasionally violent delirium. Bromides can cross the placental barrier, and have caused skin rashes in the fetus.

POTASSIUM CARBONATE • Salt of Tartar. Pearl Ash. Inorganic salt of potassium. Odorless, white powder, soluble in water but practically insoluble in alcohol. Used as an alkali in combination with potassium hydroxide (*see*) for extracting color from annatto seed (*see*). Also used in confections and cocoa products. Used in freckle lotions, liquid shampoos, vanishing creams, setting lotions, and permanent wave lotions; also in the manufacture of soap, glass, pottery, and to finish leather. Formerly employed as a diuretic to reduce body water and as an alkalizer. Irritating and caustic to human skin and may cause dermatitis of the scalp, forehead, and hands. The final report to the FDA of the Select Committee on GRAS Substances stated in 1980 that it should continue its GRAS status with no limitations other than good manufacturing practices.

POTASSIUM CASEINATE • The potassium salt of milk proteins used in ice cream, frozen custard, ice milk, and fruit sherbets. See Casein.

POTASSIUM CHLORIDE • A colorless, crystalline, odorless powder with a salty taste. A yeast food used in the brewing industry to improve brewing and fermentation and in the jelling industry. Small intestinal ulcers may occur with oral administration. Large doses ingested can cause gastrointestinal irritation, purging, weakness, and circulatory collapse. Used as a substitute for sodium chloride (*see*) in low-sodium dietary foods. The final report to the FDA of the Select Committee on

GRAS Substances stated in 1980 that it should continue its GRAS status with no limitations other than good manufacturing practices.

POTASSIUM CITRATE • A transparent or white powder, odorless, with a cool, salty taste. Used as a buffer in confections and in artificially sweetened jellies and preserves. It is a urinary alkalizer and gastric antacid. No known toxicity. The final report to the FDA of the Select Committee on GRAS Substances stated in 1980 that it should continue its GRAS status with no limitations other than good manufacturing practices.

POTASSIUM COCO HYDROLYZED PROTEIN • *See* Proteins.

POTASSIUM COCOATE • *See* Coconut Oil.

POTASSIUM CORNATE • The potassium salt of fatty acids derived from corn oil. *See* Corn Oil.

POTASSIUM GLUCONATE • The potassium salt of gluconic acid (*see*) used as a buffering agent that helps keep soda water bubbling. No known toxicity. The final report to the FDA of the Select Committee on GRAS Substances stated in 1980 that it should continue its GRAS status with no limitations other than good manufacturing practices.

POTASSIUM GLYCEROPHOSPHATE • Nutrient additive. *See* Glycerides. GRAS.

POTASSIUM HYDROXIDE • Caustic Potash. An alkali used to extract color from annatto seed, a peeling agent for tubers and fruits, also in cacao products. Occasionally used to prevent the growth of horns in calves. It is used as an emulsifier in hand lotions, as a cuticle softener, and as an alkali in liquid soaps, protective creams, shaving preparations, and cream rouges. Prepared industrially by electrolysis of potassium chloride (*see*). White or slightly yellow lumps. It may cause irritation of the skin in cuticle removers. Extremely corrosive and ingestion may cause violent pain, bleeding, collapse, and death. When applied to the skin of mice, moderate dosages cause tumors. May cause skin rash and burning. Concentrations above 5 percent can destroy fingernails as well. Good quality toilet soaps do not contain more than 0.25 percent free alkali. The FDA banned household products containing more than 10 percent potassium hydroxide. GRAS.

POTASSIUM HYPOPHOSPHATE • The final report to the FDA of the Select Committee on GRAS Substances stated in 1980 that it should continue its GRAS status with no limitations other than good manufacturing practices. *See* Phosphate.

POTASSIUM IODATE • *See* Iodine Sources. GRAS.

POTASSIUM IODIDE • Potassium salt. A dye remover and an antiseptic. Used in table salt as a source of dietary iodine. It is also in some drinking water. May cause allergic reactions. GRAS.

POTASSIUM LACTATE • Flavoring. *See* Lactic Acid. GRAS.

POTASSIUM LAURATE • The potassium salt of Lauric Acid (*see*).

POTASSIUM LAURYL SULFATE • A water softener used in shampoos. *See* Sodium Lauryl Sulfate.

POTASSIUM METABISULFITE • Potassium Pyrosulfite. White or colorless, with an odor of sulfur dioxide (*see*), it is an antioxidant, preservative, and antifermentative in breweries and wineries. Should not be used in meats or foods recognized as sources of Vitamin B_1. Also used for bleaching straw. It is also used as an antiseptic, preservative, antioxidant, and as a developing agent in dyes. Low toxicity. The final report to the FDA of the Select Committee on GRAS Substances stated in 1980 that there is no evidence in the available information that it is a hazard to the public when used as it is now and it should continue its GRAS status with limitations on the amounts that can be added to foods.

POTASSIUM-*n*-METHYLDITHIO-CARBAMATE • A bacteria-killing component in controlling microorganisms in cane sugar mills. Carbamates are used to prevent sprouting in potatoes and other products by stopping cell division, something we call mutations. Carbamate mutations may lead to defective children and to cancer. The final report to the FDA of the Select Committee on GRAS Substances stated that there is no evidence in the available information that it is a hazard to the public when used as it is now and it should continue its GRAS status with limitations on the amounts that can be added to food.

POTASSIUM MYRISTATE • The potassium salt of myristic acid (*see*).

POTASSIUM NITRATE • *See* Nitrate.

POTASSIUM NITRITE • *See* Nitrite.

POTASSIUM PALMITATE • The potassium salt of Palmitic Acid (*see*).

POTASSIUM PERMANGANATE • Dark purple or bronzelike odorless crystals with a sweet, antiseptic taste, used as a starch modifier. Dilute solutions are mildly irritating; highly concentrated solutions are caustic.

POTASSIUM PERSULFATE • White crystals, soluble in water or alcohol. Derived from potassium sulfate. Used as a flour maturing agent, for modification of starch, and as an antiseptic. Sprayed on some fruits. Strong irritant.

POTASSIUM PHOSPHATE • Monobasic, Dibasic, and Tribasic. Used as a yeast food in the brewing industry and in the production of champagne and other sparkling wines. Has been used medicinally as a urinary acidifier. No known toxicity. The final report to the FDA of the Select Committee on GRAS Substances stated in

1980 that it should continue its GRAS status with no limitations other than good manufacturing practices.

POTASSIUM POLYMETAPHOSPHATE • The final report to the FDA of the Select Committee on GRAS Substances stated in 1980 that it should continue its GRAS status with no limitations other than good manufacturing practices. *See* Potassium Phosphate for uses.

POTASSIUM PYROPHOSPHATE • Colorless, deliquescent crystals or granules, used as a sequestering, peptizing, and dispersing agent and in soaps and detergents. Low toxicity. The final report to the FDA of the Select Committee on GRAS Substances stated in 1980 that it should continue its GRAS status with no limitations other than good manufacturing practices.

POTASSIUM SALTS OF FATTY ACIDS • In foods as binders, emulsifiers, and anticaking agents. *See* Fatty Acids.

POTASSIUM SILICATE. SOLUBLE POTASH GLASS • Colorless or yellowish translucent to transparent glasslike particles. It is used for inorganic protective coatings, for phosphorous on television tubes, in detergents, as a catalyst, and in adhesives. Used as a binder in cosmetics and in soap manufacturing. Also used as a detergent and in the glass and ceramics industries. Usually very slowly soluble in cold water. No known toxicity. The final report to the FDA of the Select Committee on GRAS Substances stated in 1980 that it should continue its GRAS status with no limitations other than good manufacturing practices.

POTASSIUM SORBATE • Sorbic Acid Potassium Salt. White crystalline powder used as a preservative; a mold and yeast inhibitor; and a fungistat in beverages, baked goods, chocolate, soda fountain syrups, fresh fruit cocktail, tangerine puree (sherbet base), salads (potato, macaroni, cole slaw, gelatin), cheesecake, pie fillings, cake, cheeses in consumer-size packages, and artificially sweetened jellies and preserves. Low oral toxicity but may cause irritation of the skin. GRAS.

POTASSIUM STEARATE • Stearic Acid Potassium Salt. White powder with a fatty odor. Strongly alkaline. A defoaming agent in brewing. Also used in the manufacture of soap, hand creams, emulsified fragrances, lotions, and shaving creams. Acts as a defoaming agent. No known toxicity.

POTASSIUM SULFATE • Does not occur free in nature but is combined with sodium sulfate. Colorless or white crystalline powder, with a bitter taste. Used as a flavoring in foods. A water corrective used in the brewing industry. Used as a reagent (*see*) in cosmetics and as a salt substitute; also used as a fertilizer and a cathartic. Large doses can cause severe gastrointestinal bleeding. No known toxicity to the skin. GRAS.

POTASSIUM SULFITE • *See* Sulfites.

POTASSIUM TRIPOLYPHOSPHATE • A white crystalline solid that is used in water-treating compounds, cleaners, and fertilizers; widely used as a sequestrant (*see*) in processed foods. The final report to the FDA of the Select Committee on GRAS Substances stated in 1980 that it should continue its GRAS status with no limitations other than good manufacturing practices.

POTATO STARCH • A flour prepared from potatoes, ground to a pulp and washed of fibers. Swells in hot water to form a gel on cooling. A demulcent used in dusting powder, an emollient in dry shampoos and baby powders. With glycerin forms soothing, protective applications for eczema, skin rash, chapped skin. May cause allergic skin reactions and stuffy nose in the hypersensitive. The final report to the FDA of the Select Committee on GRAS Substances stated in 1980 that it should continue its GRAS status with no limitations other than good manufacturing practices.

POTENTIATOR • A flavor ingredient with little flavor of its own that augments or alters the flavor response, such as sodium glutamate and sodium inosinate.

PPG • Abbreviation for Propylene Glycol (*see*).

PPG BUTETH-260 THROUGH 5100 • Emulsifiers.

PPG BUTETH ETHER-200 • Emulsifier. Polymer (*see*) prepared from butyl alcohol with propylene glycol (*see* both).

PPG BUTYL ETHER-300 TO 1715 • Emulsifiers. *See* PPG Butyl Ether-200.

PPG-4-CETETH-1 OR -5 OR -10 • *See* Cetyl Alcohol.

PPG-8-CETETH -5 OR -10 OR -20 • *See* Cetyl Alcohol

PPG-10-CETYL ETHER • *See* Cetyl Alcohol.

PPG-28 CETYL ETHER • *See* Cetyl Alcohol and Propylene.

PPG-30 CETYL ETHER • A liquid nonionic surfactant (*see*). No known toxicity. *See* Cetyl Alcohol.

PPG-20-DECYLTETRADECETH-10 • *See* Decanoic Acid.

PPG-24 OR -66 GLYCERETH-24 OR -12 • *See* Glycerin.

PPG-27 AND -55 GLYCERYLETHER • *See* Glycerin and Propylene Glycol.

PPG-ISOCETYL ETHER • *See* Cetyl Alcohol.

PPG-3-ISOSTEARETH-9. • *See* Stearyl Alcohol and Propylene Glycol.

PPG-9 LAURATE • *See* Lauric acid.

PPG-20-METHYL GLUCOSE ETHER • *See* Propylene Glycol and Glucose.

PPG-3-MYRETH-11 • *See* Polyethylene Glycol and Myristic Acid.

PPG-4 MYRISTYL ETHER • *See* Fatty Alcohols.

PPG-6-C12-18 PARETH • A mixture of synthetic alcohols. *See* Fatty Alcohols.

PPG-2 SALICYLATE • *See* Dipropylene Glycol Salicylate.

PPG-9-STEARETH-3 • *See* Stearyl Alcohol.

PPG-11 OR -15 STEARYL ETHER • *See* Polypropylene Glycol and Stearyl Alcohol.

PPM • Parts per million.

PRECIPITATE • To separate out from solution or suspension. A deposit of solid separated out from a solution or suspension as a result of a chemical or physical change, as by the action of a reagent (*see*).

PREGELATINIZED STARCH • When starch and water are heated the starch molecules burst and form a gelatin. The final report to the FDA of the Select Committee on GRAS Substances stated in 1980 that it should continue its GRAS status with no limitations other than good manufacturing practices.

PRESERVATIVES • About 100 "antispoilants," which retard or prevent food from going "bad" are in common use. Preservatives for fatty products are called "antioxidants." Preservatives used in bread are labeled "mold" or "rope" inhibitors. They include sodium propionate and calcium propionate (*see* both). Preservatives to prevent mold and fungus growth on citrus fruits are called "fungicides." Among the most commonly used preservatives are sodium benzoate (*see*) to prevent the growth of microbes on cheese and syrups; sulfur dioxide (*see*) to inhibit discoloration in fruit juice concentrates; and nitrates and nitrites that are used to "cure" processed meats. In many instances a product might show no visible evidence of microbial contamination and yet contain actively growing, potentially harmful germs.

PRICKLY ASH BARK • A natural cola, maple, and root beer flavor extract from a prickly aromatic shrub or small tree bearing yellow flowers. Used in beverages, candy, and baked goods. No known toxicity. GRAS.

PRIMULA EXTRACT • The extract of various species of *Primula* taken from the rhizome and roots of the primrose or cowslip. It has been used as an expectorant, diuretic, and worm medicine. In some sensitive persons, it may cause a rash.

PROLINE, L FORM • An amino acid (*see*) used as a food supplement but classified as nonessential. Usually isolated from wheat or gelatin. L-Proline is the naturally occurring form and DL-Proline is the synthetic. GRAS.

PROPANE • A gas heavier than air; odorless when pure. It is used as a fuel and refrigerant. Cleared for use in combination with octafluorocyclobutane by a spray propellant and aerating agent for foamed and sprayed foods. Cleared for use in a spray propellant and as an aerating agent for cosmetics in aerosols. May be narcotic in high concentrations. The final report to the FDA of the Select Committee on GRAS Substances stated in 1980 that it should continue its GRAS status with no limitations other than good manufacturing practices. GRAS.

PROPANOIC ACID • *See* Propionic Acid.

PROPELLANT • A compressed gas used to expel the contents of containers in the form of aerosols. Chlorofluorocarbons were widely used because of their nonflammability. The strong possibility that they contribute to depletion of the ozone layer of the upper atmosphere has resulted in prohibition of their use for this purpose. Other propellants used are hydrocarbon gases, such as butane and propane, carbon dioxide, and nitrous oxide. The materials dispersed include shaving cream, whipping cream, and cosmetic preparations.

PROPIONALDEHYDE • Propanal. A synthetic flavoring agent that occurs naturally in apples and onions. Used in fruit flavorings for beverages, ice cream, ices, candy, and baked goods. Suffocating odor. May cause respiratory irritation.

PROPIONIC ACID • Propanoic Acid. Occurs naturally in apples, strawberries, tea, and violet leaves. An oily liquid with a slightly pungent, rancid odor. Can be obtained from wood pulp, waste liquor, and by fermentation. Used in butter and fruit flavorings for beverages, ice cream, ices, candy, baked goods, and cheese flavorings for beverages, ice cream, ices, candy, baked goods, and cheese (600 ppm). Also used as an inhibitor and preservative to prevent mold in baked goods and processed cheeses. Also used in perfume bases and as a mold inhibitor, antioxidant, and preservative in cosmetics. Its salts have been used as antifungal agents to treat skin mold. May cause migraine in those susceptible to migraines and contact with the chemical may cause skin irritations in bakery workers. Large oral dose in rats is lethal. GRAS.

PROPYL ACETATE • Colorless liquid, soluble in water, derived from propane and acetate (*see* both). It has the odor of pears. A synthetic currant, raspberry, strawberry, apple, cherry, peach, pineapple, and rum flavoring agent for beverages, ice cream, ices, candy, and baked goods. Also used in the manufacture of perfumes and as a solvent for resins. It may be irritating to the skin and mucous membranes and narcotic in high doses.

PROPYL ALCOHOL • Obtained from crude fuel oil. Alcoholic and slightly overpowering odor. Occurs naturally in cognac green oil, cognac white oil, and onion oil. A synthetic fruit flavoring for beverages, ice cream, ices, candy, and baked goods. Used instead of ethyl alcohol as a solvent for shellac, gums, resins, oils; as a denaturant (*see*) for alcohol in perfumery. Not a primary irritant, but because it dissolves fat it has a drying effect on the skin and may lead to cracking, fissuring, and infections. No adverse effects have been reported from local application as a lotion, liniment, mouthwash, gargle, or sponge bath. Mildly irritating to the eyes and mucous membranes. Ingestion may cause symptoms similar to that of ethyl alcohol (*see*).

p-PROPYL ANISOLE • A synthetic flavoring agent, colorless to pale yellow, with an anise odor. Used in licorice, root beer, spice, vanilla, wintergreen, and birch beer flavoring for beverages, ice cream, candy, and baked goods. No known toxicity.

PROPYL BENZOATE • A synthetic fruit flavoring agent for beverages, ice cream, ices, candy, and baked goods. No known toxicity.

PROPYL BUTYRATE • Contains propyl alcohol (*see*) and butyric acid (*see*). A synthetic strawberry, banana, pineapple, plum, tutti-frutti, liquor, and rum flavoring agent for beverages, ice cream, ices, candy, and baked goods. *See* Propyl Alcohol and Butryic Acid for toxicity.

PROPYL CINNAMATE • Cinnamic Acid. A synthetic berry, floral, rose, apple, grape, and honey flavoring agent for beverages, ice cream, ices, candy, baked goods, and gelatins. No known toxicity.

PROPYL FORMATE. • Formic Acid. A synthetic berry, apple, and rum flavoring agent for beverages, ice cream, ices, candy, and baked goods. *See* Formic Acid for toxicity.

PROPYL 2-FURANACRYLATE • A synthetic coffee and honey flavoring agent for beverages and candy. No known toxicity.

PROPYL 2-FUROATE • A synthetic chocolate and mushroom flavoring agent for candy, baked goods, and condiments. No known toxicity.

PROPYL GALLATE • A fine, white, odorless powder with a bitter taste used as an antioxidant for foods, fats, and oils and for potato flakes, mashed potatoes, and mayonnaise. Also used in lemon, lime, fruit, and spice flavorings for beverages, ice cream, ices, candy, baked goods, and gelatin desserts. Also used as an antioxidant in creams and lotions. Can cause stomach or skin irritation especially in people who suffer from asthma or are sensitive to aspirin. Reaffirmed as GRAS in the FDA's reevaluation in the following amounts: 0.02 percent maximum in fat or oil content of food; maximum of 0.015 percent in food prepared by the manufacturer. GRAS.

PROPYL HEPTANOATE • A synthetic berry, coffee, fruit, cognac, and rum flavoring agent for beverages, ice cream, ices, candy, liqueurs, and baked goods. No known toxicity.

PROPYL HEXANOATE • A synthetic pineapple flavoring agent for beverages, ice cream, ices, and candy. No known toxicity.

PROPYL-p-HYDROXYBENZOATE • Propylparaben. A preservative used in beverages, candy, baked goods, artificially sweetened jellies and preserves. Also used in fruit flavorings for beverages, ice cream, ices, candy, and baked goods. Less toxic than benzoic acid (*see*) or salicylic acid (*see*). Experimental animals showed no kidney or liver damage. On the FDA list for further study for short-term mutagenic, subacute, teratogenic, and reproductive effects. GRAS.

PROPYL ISOVALERATE • A synthetic strawberry, apple, banana, and peach flavoring agent for beverages, ice cream, ices, candy, and baked goods. No known toxicity.

PROPYL MERCAPTAN • A synthetic berry and onion flavoring agent for baked goods and pickles. No known toxicity.

PROPYL PHENYLACETATE • A synthetic butter, caramel, rose, fruit, and honey flavoring agent for beverages, ice cream, ices, candy, and baked goods. *See* Acetic Acid for toxicity.

PROPYL PROPIONATE • Propyl alcohol and propionic acid. A synthetic banana, cherry, melon, peach, prune, apple, plum, and rum flavoring agent for beverages, ice cream, ices, candy, and baked goods. *See* Propyl Alcohol and Propionic Acid for toxicity.

PROPYLENE GLYCOL • 1, 2-Propanediol. A clear, colorless, viscous liquid, slightly bitter tasting. In food, it is used in confectionery, chocolate products, ice cream emulsifiers, shredded coconut, beverages, baked goods, toppings, icings, and meat products to prevent discoloration during storage. Used in antifreeze in breweries and dairy establishments. It is the most common moisture-carrying vehicle other than water itself in cosmetics. It has better permeation through the skin than glycerin and is less expensive although it has been linked to more sensitivity reactions. Absorbs moisture, acts as a solvent and a wetting agent. Used in liquid makeup, foundation makeup, foundation creams, mascaras, spray deodorants, hair straighteners, liquid powders, pre-shave lotions, after-shave lotions, baby lotions, cold creams, emollients, antiperspirants, lipsticks, mouthwashes, stick perfumes, and suntan lotions. It is being reduced and being replaced by safer glycols such as butylene and polyethylene glycol. Large oral doses in animals have been reported to cause central nervous system depression and slight kidney changes. The final report to the FDA of the Select Committee on GRAS Substances stated in 1980 that it should continue its GRAS status with no limitations other than good manufacturing practices.

PROPYLENE GLYCOL ALGINATE • Kelcloid®. The propylene glycol ester of alginic acid (*see*) derived from seaweed. Used as a stabilizer, filler, and defoaming agent in food. Cleared for use in French dressing and salad dressing under the food standard regulations. Use as a stabilizer in ice cream, frozen custard, ice milk, fruit sherbet, and water ices is permitted up to 0.5 percent of the weight of the finished product. Can cause allergic reactions. The final report to the FDA of the Select Committee on GRAS Substances stated in 1980 that there is no evidence in the available information that it is a hazard to the public when used as it is now and it should continue its GRAS status with limitations on amounts that can be added to food.

PROPYLENE GLYCOL MONOSTEARATE • Cream-colored wax, which dispenses in water and is soluble in hot alcohol. It is used as a lubricating agent and emulsifier; also as a dough conditioner in baked goods. Employed as a stabilizer of essential oils. Slightly more toxic than propylene glycol (*see*) in animals, and in large doses produces central nervous system depression and kidney injury. The final report to the FDA of the Select Committee on GRAS Substances stated in 1980 that it should continue its GRAS status with no limitations other than good manufacturing practices.

PROPYLENE OXIDE • Propene Oxide. Colorless, liquid starch modifier. No known toxicity.

3-PROPYLIDENEPHTHALIDE • A synthetic fruit and spice flavoring agent for beverages, ice cream, ices, candy, and baked goods. No known toxicity.

PROPYLPARABEN • Propyl p-Hydroxybenzoate. Developed in Europe, the esters of *p*-hydroxybenzoic acid are widely used in the cosmetic industry as preservatives and bacteria and fungus killers. They are active against a variety of organisms, are neutral, low in toxicity, slightly soluble, and active in all solutions, alkaline, neutral, or acid. Used in shampoos, baby preparations, foundation creams, beauty masks, dentifrices, eye lotions, hair-grooming aids, nail creams, and wave sets. Used medicinally to treat fungus infections. Can cause contact dermatitis. Less toxic than benzoic or salicylic acid (*see* both). GRAS.

PROPYLPARASEPT • See Propyl p-Hydroxybenzoate.

a-PROPYLPHENETHYL ALCOHOL • A synthetic fruit flavoring agent for beverages, ice cream, ices, candy, and puddings. Toxicity similar to ethanol (*see*).

PROTEASE • An enzyme used as a meat tenderizer, and in sausage curing, dough conditioning, and beer haze removal. No known toxicity.

PROTECTIVE COATINGS • Antioxidants and preservatives that are used to coat cheeses, and fresh fruits and vegetables to retard spoilage. The coatings may expose consumers to hidden antibiotics or coal-tar products. Among the coating additives used are: Anoxomer; Calcium Disodium and Disodium EDTA; Coumaroneindene resin; Ethoxyquin;

Morpholine; Natamycin; Petroleum naphtha; Polyacrylamide; Synthetic paraffin and succinic derivatives; and Terpene resin; (*see* all). Citrus fruits, squash, grapes, sweet potatoes, asparagus, melons, papaya, plantain, turnips, watermelons, and nuts are commonly coated.

PROTEINS • The chief nitrogen-containing constituents of plants and animals—the essential constituents of every living cell. They are complex but by weight contain about 50 percent carbon, about 20 percent oxygen, about 15 percent nitrogen, about 7 percent hydrogen, and some sulfur. Some also contain iron and phosphorous. Proteins are colorless, odorless, and generally tasteless. They vary in solubility. They readily undergo putrefaction, hydrolysis, and dilution with acids or alkalies. They are regarded as combinations of amino acids (*see*).

PROTEIN HYDROZYLATES • Used as flavor enhancers, particularly in meat products. *See* Protein and Hydrolysis.

PROVITAMIN A • *See* Carotene.

PRUSSIATE OF SODA, YELLOW • Salt of hydrocyanic acid derived from ammonia. Anticaking agent in salt. Hydrocyanic acid is toxic by ingestion, inhalation, and skin absorption.

PSYLLIUM SEED HUSK • A stabilizer from the seed of the flea seed plant used in frozen desserts up to 0.5 percent of the weight of the finished product. No known toxicity.

PULEGONE • Found in oils of plants, principally the pennyroyal. Pleasant odor, midway between camphor and peppermint. Used in peppermint flavorings for beverages, ice cream, ices, candy, and baked goods. *See* Pennyroyal Oil for toxicity.

PULPS. FROM WOOD, STRAW, BAGASSE, OR OTHER NATURAL SOURCES • A source of cellulose in food. The wood is treated with a mixture containing mainly sodium hydroxide (*see*). Treatment removes the fibrous lignin—the resinous substance that binds the fiber that lines the cells of wood. An indirect human food additive from packaging, the FDA's reevaluation in 1976 labeled pulps. GRAS.

PYRIDINE • Occurs naturally in coffee and coal tar. Disagreeable odor; sharp taste. Used in chocolate flavorings for beverages, ice cream, ices, candy, and baked goods. Also used as a solvent for organic liquids and compounds. Once used to treat asthma, but may cause central nervous system depression and irritation of the skin and respiratory tract. After prolonged administration, kidney and liver damage may result. Pyridine is absorbed from the respiratory and gastrointestinal tract. Small oral doses in humans have produced loss of appetite, nausea, fatigue, and mental depression.

PYRIDOXINE • *See* Pyridoxine HCL.

PYRIDOXINE DIOCTENOATE • Vitamin B$_6$ Hydrochloride. Texturizer. A colorless or white crystalline powder present in many foodstuffs. A coenzyme that helps in the metabolism of amino acids (*see*) and fats. Also soothing to skin. Nontoxic.

PYRIDOXINE HYDROCHLORIDE. VITAMIN B$_6$ • A colorless or white crystalline powder added to evaporated milk base in infant foods. Present in many foodstuffs. Especially good sources are yeast, liver, and cereals. A coenzyme which helps in the metabolism of amino acids (*see*) and fat. Permits normal red blood cell formation. The final report to the FDA of the Select Committee on GRAS Substances stated in 1980 that it should continue its GRAS status with no limitations other than good manufacturing practices.

PYRIDOXINE TRIPALMITATE • Vitamin B$_6$ Tripalmitate. *See* Pyridoxine HCL.

PYROLIGNEOUS ACID AND EXTRACT • A yellow acid. Consists of 6 percent acetic acid (*see*), and small concentrations of creosote, methyl alcohol, and acetone (*see*). It is obtained by the destructive distillation of wood. Used as a synthetic flavoring in butter, butterscotch, caramel, rum, tobacco, smoke, and vanilla flavorings for beverages, ice cream, ices, candy, baked goods, puddings, and meats (300 ppm). The extract is used largely for smoking meats (300 ppm) and in smoke flavorings for baked goods (200 ppm) and alcoholic beverages. It is corrosive and may cause epigastric pain, vomiting, circulatory collapse, and death.

PYROMUCIC ALDEHYDE • *See* Furfural.

PYROPHOSPHATE. SALT OF PYROPHOSPHORIC ACID • It increases the effectiveness of antioxidants in creams and ointments. In concentrated solutions it can be irritating to the skin and mucous membranes.

PYRORACEMIC ACID • *See* Pyruvic Acid.

PYRUVALDEHYDE • A synthetic flavoring, yellowish, with a pungent odor. Formed as an intermediate in the metabolism or fermentation of carbohydrates and lactic acid (*see*). Used in coffee, honey, and maple flavorings for beverages, ice cream, ices, candy, and baked goods. No known toxicity.

PYRUVIC ACID • An important intermediate in fermentation and metabolism, it occurs naturally in coffee and when sugar is metabolized in muscle. It is reduced to lactic acid (*see*) during exertion. Pyruvic acid is isolated from cane sugar. It is a synthetic flavoring used in coffee and rum flavorings for beverages, ice cream, ices, candy, chewing gum, and baked goods. Has been used as a paste in the treatment of deep burns. No known toxicity.

Q

QUACK GRASS • A couch grass, a pernicious weed in cultivated fields. *See* Dog Grass Extract.

QUASSIA EXTRACT • Bitter Ash. Bitterwood. Yellowish white to bright yellow chips. Bitter alkaloid obtained from the wood of *Quassia amara,* a tree bearing bright scarlet flowers grown in Jamaica, the Caribbean Islands, and South America. So named for a black slave who discovered the medicinal value in the mid-eighteenth century. Slight odor, very bitter taste. Used in bitters, citrus, cherry, grape, liquor, root beer, sarsaparilla, and vanilla flavorings for beverages, baked goods, and liquors. In cosmetics, it is used chiefly as a denaturant for ethyl alcohol. Used to poison flies; to imitate hops; and as a bitter tonic and remedy for roundworms in children. Toxic to humans.

QUATERNARY AMMONIUM COMPOUNDS • A wide variety of preservatives, surfactants, germicides, sanitizers, antiseptics, and deodorants used in cosmetics. They are used less often as preservatives for food. Diluted solutions are used in medicine to sterilize the skin and mucous membranes. All the quaternary ammonium compounds can be toxic, depending upon the dose and concentrations.

QUEBRACHO BARK EXTRACT • Extract of a native Argentine tree, used in fruit, rum, and vanilla flavorings for beverages, ice cream, candy, ices, and baked goods. Closely related to the tranquilizer reserpine. Once promoted as an aphrodisiac, it can cause low blood pressure, nausea, abdominal distress, weakness, and fatigue.

QUERCITIN • The inner bark of a species of oak tree common in North America. Its active ingredient, isoquercitin, is used in forming resins and in dark brown hair dye shades but employed mainly for dyeing artificial hair pieces. Allergic reactions have been reported. *See* Rutin.

QUERCUS ALBA • *See* Oak Bark Extract.

QUICK GRASS • Triticum. *See* Dog Grass Extract.

QUILLAIA • China Bark Extract. *See* Quillaja Extract.

QUILLAJA EXTRACT • Soap Bark. Quillay Bark. Panama Bark. China Bark. The extract of the bark of *Quillaja saponaria.* The inner dried bark of a tree grown in South America. Used in fruit, root beer, and spice flavorings for beverages, ice cream, candy. Formerly used to treat bronchitis and externally as a detergent and local irritant. No known toxicity.

QUINCE SEED • The seed of a plant grown in southern Asia and Europe for its fatty oil. Thick jelly produced by soaking seeds in water. Used in fruit flavorings for beverages, ice cream, ices, and baked goods. Used in setting lotions as a suspension in skin creams and lotions, as a thickening agent in depilatories, and as an emulsifier for fragrances, hand creams, lotions, rouges, and wave sets; medicinally as a demulcent. Has been largely replaced by cheaper substitutes. It may cause allergic reactions. GRAS.

QUININE BISULFATE • Most important alkaloid of cinchona extract (*see*) from trees that grow wild in South America and are cultivated in Java. Very bitter. Used in bitters flavoring for beverages and not to exceed 83 ppm in soda. Used to treat fever and as a local anesthetic and analgesic. No known toxicity. *See* Quinine Extract.

QUININE EXTRACT • An extract of cinchona bark (*see* Cinchona Extract), which grows wild in South America. White crystalline powder, almost insoluble in water. It is used as a local anesthetic in hair tonics and sunscreen preparations. Used in bitters as flavoring for beverages in limited amounts. When taken internally, it reduces fever. It is also used as a flavoring agent in numerous over-the-counter cold and headache remedies as well as "bitter lemon" and tonic water, which may contain as much as 5 milligrams per 100 milliliters. Cinchonism, which may consist of nausea, vomiting, disturbances of vision, ringing in the ears, and nerve deafness, may occur from an overdose of quinine. Used as local anesthetic in hair tonics and sunscreen preparations. If there is a sensitivity to quinine, such symptoms can result after ingesting tonic water. Quinine more commonly causes a rash.

QUININE HYDROCHLORIDE • A synthetic flavoring agent derived from cinchona extract (*see*) and used in bitters, citrus, and fruit flavorings for beverages. Some medical use as quinine sulfate (*see*). *See* Quinine Extract for toxicity.

QUININE SULFATE • A synthetic flavoring agent derived from chinchona extract (*see*) and used in bitters flavoring for beverages. Also used medicinally to treat malaria, as an analgesic, and as a local anesthetic.

R

RACEMIC ACID • *See* Tartaric Acid.

RADISH EXTRACT • Extract of *Raphanus Sativus*. The small seeds of the radish remain viable for years. Has been used as a food since ancient times.

RAISIN-SEED OIL • Dried grapes or berries used in lubricating creams. *See* Grape-seed Oil.

RAPESEED OIL • Brownish-yellow oil from a turniplike annual herb of European origin. Widely grown as a forage crop for sheep in the United States. Canada sought clearance to sell rapeseed in the U.S. market but it was barred from the United States because it contains erucic acid, which was cited in the early 1970s as a possible source of heart problems based on the results of tests on rats. New varieties of the seeds, Canola, have been developed that have low erucic acid levels. Now, rapeseed oil is used in American salad oils, peanut butter, and some cake mixes. A distinctly unpleasant odor. It is used chiefly as a lubricant, an illuminant, and in rubber substitutes in the United States; also used in soft soaps. Can cause acnelike skin eruptions. When rats were fed a diet high in rapeseed oil over a lifetime, they showed significantly greater degenerative changes in the liver and a higher incidence of kidney damage than animals fed other vegetable oils.

RAPESEED OIL UNSAPONIFIABLES • The fraction of rapeseed oil (*see*), which is not changed into a fatty alcohol when it is saponified (heated with an alkali and acid). GRAS except in infant formula.

RASPBERRY EXTRACT • *See* Raspberry Juice.

RASPBERRY JUICE • Juice from the fresh ripe fruit grown in Europe, Asia, the United States, and Canada. Used as a flavoring for lipsticks, food, and medicines. It has astringent properties. No known toxicity.

RDA • Recommended Dietary Allowances of the Food and Nutrition Board, National Academy of Sciences—National Research Council.

REAGENT • A chemical that reacts or participates in a reaction; a substance that is used for the detection or determination of another substance by chemical or microscopical means. The various categories of reagents are colorimetric—to produce color-soluble compounds; fluxes—used to lower melting point; oxidizers—used in oxidation; precipitants—to produce insoluble compounds; reducers—used in reduction (*see*); solvents—used to dissolve water-insoluble compounds.

RED • *See* FD and C Red Nos. 3, 4, 40, and Citrus Red.

RED ALGAE • Seaweed. GRAS. *See* Algae, Red.

RED PEPPER • Cayenne Pepper. A condiment made from the pungent fruit of the plant. Used in sausage and pepper flavorings. Also used as a stimulant in hair tonics but may be an irritant and also cause allergic reactions.

RED RASPBERRY LEAF EXTRACT • An extract of the leaves of the red raspberry (*see*).

RED SAUNDERS • Red Sandalwood. Flavoring in alcoholic beverages only. No known toxicity.

REDUCED LACTOSE WHEY • GRAS. *See* Whey and Reducing Agent.

REDUCED MINERALS WHEY • GRAS. *See* Whey and Reducing Agent.

REDUCING AGENT • A substance that decreases, deoxidizes, or concentrates the volume of another substance. For instance, a reducing agent is used to convert a metal oxide to the metal itself. It also means a substance that adds hydrogen agents to another, for example, when acetaldehyde is converted to alcohol in the final step of alcoholic fermentation. It is used in foods to keep metals from oxidizing and affecting the taste or color of fats, oils, salad dressings, and other foods containing minerals.

REDUCTION • The process of reducing by chemical or electrochemical means. The gain of one or more electrons by an ion or compound. It is the reverse of oxidation.

RENNET • Rennin. Enzyme from the lining membranes of the stomach of suckling calves. Used for curdling milk in cheese-making and in junket. Sometimes as a digestant. No known toxicity. Reaffirmed GRAS in 1982.

RESINS • The brittle substance, usually translucent or transparent, formed from the hardened secretions of plants. Among the natural resins are dammar, elemi, and sandarac. Synthetic resins include polyvinyl acetate, various polyester resins, and sulfonamide resins. Resins have many uses in cosmetics. They contribute depth, gloss, flow adhesion, and water resistance. Toxicity depends upon ingredients used. *See* Gums.

RESIN, ACRYLAMIDE—ACRYLIC ACID • A clarifying agent in beet sugar and cane sugar juice. The acid is used in the synthesis of this acrylic resin. No known toxicity.

RESIN, COUMARONE—INDENE • A chewing gum base and protective coatings for citrus fruit. Coumarone is derived from coal tar and is used with a mixture of indene chiefly in the synthesis of coumarone resins. No known toxicity.

RESIN, ISOBUTYLENE • Polyisobutylene. A chewing gum base made from the chemical used chiefly in manufacturing synthetic rubber. No known toxicity.

RESIN, METHACRYLIC AND DIVINYL BENZENE • A compound of fine particle size, weakly acidic. Used as an absorbent for Vitamin B_{12} in nutritional supplement-type products. No known toxicity.

RESIN, PETROLEUM HYDROCARBON • A chewing gum base synthesized from fuel oil. No known toxicity.

RESIN, TERPENE • Alpha and Beta Pinene. A chewing gum base and coating for fresh fruits and vegetables. Pinene has the same toxicity as turpentine (*see*).

RETINOIDS • Derived from Retinoic Acid, Vitamin A, it is used to treat acne and other skin disorders. *See* Vitamin A.

RETINOL • Vitamin A (*see*).

RETINYL PALMITATE • The ester of Vitamin A and Palmitic Acid sometimes mixed with Vitamin D (*see* all).

RHATANY ROOT • A flavoring. The dried root of *Krameria triandra R*. From Peru and Brazil. Used as a cosmetics astringent. *See* Krameria Extract. No known toxicity.

RHODENAL • *See* Citronellal.

RHODINOL • A synthetic flavoring agent isolated from geranium rose oil (*see*). It has the strong odor of rose and consists essentially of geraniol and citronellol (*see* both). Used in strawberry, chocolate, rose, grape, honey, spice, and ginger ale flavorings for beverages, ice cream, ices, candy, baked goods, gelatin desserts, chewing gum, and jelly. Used also in perfumes, especially those of the rose type. No known toxicity.

RHODINYL ACETATE • Acetic Acid. An acidulant and synthetic flavoring, colorless to slightly yellow, with a light, fresh, roselike odor. Used in berry, coconut, apricot, floral, rose, and honey flavorings for beverages, ice cream, ices, candy, and baked goods. No known toxicity.

RHODINYL BUTYRATE • Butryic Acid. A synthetic raspberry, strawberry, and fruit flavoring agent for beverages, ice cream, ices, candy, baked goods, and chewing gum. No known toxicity.

RHODINYL FORMATE • Formic Acid. A synthetic flavoring, colorless to slight yellow, with a roselike odor. Used in raspberry, rose, apple, cherry, plum, pear, and pineapple flavorings for beverages, ice cream, ices, candy, baked goods, and gelatin desserts. *See* Formic Acid for toxicity.

RHODINYL ISOBUTRYATE • Isobutyric Acid. A synthetic raspberry, floral, rose, apple, pear, pineapple, and honey flavoring agent for beverages, ice cream, ices, candy, baked goods, and gelatin desserts. No known toxicity.

RHODINYL ISOVALERATE • Isovaleric Acid. A synthetic berry, floral, rose, and fruit flavoring agent for beverages, ice cream, ices, candy, and baked goods. No known toxicity.

RHODINYL PHENYLACETATE • Phenylacetic Acid. A synthetic flavoring used in beverages, ice cream, ices, candy, and baked goods. No known toxicity.

RHODINYL PROPIONATE • Propionic Acid. A synthetic berry, rose, plum, and honey flavoring agent for beverages, ice cream, ices, candy, and baked goods. No known toxicity.

RHODYMENIA PALMATA • *See* Dulse.

RHUBARB • The garden root used as a flavoring in alcoholic beverages only. Has been used as a laxative.

RHYNCHOSIA PYRAMIDALIS • A large, tropical twining plant with yellow flowers. Used as a flavoring. No known toxicity.

RIBOFLAVIN • Vitamin B$_2$. Lactoflavin. Formerly called Vitamin G. Riboflavin is a factor in the Vitamin B complex and is used in emollients. Every plant and animal cell contains a minute amount. Good sources are milk, eggs, and organ meats. It is necessary for healthy skin and respiration, protects the eyes from sensitivity to light, and is used for building and maintaining human body tissues. A deficiency leads to lesions at the corner of the mouth and to changes in the cornea. Recommended Dietary Allowances for infants is 4,000 micrograms per day and for adults, 1,300 micrograms. Its yellow to orange-yellow color is used to dye egg shells. It is permanently listed as a food color. Riboflavin and its more soluble form, riboflavin 5-phosphate, are added as enrichment to dry baby cereals, poultry stuffing, peanut butter, prepared breakfast cereals, enriched flour, enriched cornmeal, enriched corn grits, enriched macaroni, and enriched breads and rolls. GRAS.

RIBOFLAVIN-5-PHOSPHATE • A more soluble form of riboflavin (*see*). The final report to the FDA of the Select Committee on GRAS Substances stated in 1980 that it should continue its GRAS status with no limitations other than good manufacturing practices.

RIBONUCLEIC ACID • RNA. Found in both the nucleus and cytoplasm of the cell, it is the material that contains directions for the genetic code of the cell, DNA.

RICE BRAN OIL • Oil expressed from the broken coat of rice grain.

RICE BRAN WAX • The wax obtained from the broken coat of rice grain.

RICE STARCH • The finely pulverized grains of the rice plant used as an anticaking agent, thickener, and gelling agent. Also used in baby powders, face powders, and dusting powders. It is a demulcent and emollient and forms a soothing, protective film when applied. May cause mechanical irritation by blocking the pores and putrefying. May also cause an allergic reaction. The final report to the FDA of the Select Committee on GRAS Substances stated in 1980 that it should continue its GRAS status with no limitations other than good manufacturing practices.

ROCHELLE SALT • Potassium Sodium Tartrate. Used in the manufacture of baking powder and in the silvering of mirrors. Translucent crystals or white crystalline powder with cooling saline taste. Slight efflorescence in warm air. Probably used in mouthwashes, but use not identified in cosmetics. No known toxicity.

ROSA ALBA • *See* Rose, Absolute.

ROSA CANINA • *See* Rose Hips Extract.

ROSA CENTIFOLIA • *See* Rose, Absolute.

ROSE, ABSOLUTE • Same origin as for Rose Bulgarian (*see*). Used as a berry, rose, fruit, and nut flavoring agent for beverages, ice cream, ices, candy, and baked goods. No known toxicity except for allergic reactions. GRAS.

ROSE BENGAL • A bluish-red fragrant liquid taken from the rose of the Bengal region of the Asian subcontinent. Used to scent perfumes and as an edible color product to make lipstick dyes. Nontoxic.

ROSE BUDS, FLOWERS, FRUITS (HIPS), LEAVES • Flavoring. *See* Rose Extract. GRAS.

ROSE BULGARIAN • True Otto Oil. Attar of Roses. Rose Otto Bulgaria. One of the most widely used perfume ingredients, it is the essential oil, steam-distilled from the flowers of *Rosas Damascena*. The rose flowers are picked early in the morning when they contain the maximum amount of perfume and are distilled quickly after harvesting. Bulgaria is the main source of supply, but the U.S.S.R., Turkey, Syria, and Indo-China also grow it. The liquid is pale yellow and has a warm, deep floral, slightly spicy, and extremely fragrant red rose smell. It is used as a flavoring agent in loganberry, raspberry, strawberry, orange, rose, violet, cherry, grape, peach, honey, muscatel, maple, almond, pecan, and ginger ale flavorings for beverages, ice cream, ices, candy, baked goods, gelatin desserts, chewing gum, and jellies. Also used in mucilage, coloring matter, and as a flavoring in pills. May cause allergic reactions. GRAS.

ROSE EXTRACT • An extract of the various species of rose, it is used in raspberry and cola beverages and in fragrances. No known toxicity except for allergic reactions. GRAS.

ROSE GERANIUM • Distilled from any of several South African herbs grown for their fragrant leaves. Used in perfumes, and to scent toothpaste and dusting powders. May cause allergic reactions.

ROSE HIPS EXTRACT • Hipberries. Extract of the fruit of various species of wild roses, it is rich in Vitamin C and is used as a natural flavoring. Widely used by organic food enthusiasts. No known toxicity.

ROSE LEAVES EXTRACT • Derived from the leaves of the species *Rosa*. Used in raspberry and cola beverages.

ROSE OIL • Attar of Roses. The fragrant, volatile, essential oil distilled from fresh flowers. Colorless or yellow with a strong fragrant odor and taste of roses. Used in perfumes, toilet waters, and ointments. Nontoxic but may cause allergic reactions. *See* Rose Bulgarian.

ROSE OTTO BULGARIA • *See* Rose Bulgarian.

ROSELLE • Hibiscus sabdariffa. An herb cultivated in the East Indies, it is used for making tarts and jellies, and gives a tart taste to acid drinks. It is also used as a natural red food coloring for soft drinks, tea-type products, punches, apple jelly, and pectin jelly but it is not stable in carbonated beverages. No known toxicity.

ROSEMARY EXTRACT • Garden Rosemary. A flavoring and perfume from the fresh aromatic flowering tops of the evergreen shrub grown in the Mediterranean. Light blue flowers and gray green leaves. Used for beverages, condiments, and meat. It is also used in citrus, peach, and ginger flavorings for beverages, ice cream, ices, candy, baked goods, condiments, and meats. Also being studied as a natural antioxidant. A teaspoonful of the oil may cause illness in an adult, and an ounce may cause death. GRAS.

ROSIN • Colophony. Softener for chewing gum. It is a pale-yellow residue left after distilling off the volatile oil from the oleoresin obtained from various species of pine trees chiefly produced in the United States. Also used in the manufacture of varnishes and fireworks. It can cause contact dermatitis.

ROSEMARIN OFFICINALIS • *See* Rosemary.

RUBBER • Rubber as well as rubber-based adhesives are common causes of contact dermatitis. The natural gum obtained from the rubber tree is not allergenic; the offenders are the chemicals added to natural rubber gum to make it a useful product. Such chemicals are accelerators, antioxidants, stabilizers, and vulcanizers, many of which can cause allergies. Two are the most frequent but certainly not the only sensitizers.

RUBBER, BUTADIENE STYRENE • Latex. A chewing gum base. No known toxicity.

RUBBER, SMOKED SHEET • A chewing gum base. No known toxicity.

RUE OIL • A spice agent obtained from the fresh aromatic blossoming plants grown in Southern Europe and the Orient. It has a fatty odor and is used in baked goods. The oil is obtained by steam distillation and is used in fragrances and in blueberry, raspberry, coconut, grape, peach, rum, cheese, and spice flavorings for beverages, ice cream, ices, candy, baked goods, and condiments. Formerly used in medicine to treat disorders and hysteria. It is on the FDA list for study of mutagenic, teratogenic, subacute, and reproductive effects. It may cause photosensitivity. In 1976 the FDA confirmed rue as GRAS in all categories of food at a maximum use level of 2 parts per million. The final report to the FDA of the Select Committee on GRAS Substances stated in 1980 that there is no evidence in the available information that it is a hazard to the public when used as it is now and it should continue its GRAS status with limitations on amounts that can be added to food.

RUM ETHER • A synthetic flavoring, consisting of water, ethanol, ethyl acetate, methanol, ethyl formate, acetone, acetaldehyde, and formaldehyde (*see*). Used in butter, liquor, and rum flavorings for beverages, ice cream, ices, candy, baked goods, gelatin, chewing gum, and alcoholic beverages (1,600 ppm). No known toxicity.

RUTIN • Pale-yellow crystals found in many plants, particularly buckwheat. Used as a dietary supplement for capillary fragility. No known toxicity.

RYE FLOUR • Used in powders. Flour made from hardy annual cereal grass. Seeds are used for feed and in the manufacture of whiskey and bread. May cause allergic reactions.

S

SACCHARIDE HYDROLYSATE • A mixture of sugars derived from using an alkali and water on a mixture of glucose and lactose (*see*).

SACCHARIDE ISOMERATE • *See* Saccharide Hydrolysate.

SACCHARIN • An artificial sweetener in use since 1879. It is 300 times as sweet as natural sugar. Used as a sweetener for mouthwashes, dentifrices, and lipsticks. It sweetens dentifrices and mouthwashes in 0.05 to 1 percent concentration. On the FDA's top priority list to retest for mutagenic, subacute, and reproductive effects. White crystals or crystalline powder. Odorless or with a faint aromatic odor. It was used with cyclamates in the experiments that led to the ban on cyclamates. The FDA has proposed restricting saccharin to 15 milligrams per day for each kilogram of body weight or 1 gram a day for a 150-pound person. Then, on March 9, 1977, the FDA announced the use of saccharin in foods and beverages would be banned because the artificial sweetener had been found to cause malignant bladder tumors in laboratory animals. The ban was based on the findings of a study sponsored by the Canadian government that found that 7 out of 38 animals developed tumors, 3 of them malignant. In addition, 100 offspring were fed saccharin, and 14 of them developed bladder tumors. In contrast, 100 control rats were not fed saccharin and only 2 developed tumors. At the time of the FDA's announcement, Americans were consuming 5 million pounds of saccharin per year, 74 percent of it in diet soda, 14 percent in dietetic food, and 12 percent as a "tabletop" replacement for sugar. There was an immediate outcry, led vociferously by the Calorie Control Council, an organization made up of commercial producers and users of saccharin. The FDA, urged by Congress, then delayed the ban. The moratorium on prohibiting the use of saccharin has been extended indefinitely. Since 1977, however, saccharin containers carry labels warning that saccharin may be hazardous to your health.

Saccharin has exhibited mutagenic activity (genetic changes) in the early-warning Ames Test (*see*) for carcinogens. When administered orally to mice, mutagenic activity was demonstrated in the urine of these animals as well as in tissue tests. Highly purified saccharin was not mutagenic in tissue tests, but the urine of mice that had been given pure saccharin produced mutagenic effects when given to other mice. Two other sweeteners, neohesperidin dihydrochalcone and xylitol, had no such detectable mutagenic activity. Congress's Office of Technology Assessment, in view of evidence to date, strongly endorsed the scientific basis of the FDA's proposed ban. "This review of animal studies leads to the conclusion that saccharin is a carcinogen for animals," the FDA panel said. Clouding the risk of assessment, however, is that up to 20 parts per million of unknown chemical impurities contaminated those doses fed rats in the Canadian study that led to the FDA's original move. The impurities themselves proved mutagenic in the Ames Test.

On November 6, 1978, the Committee of the Institute of Medicine and National Research Council reported that it had reached the conclusion that saccharin is a potential carcinogen in humans. The extremely low potency of saccharin as a carcinogen was emphasized by the committee. However, they expressed special concern that children under 10 years of age were consuming diet sodas and other saccharin-containing products in increasing amounts. Exposure in children, the committee noted, may have special significance because of the long time required for some cancers to develop. There were some "worrisome data" regarding consumption by women of child-bearing age, children, and teenagers. The concern about fetal exposure grew out of earlier findings of increased bladder cancers in male rats fed high-saccharin diets or born to mothers who were on high-saccharin diets during pregnancy. The committee concluded that it is most likely that saccharin, acting by itself, is the carcinogenic agent, rather than any impurities that may be associated with its manufacture. The fight to keep saccharin on the market spotlighted the Delaney Amendment (*see*), which prohibits known carcinogens from being added to food, and a move to weaken that amendment persists. In 1969, Britain banned saccharin except as an artificial sweetener. In 1950, France banned it except as a non-prescription drug. Germany restricts it use to certain foods and beverages, which must state on the label that it is in the product.

SAFFLOWER GLYCERIDE • *See* Safflower Oil.

SAFFLOWER OIL • The edible oil expressed from the seed of an Old World herb that resembles a thistle, with large bright red or orange flowers. Widely cultivated for its oil, which thickens and becomes rancid on exposure to air. It is used in salad oils and shortenings, and as a vehicle for medicines. As a dietary supplement it is alleged to be a preventative in the development of atherosclerosis—fat-clogged arteries. A drug consisting of the dried flowers of safflower is used in medicine in place of saffron (*see*). Used in creams and lotions to soften the skin. No known toxicity. American safflower (American saffron) is no longer authorized for use.

SAFFRON • Crocus. Vegetable Gold. Spanish or French Saffron. It is the dried stigma of the crocus cultivated in Spain, Greece, France, and Iran. Orange-brown; strong, peculiar aromatic odor; bitterish, aromatic taste. Almost entirely employed for coloring and flavoring. It has been permanently listed for use in foods since 1966. Used in bitters, liquors, and spice flavorings for beverages, baked goods, meats, and liquors. Cleared by the USDA Meat Inspection Department for coloring sausage casing, oleomargarine, shortening, and for marking ink. The *extract* is used in honey and rum flavorings for beverages, ice cream, ices, candy, baked goods, and condiments, and it goes into yellow coloring. The coloring is used in food and has been permanently listed since 1966. Formerly used to treat skin diseases. No known toxicity. GRAS.

SAFROLE • Found in certain natural oils such as star anise, nutmeg, and ylang-ylang, it is a stable, colorless to brown liquid with an odor of sassafras and root beer. Used in the manufacture of heliotropin (*see*) and in expensive soaps and perfumes. Used as a beverage flavoring until it was banned in 1960. The toxicity of this fragrance ingredient is being questioned by the FDA. It is an animal liver carcinogen.

SAGE • The flowering tops and leaves of the shrubby mints. Spices include Greek sage and Spanish sage. The genus is *Salvia,* so named for the plant's supposed healing powers. Greek sage is used in fruit and spice flavorings for beverages, baked goods, and meats (1,500 ppm). Greek sage *oil,* obtained by steam distillation, is used in berry, grape, liquor, meat, creme de menthe, nutmeg, and sage flavorings for beverages, ice cream, ices, candy, baked goods, chewing gum, condiments, meats, and pickles. Greek sage *oleoresin* (*see*) is used in sausage and spice flavorings for condiments and meats. Spanish sage oil is used in fruit and spice flavorings for beverages, ice cream, ices, candy, baked goods, condiments, and meats. It is also used as a meat preservative. Greek sage is used in medicine. Used by herbalists to treat sore gums, mouth ulcers, and to remove warts. The Arabs believed that it prevents dying. No known toxicity. GRAS.

SAIGON CINNAMON • *See* Cinnamon.

SAIGON CINNAMON LEAF OIL • *See* Cinnamon.

ST. JOHN'S BREAD • *See* Locust Bean Gum. GRAS.

SALAD OIL • Any edible vegetable oil. Many dermatologists advise rubbing ordinary salad oils or shortenings such as Crisco® on the skin, particularly on babies and older persons. Vegetable oils are used in commercial baby preparations, cleansers, emollient creams, face powders, hair-grooming preparations, hypoallergenic cosmetics, lipsticks, nail creams, shampoos, shaving creams, and wave sets. Nontoxic.

SALICARIA EXTRACT • Spiked Loose Strife. Extract of the flowering herb *Lythrum salicaria* that has purple or pink flowers. Used since ancient Greek times as an herb that calms nerves and soothes skin.

SALICYLALDEHYDE • Salicylic Aldehyde. A synthetic flavoring made by heating phenol (very toxic) and chloroform. Occurs naturally in cassia bark. Clear, bitter almondlike odor, burning taste. White to slightly pink crystalline bitter powder. Gives a sensation of warmth on the tongue. Soluble in hot water. Used in butter flavorings for beverages, ice cream, ices, candy, baked goods, chewing gum, condiments, and liqueurs. Used chiefly in perfumery. Used as an analgesic, fungicide, and anti-inflammatory agent to soothe the skin. Lethal dose in rats is 1 gram per kilogram of body weight.

SALICYLATES • Amyl. Phenyl. Benzyl. Menthyl. Glyceryl. Dipropylene Glycol Esters. Salts of salicylic acid. Those who are sensitive to aspirin may also be hypersensitive to FD and C Yellow No. 5, a salicylate, and to a number of foods that naturally contain salicylate, such as almonds, apples, apple cider, apricots, blackberries, boysenberries, cherries, cloves, cucumbers, currants, gooseberries, grapes, nectarines, oil of wintergreen, oranges, peaches, pickles, plums, prunes, raisins, raspberries, strawberries, and tomatoes. Foods with added salicylates for flavoring may be ice cream, bakery goods (except bread), candy, chewing gum, soft drinks, Jell-o®, jams, cake mixes, wintergreen flavors. The salts are used as sunburn preventatives and antiseptics.

SALICYLIC ACID • Occurs naturally in wintergreen leaves, sweet birch, and other plants and has a sweetish taste. Synthetically prepared by heating phenol with carbon dioxide, it is used as a preservative in food products. It is also used as a preservative and antimicrobial at 0.1 to 0.5 percent in skin softeners, face masks, hair tonics, deodorants, dandruff preparations, protective creams, hair dye removers, and suntan lotions and oils. It is antipuretic (anti-itch) and antiseptic. In fact, in medicine, it is used as an antimicrobial at 2 to 20 percent concentration in lotions, ointments, powders, and plasters. It is also used in making aspirin. It can be absorbed through the skin. Absorption of large amounts may cause vomiting, abdominal pain, increased respiration, acidosis, mental disturbances, and skin rashes in sensitive individuals.

SALICYLIC ETHER • *See* Ethyl Salicylate.

SALICYLIDES • Any of several crystalline derivatives of salicylic acid (*see*) from which the water has been removed.

SALTPETER • Potassium Nitrate. Niter. *See* Nitrate, Potassium. Acute intoxication is unlikely because large doses cause vomiting and because it is rapidly excreted. Potassium poisoning disturbs the rhythm of the heart and orally poisoned animals die from respiratory failure. Prolonged exposure to even small amounts may produce anemia, methemoglobinemia (lack of oxygen in the blood), and kidney damage.

SALVIA • *See* Sage.

SAMBUCUS EXTRACT • *See* Elder Flowers.

SANDALWOOD OIL, EAST INDIAN • It is the pale-yellow, somewhat viscous, volatile oil obtained by steam distillation from the dried ground roots and wood of the plant. A strong, warm, persistent odor, soluble in most fixed oils. Used in floral, fruit, honey, and ginger ale flavorings for beverages, ice cream, ices, candy, baked goods, and chewing gum. Used in perfume. Also used for incense and as a fumigant. May produce skin rash in the hypersensitive, especially if present in high concentrations in expensive perfumes.

SANDALWOOD OIL, WEST INDIAN • Less soluble than the East Indian variety. *See* Amyris Oil.

SANDALWOOD OIL, YELLOW • Arheol. Same origin as East Indian sandalwood oil (*see*). A floral, fruit, honey and ginger ale flavoring agent for beverages, ice cream, ices, candy, baked goods, and chewing gum. No known toxicity.

SANDARAC • Used in alcoholic beverages only. Resin from a plant grown in Morocco. Light yellow, brittle, insoluble in water. Used in tooth cements, varnishes, and for gloss and adhesion in nail lacquers. No known toxicity.

SANTALOL • Alcohol from sandalwood used in fragrances. *See* Sandalwood Oil.

SANTALUM ALBUM • *See* Sandalwood Oil.

SANTALYL ACETATE • Acetic Acid. A synthetic flavoring agent obtained from sandalwood oils (*see*). Used in floral, pear, and pineapple flavorings for beverages, ice cream, ices, candy, baked goods, and chewing gum. No known toxicity.

SANTALYL PHENYLACETATE • Phenylacetic Acid. A synthetic

flavoring obtained from sandalwood oils (*see*). Used in butter, caramel, fruit, and honey flavorings for beverages, ice cream, ices, candy, and baked goods. No known toxicity.

SANTOQUIN • Ethoxyquin. A yellow liquid antioxidant and herbicide. It has been found to cause liver tumors in newborn mice. *See* Sodium Acid Pyrophosphate.

SAPONIN • Any of numerous natural glycosides—natural or synthetic compounds derived from sugars—that occur in many plants such as soapbark, soapwort, or sarsaparilla. Characterized by their ability to foam in water. Yellowish to white, acrid, hygroscopic. In powder form they can cause sneezing. Extracted from soapbark or soapwort and used chiefly as a foaming and emulsifying agent and detergent; also to reduce surface tensions, produce fine bubble lather in shaving creams, shampoos, bath oils, and dry shampoos. No known skin toxicity.

SARSAPARILLA EXTRACT • The dried root from tropical American plants. Used in cola, mint, root beer, sarsaparilla, wintergreen, and birch beer flavorings for beverages, ice cream, ices, candy, and baked goods. Still used for psoriasis; formerly used for the treatment of syphilis. No known toxicity.

SASSAFRAS BARK EXTRACT • Safrol. Safrol-free. It is the yellow to reddish-yellow volatile oil obtained from the roots of the sassafras. It is 80 percent safrole and has the characteristic odor and taste of sassafras. Used in rum and root beer flavorings for beverages, ice cream, ices, candy, and baked goods. Used in dentifrices, perfumes, soaps, and powders to correct disagreeable odors. Applied to insect bites and stings to relieve symptoms; also a topical antiseptic and used medicinally to break up intestinal gas. May produce dermatitis in hypersensitive individuals. Sassafras oil has been banned by the FDA for use in foods.

SASSAFRAS LEAVES • Safrol-free. Same origin as the bark extract. Used in soups (30,000 ppm). *See* Sassafras Bark Extract for toxicity.

SAUNDERS WHITE OIL • *See* Sandalwood Oil.

SAVORY EXTRACT • An extract of *Satureia hortensis,* an aromatic mint known as summer or winter savory. The dried leaves of summer savory is a spice used in baked goods, condiments, and meats. Summer savory oil is obtained from the dried whole plant. It is used as a spice in condiments, candy, and baked goods. Summer savory oil oleoresin (*see*) is a spice used in candy, baked goods, and condiments. Winter savory oil and oleoresin spices are used in candy, baked goods, and condiments. No known toxicity. GRAS.

SCHINUS MOLLE OIL • A natural flavoring extract from the tropical pepper tree, *Schinus molle.* Used in candy, baked goods, and condiments. No known toxicity. GRAS.

SCURVY GRASS EXTRACT • The extract of the leaves of flower stalks of *Cochlearia officinalis*. The bright green leaves of this northerly herb were collected and eaten in large quantities by European seamen to prevent scurvy. The plant has the strong odor of horseradish to which it is related. No known toxicity.

SEBACIC ACID • Decanedioic acid. Colorless leaflets, sparingly soluble in water and soluble in alcohol. Manufactured by heating castor oil with alkalies or by distillation of oleic acid (*see*). The esters of sebacic acid are used as stabilizers. No known toxicity.

SELENIUM • Yellow, solid or brownish powder, insoluble in water. Discovered in 1807 in the earth's crust. Used as a nutrient. Used in antidandruff shampoos. Can severely irritate the eyes if it gets into them while hair is being washed. Occupational exposure causes pallor, nervousness, depression, garlic odor of breath, gastrointestinal disturbances, skin rash, and liver injury in experimental animals.

SENNA, ALEXANDRIA • Flavoring from the dried leaves of *Cassia senna* grown in India and Egypt. Has been used as a cathartic.

SENSITIVITY • Hypersensitivity. An increased reaction to substance that may be quite harmless to nonallergic persons.

SENSITIZE • To administer or expose to an antigen provoking an immune response so that, on later exposure to that antigen, a more vigorous secondary response will occur.

SEQUESTERING AGENT • A preservative which prevents physical or chemical changes affecting color, flavor, texture, or appearance of a product. Ethylenediamine Tetraaceticacid (EDTA) is an example. It is used in carbonated beverages. It also prevents adverse effects of metals in shampoos.

SERINE • L and DL forms. An amino acid (*see*), nonessential, taken as a dietary supplement. It is a constituent of many proteins. *See* Proteins. On the FDA list requiring further information since 1980.

SERPENTARIA EXTRACT • Snakeroot. Snakeweed. Extracted from the roots of *Rauwolfia serpentina,* its yellow rods turn red upon drying. Used in the manufacture of resins, and as a bitter tonic. No known toxicity when applied to the skin but can affect heart and blood pressure when ingested.

SERUM ALBUMIN • The major protein component of blood plasma derived from bovines. Used as a moisturizing ingredient.

SERUM PROTEINS • *See* Serum Albumin.

SESAME • Seed and Oils. The edible seeds of an East Indian herb, which has a rosy or white flower. The seeds, which flavor bread, crackers, cakes, confectionery, and other products yield a pale-yellow, bland-tasting, almost odorless oil used in the manufacture of margarine. The oil has been used as a laxative and skin softener, and contains elements active against lice. Bland taste flavoring. May cause allergic reactions, primarily contact dermatitis. GRAS.

SESQUITERPENE LACTONES • In recent years, more than 600 plants have been identified as containing these substances and more than 50 are known to cause allergic contact dermatitis. Among them are arnica, chamomile, and yarrow (*see* all).

SHADDOCK EXTRACT • An extract of *Citrus grandis* and named for a 17th-century sea captain who brought the seeds back from the East Indies to Barbados. Shaddock is a very large, thick-rinded, pear-shaped citrus fruit related to and largely replaced by the grapefruit. No known toxicity.

SHARK-LIVER OIL • A rich source of Vitamin A believed to be beneficial to the skin. A brown fatty oil obtained from the livers of the large predatory fish. Used in lubricating creams and lotions. No known toxicity.

SHEA BUTTER • The natural fat obtained from the fruit of the karite tree, *Butyrosperum parkii*. Also called karite butter, it is chiefly used as a food but also used in soap and candles. No known toxicity.

SHEA BUTTER UNSAPONIFIABLES • The fraction of shea butter which is not saponified during processing, that is, not turned into fatty alcohol.

SHELLAC • A resinous excretion of certain insects feeding on appropriate host trees, usually in India. As processed for marketing, the lacca, which is formed by the insects, may be mixed with small amounts of arsenic trisulfide for color and with rosin. White shellac is free of arsenic. Shellac is used as a candy glaze and polish up to 0.4 percent. Also used in hair lacquer and on jewelry and accessories. May cause allergic contact dermatitis.

SHELLAC WAX • Bleached refined shellac. *See* Shellac.

SHORTENINGS • A fat such as a butter, lard, or vegetable oil used to make cake, pastry, bread, etc., light and flaky. *See* Salad Oils.

SIBERIAN FIR OIL • *See* Pine Needle Oil.

SILICA AEROGEL • Silicon Dioxide. A fine, white powder, slightly soluble in water, that occurs abundantly in nature and is 12 percent of all rocks. Sand is a silica. Chemically and biologically inert, it is used as an antifoaming agent in beverages and as a surface-active agent. Used chiefly in manufacture of glass. Upon drying and heating in a vacuum, hard transparent porous granules are formed that are used in absorbents and adsorbent material in toilet preparations, particularly skin-protectant creams. Also used as a coloring agent. *See* Silicones. The final report to the FDA of the Select Committee on GRAS Substances stated in 1980 that it should continue its GRAS status with no limitations other than good manufacturing practices.

SILICATES • Salts or esters derived from silicic acid (*see*). Any of numerous insoluble complex metal salts that contain silicon and oxygen and that constitute the largest group of minerals, and with quartz made up of the greater part of the earth's crust (as rocks, soils, and clays). Contained in building materials such as cement, concrete, bricks, and glass. No known toxicity.

SILICIC ACID • Silica Gel. White gelatinous substance obtained by the action of acids on sodium silicate (*see*). Odorless, tasteless, inert, white fluffy powder when dried. Insoluble in water and acids. Absorbs water readily. Used in face powders, dentifrices, creams, talcum powders as an opacifier. Soothing to skin. No known toxicity.

SILICON DIOXIDE • Silica. Transparent, tasteless crystals or powder, practically insoluble in water. Occurs in nature as agate, amethyst, chalcedony, cristobalite, flint, quartz, sand, and tridymite. Used as a defoamer in beer production. Cleared for use as a food additive and as an anticaking agent at a level not to exceed 2 percent in salt and salt substitutes, in BHT (*see* Butylated Hydroxytoluene), in vitamins up to 3 percent, in urea up to 1 percent, in sodium propionate up to 1 percent (*see* all). Also used in ceramics and in scouring and grinding compounds. Prolonged inhalation of the dust can injure lungs. The final report to the FDA of the Select Committee on GRAS Substances stated in 1980 that it should continue its GRAS status with no limitations other than good manufacturing practices.

SILICONES • Any of a large group of fluid oils, rubbers, resins, and compounds derived from silica (*see*), and which are water repellent, skin adherent, and stable over a wide range of temperatures. Used as an anticaking agent in foods and in waterproofing and lubrication. Used in after-shave preparations, hair-waving preparations, nail driers, hair straighteners, hand lotions, and protective creams. Used commercially in waterproofing and lubrication. No known toxicity when used externally.

SIMPLESSE® • A fat substitute developed by the same company that brought you Nutra-sweet. It is made from egg and milk protein. It can be used, according to the company, in margarine, ice cream, salad dressings, and yogurt. It cannot be used in baked food. Its introduction was delayed by the FDA, which said in 1988 that even though Simplesse was made from natural food, it should be premarket tested for safety.

SLOE BERRIES • Blackthorn Berries. The fruit of the common juniper. The extract is a natural flavoring used in berry, plum, and liquor flavorings for beverages, ice cream, ices, candy, baked goods, and cordials (up to 43,000 ppm). Sloe gin is flavored with sloe berries. No known toxicity. GRAS.

SMALLAGE • *See* Lovage.

SMELLAGE • *See* Lovage.

SMOKE FLAVORING SOLUTIONS • Condensates from burning hardwood in a limited amount of air. The solutions are used to flavor various foods, primarily meats, and as an antioxidant to retard bacterial growth. It is also permitted in cheese and smoke-flavored fish. The Select Committee of the Federation of American Societies from Experimental Biology (FASEB), under contract to the FDA, concluded that smoke flavorings in general pose no hazard to the public when used at current levels and under present procedures but uncertainties exist which require further study. The committee also said there are insufficient data upon which to base an evaluation of smoked yeast flavoring, produced by exposing food-grade yeast to wood smoke. It is used to flavor soups, cheese, crackers, dip, pizza, and seasoning mixes.

SMOKED SHEET RUBBER • A chewing gum base. No known toxicity.

SNAKEROOT OIL • Canadian Oil. Derived from the roots of the plant which had a reputation for curing snakebites. Grown from Canada to North Carolina and Kansas. Used in ginger, ginger ale, wintergreen, and birch beer flavorings for beverages, ice cream, ices, candy, baked goods, and condiments. No known toxicity.

SOAP • Sodium Oleate and Sodium Palmitate. Any salt of a fatty acid usually made by saponification of a vegetable oil with caustic soda. The oldest cleanser, usually a mixture of sodium salts of various fatty acids. In liquid soaps, potassium instead of sodium salts is used. Bar soaps vary in contents from brand to brand, depending on the fats or oils used. Sodium hydroxide makes a strong soap; fatty acids, a mild soap. So-called "neutral soaps" actually are alkaline, with pH around 10 (compared to skin, which is 5 to 6.5 pH) when dissolved in water. Soaps are usually in toothpastes, tooth powder, and shaving creams. Hard soap consists largely of sodium oleate or sodium palmitate and is used medicinally as an antiseptic, detergent, or suppository. Many people are allergic to soaps. They may also be drying to the skin, irritate the eyes, and cause rashes, depending upon ingredients. GRAS for food packaging.

SOAPBARK • *See* Quillaja.

SODIUM ACETATE • Sodium Salt of Acetic Acid. A preservative and alkalizer in cosmetics. Transparent crystals highly soluble in water. Used as a preservative in licorice candy. In industrial forms, it is used in photography and dyeing processes and in foot warmers because of its heat retention ability. Medicinally it is used as an alkalizer and as a diuretic to reduce body water. No known toxicity.

The final report to the FDA of the Select Committee on GRAS Substances stated in 1980 that it should continue its GRAS status with no limitations other than good manufacturing practices.

SODIUM ACID PHOSPHATE • A sequestrant in cheeses and frozen desserts. GRAS. *See* Sodium Acid Pyrophosphate.

SODIUM ACID PYROPHOSPHATE (SAP) • A white mass or free-flowing powder used as a buffer. It is a slow-acting acid constituent of a leavening mixture for self-rising and prepared cakes, doughnuts, waffles, muffins, cupcakes, and other types of flours and mixes. Also used in canned tuna fish. The U.S. Department of Agriculture has proposed that SAP be added to hot dogs and other sausages to accelerate the development of a rose-red color, thus cutting production time by some 25 to 40 percent. It is related to phosphoric acid, which is sometimes used as a gastric acidifier. No known toxicity. The final report to the FDA of the Select Committee on GRAS Substances stated in 1980 that it should continue its GRAS status with no limitations other than good manufacturing practices.

SODIUM ACID SULFITE • *See* Sodium Bisulfite.

SODIUM ALGINATE • Dissolves in water to form a viscous, colloidal solution and is used in cosmetics as a stabilizer, thickener, and emulsifier. An emollient used in baby lotions, hair lacquers, wave sets, and shaving creams. It is the sodium salt of alginic acid extracted from brown seaweed. Occurs as a white to yellowish fibrous or granular powder, nearly odorless and tasteless. No known toxicity. GRAS.

SODIUM ALUM • *See* Alum.

SODIUM ALUMINATE • A strong alkaline employed in the manufacture of lake colors used in foods (*see* FD and C Lakes). Also used in water-softening and printing. The final report to the FDA of the Select Committee on GRAS Substances stated in 1980 that it should continue its GRAS status with no limitations other than good manufacturing practices.

SODIUM ALUMINOSILICATE • A chemical substance used in dental compounds, colored lakes (*see* FD and C Lakes) for foods, and in washing compounds. The final report to the FDA of the Select Committee on GRAS substances stated in 1980 that it should continue its GRAS status with no limitations other than good manufacturing practices.

SODIUM ALUMINUM PHOSPHATE • A white, odorless powder, insoluble in water, used as a buffer in self-rising flour. Used with sodium bicarbonate (*see*). Used also in various cheeses. No known toxicity. The final report to the FDA of the Select Committee on GRAS Substances stated in 1980 that it should continue its GRAS status with no limitations other than good manufacturing practices.

SODIUM ALUMINUM SULFATE • A bleaching agent for flour at no more than 6 parts by weight alone, or in combination with potassium aluminum, calcium sulfate, and other compounds. No known toxicity.

SODIUM ASCORBATE • Vitamin C Sodium. Aside from its use in Vitamin C preparations, it can serve as an antioxidant in chopped meat and other foods to retard spoiling; also used in curing meat. No known toxicity. The final report to the FDA of the Select Committee on GRAS Substances stated in 1980 that it should continue its GRAS status with no limitations other than good manufacturing practices. *See* Ascorbic Acid.

SODIUM BENZOATE • White, odorless powder or crystals; sweet, antiseptic taste. Works best in slightly acid media. Used as a flavoring and in liver function tests and as a preservative in margarine, codfish, bottled soft drinks, maraschino cherries, mincemeat, fruit juices, pickles, confections, fruit jelly preserves, and jams. Also used in the ice for cooling fish. An antiseptic and preservative used in eye creams, vanishing creams, and toothpastes. White odorless powder or crystals with a sweet antiseptic taste. Once used medicinally for rheumatism and tonsillitis. No known toxicity for external use.

SODIUM BICARBONATE • Bicarbonate of Soda. Baking Soda. An alkali prepared by the reaction of soda ash with carbon dioxide and used in prepared pancakes, biscuits, and muffin mixes; a leavening agent in baking powders; in various crackers and cookies; to adjust acidity in tomato soup, ices, and sherbets, in pastes and beverages; in syrups for frozen products; confections; and self-rising flours. Also used in corn-meals and canned peas. Also used in effervescent bath salts, mouthwashes, and skin-soothing powders. Its white crystals or powder are used as a gastric antacid, an alkaline wash, and a treatment for burns. Used also as a neutralizer for butter, cream, milk, and ice cream. Essentially harmless to the skin but when used on very dry skin in preparations that evaporate, it leaves an alkaline residue that may cause irritation. It may alter the urinary excretion of other drugs, thus making those drugs either more toxic or less effective. GRAS.

SODIUM BISULFATE • Sodium Acid Sulfite. Sodium Hydrogen Sulfite. Colorless or white crystals fused in water, with a disagreeable taste. It is used as a disinfectant in the manufacture of soaps, in perfumes, and in foods and pickling compounds. *See* Sulfite.

SODIUM BISULFITE • Sodium Acid Sulfite. An inorganic salt. It is a white powder with a disagreeable taste and it is used as bleaching agent in ale, wine, beer, and other food products. Commercial bisulfite consists chiefly of sodium metabisulfite (*see*). It is used as an antiseptic, as an antifermentative in cosmetic creams, mouthwashes, bleaches, perfumes, and hair dyes, to treat parasitic skin diseases, and to remove warts. In its aqueous solution, it is an acid. Concentrated solutions are highly irritating to the skin and mucous membranes. Sodium bisulfite can cause changes in the genetic material of bacteria and is a suspect mutagen. Not permitted in meats and other sources of vitamin B_1, strong irritant to the skin and tissue. The Select Committee on GRAS Substances found it did not present a hazard at present use levels but that additional data would be needed if higher use occurred. The committee said in 1980 that it should continue as GRAS with limitations on the amounts that can be added to food.

SODIUM BROMATE • Inorganic salt. Colorless, odorless crystals that liberate oxygen. Used as a solvent. *See* Potassium Bromate for toxicity.

SODIUM CALCIUM ALUMINOSILICATE • Used to prevent salt and dry mixes from caking. No known toxicity. The final report to the FDA of the Select Committee on GRAS Substances stated in 1980 that it should continue its GRAS status with no limitations other than good manufacturing practices.

SODIUM CAPRYL LACTYLATE • *See* Palm Oil.

SODIUM CAPRYLATE • *See* Palm Oil.

SODIUM CARBONATE • Soda Ash. Small odorless crystals or powder that occurs in nature in ores and is found in lake brines or seawater. Absorbs water from the air. Used as a neutralizer for butter, cream, fluid milk, and ice cream; in the processing of olives before canning; and in cocoa products. Has an alkaline taste and is used as an antacid and reagent in permanent wave solutions, soaps, mouthwashes, shampoos, foot preparations, bath salts, and vaginal douches. A strong alkali used as lye. It is used to treat skin rashes and as a water softener. It is the cause of scalp, forehead, and hand rashes when the hypersensitive use cosmetics containing it. Ingestion of large quantities may produce corrosion of the gastrointestinal tract, vomiting, diarrhea, circulatory collapse, and death. The final report to the FDA of the Select Committee on GRAS Substances stated in 1980 that it should continue its GRAS status with no limitations other than good manufacturing practices.

SODIUM CARBOXYMETHYLCELLULOSE • Made from a cotton by-product, it occurs as a white powder or granules. Used as a stabilizer, thickener, gelling agent and nonnutritive bulking aid. Used to prevent water loss, make food opaque, and texturize food. Found in ice cream, beverages, confections, baked goods, icings, toppings, chocolate milk, chocolate-flavored beverages, gassed cream (pressure-dispensed whipped cream), syrup for frozen products, variegated mixtures, cheese spreads, and in certain cheeses. Also used in French dressing, artificially sweetened jellies, and preserves, gelling ingredients, and mix-it-yourself and powdered drinks. Medicinally used as a laxative (1.5 grams orally), antacid (15–30 milligrams of 5-percent solution), and in pharmacies for preparing suspensions. As used in setting lotions, it is an artificial gum that dries and leaves a film on the hair. Prepared by treating alkali cellulose with sodium chloroacetate. Can cause digestive disturbances. *See* Cellulose Gums. GRAS.

SODIUM CARRAGEENAN • Sodium salt of carrageenan (*see*).

SODIUM CASEINATE • Casein. The soluble form of milk protein in which casein is partially neutralized with sodium hydroxide and used as a texturizer in ice cream, frozen custard, ice milk, and sherbet. Cleared by the USDA Meat Inspection Department for use in imitation sausage, nonspecific loaves, soups, and stews. No known toxicity. GRAS. The final report to the FDA of the Select Committee on GRAS Substances stated in 1980 that it should continue its GRAS status with no limitations other than good manufacturing practices.

SODIUM CASTORATE • The sodium salt of the fatty acids derived from castor oil (*see*).

SODIUM CHLORIDE • Common table salt. In addition to seasoning, it is used as a pickling agent, a preservative for meats, vegetables, butter. Prevents browning in cut fruit. Used as an astringent and antiseptic in mouthwashes, dentifrices, bubble baths, soap, bath salts, and eye lotions. It consists of opaque white crystals. Odorless, with a characteristic salty taste, and absorbs water. Used topically to treat inflamed lesions. Diluted solutions are not considered irritating, but upon drying, water is drawn from the skin and may produce irritation. Salt workers have a great deal of skin rashes. Also reported to irritate the roots of the teeth when used for a long time in dentifrices. Not considered toxic but can adversely affect persons with high blood pressure and kidney disease. The final report to the FDA of the Select Committee on GRAS Substances stated in 1980 that it should continue its GRAS status with no limitations other than good manufacturing practices.

SODIUM CHLORITE • A powerful oxidizer prepared commercially and used to modify food starch (*see* Modified Starch) up to 0.5 percent. Used as a bleaching agent for textiles and paper pulp and in water purification. Toxicity depends on concentration.

SODIUM CITRATE • White odorless crystals, granules, or powder with a cool salty taste. Stable in air. Prevents "cream plug" in cream and "feathering" when cream is used in coffee, an emulsifier in ice cream, processed cheese, evaporated milk; a buffer to control acidity and retain carbonation in beverages, in frozen fruit drinks, confections, fruit jellies, preserves, and jams. It attaches itself to trace metals present in water and inhibits their entering living cells. Proposed as a replacement for phosphates in detergents but also causes algal growth and removes the necessary trace metals from water as well as the toxic ones. Used as a sequestering agent (*see*) to remove trace metals in solutions and as an alkalizer in cosmetic products. Can alter urinary excretion of other drugs, thus making those drugs either less effective or more toxic. The final report to the FDA of the Select Committee on GRAS Substances stated in 1980 that it should continue its GRAS status with no limitations other than good manufacturing practices.

SODIUM COCOATE • *See* Coconut Oil.

SODIUM COCOYL GLUTAMATE • A softener. *See* Glutamate.

SODIUM DEHYDROACETATE. • Dehydroacetic Acid. A preservative; white, odorless, powdered, with an acrid taste. Used in cut or peeled squash and as a plasticizer, fungicide, and bactericide in antienzyme toothpaste. Used as a plasticizer, fungicide, and bacteria killer in cosmetics; also an antienzyme ingredient in dentifrices, allegedly to prevent decay, and a kidney tube blocking agent. Can cause impaired kidney function. Large doses can cause vomiting, ataxia, and convulsions. There are no apparent allergic skin reactions.

SODIUM DIACETATE • A compound of sodium acetate and acetic acid (*see*); a white crystalline solid. Smells like vinegar. Used as a preservative. Inhibits molds and rope-forming bacteria in baked goods. No known toxicity. The final report to the FDA of the Select Committee on GRAS Substances stated in 1980 that it should continue its GRAS status with no limitations other than good manufacturing practices.

SODIUM DIALKYLPHENOXYBENZENEDISULFONATE • Used in lye mixtures for peeling fruits and vegetables.

SODIUM DODECYLBENZENESULFONATE • Used in commercial detergents to treat raw food products, which is followed by water rinsing. An anionic detergent used in cosmetic bath products, and in creams. It may irritate the skin. Will cause vomiting if swallowed.

SODIUM ERYTHORBATE • Sodium Isoascorbate. A white odorless powder used as an antioxidant in pickling brine up to 7.5 ounces per 100 gallons and in meat products up to ¾ of an ounce per 100 pounds. Also used in beverages and baked goods; in cured cuts and cured, pulverized products to accelerate color fixing in curing. No known toxicity. The final report to the FDA of the Select Committee on GRAS Substances stated in 1980 that it should continue its GRAS status with no limitations other than good manufacturing practices.

SODIUM 2-ETHYL 1-HEXYLSULFATE • A component of a commercial detergent for washing raw foods, followed by water rinsing. No known toxicity.

SODIUM FERRIC EDTA • Prepared from disodium ethylenediaminetetraacetic acid and ferric nitrate. Used as an iron source. The final report to the FDA of the Select Committee on GRAS Substances stated in 1980 that there were insufficient relevant biological and other studies upon which to base an evaluation of it when it is used as a food ingredient. Nothing new has been reported by the FDA since. *See* Iron Salts.

SODIUM FERRICITROPYROPHOSPHATE • A white powder used in food enrichment. It is less prone to induce rancidity than other orthophosphates. The final report to the FDA of the Select Committee on GRAS Substances stated in 1980 that there were insufficient relevant biological and other studies upon which to base an evaluation of it when it is used as a food ingredient. Nothing new has been reported by the FDA since. *See* Iron Salts.

SODIUM GLUTAMATE • The monosodium salt of the L-form of glutamic acid. *See* Glutamic Acid.

SODIUM GLUCONATE • Gluconic Acid. Sodium Salt. A pleasant smelling compound, it is used as a sequestering agent (*see*). The final report to the FDA of the Select Committee on GRAS Substances stated in 1980 that it should continue its GRAS status with no limitations other than good manufacturing practices.

SODIUM GLYCERYL OLEATE PHOSPHATE • *See* Glyceryl Monostearate.

SODIUM HEXAMETAPHOSPHATE • Sodium Polymetaphosphate. Graham's Salt. An emulsifier, sequestering agent (*see*), and texturizer. Used in breakfast cereals, angel food cake, flaked fish, ice cream, ice milk, beer, bottled beverages, reconstituted lemon juice, puddings, processed cheeses, and artificially sweetened jellies. Used in foods and potable water to prevent scale formation and corrosion. Because it keeps calcium, magnesium, and iron salts in solution, it is an excellent water softener and detergent. Used in bath salts, bubble baths, permanent wave neutralizers, and shampoos. Phosphorous is an essential nutrient, but it has to be in balance with other minerals such as calcium in the diet. Too much phosphorous in foods could lead to an imbalance and adversely affect bones, kidney, and heart. Lethal dose in dogs is 140 milligrams per kilogram of body weight. Used in Calgon®, Giltex®, and other such products. The final report to the FDA of the Select Committee on GRAS Substances stated in 1980 that it should continue its GRAS status for packaging with no limitations other than good manufacturing practices.

SODIUM HYALURONATE • The sodium salt of hyaluronic acid. From the fluid in the eye, it is used as a gelling agent. No known toxicity.

SODIUM HYDROSULFATE • Sodium Dithionate. A bacterial inhibitor and antifermentative. Slight odor. White or grayish-white crystalline powder that oxidized in air. No known toxicity to the skin.

SODIUM HYDROSULFITE • A bacterial inhibitor and antifermentative in the sugar and syrup industries. Slight odor. No known toxicity. The final report to the FDA of the Select Committee on GRAS Substances stated in 1980 that it should continue its GRAS status with no limitations other than good manufacturing practices.

SODIUM HYDROXIDE • Caustic Soda. Soda Lye. An alkali and emulsifier. Readily absorbs water. Used as a modifier for food starch, a glazing agent for pretzels, and a peeling agent for tubers and fruits. An alkali and emulsifier in liquid face powders, soaps, shampoos, cuticle removers, hair straighteners, shaving soaps, and creams. The FDA banned use of more than 10 percent in household liquid drain cleaners. If too much alkali is used dermatitis of the scalp may occur. Its ingestion causes vomiting, prostration, and collapse. Inhalation causes lung damage. The final report to the FDA of the Select Committee on GRAS Substances stated in 1980 that it should continue its GRAS status for packaging with no limitations other than good manufacturing practices.

SODIUM HYDROXIDE GELATINIZED STARCH • Starch (*see*) that has been gelatinized with sodium hydroxide. The final report to the FDA of the Select Committee on GRAS Substances stated in 1980 that there were insufficient relevant biological and other studies upon which to base an evaluation of it when it is used as a food ingredient. Nothing new has been reported since.

SODIUM HYPOCHLORITE • A preservative used in the washing of cottage cheese curd. Also used medically as an antiseptic for wounds. Ingestion may cause corrosion of mucous membranes, esophageal or gastric perforation. The aqueous solutions are Eau de Javelle, Clorox, Dazzle.

SODIUM HYPOPHOSPHATE • White crystals, soluble in water, used as a sequestering agent (*see*). The final report to the FDA of the Select Committee on GRAS Substances stated in 1980 that it should continue its GRAS status with no limitations other than good manufacturing practices.

SODIUM INOSINATE • *See* Inosinate.

SODIUM IRON PYROPHOSPHATE • *See* Sodium Pyrophosphate.

SODIUM ISOASCORBATE • *See* Erythrobic Acid.

SODIUM ISOSTEROYL LACTYLATE • The sodium salt of isostearic acid and lactyl lactate. *See* Stearic Acid and Lactic Acid.

SODIUM LACTATE • Plasticizer substitute for glycerin. Colorless, thick, odorless liquid miscible with water, alcohol, and glycerin. It is used as an antioxidant, bodying agent, and humectant. Solution is neutral. Used medicinally as a systemic and urinary alkalizer. No known toxicity. GRAS.

SODIUM LAURETH SULFATE • The sodium salt of sulfated ethoxylated lauryl alcohol, widely used as a water softener, and in baby and other nonirritating shampoos as a wetting agent and cleansing agent. *See also* Surfactants.

SODIUM LAUROYL GLUTAMATE • A softener. *See* Glutamate.

SODIUM LAURYL SULFATE (SLS) • A detergent, wetting agent, and emulsifier. It is used to treat raw foods, followed by a water rinsing. It is employed as a whipping aid in cake mixes and dried egg products. Also used in bubble baths, emollient creams, cream depilatories, hand lotions, cold permanent waves, soapless shampoos, and toothpastes. Prepared by sulfation of lauryl alcohol followed by neutralization with sodium carbonate. Faint fatty odor; also emulsifies fats. May cause drying of the skin because of its degreasing ability and is an irritant to the skin. On the FDA list for further studies on the safety of this widely used additive.

SODIUM MAGNESIUM SILICATES • *See* Silicates.

SODIUM METABISULFITE • An inorganic salt. A bacterial inhibitor in wine, ale, and beer; an antifermentative in sugar and syrups; a preservative for fruit and vegetable juices; antibrowning agent in cut fruits, frozen apples, dried fruits, prepared fruit-pie mix, peeled potatoes, and maraschino cherries. The final report to the FDA of the Select Committee on GRAS Substances stated in 1980 that the additive did not present a hazard when used at present levels but that increased use would require additional safety data. *See* Sulfites.

SODIUM METAPHOSPHATE • Graham's Salts. A dough conditioner. Used in dental polishing agents, detergents, water softeners, sequestrants, emulsifiers, food additives, and textile laundering. The final report to the FDA of the Select Committee on GRAS Substances stated in 1980 that it should continue its GRAS status with no limitations other than good manufacturing practices. *See* Sodium Hexametaphosphate.

SODIUM METASILICATE • An alkali usually prepared from sand and soda ash. Used as a peeling solution for peaches and as a denuder for tripe ''in amounts sufficient for the purpose.'' Used in detergents. Caustic substance, corrosive to the skin, harmful if swallowed, and cause of severe eye irritations. Preserves eggs in egg shampoos.

SODIUM METHYL COCOYL TAURATE • *See* Ox Bile.

SODIUM METHYL NAPHTHALENE SULFONATE • Used in solutions for peeling fruits and vegetables with a water rinse and in detergents. *See* Sulfated Oil.

SODIUM METHYL OLEOYL TAURATE • *See* Ox Bile.

SODIUM n-METHYL-n-OLEYL TAURATE • *See* Ox Bile.

SODIUM METHYL SULFATE • Used in processing of pectin (*see*). No known toxicity.

SODIUM MONOALKYLPHENOXYBENZENEDISULFONATE • Used in lye for peeling fruits and vegetables. No known toxicity.

SODIUM MYRISTATE • *See* Myristic Acid.

SODIUM MYRISTOYL ISETHIONATE • *See* Myristic Acid.

SODIUM NITRATE • *See* Nitrate.

SODIUM NITRITE • *See* Nitrite.

SODIUM OLEATE • Sodium salt of oleic acid. White powder, fatty odor, alkaline. Used in soaps. The final report to the FDA of the Select Committee on GRAS Substances stated in 1980 that it should continue its GRAS status for packaging with no limitations other than good manufacturing practices. No known toxicity.

SODIUM PALMATE • Sodium salt of palmitic acid (*see*).

SODIUM PANTOTHENATE • Vitamins D_1 and D_2. Used as a dietary supplement. The final report to the FDA of the Select Committee on GRAS Substances stated in 1980 that it should continue its GRAS status with no limitations other than good manufacturing practices.

SODIUM PECTINATE • A stabilizer and thickener for syrups for frozen products, ice cream, ice milk, confections, fruit sherbets, French dressing and other salad dressings, fruit jelly preserves, jams. Used in quantities which "reasonably compensate the deficiency, if any, of natural pectin content of the fruit ingredients." No known toxicity. GRAS.

SODIUM PHOSPHATE • Buffer and effervescent used in manufacture of nail enamels and detergents. White crystalline or granular powder, stable in air. Without water, it can be irritating to the skin but has no known skin toxicity. The final report to the FDA of the Select Committee on GRAS Substances stated in 1980 that it should continue its GRAS status with no limitations other than good manufacturing practices. *See* Phosphorous Sources.

SODIUM PHOSPHOALUMINATE • The acid salt of phosphoric acid. An ingredient of baking powders and other leavening mixtures. GRAS for packaging. *See* Phosphoric Acid for toxicity.

SODIUM POTASSIUM TARTRATE • Rochelle Salt. A buffer for confections, fruit jelly, preserves, and jams. For each 100 pounds of saccharin in the above products 3 ounces of sodium potassium tartrate is used. Also used in cheese. Used medicinally as a cathartic. No known toxicity. GRAS.

SODIUM PROPIONATE • Colorless or transparent odorless crystals that gather water in moist air. Used as a preservative in cosmetics and foodstuffs to prevent mold and fungus. Used in baked goods, frostings, confections, and gelatin. It has been used to treat fungal infections of the skin, but can cause allergic reactions. GRAS.

SODIUM PYROPHOSPHATE • Used to decrease the amount of cooked-out juices in canned hams, pork shoulders, and bacon at 5 percent phosphate in pickle; 0.5 percent phosphate in product (only clear solution may be injected into hams). It is also used in cold-water puddings and processed cheese. It is an emulsifier salt and a texturizer as well as a sequestrant. The FDA labeled it GRAS for use as a sequestrant.

SODIUM RIBOFLAVIN PHOSPHATE • A B vitamin containing sodium phosphate (*see*).

SODIUM SACCHARIN • An artificial sweetener in dentifrices, mouthwashes, and lipsticks. In use since 1879. Pound for pound it is 300 times as sweet as natural sugar but leaves a bitter aftertaste. It was used along with cyclamates in the experiments that led to the ban on cyclamates in 1969. The FDA has proposed restricting saccharin to 15 milligrams per day for each kilogram of body weight or one gram a day for 150-pound person. On the FDA's priority list for further safety testing.

SODIUM SALT • *See* Sodium Benzoate.

SODIUM SESQUICARBONATE • Lye. White crystals, flakes, or powder produced from sodium carbonate. Soluble in water. Used as a neutralizer for butter, cream, fluid milk, ice cream, in the processing of olives before canning, cacao products, and canned peas. Used as an alkalizer in bath salts, shampoos, tooth powders, and soaps. Irritating to the skin and mucous membranes. May cause allergic reaction in the hypersensitive. The final report to the FDA of the Select Committee on GRAS Substances stated in 1980 that it should continue its GRAS status with no limitations other than good manufacturing practices.

SODIUM SILICATE • Water Glass. Soluble Glass. An anticaking agent preserving eggs, detergents in soaps, depilatories, and protective creams. Consists of colorless to white or grayish-white crystallike pieces or lumps. These silicates are almost insoluble in cold water. Strongly alkaline. As a topical antiseptic, can be irritating and caustic to the skin and mucous membranes. If swallowed it causes vomiting and diarrhea. The final report to the FDA of the Select Committee on GRAS Substances stated in 1980 that it should continue its GRAS status with no limitations other than good manufacturing practices.

SODIUM SILICO ALUMINATE • Anticaking agent used in table salt up to 2 percent; dried egg yolks up to 2 percent; in sugar up to 1 percent; and in baking powder up to 5 percent. Slightly alkaline. No known toxicity. *See* Silicates.

SODIUM SOAP • *See* Sodium Stearate.

SODIUM SORBATE • A food preservative. The final report to the FDA of the Select Committee on GRAS Substances stated in 1980 that it should continue its GRAS status with no limitations other than good manufacturing practices. *See* Calcium Sorbate.

SODIUM STEARATE • Alkaline; 92.82 percent stearic acid (*see*). Used as an emulsifier in foods. A fatty acid used in deodorant sticks, stick perfumes, toothpastes, soapless shampoos, and shaving lather. A white powder with a soapy feel and a slight tallowlike odor. Slowly soluble in cold water or cold alcohol. Also a waterproofing agent and has been used to treat skin diseases and in suppositories. One of the least allergy-causing of the sodium salts of fatty acids. Nonirritating to the skin.

SODIUM STEAROYL LACTYLATE • *See* Lactic Acid.

SODIUM STEARYL FUMARATE • A fine white powder used as a dough conditioner in yeast and leavened bakery products in amounts not exceeding 0.5 percent by weight of flour used. Also used as a conditioning agent in dehydrated potatoes in an amount not exceeding 1 percent by weight. No known toxicity.

SODIUM STEAROYL-2-LACTYLATE • The sodium salt of a lactylic ester of fatty acid. Prepared from lactic acid and fatty acids. It is used as an emulsifier, plasticizer, or surface active agent in an amount not greater than required to produce the intended physical or technical effect, and where standards of identity do not preclude use, in the following: bakery mixes, baked products, cake icings, fillings and toppings, dehydrated fruits and vegetables, dehydrated fruit and vegetable juices; frozen desserts, liquid shortenings for household use; pancake mixes, precooked instant rice, pudding mixes, solid-state edible vegetable fat–water emulsions used as substitutes for milk or cream in coffee; and with shortening and edible fats and oils when such are required in the foods listed above. *See* Lactic Acid for toxicity.

SODIUM SULFATE • Salt cake. Occurs in nature as the minerals mirabilite and nardite. Used in chewing-gum base and to preserve tuna fish and biscuits. Used medicinally to reduce body water. Used chiefly in the manufacture of dyes, soaps, and detergents. It is a reagent (*see*) and a precipitant; mildly saline in taste. Usually harmless when applied in toilet preparations. May prove irritating in concentrated solutions if applied to the skin, permitted to dry, and then remain. May also enhance the irritant action of certain detergents. Taken by mouth it stimulates gastric mucous production and sometimes inactivates a natural digestive juice—pepsin. Fatally poisoned animals show only diarrhea and intestinal bloating with no gross lesions outside the intestinal tract.

SODIUM SULFIDE • Composition in chewing gum base. Crystals or granules that easily absorb water prepared from ammonia. Also used in dehairing hides and wool pulling, engraving, and cotton printing.

SODIUM SULFITE • White to tan-pink, odorless or nearly odorless powder having a cooling, salty, sulfurlike taste. An antiseptic, preservative, and antioxidant used as a bacterial inhibitor in wine brewing, and distilled-beverage industries. Also an antifermentative in the sugar and syrup industries and a browning inhibitor in cut fruits, used in frozen apples, dried fruit, prepared fruit pie mix, peeled potatoes, maraschino cherries, dried fruits, and glacéed fruits. Used to bleach straw, silk, and wool; a developer in photography; treats upset stomachs and combats fungus infections. Also used in hair dyes. Foods and drinks containing sulfites may release sulfur dioxide. If this is inhaled by people who suffer from asthma it can trigger an asthmatic attack. Sulfites are known to cause stomach irritation, nausea, diarrhea, skin rash, or swelling in sulfite-sensitive people. People whose kidneys or livers are impaired may not be able to produce the enzymes which break down sulfites in the body. Sulfites may destroy thiamin and consequently are not added to foods which are sources of this B vitamin. The final report to the FDA of the Select Committee on GRAS Substances stated in 1980 that it did not present a hazard when used at present levels but that additional data would be necessary if significant increase in consumption occurred. *See* Sulfites.

SODIUM SULFO-ACETATE DERIVATIVES • Used as emulsifiers in margarine. *See* Sodium Sulfate.

SODIUM TARTRATE • A laxative, sequestrant, chemical reactant, and stabilizer in cheese and artificially sweetened jelly. *See* Tartaric Acid. GRAS.

SODIUM TAUROCHOLATE • Taurocholic Acid. The chief ingredient of the bile of carnivorous animals. Used as an emulsifier in dried egg white up to 0.1 percent. It is a lipase accelerator. Lipase is a fat-splitting enzyme in the blood, pancreatic secretion, and tissues. No known toxicity.

SODIUM TETRAPHOSPHATE • Sodium Polyphosphate. Used as a sequestering agent. The final report to the FDA of the Select Committee on GRAS Substances state in 1980 that it should continue its GRAS status with no limitations other than good manufacturing practices. *See* Phosphates.

SODIUM THIOSULFATE • An antioxidant used to protect sliced potatoes and uncooked French fries from browning and as a stabilizer for potassium iodide in iodized salt. Also used to neutralize chlorine and to bleach bone. It is an antidote for cyanide poisoning and has been used in the past to combat blood clots; used to treat ringworms and mange in animals. Poorly absorbed by the bowel. The final report to the FDA of the Select Committee on GRAS Substances stated in 1980 that it should continue its GRAS status with no limitations other than good manufacturing practices.

SODIUM *p*-TOLUENE SULFOCHLORAMINE • Chloramine T. Water-purifying agent and a deodorant used to remove weed odor in cheese. Suspected of causing rapid allergic reaction in the hypersensitive. Poisoning by Chloramine T is characterized by pain, vomiting, sudden loss of consciousness, circulatory and respiratory collapse, and death.

SODIUM TOLUENESULFONATE • Methylbenzenesulfonic Acid, Sodium Salt. An aromatic compound that is used as a solvent. *See* Benzene.

SODIUM TRIMETHAPHOSPHATE • A starch modifier. *See* Sodium Metaphosphate.

SODIUM TRIPOLYPHOSPHATE • STPP. A texturizer and sequestrant cleared for use in food starch modifiers. A water softener. Also cleared by the USDA Meat Inspection Department to preserve meat by decreasing cooked-out juices in canned hams, pork shoulders, chopped ham, and bacon. Also used as a dilutant for Citrus Red No. 2 (*see* FD and C Citrus Red No. 2). It may deplete the body of calcium if taken in sufficient amounts and such a case of low calcium was reported in a patient poisoned with water softener. Used in bubble baths and as a texturizer in soaps. It is a crystalline salt, moderately irritating to the skin and mucous membranes. Ingestion can cause violent purging. The final report to the FDA of the Select Committee on GRAS Substances stated in 1980 that it should continue its GRAS status for packaging with no limitations other than good manufacturing practices. *See* Sodium Phosphate. GRAS.

SOLUBILIZATION • The process of dissolving in water such substances as fats and liquids that are not readily soluble under standard conditions by the action of a detergent or similar agent. Technically, a solubilized product is clear because the particle side of an emulsion is so small that light is not bounced off the particles.

SOLVENT • A liquid capable of dissolving or dispensing one or more substances. Ethylene Dichloride (*see*) is an example of a solvent.

SORBATE, CALCIUM • *See* Calcium Sorbate.

SORBIC ACID • Acetic acid. Hexadienic Acid. Hexadienoic Acid. Sorbistat. A white, free-flowing powder obtained from the berries of the mountain ash. It is also made from chemicals in the factory. It is used in cosmetics as a preservative and humectant. A mold and yeast inhibitor, it is used in foods, especially cheeses and beverages. It is also used in baked goods, chocolate syrup, fresh fruit cocktail, soda-fountain type syrups, tangerine puree (sherbet base), salads (potato, macaroni, cole slaw, gelatin), cheesecake, pie fillings, cake, cheese in consumer-size packages, and artificially sweetened jellies and preserves. Percentages range from 0.003 percent in beverages to 0.2 percent in cheeses. Used as a replacement for glycerin in emulsions, ointments, embalming fluids, mouthwashes, dental creams, and various cosmetic creams. A binder for toilet preparations and plasticizers. Produces a velvetlike feel when rubbed on skin. In large amounts, sticky. Practically nontoxic but may cause skin irritation in susceptible people. When injected under the skin in 2,600-milligram doses per kilogram of body weight, it caused cancer in rodents. The final report to the FDA of the Select Committee on GRAS Substances stated in 1980 that it should continue its GRAS status with no limitations other than good manufacturing practices.

SORBITAN DIOLEATE • The diester of oleic acid and hexitol anhydrides derived from sorbitol. *See* Sorbitan Fatty Acid Esters.

SORBITAN DIISOSEATE • The diester of Isostearic Acid and Hexitol. *See* Sorbitan Fatty Acid Esters.

SORBITAN FATTY ACID ESTERS • Mixture of fatty acids (*see*) and esters of sorbitol (*see*) and sorbitol with the water removed. Widely used in the food and cosmetic industry as emulsifiers and stabilizers. Also used to prevent irritation from other cosmetic ingredients.

SORBITAN ISOSTEARATE • *See* Sorbitan Fatty Acid Esters.

SORBITAN LAURATE • Span 20®. Oily liquid, insoluble in water, soluble in alcohol and oils. An emulsifier in cosmetic creams and lotions; a stabilizer of essential oils in water. No known toxicity.

SORBITAN MONOOLEATE • Polysorbate 80. An emulsifying agent for special dietary products and pharmaceuticals, a defoamer in yeast production, and a chewing gum plasticizer. An unintentionally administered daily dose of 19.2 grams per kilogram of body weight for two days to a four-month-old baby caused no harm except loose stools.

SORBITAN MONOPALMITATE • An emulsifier and flavor-dispersing agent used as an alternate for sorbitan monostearate (*see*) in cake mixes. No known toxicity.

SORBITAN MONOSTEARATE • An emulsifier, defoaming, and flavoring dispersing agent. Used in cakes and cake mixes, whipped vegetable oil toppings, cookie coatings, cake icings and fillings, solid-state edible vegetable fat–water emulsions used as substitutes for milk or cream in coffee, coconut spread, beverages, confectionery, baked goods. Percentages range from 1 to 0.0006 percent. No single dose is known to be lethal in animals, and humans have been fed a daily single dose of 20 grams without harm.

SORBITAN OLEATE • Sorbitan Monooleate. An emulsifying agent, defoaming agent, and plasticizer. No known toxicity.

SORBITAN PALMITATE • Span 40®. Derived from sorbitol (*see*). An emulsifier in cosmetics creams and lotions, a solubilizer of essential oils in water. Light yellow wax, insoluble in water, soluble in solvents. No known toxicity.

SORBITAN SESQUIOLEATE • An emulsifier. *See* Sorbitol and Oleic Acid.

SORBITAN SEQUISTEARATE • *See* Sorbitan Stearate.

SORBITAN STEARATE • Sorbitan Monostearate. An emulsifier in cosmetic creams and lotions, a solubilizer of essential oils in water. Used in antiperspirants, deodorants, cake makeup, hand creams, hair tonics, rouge, and suntan creams. Manufactured by reacting edible commercial stearic acid with sorbitol (*see* both). Light-cream to tan colored, hard waxy solid, with a bland odor and taste. No known toxicity. *See* Sorbitol.

SORBITAN TRIISOSTEARATE • *See* Stearic Acid.

SORBITAN TRIOLEATE • *See* Sorbitol.

SORBITAN TRISTEARATE • An emulsifier and alternate for sorbitan stearate (*see*). No known toxicity.

SORBITOL • An alcohol first found in the ripe berries of the mountain ash; it also occurs in other berries (except grapes), and in cherries, plums, pears, apples, seaweed, and algae. Consists of white hygroscopic powder, flakes, or granules with a sweet taste. It is a texturizing agent, humectant, anticaking agent, and sequestrant. A sugar substitute for diabetics. Used as a thickener in candy, in vegetable oils as a sequestrant, as a stabilizer and sweetener in frozen desserts for special dietary purposes, as a humectant and texturizing agent in shredded coconut and dietetic fruits and soft drinks. Gives a velvety feel to skin. Used as a replacement for glycerin in emulsions, ointments, embalming fluid, mouthwashes, dental creams, and various cosmetic creams. A binder for toilet preparations and a plasticizer. Also used in hair sprays, beauty masks, cuticle removers, foundation cake makeup, hand lotions, liquid powders, dentifrices, after-shave lotions, deodorants, antiperspirants, shampoos, and rouge; in writing inks, to ensure a smooth flow from the point of the pen; and in pharmaceutical preparations to increase the absorption of vitamins. Medicinally used to reduce body water and for intravenous feedings. No known toxicity if taken externally. However, if ingested in excess, it can cause diarrhea and gastrointestinal disturbances; also it may alter the absorption of other drugs making them less effective or more toxic. Labels of foods that may be consumed in excess of 50 grams of sorbitol per day must bear the label, "Excess consumption may have a laxative effect."

SORBOSE • Derived from sorbitol (*see*) by fermentation. Used in manufacture of Vitamin C (accounts for nearly 1000 tons of ascorbic acid [*see*] produced yearly). No known toxicity. The final report to the FDA of the Select Committee on GRAS Substances stated in 1980 that it should continue its GRAS status for packaging with no limitations other than good manufacturing practices.

SORBUS EXTRACT • Service Tree Extract. The extract of *Sorbus domestica*. An extract was used by the Indians to make a wash for sore and blurred eyes from the sun as from climbing and hiking, and from dust.

SORGHUM • The second most widely grown feed grain in the United States. Only 2 to 3 percent of the crop is used for human food in America but it is the reverse in Africa and Asia. However, a new high-lysine sorghum plant has been developed that is twice as nutritious in protein as the common variety and is 50 percent richer in lysine, the essential amino acid. The syrup, produced by evaporation from the stems and the juice, resembles cane sugar but contains a high proportion of invert sugar (*see*) as well as a starch and dextrin (*see* both). Very sweet, it is used as a texturizer and sweetener in foods. No known toxicity.

SORGHUM GRAIN SYRUP • Produced from the dried sorghum juice. *See* Sorghum.

SORREL EXTRACT • Rumex Extract. An extract of the various species of *Rumex*. The Europeans imported this to the Americas and the Indians adopted it. Originally the root was used as a laxative and as a mild astringent. It was also used for scabs on the skin and as a dentifrice. It was widely used by American medical circles in this century to treat skin diseases.

SOY EXTRACT • *See* Soybean Oil.

SOY FLOUR • *See* Soybean Oil.

SOY STEROL • *See* Soybean Oil.

SOY ACID • *See* Soybean Oil.

SOYA HYDROXYETHYL IMIDAZOLINE • *See* Ethylenediamine and Urea.

SOYAMIDE DEA • *See* Soybean Oil.

SOYAMINE • *See* Soybean Oil.

SOYBEAN OIL • Flour extracted from the seeds of plants grown in eastern Asia, especially Manchuria, and the midwestern United States. The oil is made up of 40 percent protein, 17 percent carbohydrates, 18 percent oil, and 4.6 percent ash. It contains ascorbic acid, Vitamin A, and thiamine. Pale yellow to brownish yellow. Also used in the manufacture of margarine. Debittered soybean flour contains practically no starch and is widely used in dietetic foods. Soybean oil is used in defoamers in the production of beet sugar and yeast, in the manufacture of margarine, shortenings, candy, and soap. Soybean is used in many products including MSG, dough mixes, Lea and Perrins Sauce, Heinz's Worcester Sauce, La Choy Oriental Show You Sauce, soy sauce, salad dressings, pork link sausages, luncheon meats, hard candies, nut candies, milk and coffee substitutes. It is made into soybean milk, soybean curd, and soybean cheese. Used in manufacture of soaps, shampoos, and bath oils. About 300 million bushels of soybean are grown yearly in the U.S.A., one third more than in China. May cause allergic reactions, including hair damage and acnelike pimples. The final report to the FDA of the Select Committee on GRAS Substances stated in 1980 that it should continue its GRAS status with no limitations other than good manufacturing practices.

SOYBEAN OIL UNSAPONIFIABLES • The fraction of soybean oil which is not saponified (turned into fatty alcohol) in the refining of soybean oil fatty acids.

SOY SAUCE • Fermented or Hydrolyzed   A hydrolysis product of soybeans. A combination of mold fermentation and acid hydrolysis is used. The molds employed are *Aspergillus flavus, A. niger,* and *A. oryzae.* Soy sauce consists of a mixture of amino acids, peptides, polypeptides, peptones, simple proteins, purines, carbohydrates, and other organic compounds suspended in an 18-percent sodium chloride solution. In 1983, some manufacturers began producing soy sauce with a lower salt content. Used directly on food as a flavoring. The final report to the FDA of the Select Committee on GRAS Substances stated in 1980 that there is no evidence in the available information that it is a hazard to the public when used as it is now and it should continue its GRAS status with limitations on the amounts that can be added to food.

SOY STEROL • *See* Soybean Oil.

SOY STEROL ACETATE • *See* Soybean Oil and Acetate.

SPANISH HOPS • *See* Ditanny of Crete.

SPANISH ORIGANUM • *See* Origanum Oil.

SPEARMINT • Garden Mint. Green Mint.   It is the essential volatile oil obtained by steam distillation from the fresh above-ground parts of the flowering plant grown in the United States, Europe, and Asia. It is colorless, yellow or yellow green with the characteristic taste and odor of spearmint. The oil (principal active constituent contains at least 50 percent carvone; *see*), obtained by steam distillation of the flowering plant. The fresh ground parts of the aromatic herb is used in spearmint flavoring for beverages, meats, and condiments (1,000 ppm). Widely cultivated in the United States, it is used in butter, caramel, citrus, fruit, garlic, soy, and spice flavorings for beverages, ice cream, ices, candy, baked goods, condiments (100,000 ppm), fats, oils, and icings (50,000 ppm). Has been used to break up intestinal gas. Used in perfumes, perfumed cosmetics, and toothpaste. May cause allergic reactions such as skin rash. GRAS.

SPEEDWELL • Used in shampoos. It is an herb, a common hairy perennial grown in Europe, with pale-blue or lilac flowers. It has a reputation among herbalists of inducing sweating and restoring healthy body functions; also an expectorant tonic, a treatment for hemorrhages, and a medication for skin diseases. No known toxicity.

SPERM OIL • Hydrogenated (*see*). Obtained from the sperm whale. Yellow, thin liquid; slightly fishy odor if not of good quality. Used as a releasing agent or lubricant in baking pans and as a coating on fresh citrus fruits. Also as an industrial lubricant. No known toxicity.

SPIKE LAVENDER OIL • French Lavender. Used in perfumes. A pale yellow stable oil obtained from a flower grown in the Mediterranean region. A lavenderlike odor. Used in fruit, floral, mint, and spice flavorings for beverages, ice cream, ices, candy, and baked goods. Used in cologne, toilet water, blended with lavender oil, soaps, and varnishes. Used also for fumigating to keep moths from clothes and in food and beverage flavorings. No known toxicity. GRAS.

SPINACH EXTRACT • An extract of the leaves of spinach, *Spinacea oleracea*.

SPIRAEA EXTRACT • Queen Meadow. An extract from the flowers of *Spiraea ulmaria*. Contains an oil similar to wintergreen (*see*). The roots are rich in tannic acid (*see*).

SPIRAL FLAG OIL • *See* Costus Root Oil.

SPIRIT OF NITROUS ETHER • *See* Ethyl Nitrite.

SPRUCE NEEDLES AND TWIGS • Flavorings. *See* Spruce Oil.

SPRUCE OIL • Colorless to light yellow, pleasant smelling oil obtained from the needles and twigs of various spruces and hemlocks used chiefly for scenting soaps and cosmetics but also used as a flavoring. No known toxicity. *See* Hemlock Oil.

SQUALENE • Obtained by hydrogenation of shark-liver oil. Stable in air and oxygen. Occurs in smaller amounts in olive oil, wheat germ oil, rice bran oil. A faint agreeable odor, tasteless, miscible with vegetable and mineral oils, organic solvents, and fatty substances. Insoluble in water. A lubricant and perfume fixative. A bactericide, an intermediate (*see*) in hair dyes, and used in surface-active agents. No known toxicity.

STABILIZER • A substance added to a product to give it body and to maintain a desired texture or consistency. Chocolate milk needs a stabilizer to keep the particles of chocolate from settling to the bottom of the container. Calcium (*see*) is used as a stabilizer in canned tomatoes to keep them from falling apart. Among the most widely used stabilizers are the gums, such as gum arabic and agar-agar (*see* both).

STANNOUS CHLORIDE • Tin Dichloride   An antioxidant, soluble in water, and a powerful reducing agent, used in canned asparagus, canned soda (11 ppm), and other foods. Used to revive yeast. Low systemic toxicity but may be irritating to the skin and mucous membranes. On the FDA list for further study of mutagenic, teratogenic, subacute and reproductive effects since 1980. GRAS.

STAR ANISE • Chinese Anis.   Fruit of *Illicium verum* from China, called star because of the fruit's shape. The *extract* is used in fruit, licorice, anise, liquor, sausage, root beer, sarsaparilla, vanilla, wintergreen, and birch beer flavorings for beverages, ice cream, ices, candy, meats (1,000 ppm), and liqueurs. The *oil* is used in blackberry, peach, licorice, anise, liquor, meat, root beer, spice, wintergreen, and birch beer flavorings for beverages, ice cream, ices, candy, baked goods, meats, syrups, and liqueurs. The fruit is a source of anise oil (*see* Anise). Star anise has been used as an expectorant and carminative. Japanese star anise is *Illicium anisatum* and contains a toxic lactone called anisatin, unknown in the Chinese variety. No known toxicity. GRAS.

STARCH • Acid Modified. Pregelatinized and Unmodified.   Starch is stored by plants and is taken from grains of wheat, potatoes, rice, corn, beans, and many other vegetable foods. Insoluble in cold water or alcohol but soluble in boiling water. Comparatively resistant to naturally occurring enzymes, and this is why processors "modify" starch to make it more digestible. Starch is modified with propylene oxide, succinic anhydride, 1-octenyl succinic anhydride, aluminum sulfate, or sodium hydroxide (*see* all). Starch is a major component of cereals and many vegetables. The average United States diet has about 180 grams per person daily. Modified starch contributes about a gram per person per day. The source of starch and the type of modification are not usually identified on the label, since the FDA does not require it. The modified starches used in foods are most often bleached starch, acetylated distarch adipate, distarch phosphate, acetylated distarch phosphate, and hydroxypropyl distarch phosphate. The latter three are commonly used in baby foods. Starch is also used in dusting powders, dentifrices, hair colorings, rouge, dry shampoos, baby powders, emollients, and bath salts. Soothing to the skin and used to treat rashes. Used internally as a gruel for persons with diarrhea. Allergic reaction to starch in toilet goods includes stuffy nose and other symptoms due to inhalation. Absorbs moisture and swells, causing blocking and distention of the pores leading to mechanical irritation. Particles remain in pores and putrefy, accelerated by sweat. The final report to the FDA of the Select Committee on GRAS Substances said there was no information that starch acetate was hazardous to the public when used as it is now and it should continue its GRAS status with limitations on amounts that can be added to food. On the other hand, starch sodium succinate, starch sodium octenyl succinate, and starch sodium hypochlorite oxidized were said not to demonstrate a hazard to the public at current use levels, but uncertainties do exist, requiring additional studies to be conducted. However, GRAS status continues while tests are being completed and evaluated. Acid-modified and pregelatinized starches were said in the final report to be GRAS, requiring no limitations other than good manufacturing practices.

STARCH/ACRYLATES/ACRYLAMIDE COPOLYMER • *See* Starch and Acrylic Acid.

STARCH DIETHYLAMINOETHYL ETHER • *See* Starch.

STEARAMIDE • An emulsifier. Colorless leaflets, insoluble in water. No known toxicity. *See* Stearic Acid.

STEARAMINE • *See* Stearic Acid.

STEARMINE OXIDE • *See* Stearyl Alcohol.

STEARATES • See Stearic Acid.

STEARETH-2 • A polyoxyethyl (*see*) ether of fatty alcohol. The oily liquid is used as a surfactant (*see*) and emulsifier (*see*). No known toxicity.

STEARETH-4 THROUGH -100 • The polyethylene glycol ethers of stearyl alcohol. The number indicates the degree of liquidity; the higher, the more solid. *See* Steareth-2.

STEARIC ACID • Octadecanoic Acid. Occurs naturally in some vegetable oils, cascarilla bark extract, and as a glyceride (*see*) in tallow and other animal fats and oils. A white waxy natural fatty acid, it is the major ingredient used in making bar soap and lubricants. Prepared synthetically by hydrogenation (*see*) of cottonseed and other vegetable oils. Slight tallowlike odor. Used in butter and vanilla flavorings for beverages, baked goods, and candy (4,000 ppm). Also a softener in chewing gum base. Also used in deodorants and antiperspirants, liquid powders, foundation creams, hand creams, hand lotions, liquefying creams, hair straighteners, protective creams, shaving creams, and soap. A large percentage of all cosmetic creams on the market contains it. It gives pearliness to hand creams. It is also for suppositories. It is a possible sensitizer for allergic people. The final report to the FDA of the Select Committee on GRAS Substances stated in 1980 that it should continue its GRAS status with no limitations other than good manufacturing practices. In 1988, University of Texas researchers reported in *The New England Journal of Medicine* that it did not raise blood cholesterol levels as much as other saturated fats. *See* Fatty Acids.

STEARYL ACETATE • The ester of stearyl alcohol and acetic acid (*see* both).

STEARYL ALCOHOL • Stenol. A mixture of solid alcohols prepared from sperm whale oil. Unctuous white flakes, insoluble in water, soluble in alcohol and ether. Can be prepared from sperm whale oil. A substitute for cetyl alcohol (*see*) to obtain a firmer product at ordinary temperatures. Used in pharmaceuticals, cosmetic creams, for emulsions, as an antifoam agent, and lubricant; also in depilatories, hair rinses, and shampoos. No known toxicity.

STEARYL BETAINE • *See* Surfactants and Stearic Acid.

STEARYL CAPRYLATE • The ester of stearyl alcohol and citric acid (*see* both).

STEARYL CITRATE • The ester of stearyl alcohol and citric acid (*see* both). A metal scavenger to prevent adverse effects of trace metals in foods and an antioxidant to prevent rancidity in oleomargarine. *See* Citrate Salts for toxicity. The final report to the FDA of the Select Committee on GRAS Substances stated in 1980 that it should continue its GRAS status with no limitations other than good manufacturing practices.

STEARYL ERUCATE • *See* Stearyl Alcohol and Erucic Acid.

STEARYL GLYCYRRHETINATE • The ester of stearyl alcohol and glycyrrhetinate. The ester of stearyl alcohol and glycrrhetinic acid (*see* both).

STEARYL HEPTANOATE • The ester of stearyl alcohol and heptanoic acid. Used as a wax. *See* Stearyl Alcohol and Heptanoic Acid.

STEARYL LACTATE • An emulsifier that occurs in tallow and other animal fats as well as vegetable oils. Used to emulsify shortening in non-yeast-leavened bakery products and pancake mixes. Also used to emulsify cakes, icing, and fillings. No known toxicity mixes. No known toxicity.

STEARYL MONOGLYCERIDYL CITRATE • The soft, practically tasteless, off-white, waxy solid used as an emulsion stabilizer in shortening with emulsifiers. Not over 0.15 percent in food. It is prepared by the chemical reaction of citric acid on monoglycerides of fatty acids (*see*). No known toxicity.

STEARYL OCTANOATE • The ester of stearyl alcohol and 2-ethylhexanoic acid. *See* Stearyl Alcohol.

STEARYL STEARATE • The ester of stearyl alcohol and stearic acid (*see* both).

STEARYL STEAROYL STEARATE • *See* Stearyl Alcohol.

STEARYLDIMETHYL AMINE • *See* Stearyl Alcohol.

STERCULEN • Sterculia. *See* Karaya Gum.

STERCULIA GUM • GRAS. *See* Karaya Gum.

STEROIDS • Class of compounds that includes certain drugs of hormonal origin, such as cortisone, and used to treat the inflammations caused by allergies.

STEROL • Any class of solid complex alcohols from animals and plants. Cholesterol is a sterol and is used in hand creams. Sterols are lubricants in baby preparations, emollient creams, and lotions, emulsified fragrances, hair conditioners, hand creams, and hand lotions. No known toxicity.

STONEROOT • Horse Balm. Used for its constituents of resin, saponin, and tannic acid (*see* all). An erect smooth perennial; a strong scented herb of eastern North America with pointed leaves. It produces a chocolate-colored powder with a peculiar odor and bitter astringent taste. Soluble in alcohol. No known toxicity.

STORAX • Styrax. Sweet Oriental Gum. Used in perfumes. It is the resin obtained from the bark of an Asiatic tree. Grayish brown, fragrant semiliquid, containing styrene and cinnamic acid (*see* both). Once used in medicine as a weak antiseptic and as an expectorant. Used in strawberry, fruit, and spice flavorings for beverages, ice cream, ices, candy, baked goods, chewing gum, and toppings. Moderately toxic when ingested. Can cause urinary problems when absorbed through the skin. Can cause skin irritation, welts, and discomfort when applied topically. A common allergen.

STPP • *See* Sodium Tripolyphosphate.

STRAWBERRY ALDEHYDE • Synthetic flavoring. Little information available.

STRAWBERRY EXTRACT • *See* Strawberry Juice.

STRAWBERRY JUICE • Fresh ripe strawberries are reputed to contain ingredients that soften and nourish the skin. Widely used in natural cosmetics today. No scientific evidence of benefit or harm.

STRAWFLOWER EXTRACT • The extract of *Helichrysum italicum,* grown for its bright-yellow strawlike flowers. Used in coloring.

STRONTIUM HYDROXIDE • Used chiefly in making soaps and greases in cosmetics. Colorless, water-absorbing crystals or white powder. Absorbs carbon dioxide from the air. Very alkaline in solution. Also used in refining beet sugar and separating sugar from molasses. Irritating when applied to the skin.

STYRACIN • *See* Cinnamyl Cinnamate.

STYRAX • *See* Storax.

STYRENE • Obtained from ethylbenzene by taking out the hydrogen. Colorless to yellowish oil liquid with a penetrating odor. Used in the manufacture of cosmetic resins and in plastics. May be irritating to the eyes and mucous membranes, and in high concentrations it is narcotic.

STYRYL CARBINOL • *See* Cinnamyl Alcohol.

SUBACUTE • A zone between acute and chronic or the process of a disease that is not overt. Subacute endocarditis, for example, is an infection of the heart. It is usually due to a "strep germ" and may follow temporary infection after a tooth extraction.

SUBSTITUTE • Means the product is equivalent to the food it resembles. *See* Imitation.

SUCCINIC ACID • Occurs in fossils, fungi, lichens, etc. Prepared from acetic acid (*see*). Odorless; very acid taste. The acid is used as a plant growth retardant. A buffer and neutralizing agent in food processing. A germicide and mouthwash and used in perfumes and lacquers; also a buffer and neutralizing agent. Has been employed medicinally as a laxative. No known toxicity in cosmetic use. Large amounts injected under the skin of frogs kills them. The final report to the FDA or the Select Committee on GRAS Substances stated in 1980 that it should continue its GRAS status with no limitations other than good manufacturing practices.

SUCCINIC ANHYDRIDE • A starch modifier up to 4 percent. *See* Succinic Acid.

SUCCINISTEARIN • Stearoyl Propylene Glycol Hydrogen Succinate. Emulsifier in or with shortenings and edible oils used in cakes, cake mixes, fillings, icings, pastries, and toppings. *See* Succinic Acid.

SUCCINYLATED MONOGLYCERIDES • Surfactant (*see*) used as a dough conditioner to add loaf volume and firmness. *See* Glycerides and Succinic Acid.

SUCROSE • Sugar. Cane Sugar. Saccharose. A sweetening agent and food, a starting agent in fermentation production, a preservative and antioxidant in pharmacy, a demulcent, and a substitute for glycerin (*see*). Table sugar can stimulate the production of fat in the body, apart from its calorie content in the diet, and may be particularly fat-producing in women using contraceptive pills. Workers who handle raw sugar often develop rashes and other skin problems. Sugar when it oxidizes with sweat draws water from the skin and causes chapping and cracking. Infections, erosions, and fissures around the nails can occur. No known toxicity in cosmetics. The final report to the FDA of the Select Committee on GRAS Substances stated in 1980 that it should continue its GRAS status with no limitations other than good manufacturing practices.

SUCROSE BENZOATE • *See* Benzoic Acid.

SUCROSE DISTEARATE • A mixture of sucrose and lauric acid (*see* both).

SUCROSE FATTY ACID ESTERS • Derived from sucrose (*see*) and edible tallow, the FDA gave permission in 1982 for their use as components of protective coatings for fruits.

SUCROSE LAURATE • A mixture of sucrose and lauric acid (*see* both).

SUCROSE OCTAACETATE • Prepared from sucrose (*see*). A synthetic flavoring used in bitters, spice, and ginger ale flavorings for beverages. Used in adhesives; a denaturant for alcohol. No known toxicity.

SUCROSE POLYESTER • *See* Olestra.

SUCROSE STEARATE • A mixture of sucrose and stearic acid (*see* both).

SUGAR • *See* Sucrose.

SUGAR BEET EXTRACT • A flavoring in foods. *See* Sucrose.

SULFAMIC ACID • A strong white crystalline acid used chiefly as a weed killer, in cleaning metals, and as a softening agent. Used as a plasticizer and fire retardant for paper and other cellullose products; as a stabilizing agent for chlorine and hypochlorite, bleaching paper pulp, and as a catalyst for ureaformaldehyde resin. A cleaning agent in cosmetics and used in the manufacture of hair dyes. Toxic by ingestion. Moderately irritating to the skin and mucous membranes.

SULFATED OIL • Sulphated Oil. A compound to which a salt of sulfuric acid has been added to help control the acid-alkali balance.

SULFATED TALLOW • Fat from fatty tissues of sheep and cattle which becomes solid at 40 to 46° F. It is a defoaming agent in yeast and beet sugar production in "amounts reasonably required to inhibit foaming." *See* Tallow Flakes for toxicity.

SULFITE DIOXIDE • *See* Sulfites.

SULFITES • Sodium, Potassium, and Ammonium. Preservatives, antioxidants, and antibrowning agents used in foods. There are six sulfiting agents that are currently listed as GRAS chemical preservatives. They are sulfur dioxide, sodium sulfite, sodium and potassium bisulfite, and sodium and potassium metabisulfite (*see* all). Under the current listing, sulfiting agents may be used as preservatives in any food except meat or food that is a recognized source of Vitamin B_1. These agents have been used in many processed foods and in cafeterias and restaurants to prevent fruits, green vegetables, potatoes, and salads from turning brown, as well as to enhance their crispness.

The FDA had sulfiting agents under review in 1983. As part of this review, a proposal to affirm the GRAS status of sulfur dioxide, sodium bisulfite, and sodium and potassium metabisulfite with specific use limitations, was published in the *Federal Register* of July 9, 1982. The agency did not propose to affirm the GRAS status of sodium sulfite and potassium bisulfite because it had no evidence to determine their current use in food.

Reactions to sulfites can include acute asthma attacks, loss of consciousness, anaphylactic shock, diarrhea, and nausea occurring soon after ingesting sulfiting agents. There have been seventeen deaths that the FDA has determined were "probably or possibly" associated with sulfites. The FDA banned the use of the preservative on fresh fruits and vegetables and at this writing is reviewing a proposal to prohibit it on fresh, precut potatoes. The FDA decided in 1988 against extending its ban on the use of sulfites to a variety of foods sold in supermarkets and served in restaurants, including wine, dried fruit, some seafood, and condiments. Sulfites must be declared on the labels of wine and packaged foods sold in supermarkets when they are added in excess of 10 parts per million.

A citizens' petition was submitted by the Center for Science in the Public Interest, Washington, D.C., on October 28, 1982, that asked the agency to restrict the use of sulfiting agents to a safe residue level in food or require labels on those food products in which sulfiting agents must be used at higher levels to perform essential public health functions.

In the meantime, the California Grape and Tree Fruit League recommended that the Food and Drug Administration affirm as GRAS sulfiting agents used in sulfur dioxide fumigation within specific limitations and include its use as an ingredient to treat fresh grapes. Stating that the compound is essential to the marketing, transport, storage, and export of table grapes, the group claimed lack of any known substitute for the gaseous compound effective in preventing mold-rot and other storage fungi and in prolonging storage life. A spokesperson for the Wine Institute, which represents 460 domestic wine makers, said that many of the sulfur compounds in wine are natural parts of fermentation, but they also are added to many wines.

In addition to wines, beer, cocktail mixes and wine coolers, sulfites are often added to:

• Baked goods—cookies, crackers, mixed with dried fruits or vegetables, pie crusts, pizza crusts, quiche crusts, and flour tortillas.

• Beverage bases—dried citrus fruit beverage mixes.

• Condiments and relishes—horseradish, onion and pickle relishes, pickles, olives, salad dressing mixes, and wine vinegar.

• Confections and frostings—brown, raw, powdered or white sugar derived from sugar beets.

• Dairy product analogs—filled milk (skim milk enriched in fat content by the addition of vegetable oils).

• Fish and shellfish—canned clams; fresh, frozen, canned and dried shrimp; frozen lobster; scallops and dried cod.

• Fresh fruits and vegetables—all banned by FDA regulation except fresh precut potatoes.

• Processed fruits—canned, bottled or frozen fruit juices (including lemon, lime, grape, apple); dried fruit; canned, bottled or frozen dietetic fruit or fruit juices; maraschino cherries and glazed fruit.

SULFOACETATE DERIVATIVES OF MONOGLYCERIDES AND DIGLYCERIDES • Used as emulsifiers. The final report to the FDA of the Select Committee on GRAS Substances stated in 1980 that there were insufficient relevant biological and other studies upon which to base an evaluation of them when they are used as food ingredients.

SULFO-*p*-TOLUENE • Sodium Chloramine. A water-purifying agent and a deodorant used to remove onion and weed odors in cheese. Toluene may cause mild anemia and is narcotic in high concentrations.

SULFUR DIOXIDE • A gas formed when sulfur burns. Used to bleach vegetable colors and to preserve fruits and vegetables; a disinfectant in breweries and food factories; a bleaching agent in gelatin, glue, and beet sugars; an antioxidant, preservative, and antibrowning agent in wine, corn syrup, table syrup, jelly, dried fruits, brined fruit, maraschino cherries, beverages, dehydrated potatoes, soups, and condiments. Should not be used on meats or on food recognized as a source of Vitamin A because it destroys the vitamin. Very poisonous, highly irritating. Often cited as an air pollutant. Inhalation produces respiratory irritation and death when sufficiently concentrated. The final report to the FDA of the Select Committee on GRAS Substances stated in 1980 there is no evidence in the available information that it is a hazard to the public when used as it is now and it should continue its GRAS status with limitations on amounts that can be added to food.

SULFURIC ACID • Oil of Vitriol. A clear, colorless, odorless, oily acid used to modify starch and to regulate acid-alkalinity in the brewing industry. It is very corrosive and produces severe burns on contact with the skin and other body tissues. Inhalation of the vapors can cause serious lung damage. Dilute sulfuric acid has been used to stimulate appetite and to combat over alkaline stomach juices. It is used as a topical caustic in cosmetic products. If ingested undiluted, it can be fatal. The final report to the FDA of the Select Committee on GRAS Substances stated in 1980 that it should continue its GRAS status with no limitations other than good manufacturing practices.

SUNFLOWER SEED OIL • Oil obtained by milling the seeds of the large flower produced in the U.S.S.R., India, Egypt, and Argentina. A bland, pale-yellow oil, it contains amounts of Vitamin E (*see* Tocopherols) and forms a "skin" after drying. Used in food and salad oils, and in resin and soap manufacturing. No known toxicity.

SUNFLOWER SEED OIL GLYCERIDE • *See* Sunflower Seed Oil and Glycerides.

SUNSET YELLOW • A monoazo color. The name can be used only when applied to batches of uncertified color. The CTFA adopted name for certified (*see*) batches is FD and C Yellow No. 6 (*see*).

SUPERGLYCERINATED FULLY HYDROGENATED RAPESEED OIL • Used in some margarines and emulsions. *See* Rapeseed Oil, Glycerin, and Hydrogenation.

SURFACE-ACTIVE AGENT • *See* Surfactants.

SURFACTANTS • These are wetting agents. They lower water's surface tension, permitting water to spread out and penetrate more easily. These surface-active agents are classified by whether or not they ionize in solution and by the nature of their electrical charges. There are four major categories—anionic, nonionic, cationic, and amphoteric. *Anionic surfactants,* which carry a negative charge, have excellent cleaning properties. They are stain and dirt removers in household detergents, powders, and liquids and in toilet soaps. *Nonionic surfactants* have no electrical charge. Since they are resistant to hard water and dissolve in oil and grease, they are especially effective in spray-on oven cleaners. *Cationic surfactants* have a positive charge. These are primarily ammonia derivatives and are antistatic and sanitizing agents used as friction reducers in hair rinses and fabric softeners. *Amphoteric surfactants* may be either negatively charged or positively charged depending on the activity or alkalinity of the water. They are used for cosmetics where mildness is important, such as in shampoos and lotions. Surfactants may be classified as emulsifiers, dispersants, wetting and foaming agents, detergents, viscosity modifiers, and stabilizers. For example, in peanut butter, a surfactant keeps oil and water mixtures from separating; in cosmetics, it makes lotions more spreadable; salad dressings and cheeses are thickened by surfactants which make them pour better.

SWEET BIRCH • *See* Methyl Salicylate.

SWEET CLOVER EXTRACT • The extract of various species of *Melilotus,* grown for hay and soil improvement. It contains coumarin (*see*) and is used as a scent to disguise bad odors.

SWEET FLAG • Calamus. Sweet Cane. Dried rhizome of *acorus calamus* cultivated in Burma and Sri Lanka. It contains tannins (*see*) and sugars. Used as a flavoring agent. May cause allergic reactions.

SWEET MARJORAM OIL • Marjoram Pot. Used in perfumery and hair preparations. The natural extract of the flowers and leaves of two varieties of the fragrant marjoram. Also a food flavoring. No known toxicity.

SYLVIC ACID • *See* Abietic Acid.

SYNTHETIC • Made in the laboratory and not by nature. Vanillin, for example, made in the laboratory, may be identical to vanilla extracted from the vanilla bean but vanillin cannot be called "natural."

SYNTHETIC BEESWAX • A mixture of alcohol esters.

SYNTHETIC FATTY ALCOHOLS • Made from fatty alcohols (*see*) obtained by distillation. Used as substitutes for naturally derived fatty acids (*see*).

SYNTHETIC GLYCERIN • *See* Glycerin.

SYNTHETIC JOJOBA OIL • *See* Jojoba Oil.

SYNTHETIC PARAFFIN AND SUCCINIC DERIVATIVES • Used as a coating on fresh citrus, muskmelons, and sweet potatoes. *See* Paraffin Wax and Succinic Acid.

SYNTHETIC WAX • A hydrocarbon wax derived from various oils.

T

TAGETES • Meal, Extract, and Oil. The *meal* is the dried, ground flower petals of the Aztec marigold, a strong-scented, tropical American herb, mixed with no more than 0.3 percent ethoxyquin, a herbicide and antioxidant. The *extract* is taken from tagetes peels. Both the meal and the extract are used to enhance the yellow color of chicken skin and eggs. They are incorporated in chicken feed, supplemented sufficiently with yellow coloring xanthophyll. The coloring has been permanently listed since 1963 but is exempt from certification. The oil is extracted from the Aztec flower and used in fruit flavorings for beverages, ice cream, ices, candy, baked goods, gelatin, desserts, and condiments. No known toxicity.

TALC • French Chalk. The lumps are known as soapstone of steatite. An anticaking agent added to vitamin supplements to render a free flow; also to chewing gum base. Gives a slippery sensation to powders and creams. Talc is finely powdered native magnesium silicate, a mineral. The main ingredient of baby and bath powders, face powders, eye shadows, liquid powders, protective creams, dry rouges, face masks, foundation cake makeups, skin fresheners, foot powders, and face creams. It usually has small amounts of other powders such as boric acid or zinc oxide added as a coloring agent. Prolonged inhalation can cause lung problems because it is similar in chemical composition to asbestos, a known lung irritant and cancer-causing agent. There is no known acute toxicity, but there is a question about its being a cancer-causing agent upon ingestion. It is suspected that the high incident of stomach cancer among the Japanese is due to the fact that the Japanese prefer that their rice be treated with talc. Furthermore, talc-based powders have been linked to ovarian cancer. In Boston's Brigham and Women's Hospital, of 215 women with ovarian cancer, 32 had used talcum powder on their genitals and sanitary napkins. Talc easily works its way up the reproductive tract. Eventually, a few particles reach the ovary and may set the stage for cancer. Other factors considered in the study, the risk of ovarian cancer was raised to 3.28 times greater for women who use talc than for women who don't. Daniel Cramer, M.D., the obstetrician-gynecologist who wrote of the findings in the journal *Cancer*, said further studies are needed before doctors could recommend that women should not use talc but said that he, himself, advises patients to use other products such as cornstarch-based powders or creams. Talcum powder has been reported to cause coughing, vomiting, or even pneumonia when it is used carelessly and inhaled by babies. GRAS for packaging.

TALL OIL • Liquid Rosin. A by-product of the wood pulp industry. *Tall* is Swedish for "pine." Dark-brown liquid. Acrid odor. A fungicide and cutting oil. It may be a milk irritant and sensitizer. The final report to the FDA of the Select Committee on GRAS Substances stated in 1980 that it should continue its GRAS status with no limitations other than good manufacturing practices.

TALL OIL BENZYL HYDROXYETHYL IMIDAZOLINIUM CHLORIDE • *See* Quaternary Ammonium Compounds and Tall Oil.

TALL OIL ROSIN AND GLYCEROL ESTER • Softener for chewing gum base. *See* Tall Oil.

TALLAMIDE DEA • *See* Tall Oil.

TALLAMPHOPROPIONATE • (*See*) Tall Oil.

TALLOW ACID • *See* Tallow Flakes.

TALLOW AMIDE • *See* Tallow Flakes.

TALLOW AMINE • *See* Tallow Flakes.

TALLOW AMINE OXIDE • (*See*) Tallow Flakes.

TALLOW FLAKES • Suet. Dripping. The fat from the fatty tissue of bovine cattle and sheep in North America. White, almost tasteless when pure, and generally harder than grease. Used as a defoaming agent in yeast and beet sugar production. In miniature pigs in one year, feeding tallow caused moderate to severe atherosclerosis (clogging of the arteries) similar to lesions in humans. Used in shaving creams, lipsticks, shampoos, and soaps. May cause eczema and blackheads. The final report to the FDA of the Select Committee on GRAS Substances stated in 1980 that it should continue its GRAS status for packaging with no limitations other than good manufacturing practices.

TALLOW GLYCERIDES • A mixture of triglycerides (fats) derived from tallow.

TALLOW IMDAZOLINE • *See* Tallow Flakes.

TALLOWAMIDE DEA AND MEA • *See* Tallow Flakes.

TALLOW AMIDOPROPHYLAMINE OXIDE • *See* Tallow Flakes.

TALLOWETH-6 • *See* Tallow Flakes.

TAMARIND EXTRACT • The extract of *Tamarindus indica*, a large tropical tree grown in the East Indies and Africa. Preserved in sugar or syrup, it is used as a natural fruit flavoring. The pulp contains about 10 percent tartaric acid (*see*). Has been used as a cooling laxative drink. No known toxicity. GRAS.

TANGERINE OIL • The oil obtained by expression from the peels of the ripe fruit from several related tangerine species. Reddish orange, with a pleasant orange aroma. Used in blueberry, mandarin, orange, tangerine, and other fruit flavorings for beverages, ice cream, ices, candy, baked goods, gelatin desserts, and chewing gum. No known toxicity. GRAS.

TANNIC ACID • It occurs in the bark and fruit of many plants, notably in the bark of the oak and sumac, and in cherries, coffee, and tea. It is used to clarify beer and wine, and as a refining agent for rendered fats. As a flavoring it is used in butter, caramel, fruit, brandy, maple, and nut flavorings for beverages, ice cream, ices, candy, baked goods, and liquor (1,000 ppm). Used medicinally as a mild astringent and when applied it may turn the skin brown. Used in sunscreen preparations, eye lotions, and antiperspirants. Tea contains tannic acid, and this explains folk use of tea as an eye lotion. Excessive use in creams or lotions in hypersensitive persons may lead to irritation, blistering, and increased pigmentation. Low toxicity orally but large doses may cause gastric distress. Can cause tumors and death by injection, but not, evidently, by ingestion. The final report to the FDA of the Select Committee on GRAS Substances stated in 1980 that there is no evidence in the available information that it is a hazard to the public when used as it is now and it should continue its GRAS status with limitations on the amount that may be added to food.

TANNIN • Used in alcoholic beverages only. *See* Tannic Acid.

TANSY • A common herb which the Greeks believed prolonged life. Strong aromatic odor and bitter taste. Flavoring used in alcoholic beverages only. No known toxicity.

TAPIOCA STARCH • A preparation of cassava, the tapioca plant. Used for thickening liquid foods such as puddings, juicy pies, and soups. No known toxicity. The final report to the FDA of the Select Committee on GRAS Substances stated in 1980 that it should continue its GRAS status with no limitations other than good manufacturing practices.

TAR OIL • The volatile oil distilled from wood tar, generally from the family *Pinaceae*. Used externally to treat skin diseases, the principal toxic ingredients are phenols (very toxic) and other hydro-carbons such as the naphthalenes. Toxicity estimates are hard to make because even the U.S. Pharmacopoeia does not specify the phenol content of official preparations. However, if ingested, it is estimated that one ounce would kill. *See* Pine Tar Oil, which is a rectified tar oil used as a licorice flavoring.

TARA GUM • Peruvian Carob. Obtained by grinding the en-dosperms of the seeds of an evergreen tree common to Peru. The whitish-yellow, nearly odorless powder that is produced is used as a thickening agent and stabilizer. No known toxicity. *See* Locust Bean Gum.

TARAXACUM ERYTHROSPERUMUM • *See* Dandelion Leaf and Root.

TARRAGON • Derived from the dried leaves of a small European perennial wormwood herb. Pale yellow oil grown for its aromatic, pungent foliage. Used in making pickles and vinegar. Also used in perfumery. No known toxicity. GRAS.

TARS • An antiseptic, deodorant, and bug killer. Any of the various dark brown or black bituminous, usually odorous, viscous liquids or semiliquids obtained by the destructive distillation of wood, coal, peat, shale, and other organic materials. Used in hair tonics and shampoos and as a licorice food flavoring. May cause allergic reactions.

TARTARIC ACID • Sodium Tartrate. Sodium Potassium Tartrate. Rochelle Salts. Described in ancient times as being a residual of grape fermentation. Widely distributed in nature in many fruits but usually obtained as a by-product of wine making. Consists of colorless or translucent crystals or a white fine to granular crystalline powder, which is odorless and has an acid taste. It is the acidic constituent of some baking powders and is used to adjust acidity in frozen dairy products, jellies, bakery products, beverages, confections, dried egg whites, food colorings, candies, and artificially sweetened preserves up to 4 percent. Used as a sequestrant, especially in wines, as an emulsifier, and as a grape and sour flavoring for candies, canned sodas and colas, preserves, baked goods, dried egg white, lemon meringue pie mix, pasteurized processed cheese, cheese food and cheese spread, and some types of baking powder. Effervescent acid used in bath salts, denture powders, nail bleaches, hair-grooming aids, hair rinses, depilatories, and hair coloring. In strong solutions it may be mildly irritating to the skin. Large amounts may have a laxative effect. GRAS.

TARTRATE, SODIUM POTASSIUM • The final report to the FDA of the Select Committee on GRAS Substances stated in 1980 that it should continue its GRAS status with no limitations other than good manufacturing practices. *See* Sodium Potassium Tartrate.

TARTRAZINE • FD and C Yellow No. 5. Bright orange-yellow powder used in foods, drugs, and cosmetics, and as a dye for wool and silk. Those allergic to aspirin are often allergic to tartrazine. Allergies have been reported in persons eating sweet corn, soft drinks, and cheese crackers—all colored with Yellow No. 5. It is derived from coal tar.

TAURINE • An amino acid found in almost every tissue of the body and high in human milk. Most infant soy protein formulas are now supplemented with taurine. Taurine is almost absent from vegetarian diets. It is believed necessary for healthy eyes and it is an anitoxidant.

TAUROCHOLIC ACID • Cholic Acid. Cholyltaurine. Occurs as a sodium salt in bile. It is formed by the combination of the sulfur-containing amino acid, taurine, and cholic acid. It aids digestion and absorption of fats. It is used as an emulsifying agent in foods. The final report to the FDA of the Select Committee on GRAS Substances stated in 1980 that it should continue its GRAS status with no limitations other than good manufacturing practices.

TBHQ • *See* Tertiary Butylhydroquinone.

TEA • The abbreviation for Triethanolamine.

TEA • The leaves, leaf buds, and intermodes of plant shaving leaves and fragrant white flowers, prepared and cured to make an aromatic beverage. Cultivated principally in China, Japan, Sri Lanka, and other Asian countries. Tea is a mild stimulant and its tonic properties are due to the alkaloid caffeine; tannic acid (*see*) makes it astringent. Used by natural cosmeticians to reduce the puffiness around the eyes. No known toxicity.

TEA EXTRACT • Essential oil. *See* Tea. GRAS.

TEA-EDTA • *See* Ethylenediamine Tetraacetic Acid.

TEA-HYDROGENATED TALLOW GLUTAMATE • A softener. *See* Glutamate.

TEA-LAUROYL GLUTAMATE • A softener. *See* Glutamate.

TEA SORBATE • *See* Triethanolamine and Sorbic Acid.

TEA-STEARATE • *See* Triethanolamine and Stearic Acid.

TEA-SULFATE • *See* Triethanolamine and Sulfuric Acid.

TERATOGENIC • From the Greek *terat* (monster) and Latin *genesis* (origin); the origin or cause of a monster, or defective fetus.

TERPENE RESIN • Derived from wood, it is used as a moisture barrier on soft gelatin capsules and on Vitamin C powders. Terpenes are common allergens.

TERPENES • A class of unsaturated hydrocarbons *see*. Its removal from products improves their flavor and gives them a more stable, stronger odor. However, some perfumers feel that the removal of terpenes destroys some of the original odor. Has been used as an antiseptic. No known toxicity.

TERPINEOL • A colorless, viscous liquid with a lilaclike odor, insoluble in mineral oil and slightly soluble in water. It is primarily used as a flavoring agent but is also employed as a denaturant to make alcohol undrinkable. It has been used as an antiseptic. It can be a sensitizer.

TERPINOLENE • A synthetic citrus and fruit flavoring agent for beverages, ice cream, ices, candy, and baked goods. See Turpentine for toxicity.

TERPINYL ACETATE • Colorless liquid, odor suggestive of bergamot and lavender. Occurs naturally in cardamon. Slightly soluble in water and glycerol. Derived by heating terpineol with acetic acid (see both). Used in berry, lime, orange, cherry, peach, plum, and meat flavorings for beverages, ice cream, ices, candy and baked goods. See Turpentine for toxicity.

TERPINYL ANTHRANILATE • A synthetic fruit flavoring agent. Derived by heating terpineol with anthranilic acid. Used as a synthetic fruit flavoring agent for beverages, ice cream, ices, candy, and baked goods. See Turpentine for toxicity.

TERPINYL BUTYRATE • A synthetic fruit flavoring agent. Derived by heating terpineol with butyric acid (see both). Used as a synthetic fruit flavoring agent for beverages, ice cream, ices, candy, chewing gum, and baked goods. See Turpentine for toxicity.

TERPINYL CINNAMATE • A synthetic fruit flavoring agent. Derived by heating terpineol with cinnamic acid (see both). Used as a synthetic fruit flavoring agent for beverages, ice cream, ices, candy, and baked goods. See Turpentine for toxicity.

TERPINYL FORMATE • Formic Acid. A synthetic fruit flavoring agent. Derived by heating terpineol with formic acid (see both). Used as a synthetic fruit flavoring agent for beverages, ice cream, ices, candy, liqueurs, and baked goods. See Turpentine for toxicity.

TERPINYL ISOBUTRYATE • A synthetic fruit flavoring agent. Derived by heating terpineol with isobutryic acid (see both). Used as a synthetic fruit flavoring agent for beverages, ice cream, ices, candy, and baked goods. See Turpentine for toxicity.

TERPINYL ISOVALERATE • A synthetic fruit flavoring agent. Derived by heating terpineol with isovaleric acid (see both). Used as a synthetic fruit flavoring agent for beverages, ice cream, ices, candy, and baked goods. See Turpentine for toxicity.

TERPINYL PROPIONATE • A synthetic fruit flavoring agent, colorless with a lavender odor. Derived by heating terpineol with propionic acid see both. Used as a synthetic fruit flavoring agent for beverages, ice cream, ices, candy, and baked goods. See Turpentine for toxicity.

TERA JAPONICA • See Catechu Extract.

TERTIARY BUTYLHYDROQUINONE • TBHQ. This antioxidant was put on the market after years of pushing by food manufacturers to get it approved. It contains the petroleum-derived butane and is used either alone or in combination with the preservative-antioxidant butylated hydroxyanisole (BHA) and/or butylated hydroxytoluene (BHT) (*see* both). Hydroquinone combines with oxygen very rapidly and becomes brown when exposed to air. The FDA said that TBHQ must not exceed 0.02 percent of its oil and fat content. Death has occurred from the ingestion of as little as 5 grams. Ingestion of a single gram (a thirtieth of an ounce) has caused nausea, vomiting, ringing in the ears, delirium, a sense of suffocation, and collapse. Industrial workers exposed to the vapors—without obvious systemic effects—suffered clouding of the eye lens. Application to the skin may cause allergic reactions.

TETRADECANAL • *See* Myristaldehyde.

TETRADECANOIC ACID • *See* Ethyl Myristate.

TETRADECYL ALDEHYDE • *See* Myristaldehyde.

TETRAHYDROFURFURYL ACETATE • *See* Furfural.

TETRAHYDROFURFURYL ALCOHOL • A liquid that absorbs water and is flammable in air. A solvent for cosmetic fats, waxes, and resins. Mixes with water, ether, and acetone. Mildly irritating to the skin and mucous membranes. *See* Furfural.

TETRAHYDROFURFURYL BUTYRATE • Burtyric acid. A synthetic chocolate, honey, and maple flavoring agent for beverages, ice cream, ices, candy, and baked goods. May be irritating to the skin and mucous membranes.

TETRAHYDROFURFURYL PROPIONATE • Propionic Acid. A synthetic chocolate, honey, and maple flavoring agent for beverages, ice cream, ices, candy, and baked goods. Also used as a solvent for intra venous drugs. Moderately irritating to skin and mucous membranes.

TETRAHYDROGERANYL HYDROXYL STEARATE • *See* Stearic Acid and Hydroxylation.

TETRAHYDROXYPROPYL ETHYLENEDIAMINE • Clear, colorless, thick liquid, a component of the bacteria-killing substance in sugar cane. It is strongly alkaline and is used as a solvent and preservative. It may be irritating to the skin and mucous membranes and may cause skin sensitization.

TETRAKIS(HYDROXYMETHYL)PHOSPHONIUMCHLORIDE • Catalyst, humectant, emulsifier, and plasticizer. No known toxicity.

TETRAMETHYL DECYNEDIOL • *See* Fatty Alcohols.

TETRAMETHYLTHIURAM • Sprayed on some bananas. Seed disinfectant; fungicide; bacteriostat in soap. Can cause contact dermatitis. Irritating to mucous membranes.

TETRAPOTASSIUM PHOSPHATE • TKPP. An emulsifier. *See* Tetrasodium Pryrophosphate.

TETRAPOTASSIUM PYROPHOSPHATE • An emulsifier. *See* Tetrasodium Pryrophosphate.

TETRASODIUM EDTA • Sodium Edetate. Powdered sodium salt that reacts with metals. A sequestering agent and chelating agent (*see* both) used in cosmetic solutions. Can deplete the body of calcium if taken internally. *See* Ethylenediamine Tetraacetic Acid. No known toxicity on the skin.

TETRASODIUM PYROPHOSPHATE • TSPP. Used in cheese emulsification, and as a sequestering agent in cheese and ice cream. Also used in cleansing compounds, oil-well drilling, water treatment, and as a general sequestering agent to remove rust stains. A sequestering agent, clarifying agent, and buffering agent for shampoos. Produced by molecular dehydration of dibasic sodium phosphate. Insoluble in alcohol. A water softener in bath preparations. It is alkaline and irritating and ingestion can cause nausea, diarrhea, and vomiting. GRAS for packaging.

TEXTURIZER • A chemical used to improve the texture of various foods. For instance, canned tomatoes, canned potatoes, and canned apple slices tend to become soft and fall apart, unless the texturizer calcium chloride (*see*), for example, or its salts are added which keep the product firm.

TFC • Triclof/ucarban. A disinfectant used in cosmetics. No known toxicity.

THALOSE™ • A blend of food-grade acidulants *see* that contains propylene glycol, the acids—citric, lactic, phosphoric, and tartaric (*see* all)—and water and salt. Adding this compound to sugar permits a reduction in the amount of sugar required to achieve a desired sweetness (1 ounce of liquid Thalose added to 32 pounds of sugar causes the perceived sweetness to be increased by 90 percent). One pint added to sugar will result in a saving of 500 pounds of sugar without reducing sweetness. Thalose itself is not sweet and does not alter the flavor or aroma of the foods to which it is added. It does not contribute calories but will reduce the caloric level of the end product by lowering the amount of carbohydrates in the compound. Thalose can be used in beverages, bakery and confectionery products, and in ice cream, as long as the physical properties of the sugar are not needed (sugar is often used as a thickening agent and texturizer). All of the substances contained in this extender are GRAS and comply with the FDA provision for food-grade ingredients.

THAMNIDIUM ELEGANS • A grayish-white mold used for aging meat. It is related to the tropical bread mold. No known toxicity.

THBP • *See* 2,4,5-Trihydroxybutylzophenone. Anitoxidant in fats and oils.

THEINE • *See* Caffeine.

THEOBROMA OIL • Cacao Butter. Cocoa Butter. Yellowish-white solid with chocolatelike taste and odor. Derived from the cacao bean. Widely used in confections, suppositories, and pharmaceuticals, and in soaps and cosmetics. No known toxicity but may cause allergic reactions in the sensitive.

THIAMINE HYDROCHLORIDE • Vitamin B_1. A white crystalline powder used as a dietary supplement in prepared breakfast cereals, peanut butter, poultry, stuffing, baby cereals, skimmed milk, bottled soft drinks, enriched flours, enriched farina, corn meal, enriched macaroni and noodle products, and enriched bread and rolls. Acts as a helper in important energy-yielding reactions in the body. Practically all B_1 sold is synthetic. The vitamin is destroyed by alkalies and alkaline drugs such as phenobarbital. No known toxicity. GRAS.

THIAMINE NITRATE • A B vitamin. A white crystalline powder used as a diet supplement and to enrich flour. No known toxicity. GRAS

THIBETOLIDE® • *See* Pentadecalactone.

THICKENERS • Many natural gums and starches are used to add body to mixtures. Pectin *see*, for instance, which is used in fruits naturally low in this gelling agent, enables manufacturers to produce jams and jellies of a marketable thickness. Algin (*see* Alginates) is used to make salad dressings that will not be runny. Also used to add body to lotions and creams. Those usually employed include such natural gums as sodium alginate and pectins.

2-THIENYL MERCAPTAN • A synthetic flavoring agent that occurs naturally in coffee. Used in coffee flavoring for candy and baked goods. No known toxicity.

THIETHYL CITRATE • An antioxidant used primarily in dried egg whites. *See* Citric Acid. GRAS.

THIODIPROPIONIC ACID • An acid freely soluble in hot water, alcohol, and acetone. Used as an antioxidant in general food use. Percent of fat or oil, including essential oil content of food, is up to 0.02. Used also for soap products and polymers (*see*) of ethylene. The final report to the FDA of the Select Committee on GRAS Substances stated in 1980 that there is no evidence in the available information that it is a hazard to the public when used as it is now and it should continue its GRAS status with limitations on the amounts that can be added to food.

THIOLLYL ETHER • *See* Allyl Sulfide.

THISTLE, BLESSED • Holy Thistle. Extract of the prickly plant.

Cleared for use as a natural flavoring in alcoholic beverages. No known toxicity.

THREONINE • L form. An essential amino acid (*see*); the last to be discovered (1935). Prevents the buildup of fat on the liver. Occurs in whole eggs, skim milk, casein, and gelatin. On the FDA list for further study. GRAS.

THUJA OIL • *See* White Cedar Leaf Oil.

THYME OIL • It is a seasoning from the dried leaves and flowering tops of the wild creeping thyme grown in Eurasia and throughout the United States. Colorless, yellow, or red, with a pleasant odor. Used in sausage, spice, and thyme flavorings for beverages, ice cream, ices, candy, baked goods, chewing gum, condiments, meats, and soups. Used to flavor toothpaste, mouthwashes, and to scent perfumes, after-shave lotions, and soap. Used as a flavoring in cough medicines. May cause contact dermatitis and hayfever. Gras.

THYME, WHITE OIL • Obtained from the plant and used in fruit, liquor, and thyme. Used in fruit, peppermint, and spice flavorings for beverages, ice cream, ices, candy, baked goods, and chewing gum. Oral dose as medicine is 0.067 grams. It can cause vomiting, diarrhea, dizziness, and cardiac depression when taken in sufficient amounts. GRAS.

THYMOL • Obtained from the essential oil of lavender, origanum oil, and other volatile oils. It destroys mold, preserves anatomical specimens, and is a topical antifungal agent with a pleasant aromatic odor. Used in fruit, peppermint, and spice flavorings, for beverages, ice cream, ices, candy, baked goods, and chewing gum. Used in mouth washes, and to scent perfumes, after-shave lotions, and soap. It is omitted from hypoallergenic cosmetics because it can cause allergic reactions. Oral dose as medicine is 0.067 grams. It can cause vomiting, diarrhea, dizziness, and cardiac depression when taken in sufficient amounts.

THYMUS CAPITATUS • Flavoring.

TIGLIC ACID • *See* Allyl Tiglate.

TIPA • The abbreviation for Triisopropanolamine.

TIPA-STEARATE • *See* Stearic Acid.

TITANIUM DIOXIDE • Occurs naturally in minerals. Used chiefly as a white pigment and as an opacifier; also a white pigment for candy, gum, and marking ink. The amount of dioxide may not exceed 1 percent by weight of food. A pound has been ingested without apparent ill effects. The greatest covering and tinting power of any white pigment used in bath powders, nail whites, depilatories, eye liners, white eye shadows, antiperspirants, face powders, protective creams, liquid powders, lipsticks, hand lotions, and nail polish. In high concentrations the dust may cause lung damage. It has been permanently listed for use as a food color with a limit of 1 percent by weight of finished food since 1966.

TITANIUM HYDROXIDE • *See* Titanium Dioxide.

TOCOPHEROLS • Vitamin E. Obtained by the vacuum distillation of edible vegetable oils. Protects fat in the body's tissues from abnormal breakdown. Experimental evidence shows Vitamin E may protect the heart and blood vessels and retard aging. Used as a dietary supplement and as an antioxidant for essential oils, rendered animal fats, or a combination of such fats with vegetable oils. Helps form normal red blood cells, muscle, and other tissues. The final report to the FDA of the Select Committee on GRAS Substances stated in 1980 that it should continue its GRAS status with no limitations other than good manufacturing practices.

TOCOPHERYL SUCCINATE • Vitamin E Succinate. Obtained by the distillation of edible vegetable oils and used as a dietary supplement and as an antioxidant for fats and oils. No known toxicity.

TOLERANCE • The ability to live with an allergen.

TOLU BALSAM • Extract and Gum. Extract from the Peruvian or Indian plant. Contains cinnamic acid and benzoic acid (*see* both). Used in butter, butterscotch, cherry, and spice flavorings for beverages, ice cream, ices, candy, baked goods, and chewing gum. The gum is used in fruit, maple, and vanilla flavorings for beverages, ice cream, ices, candy, baked goods, and syrups. Mildly antiseptic and may be mildly irritating to the skin.

a-**TOLUALDEHYDE** • *See* Phenylacetaldehyde.

TOLUALDEHYDE GLYCERYL ACETAL • A synthetic chocolate, fruit, cherry, coconut, and vanilla flavoring agent for beverages. Ice cream, ices, candy, and baked goods. No known toxicity.

TOLUALDEHYDES (MIXED *o, m, p*) • Synthetic berry, loganberry, fruit, cherry, muscatel, peach, apricot, nut, almond, and vanilla flavorings for beverages, ice cream, ices, candy, baked goods, chewing gum, gelatin desserts, and maraschino cherries. No known toxicity.

TOLYL ACETATE • Acetic Acid. A synthetic butter, caramel, fruit, honey, nut and spice flavoring for beverages, ice cream, ices, candy, baked goods, chewing gum, and gelatin desserts. No known toxicity.

o-**TOLYL ACETATE** • Acetic Acid. A synthetic butter, caramel, fruit, honey, and cherry flavoring for beverages, ice cream, ices, candy, baked goods, chewing gum, and gelatin desserts. No known toxicity.

p-**TOLYL ACETATE** • Acetic Acid. A synthetic butter, caramel, fruit, honey, nut, and spice flavoring for beverages, ice cream, ices, candy, baked goods, chewing gum, and condiments. No known toxicity.

4-(p-TOLYL)-2-BUTANONE • A synthetic fruit flavoring for beverages, ice cream, ices, candy, and baked goods. No known toxicity.

a-TOLYL ISOBUTYRATE • A synthetic fruit flavoring for beverages, ice cream, ices, candy, and baked goods. No known toxicity.

p-TOLYL LAURATE • Dodecanoic Acid. A synthetic butter, caramel, fruit, honey, and nut flavoring for beverages, ice cream, ices, candy, and baked goods. No known toxicity.

p-TOLYL PHENYLACETATE • A synthetic butter, caramel, fruit, honey, and nut flavoring for beverages, ice cream, ices, candy, and baked goods. No known toxicity.

2-(p-TOYL) PROPIONALDEHYDE • A synthetic caraway flavoring agent for beverages, ice cream, ices, candy, baked goods, and liqueurs. No known toxicity.

TOLYLACETALDEHYDE • A synthetic berry, loganberry, fruit, cherry, muscatel, peach, apricot, nut, almond, and vanilla flavoring agent for beverages, ice cream, ices, candy, baked goods, gelatin desserts, chewing gum, and maraschino cherries. No known toxicity.

TOLYLACETALDEHYDE • A synthetic honey and nut flavoring for beverages, ice cream, ices, candy, and baked goods. No known toxicity.

TOMATO EXTRACT • Tomatine. Extract from the fruit of the tomato, *Solanum esculentum*. Used as a fungicide and as a precipitating agent. Nontoxic.

TONKA • Tonka Bean. Coumarouna Bean. Black-brownish seeds with a wrinkled surface and brittle shining or fatty skins. A vanillalike odor and a bitter taste. Used in the production of natural courmarin (*see*), flavoring extracts, and toilet powders. Banned in foods.

TORMENTIL EXTRACT • The extract of the roots of *Potentilla erecta*.

TORTUA YEAST • Dried *candida utils*. Flavoring in food. *See* Yeast.

TRAGACANTH • *See* Gum Tragacanth. GRAS.

TRIACETIN • Glyceryl Triacetate. Primarily a solvent for hair dyes. Also a fixative in perfume and used in toothpaste. A colorless, somewhat oily liquid with a slight fatty odor and a bitter taste. Obtained from adding acetate to glycerin (*see* both). Soluble in water and miscible with alcohol. No known toxicity in above use. Large subcutaneous injections are lethal to rats. GRAS

TRIBASIC CALCIUM PHOSPHATE • Tricalcium Diorthophosphate. Tricalcium Phosphate. An anticaking agent, calcium supplement in grain products used in packaged cake mixes, candy, baked goods, gelatin desserts, powdered beverage mixes, seasoning mixes and powdered soups, and sugar. Too much phosphorous in the form of phosphates from processed foods could upset the body's mineral balance, particularly calcium, and could adversely affect teeth, bones, and kidneys.

TRIBUTYL ACETYLCITRATE • A synthetic fruit flavoring agent for beverages. No known toxicity.

TRIBUTYL CITRATE • The triester of butyl alcohol and citric acid (*see* both), it is a pale-yellow, odorless liquid used as a plasticizer, antifoam agent, and solvent for nitrocellulose. Low toxicity.

TRIBUTYLCRESYLBUTANE • Used as a stabilizer. *See* Phenol.

TRIBUTYRIN • Glyceryl Tributyrate. A colorless, somewhat oily liquid that occurs naturally in butter. It has a characteristic odor and bitter taste. It is a soluble in alcohol. Used as a flavoring agent in beverages, ice cream, candy, baked goods, margarine, and puddings. No known toxicity.

TRICALCIUM PHOSPHATE • The calcium salt of phosphate (*see*). An anticaking agent in table salt and vanilla powder, and a dietary supplement. Used as a bleaching agent in flour at not more than six parts per million by weight alone or in combination with potassium alum, calcium sulfate (*see*), and other compounds. Also used as a polishing agent in dentifrices. No known toxicity. *See* Calcium Phosphate. GRAS

TRICALCIUM SILICATE • Used in table salt and baking powder as an anticaking agent up to 2 percent. On the FDA list to be studied for subacute, mutagenic, teratogenic, and reproductive effects. No known toxicity. GRAS.

TRICETETH-5 PHOSPHATE • *See* Phosphoric Acid and Ceteth-5.

TRICHLOROETHYLENE (TCE) • Residue in decaffeinated coffee powder. Used in spice oleoresins as a solvent. Moderate exposure can cause symptoms similar to alcohol inebriation, and its analgesic and anesthetic properties make it useful for short operations. High concentrations have a narcotic effect. Deaths have been attributed to irregular heart rhythm. Tests conducted by the National Cancer Institute showed that this chlorinated hydrocarbon caused cancer of the liver in mice. Rats failed to show significant response, a fact which may be attributed to the cancer-resistance of the strain used. Despite the species difference in cancer response, the NCI concluded that the TCE test clearly showed the compound caused liver cancer in mice. The finds are considered definitive for animal studies and serve as a warning of possible carcinogenicity in humans. However, the extent of the possible human risk cannot be predicted reliably on the basis of these studies alone. A related compound, vinyl chloride (*see*), does cause liver cancer in humans.

2-TRIDECENAL • A synthetic citrus and flavoring for beverages, ice cream, ices, candy, baked goods, and chewing gum. No known toxicity.

TRIDECYL ALCOHOL • Derived from tridecane, a paraffin hydrocarbon obtained from petroleum. Used as an emulsifier in cosmetic creams, lotions, and lipsticks. No known toxicity.

TRIETHANOLAMINE • A coating agent for fresh fruit and vegetables and widely used in surfactants (*see*) and as a dispersing agent and detergent in hand and body lotions, shaving creams, soaps, shampoos, and bath powders. Its principal toxic effect in animals has been attributed to over alkalinity. Gross pathology has been found in the gastrointestinal tract in fatally poisoned guinea pigs. It is an irritant.

TRIETHANOLAMINE STEARATE • Made from ethylene oxide. Used in brilliantines, cleansing creams, foundation creams, hair lacquers, liquid makeups, fragrances, liquid powders, mascara, protective creams, baby preparations, shaving creams and lathers, and preshave lotions. A moisture absorber, viscous, used in making emulsions. Cream-colored, turns brown on exposure to air. May be irritating to the skin and mucous membranes, but less so than many other amine oxides (*see*).

TRIETHYL CITRATE • Citric Acid. Ethyl Citrate. A plasticizer in nail polish. Odorless, practically colorless, bitter; also used in dried egg as a sequestering agent (*see*), and to prevent rancidity. Citrates may interfere with laboratory tests for blood, liver, and pancreatic function, but no known skin toxicity. The final report to the FDA of the Select Committee on GRAS Substances stated in 1980 that it should continue its GRAS status with no limitations other than good manufacturing practices.

TRIETHYLENE GLYCOL • Used in stick perfume. Prepared from ethylene oxide and ethylene glycol (*see* both). Used as a solvent. *See* Polyethylene Glycol for toxicity.

2-4-5 TRIHYDROXYBUTYROPHENONE (THBP) • An antioxidant used alone or in combination with other antioxidants, total antioxidant not to exceed 0.02 percent of the oil or fat content of any product. Also used in the manufacture of food packaging materials, with a limit of 0.005 percent in food. On the FDA list for further study of this widely used additive.

TRIHYDROXY STEARIN • Isolated from cork and used as a thickener. No known toxicity.

TRIISOPROPANOLAMINE • A crystalline white solid. A mild base used as an emulsifying agent. A component of a coating used for fresh fruits and vegetables. No known toxicity.

TRIISOSTEARIN • *See* Glycerin and Isostearic Acid.

TRILAURIN • *See* Lauric Acid.

TRILAURYL CITRATE • *See* Lauryl Alcohol and Citric Acid.

2,6,6-TRIMETHYL-2-CYCLONEHEXANE-1-ONE • Nicomol. Crystals from dilute acetic acid. Odorless and tasteless. Breaks down fats. No known toxicity.

TRIPOLYPHOSHPATE • A phosphorus salt. A sequestering agent (*see*) in foods and a food additive. Used to soften water, as an emulsifier, and a dispersing agent. A buffering agent in shampoos. Can be irritating because of its alkalinity. May cause esophageal stricture if swallowed. Moderately irritating to the skin and mucous membranes. Ingestion can cause violent vomiting.

TRISODIUM EDTA • *See* Tetrasodium EDTA.

TRISODIUM HEDTA • Mineral suspending agents. *See* Sequestrants.

TRISODIUM HYDROXY EDTA • *See* Tetrasodium EDTA.

TRISODIUM HYDROXYETHYL ETHLENEDIAMINETRIACETATE • *See* Tetrasodium EDTA.

TRISODIUM NTA • *See* Sequestrants.

TRISODIUM PHOSPHATE • Obtained from phosphate rock. Highly alkaline. Used in shampoos, cuticle softeners, bubble baths, and bath salts for its water-softening and cleaning actions. Phosphorous was formerly used to treat rickets and degenerative disorders and is now used as a mineral supplement for foods; also in incendiary bombs and tracer bullets. Can cause skin irritation from alkalinity.

TRISTEARIN • Present in many animal and vegetable fats, especially hard ones like tallow and cocoa butter, it is used in surfactants, quaternary ammonium compounds, and emollients. No known toxicity.

TRISTEARYL CITRATE • The triester of stearyl alcohol and citric acid (*see* both).

TRITICALE • A manmade cross between wheat (*see* Dog Grass, Triticum) and rye (secale), but more nutritious than wheat. The protein content of bread made with it is 10 percent higher and its essential amino acid, lysine (*see*), exceeds wheat bread by 50 percent. The crop is the result of seven years' development and is being offered both as an ingredient and as a basic food substance. A number of novel products are being made from it, including ethnic breads. Two slices of Tritibread (made with triticale) supply 12 percent of the U.S. Recommended Daily Allowance for protein, 30 percent for thiamine, and 10 percent for riboflavin, niacin, and iron. Tritibread is intended for baked goods, ready-to-eat cereals, and malt products; also as a thickener, emulsifier, fortifier, and supplement. Once accepted, triticale can be an important nutritious addition to the food supply.

TRITICUM • *See* Dog Grass. GRAS.

TROMETHAMINE • Made by the reduction (*see*) of nitro compounds, it is a crystalline mass used in the manufacture of surface-active agents (*see*). Used as an emulsifying agent for cosmetic creams and lotions, mineral oil, and paraffin wax emulsions. Used medicinally to correct an overabundance of acid in the body. No known toxicity.

TRUE FIXATIVE • This holds back the evaporation of the other materials. Benzoin is an example. *See* fixatives.

TRYPTOPHAN • A tremendous amount of research is now in progress with this amino acid (*see*). First isolated in milk in 1901, it is now being studied as a means to calm hyperactive children, induce sleep, and fight depression and pain. Although it is sold over the counter, it is not believed to be completely harmless and has been suspected of being a cocarcinogen and to affect the liver when taken in high doses. Like niacin, it is capable of preventing and curing pellagra. It is a partial precursor of the brain hormone serotonin and is indispensable for the manufacture of certain cell proteins. In cosmetics, it is used to increase the protein content of creams and lotions. The FDA called for further study of this additive. GRAS.

TUBEROSE EXTRACT • Derived from a Mexican bulbous herb commonly cultivated for its spike of fragrant white single or double flowers that resemble small lilies. Used in peach flavorings for beverages, ice cream, ices, candy, and baked goods. Tuberose is used in perfumes. Can cause allergic reactions. GRAS.

TUNU EXTRACT • Tuno. From a Central American tree closely related to the rubber tree. Cleared for use as a natural masticatory substance of vegetable origin in chewing gum base. No known toxicity.

TUMIRIC • *See* Turmeric

TURMERIC • Derived from an East Indian herb. An aromatic pepperlike but somewhat bitter taste. The cleaned, boiled, sun-dried, pulverized root is used in coconut, ginger ale, and curry flavorings for puddings, condiments, meats, soups, and pickles; also for yellow coloring used to color sausage casings, oleomargarine, shortening, and marking ink. The *extract* is used in fruit, meat, and cheese flavorings for beverages, condiments, meats, soup bases, and pickles. The *oleoresin* (*see*) is obtained by extraction with one or more of the solvents acetone, ethyl alcohol, ethylene dichloride (*see* all), and others. It is used in spice flavorings for condiments, meats, pickles, and brine. Both turmeric and its oleoresin have been permanently listed for coloring food since 1966. No known toxicity. GRAS.

TURPENTINE • Gum and Steam Distilled. Any of the various resins obtained from coniferous trees. A yellowish, viscous exudate with a characteristic smell, both forms are used in spice flavorings for baked goods. Steam-distilled turpentine is used also in candy. Also used as a solvent in hair lotions, waxes, perfume soaps, and to soothe skin. It is the oleoresin from a species of pines. Readily absorbed through the skin. Irritating to the skin and mucous membranes. In addition to be a local skin irritant, it can cause allergic reactions. In addition, it is a central nervous system depressant. Death is usually due to respiratory failure. As little as 15 milliliters has killed children.

TYROSINE • L form.   Widely distributed amino acid (*see*), termed nonessential because it does not seem to be necessary for growth. It is used as a dietary supplement. It is a building block of protein and is used in cosmetics to help creams penetrate the skin. The FDA has asked for further study of this additive. GRAS.

U

2,3-UNDECADIONE • A synthetic butter flavoring agent for beverages, ice cream, ices, candy, and baked goods. No known toxicity.

γ-UNDECALACTONE • Peach Aldehyde.   Colorless to light yellow liquid with a peachy odor. Derived from undecylenic acid with sulfuric acid. A synthetic fruit flavoring, colorless or yellow, with a strong peach odor. Used for beverages, ice cream, ices, candy, baked goods, gelatin desserts, and chewing gum. Used also in perfumery. No known toxicity.

UNDECANAL • A synthetic flavoring agent. Colorless to slightly yellow, with a sweet, fatty odor. Used in lemon, orange, rose, fruit, and honey flavorings for beverages, ice cream, ices, candy, baked goods, and chewing gum. No known toxicity.

9-UNDECANAL • A synthetic citrus and fruit flavoring for beverages, ice cream, ices, candy, baked goods, and chewing gum. No known toxicity.

10-UNDECANAL • A synthetic citrus, floral, and fruit flavoring agent for beverages, ice cream, ices, and candy. No known toxicity.

2-UNDECANONE • A synthetic flavoring agent that occurs naturally in rue and hops oil. Used in citrus, coconut, peach, and cheese flavorings for beverages, ice cream, ices, candy, baked goods, and puddings. No known toxicity.

1-UNDECANOL • Colorless liquid with a citrus odor used in perfumery and as a flavoring. *See* Undecylenic Acid.

2-UNDECANOL • Antifoaming agent, perfume fixative, and plasticizer. *See* Undecylenic Acid.

10-UNDECEN-1-YL ACETATE • A synthetic citrus and fruit flavoring agent for beverages, ice cream, ices, candy, and baked goods. No known toxicity.

UNDECYL ALCOHOL • A synthetic lemon, lime, orange, and rose flavoring agent for beverages, ice cream, ices, candy, and baked goods. No known toxicity.

UNDECYLENIC ACID • Occurs in sweat. Obtained from ricinoleic acid, an unsaturated fatty acid (*see*). A liquid or crystalline powder, with an odor suggestive of perspiration or citrus. Used as a fungicide, in perfumes, as a flavoring, and as a lubricant additive in cosmetics. Has been given orally but it causes dizziness, headaches, and stomach upset. No known toxicity for the skin.

UNDECYLENYL ALCOHOL • Colorless liquid with a citrus odor. Used in perfumes. It is combustible but has a low toxicity.

UNDECYLIC ACID • *See* Undecylenic Acid.

UNDECYLPENTADECANOL • *See* Fatty Alcohols.

UNSAPONIFIABLE OLIVE OIL • The oil fraction that is not broken down in the refining of olive fatty acids.

UNSAPONIFIABLE RAPESEED OIL • The oil that is not broken down in the refining of rapeseed oil fatty acids.

UNSAPONFIABLE SHEA BUTTER • The fraction of shea butter that is not broken down during processing.

UNSAPONIFABLE SOYBEAN OIL • The fraction of soybean oil that is not broken down in the refining recovery of soybean oil fatty acids.

UREA • Carbamide.   A product of protein metabolism and excreted from human urine. Used in yeast food and wine production up to 2 pounds per gallon. It is used to "brown" baked goods such as pretzels, and consists of colorless or white, odorless crystals that have a cool salty taste. An antiseptic and deodorizer used in liquid antiperspirants, ammoniated dentifrices, roll-on deodorants, mouthwashes, hair colorings, hand creams, lotions, and shampoos. Medicinally, urea is used as a topical antiseptic and as a diuretic to reduce body water. Its largest use, however, is a fertilizer, and only a small part of its production goes into the manufacture of other urea products. No known toxicity. The final report to the FDA of the Select Committee on GRAS Substances stated in 1980 that it should continue its GRAS status with no limitations other than good manufacturing practices.

UREASE • An enzyme that hydrolyzes urea (*see*) to ammonium carbonate (*see*).

UROCANIC ACID • Prepared from L-histidine (*see*).

UNSATURATED FATS • Fats are composed of carbon, hydrogen, and oxygen. They can be liquid or solid, depending on the type of fatty acids. Food fats are made up of three types of fatty acids that influence cholesterol levels in blood: saturated, monounsaturated, and polyunsaturated. Highly saturated fats are usually animal fats. With the exception of a few vegetable fats, such as palm and coconut oils, they are hard at room temperature and have the maximum number of hydrogen atoms attached to their carbon atoms. Saturated fats tend to raise blood cholesterol levels. Unsaturated fats, found mostly in plant foods, are short two or more hydrogen atoms, so they are usually liquid at room temperature. Unsaturated fats are further divided into two types: monounsaturated (two hydrogen atoms short of saturation) and polyunsaturated (four or more hydrogen atoms short of saturation). Monounsaturated fats, such as olive oil, and polyunsaturated fats, such as corn and soybean oils, tend to reduce the level of cholesterol in the blood.

USNIC ACID • Antibacterial compound found in lichens. Pale yellow, slightly soluble in water. No known toxicity.

V

VALERAL • *See* Valeraldehyde.

VALERALDEHYDE • Pentanal. A synthetic flavoring agent which occurs naturally in coffee extract. Used in fruit and nut flavorings for beverages, ice cream, ices, candy, and baked goods. Has narcotic properties and is a mild irritant.

VALERIAN • *See* Valeric Acid.

VALERIC ACID • Occurs naturally in apples, cocoa, coffee, oil of lavender, peaches, and strawberries. A synthetic flavoring agent used in butter, butterscotch, fruit, rum, and cheese flavorings for beverages, ice cream, ices, candy, and baked goods. Colorless, with an unpleasant odor. Usually distilled from valerian root. Used in the manufacture of perfumes. Some of its salts are used in medicine. No known toxicity.

VALERIC ALDEHYDE • *See* Valeraldehyde.

VALEROLACTONE • A synthetic vanilla flavoring agent for beverages, ice cream, ices, candy, and baked goods. No known toxicity.

VALINE • L form. An essential amino acid (*see*). Occurs in the largest quantities in fibrous protein. It is indispensable for growth and nitrogen balance. Used in suntan lotions. No known toxicity in cosmetics but the FDA asked for further study of this ingredient as a food additive in 1980. Nothing new has been reported. GRAS.

VANADIUM TETRACHLORIDE • Derived from chlorination of fer-rovanadium. Catalyst. Toxic by ingestion, inhalation, and skin absorption.

VANAY® • *See* Triacetin.

VANILLA EXTRACT • Extracted from the full-grown unripe fruit of the vanilla plant of Mexico and the West Indies. Contains not less than 35 percent aqueous ethyl alcohol (*see*) and one or more of the following ingredients: glycerin, propylene glycol, sugar (including invert sugar), and corn syrup. Used in many food and beverages as flavorings. No known toxicity. GRAS.

VANILLAL • *See* Ethyl Vanillin.

VANILLIN • Occurs naturally in vanilla extract (*see*) and potato parings but is an artificial flavoring. Odor and taste of vanilla. Make synthetically from eugenol (*see*); also from the waste of the wood pulp industry. One part vanillin equals 400 parts vanilla pods. Used in butter, chocolate, fruit, root beer, and vanilla flavorings for beverages, ice cream, ices, candy, baked goods, gelatin desserts, puddings, syrups (30,000 ppm), toppings, margarine, chocolate products, and liqueurs. The lethal dose in mice is 3 grams (30 grams to the ounce) per kilogram of body weight. A skin irritant that produces a burning sensation and eczema. May also cause pigmentation of the skin. GRAS.

VANILLIN ACETATE • Vanillin. A synthetic spice and vanilla flavoring agent for beverages, ice cream, ices, candy, and baked goods. No known toxicity.

VERATRALDEHYDE • A synthetic fruit, nut, and vanilla flavoring agent for beverages, ice cream, ices, candy, baked goods, and puddings. Derived from vanillin. May have narcotic and irritant effects but no specific data.

VEGETABLE GUMS • Includes derivatives from quince seed, karaya, acacia, tragacanth, Irish moss, guar, sodium alginate, potassium alginate, ammonium alginate, and propylene glycol alginate. All are subject to deterioration and always need a preservative. The gums function as liquid emulsions, that is, they thicken cosmetic products and make them cream. No known toxicity other than allergic reactions in hypersensitive persons.

VEGETABLE JUICE • Used in food colorings consistent with good manufacturing practices. Permanently listed for coloring since 1966.

VEGETABLE OILS • Peanut, sesame, olive, and cottonseed oil obtained from plants and used in baby preparations, cleansing creams, emollient creams, face powders, hair-grooming aids, hypoallergenic cosmetics, lipsticks, nail creams, shampoos, shaving creams, and wave sets. No known toxicity.

VEGETABLE OILS, BROMINATED • Flavoring in fruit and beverages where not prohibited by standards (standard recipes). *See* Bromates and Vegetables Oils.

VERONICA • Extract of Veronica, a small herb of wide distribution that has pink or white flowers. Flavoring in alcoholic beverages only. No known toxicity.

VERVAIN, EUROPEAN • Verbena. A class of medicinal plants used as a flavoring in alcoholic beverages only. No known toxicity.

VETIVER OIL • Vetiverol. Khus-Khus. Stable brown to reddish brown oil from the roots of a fragrant grass. It has an aromatic to harsh woodsy odor. Used as a flavoring in foods and as a scent in soaps and perfumes. No known toxicity.

VIBURNUM EXTRACT • Haw Bark. Black Extract. Extract of the fruit of a hawthorn shrub or tree. Used in fragrances and in butter, caramel, cola, maple, and walnut flavorings for beverages. Has been used as a uterine antispasmodic. No known toxicity.

VIBURNUM PRUNIFOLIUM • *See* Viburnum Extract.

VINEGAR • Used for hundreds of years to remove lime soap after shampooing. It is a solvent for cosmetic oils and resins. Vinegar is about 4 to 6 percent acetic acid. Acetic acid occurs naturally in apples, cheese, grapes, milk, and other foods. No known toxicity but may cause an allergic reaction in those allergic to corn.

VINEGAR NAPHTHA • *See* Ethyl Acetate.

VINYL ACETATE • A starch modifier not to exceed 2.5 percent in modified starch (*see*). Vapors in high concentration may be narcotic; animal experiments show low toxicity.

VINYL CHLORIDE • Chlorethylene. Prepared from ethylene dichloride and alcoholic potassium, it is a colorless gas that becomes liquid upon freezing. It is one of the most frequently used vinyl compounds and is a very hazardous chemical by all avenues of exposure. It may be narcotic in high concentrations. If spilled on the skin, rapid evaporation causes local frostbite. It is a known cancer-causing agent, and, because of that, it has been banned from aerosol sprays. It is used for many polyvinyl compounds in paper coating, adhesives, and refrigerants. It is permitted by the FDA for use in adhesives and in food contact coatings.

VIOLA ODORATA • See Violet Extract.

VIOLAXANTHIN • Natural orange-red coloring isolated from yellow pansies and Valencia orange peel. Soluble in alcohol. *See* Xanthophyll. No known toxicity.

VIOLET EXTRACT • Flowers and Leaves. Green liquid with typical odor of violet. It is taken from the plant widely grown in the United States. Used in berry, violet, and fruit flavorings for beverages, ice cream, ices, candy, and baked goods. Also in face powders, and for coloring inorganic pigments. May produce skin rash in the allergic. No known toxicity. GRAS.

VIOLET LEAVES, ABSOLUTE • Essential Oil. *See* Violet Extract. GRAS.

VIRIDINE • *See* Phenylacetaldehyde Dimethyl Acetal.

VITAMIN A • Acetate and Palmitate. A yellow viscous liquid insoluble in water. An anti-infective, antixerophthalmic vitamin, essential to growth and development. Deficiency leads to retarded growth in the young, diminished visual acuity, night blindness, and skin problems. Insoluble in water. Toxic when children or adults receive more than 100,000 units daily over several months. Recommended daily dietary allowance is 1,500 units for infants, 4,500 units for adults, and 2,000–3,500 units for children. It is used to fortify Mellorine (vegetable-fat imitation ice cream), skim milk, dietary infant formula, blue cheese, Gorgonzola cheese, milk, and oleomargarine (1 pound of margarine contains 15,000 units USP of Vitamin A). Vitamin A is also used in lubricating creams and oils for its alleged skin-healing properties. Can be absorbed through the skin. The final report to the FDA of the Select Committee on GRAS Substances stated in 1980 that it should continue its GRAS status with no limitations other than good manufacturing practices. *See* also Retinoids and Retin-A.

VITAMIN B$_{12}$ • *See* Cyanocobalamin.

VITAMIN C • *See* Ascorbic Acid.

VITAMIN D$_2$ • Calciferol. A pale yellow oily liquid, odorless, tasteless, insoluble in water. Nutritional factor added to prepared breakfast cereals, mellorine (vegetable-fat imitation ice cream), Vitamin D milk, evaporated and skim milks, margarine, infant dietary formulas, enriched flour, self-rising flour, enriched corn meal and grits, enriched macaroni and noodle products (250–1,000 units USP), enriched farina and enriched bread, rolls, etc. Vitamin D speeds the body's production of calcium and has been found to cause calcium deposits and facial deformities and subnormal IQs in children of mothers given too much Vitamin D. Nutritionists recommend 400 units per day for pregnant women. Some women taking vitamin pills and vitamin-enriched milk and foods consume as much as 2,000 to 3,000 units daily. Used for its alleged skin-healing properties in lubricating creams and lotions. The absence of Vitamin D in the food of young animals can lead to rickets, a bone affecting condition. It is soluble in fats and fat solvents and is present in animal fats. Absorbed through the skin, its value in cosmetics has not been proven. No known toxicity to the skin. The final report to the FDA of the Select Committee on GRAS Substances stated in 1980 that there is no evidence in the available information that it is a hazard to the public when used as it is now and it should continue its GRAS status with limitations on amounts that can be added to food.

VITAMIN D$_3$ • Activated 7-Dehydrocholesterol. Approximately as effective as Vitamin D$_2$ (*see*). The final report to the FDA of the Select Committee on GRAS Substances stated in 1980 that there is no evidence in the available information that it is a hazard to the public when used as it is now and it should continue its GRAS status with limitations on the amounts that can be added to food.

VITAMIN E • *See* Tocopherols.

VITAMIN E ACETATE • *See* Tocopherols.

VITAMIN E SUCCINATE • *See* Tocopherols.

VITAMIN G • *See* Riboflavin.

VITAMIN H • *See* Biotin.

VIVERRA CIVETTA SCHREBER • *See* Civet, Absolute.

VIVERRA ZIBETHASCHREBER • *See* Civet, Absolute.

W

WALNUT EXTRACT • An extract of the husk of the nut of *Juglans spp.,* the Enlgish walnut tree. Used in walnut flavorings for beverages, ice cream, ices, candy, and baked goods. Also used for brown coloring. No known toxicity.

WALNUT OIL • *See* Walnut Extract.

WALNUT SHELL POWDER • The ground shell of English Walnuts, *Juglans regia. See* Walnut Extract.

WATERCRESS EXTRACT • Extract obtained from *Nasturtium officinalis.*

WAXES • Obtained from insects, animals, petroleum, and plants. Waxes made in the United States are vegetable, petroleum or bug based. One of the most common vegetable waxes, carnauba (*see*), is made from a palm leaf. Waxes from petroleum are the same as those used as chewing gum bases. The ''shellac'' used on some products is made from the secretion of the lac bug, native to Pakistan and India. More than 20 varieties of fruits and vegetables, including cantaloupes, eggplants, oranges, peaches, persimmons, squash, cucumbers, sweet potatoes, and tomatoes are being waxed. Waxing reduces the loss of moisture and keeps produce from dehydration. Some waxes are cosmetic. For example, oranges are waxed because consumers prefer a shiny surface rather than the natural dull matte of the rind. A wide application in the manufacture of cosmetics. Beeswax, for instance, is a substance secreted by the bee's special glands on the underside of its abdomen. The wax is glossy and hard but plastic when warm. Insoluble in water but partially soluble in boiling alcohol. Used in candy and vegetable coatings as well as by packaging. Waxes are generally nontoxic but may cause allergic reactions in the hypersensitive depending upon the source of the wax. It is also difficult to know which items have been waxed. Some foreign imports may use beef tallow, for example, which is undesirable in vegetarian or kosher diets. In many cases, pesticides and fungicides are added to waxes to help prevent decay. The FDA does have regulations requiring all waxed products at the supermarket to be labeled as such, either with a card listing the specific ingredients in the wax above the bin or on the bin or container itself. Have you seen such as listing? Some companies, according to Cornell University professor of food science Joseph Regenstein, Ph.D., switch waxes three times a day depending on environmental conditions.

WAX, PARAFFIN • Coating for certain cheeses. *See* Paraffins.

WAXY MAIZE • Corn starch. The soft, sticky material from the inside the corn kernel. The final report to the FDA of the Select Committee on GRAS Substances stated in 1980 that it should continue its GRAS status with no limitations other than good manufacturing practices.

WETTING AGENT. • Any of numerous water-soluble agents that promote spreading of a liquid on a surface or penetration into a material such as skin. It lowers surface tension for better contact and absorption. *See* Surfactants.

WHEAT • A cereal grain that yields a fine white powder. Wheat is avoided by some allergic people. Bread, cakes, crackers, cookies, pretzels, pastries, and noodles are made of wheat; also, breakfast foods such as Cream of Wheat, Pablum, Grapenuts, Wheaties, Puffed Wheat, Shredded Wheat, and bran; sauces, soups, gravies; Postum, Ovaltine, Malted milk; sausages, hamburger, and meat loaf. Nontoxic.

WHEAT BRAN • The broken coat of *Triticum aestivum*. About 14.5 percent of the kernel. In addition to indigestible cellulose, it contains 86 percent of the niacin; 73 percent of the pyridoxine; 50 percent of pantothenic acid; 42 percent of the riboflavin; 33 percent of thiamine; and 19 percent of protein. *See* Wheat Germ.

WHEAT BRAN LIPIDS • An extract of the coat of wheat. *See* Wheat Germ.

WHEAT FLOUR • Milled from the kernels of wheat, *Tricticum aestivum*. *See* Wheat Starch.

WHEAT GERM • The golden germ of the wheat is high in Vitamin E. About 2.5 percent of the whole wheat kernel. The germ contains about 64 percent of the thiamine; 26 percent of the riboflavin; and 21 percent of the pyridoxine. *See* Tocopherols.

WHEAT GERM EXTRACT • *See* Tocopherols.

WHEAT GERM GLYCERIDES • *See* Tocopherols.

WHEAT GERM OIL • *See* Tocopherols.

WHEAT GERMAMIDOPROPYLAMINE • *See* Tocopherols.

WHEAT GERMAMIDOPROPYL BETAINE • *See* Surfactants.

WHEAT GERMAMIDOPROPYL DIMETHYLAMINE LACTATE • *See* Tocopherols.

WHEAT GLUTEN • A mixture of proteins present in wheat flour and obtained as an extremely sticky yellowish gray mass by making a dough and then washing out the starch. It consists almost entirely of two proteins, gliadin and glutenin. It contributes to the porous and spongy structure of bread. Used in powders and creams as a base. No known toxicity.

WHEAT STARCH • A product of cereal grain. It swells when water is added. A minor part of starch production in the U.S. Used as a demulcent, emollient, and in dusting and face powders. May cause allergic reactions such as red eyes and stuffy nose. The final report to the FDA of the Select Committee on GRAS Substances stated in 1980 that it should continue its GRAS status with no limitations other than good manufacturing practices.

WHEY • The serum that remains after removal of fat and casein (*see*) from milk. Used to make cheese. GRAS. *See* Whey Protein.

WHEY PROTEIN • Milk Serum. Serum Lactis. The water part of milk remaining after the separation of casein (*see*). Cleared by the U.S. Department of Agriculture's Meat Inspection Department to bind and extend imitation sausage, and for use in soups and stews. It is used in emollients. No known toxicity. GRAS.

WHITE CEDAR LEAF OIL • Oil of Arborvitae. Stable, pale yellow volatile oil obtained by steam distillation from the fresh leaves and branch ends of the eastern *arborvitae*. Has a strong camphoraceous and sagelike scent. Used as a perfume and scent for soaps and room sprays. Also used as a flavoring agent. Soluble in most fixed oils. *See* Cedar for toxicity.

WHITE FLAG EXTRACT • *See* Orris.

WHITE LILY EXTRACT • Extract of the bulbs of *Lilium candidum*. Edible bulbs that were made into soup by the Indians, the lily is used in perfumery.

WHITE MINERAL OIL • Obtained from petroleum and used in baked goods. *See* Mineral Oil.

WHITE NETTLE EXTRACT • Obtained from the flowers of *Lamium album*. *See* Nettles.

WILD CHERRY • Wild Black Cherry Bark. The dried stem bark collected in autumn in North America. Used in cherry flavorings for food, lipsticks, and medicines. Also used as a sedative and expectorant medicinally. No known toxicity. GRAS.

WILD GINGER • Canadian Oil. *See* Snakeroot Oil.

WILD MARJORAM EXTRACT • Extract of the flowering ends of *Origanum vulgare*. Yellow or greenish-yellow liquid containing about

40 percent terpenes (see). Used in flavoring and perfumery. See Marjoram Oil.

WILD MINT EXTRACT • Extract of the leaves and tender twigs of *Mentha arvensis*. The Cheyenne Indians prepared a decoction of the ground leaves and stems of wild mint and drank the liquid to check nausea. Pulegone and thymol (see) are derived from an oil of wild mint. Its odor resembles peppermint. Used in flavoring. See Peppermint.

WILD THYME EXTRACT • The flowering tops of plant grown in Eurasia and throughout the United States. The dried leaves are used as a seasoning in foods and in emollients and fragrances. Has also been used as a muscle relaxant. No known toxicity. GRAS.

WILLOW LEAF EXTRACT • The extract of the leaves of the willow tree species, *Salix*. The willow has been used for pain-relieving and fever-lowering properties since ancient Greece. The American Indians used willow baths to cool fevers and indeed, the extract of willows contain salicylic acid, a close cousin of aspirin.

WINTERGREEN OIL • Extract and Oil. Menthyl Salicylate. Checkerberry Extract. Obtained naturally from betula, sweet birch, or teaberry oil. Present in certain leaves and bark but usually prepared by treating salicylic acid with methanol (see both). Wintergreen *extract* is used in root beer and wintergreen flavorings for beverages and candy (5,000 ppm). The *oil* is used for checkerberry, raspberry, teaberry, fruit, nut, root beer, sassafras, spice, and wintergreen flavorings for beverages, ice cream, ices, candy, baked goods (1500 ppm), and chewing gum (3900 ppm). Used in toothpaste, tooth powder, and perfumes. Wintergreen is a strong irritant. Ingestion of relatively small amounts may cause severe poisoning and death. Average lethal dose in children is 10 milliters and in adults, 30 milliliters. It is very irritating to the mucous membranes and skin and can be absorbed rapidly through the skin. Like other salicylates, it has a wide range of interaction with other drugs, including alcohol, antidiabetic medications, Vitamin C, and tranquilizers.

WOOD ROSIN • The exudate from a living Southern pine tree. Pale yellow to amber, slight turpentine odor. Used as a coating for fresh citrus fruits. No known toxicity.

WOODRUFF • Master of the Woods. Used as a flavoring in alcoholic beverages only. Made of the leaves of the herb grown in Europe, Siberia, North Africa, and Australia. It is a symbol of spring, and has a clean fresh smell. No known toxicity.

WORMWOOD • Absinthium. A European woody herb with a bitter taste, used in bitters and liquor flavoring for beverages and liquors. The *extract* is used in bitters, liquor, and vermouth flavorings for beverages, ice cream, candy, and liquors, and in making absinthe.

The *oil* is a dark-green to brown and a narcotic substance. Used in bitters, apple, vermouth, and wine flavorings for beverages, ice cream, ices, candy, baked goods, and liquors. In large doses or frequently repeated doses, it is a narcotic poison, causing headache, trembling, and convulsions. Ingestion of the volatile oil or of the liquor, absinthe, may cause gastronintestinal symptoms, nervousness, stupor, coma, and death.

X

XANTHAN GUM • A gum produced by a pure culture fermentation of a carbohydrate with *Xanthomonas campestris*. Also called corn sugar gum. The United States Agriculture Department has asked for the use of xanthan gum as a necessary ingredient in packaging meat and poultry products. It is now used to thicken, suspend, emulsify, and stabilize water-based foods, such as dairy products and salad dressings. It is also used as a "pseudoplasticizer" in salad dressings to help them pour well. No known toxicity.

XANTHENE • Colorants are divided into acid and basic groups. They are the second largest category of certified colors. The acids are derived from fluorescein. The quinoid acid type is represented by FD and C Red No. 3, erythrosine, used frequently in lipsticks. The phenolic formulations, often called "bromo acids," is represented by D & C Red No. 2, used to "stain" lips. The only basic type certified is D and C Red No. 19, also called Rhodamine B.

XANTHOPHYLL • Vegetable Lutein. A yellow coloring originally isolated from egg yolk, now isolated form petals of flowers. Occurs also in colored feathers of birds. One of the most widespread carotenoid alcohols (a group of red and yellow pigments) in nature. Provisionally listed for use in food. Although carotenoids can usually be turned into Vitamin A, xanthophyll has no Vitamin A activity.

XANTHOXYLUM AMERICANUM (ZANTHOXYLUM) • Ash Bark. Toothache Tree. Angelica Tree   The dried bark or berries of this tree, which grows in Canada, south of Virginia, and Missouri, is used to ease the pain of toothaches, to soothe stomachs, and as a antidiarrheal medicine. No known toxicity. A member of the rue family.

XYLITOL • Formerly made from birchwood, but now made from waste products from the pulp industry. It still costs more than sugar and it is not calorie-free. Xylitol was reported by the Finnish, who have the most experience with it, to have a diuretic effect but this has not been substantiated in England and the United States. It is used in chewing gum and as an artificial sweetener. It has been reported to sharply reduce cavities in teeth. The reason is that, unlike sugar, it doesn't ferment in the mouth. Therefore, it is sold for foods that stay in the mouth for some time, such as gum, toffee, and mints. FDA preliminary reports cited it as a possible cancer-causing agent. Xylitol is now used in eleven European countries and the United States and Canada. It is also used in large amounts in the Soviet Union as a diabetic sweetener. Xylitol has been evaluated by the Joint FAO/WHO Expert Committee on Food Additives in Geneva, April 11–20, 1983. On the basis of submitted data, the committee accepted that the adverse effects observed in British studies in which cancer-prone rats were fed large doses of xylitol were species-specific and cannot be extrapolated to humans. Therefore, no limit on daily intake was set and no additional toxicological studies were recommended. It can cause stomach upsets when taken in large amounts. It may be of benefit to diabetics since xylitol metabolization does not involve insulin.

Y

YARA YARA • *See B*-Naphthyl Methyl Ether.

YARROW • Milfoil. A strong-scented, spicy, wild herb used in liquor, root beer, and spice flavorings for beverages and liquor. Also used in shampoos. Its astringent qualities have caused it to be recommended by herbalists for greasy skins. According to old herbal recipes, it prevents baldness when the hair is washed regularly with it. Used medicinally as an astringent, tonic, and stimulant. May cause a sensitivity to sunlight and artificial light, in which the skin breaks out and swells.

YEAST • A fungus that is a dietary source of folic acid. It produces enzymes that will convert sugar to alcohol and carbon dioxide. It is used in enriched farina, enriched corn meal, and corn grits, and in bakery products. It is also used in hot dogs, hamburger and frankfurter buns and rolls, pretzels, milk fortified with vitamins, meat fried in cracker crumbs, mushrooms, truffles, cheeses of all kinds, vinegars, catsup, barbecue sauce, fermented brews, and all dried fruits. Any yeast is a type of one-celled fungus. Ordinary yeast produces the enzymes invertase and zymase, which eventually convert cane sugar to alcohol and carbon dioxide in the fermentation process. Some of the living organisms pressed into damp, starch, or other absorbent material give a product known as "baker's yeast," which is not as potent as brewer's yeast. No known toxicity. GRAS.

YEAST AUTOLYZATES • Concentrated soluble components of hydrolyzed brewer's or baker's yeasts, a by-product of brewing. They provide a good source of B vitamins. The final report to the FDA of the Select Committee on GRAS Substances stated in 1980 that while no evidence in the available information on it demonstrates a hazard to the public at current use levels, uncertainties exist, requiring that additional studies be conducted. The FDA said GRAS status should continue while tests were being completed and evaluated. Nothing new has been reported since.

YEAST EXTRACT • *See* Yeast.

YEAST-MALT SPROUT EXTRACT • Flavor enhancer. *See* Yeast.

YELLOW NO. 5 • All foods containing this coloring, which is the most widely used color additive in food, drugs, and cosmetics, are supposed to identify it on the label. The FDA ordered this so that those allergic to it could avoid it. *See* also Tartrazine and Salicylates.

YELLOW PRUSSIATE OF SODA • Sodium Ferrocyanide. An anti-caking agent, it is used in table salt to prevent the formation of clumps and keep it free flowing. The additive is produced by heating sodium carbonate and iron with organic materials. The average daily diet in the United States contains 0.6 milligrams of sodium ferrocyanide per person. The UN Joint FAO/WHO Expert Committee on Food Additives considers 1.5 milligrams daily an acceptable and safe intake for a 132-pound human.

YELLOW WAX • *See* Beeswax.

YERBA SANTA FLUID EXTRACT • Holy Herb. Fruit flavoring derived from evergreen shrubs grown in California. Used in beverages, ice cream, ices, candy, and baked goods, and to mask the bitter taste of drugs. Also used as an expectorant. No known toxicity.

YLANG-YLANG OIL • A light yellow very fragrant liquid obtained in the Philippine Islands from flowers. Used in raspberry, cola, violent, cherry, rum, and ginger ale flavorings for beverages, ice cream, ices, candy, baked goods, chewing gum, and icing. Used in perfumes, cosmetics, and soap. No known toxicity. GRAS.

YOGURT • A dairy product produce by the action of bacteria or yeast on milk. No known toxicity. Supposedly has emollient properties.

YUCCA EXTRACT • Mohave Extract. Joshua Tree. Adam's Needle. Derived from a southwestern United States plant and used as a base for organic cosmetics and as a root beer flavoring for beverages, ices, and ice cream. No known toxicity.

Z

ZANTHOXYLUM • *See* Xanthoxylum.

ZEIN • The protein of corn. Contains 17 amino acids. A by-product of corn processing, it is used to coat food and in label varnishes and microencapsulation fibers. Also used in face masks, nail polishes, and as a plasticizer. No known toxicity. GRAS.

ZEODARY • A bark extract from the East Indies used as a bitters and ginger ale flavoring for beverages. No known toxicity. GRAS.

ZINC • A white brittle metal insoluble in water and soluble in acids or hot solutions of alkalies. It is a mineral source and added as a nutrient to food. Widely used as an astringent for mouthwashes and as a reducing agent (*see*) and reagent (*see*). Ingestion of the salts can cause nausea and vomiting. It can cause contact dermatitis. *See* Zinc Chloride.

ZINC ACETATE • The zinc salt of acetic acid (*see*) used in medicine as a dietary supplement and as a cross-linking agent for polymers (*see*). For toxicity, *see* Zinc. GRAS.

ZINC BORATE • The inorganic salt of zinc oxide and boric oxide, it is used as a fungistat and mildew inhibitor. *See* Zinc.

ZINC CARBONATE • A cosmetic coloring agent, it is a crystalline salt of zinc occurring in nature as smithsonite. *See* Zinc for Toxicity. GRAS.

ZINC CHLORIDE • Butter of Zinc. A zinc salt used as an antiseptic and astringent in shaving creams, dentifrices, and mouthwashes. Odorless and water absorbing; also a deodorant and disinfectant. Can cause contact dermatitis and is mildly irritating to the skin. Can be absorbed through the skin. GRAS.

ZINC GLUCONATE • GRAS. *See* Zinc.

ZINC GLUTAMATE • The zinc salt of glutamic acid. (*see*).

ZINC METHIONINE SULFATE • *See* Zinc.

ZINC OXIDE • GRAS. *See* Zinc.

ZINC RESINATE • The zinc salt of rosin (*see*).

ZINC RICINOLEATE • The zinc salt of ricinoleate. Used as a fungicide, emulsifier, and stabilizer. *See* Zinc and Castor Oil.

ZINC ROSINATE • The zinc salt of rosin (*see*).

ZINC STEARATE • Prepared from Stearic Acid (*see*), it is used as a water-proofing agent. GRAS. *See* Zinc.

ZINC SULFATE. • White Vitriol. The reaction of sulfuric acid with zinc. Used in paper. Mild crystalline zinc salt used in shaving cream, eye lotions, astringents, styptic, as a gargle spray, skin tonic, and after-shave lotion. Used medicinally as an emetic. Irritating to the skin and mucous membranes. May cause an allergic reaction. Injection under the skin of 2.5 milligrams per kilogram of body weight caused tumors in rabbits. *See* Zinc. GRAS.

ZINGERONE • A synthetic flavoring occurring naturally in ginger.

Used in fruit, root beer, sarsaparilla, spice, ginger ale, wintergreen, and birch beer flavorings for beverages, ice cream, ices, candy, baked goods, and chewing gum. No known toxicity.

ZINGIBER OFFICINALE ROSC • *See* Ginger.

ZINGIBERONE • *See* Zingerone.

BIBLIOGRAPHY

Adams, Catherine F., *Nutritive Value of American Foods in Common Units*. Washington, D.C.: Agriculture Handbook No. 456, U.S. Department of Agriculture, 1975.

Bowes, Helen N., and Charles F. Church, *Food Values of Portions Commonly Used*, 11th ed., rev. Philadelphia: J.B. Lippincott Co., 1970.

Chemicals Used in Food Processing. Washington, D.C.: National Academy of Sciences, Publication 1274, 1965.

Code of Federal Regulations, Food and Drugs, Parts 170–199, rev./ April 1, 1988.

The Condensed Chemical Dictionary, 11th ed. Revised by N. Irving Sax and Richard J. Lewis, Sr. New York: Van Nostrand Reinhold, 1987.

Done, Alan, *Toxic Reactions to Common Household Products*. Paper read at the Symposium on Adverse Reactions sponsored by the Drug Service Center for Disease Control, December 1976, San Francisco.

Fisher, Alexander A., *Contact Dermatitis*, 3rd. ed. Philadelphia: Lea & Febiger, 1986.

Food Chemicals Codex. First ed. Washington D.C. National Academy of Sciences, Publication 1406, 1966.

Gleason, Marion N., et al., *Clinical Toxicology of Commercial Products*. Baltimore: The Williams & Wilkins Co., 1969.

Gordon, Lesley, *A Country Herbal*. New York: Mayflower Books, 1980.

Handbook of Food Additives. Edited by Thomas E. Furia. Cleveland: The Chemical Rubber Co., 1971.

Martin, Eric W., et al., *Hazards of Medications*. Philadelphia: J.B. Lippincott Co., 1971.

The Merck Index, 8th, 9th, and 10th editions. Rahway, N.J.: Merck, Sharp and Dohme Research Laboratories, 1983.

The Merck Manuul, 15th cdition. Edited by Robert Berkow, M.D. Rahway, N.J.: Merck, Sharp and Dohme Research Laboratories, 1987.

Miall, L. Mackenzie, and D. W. A. Sharp, *A New Dictionary of Chemistry*, 4th ed. New York: John Wiley & Sons, Inc., 1968.

Physicians' Desk Reference. Oradell, N.J.: Medical Economics, 1988.

Present Knowledge in Nutrition, 5th ed. Washington, D.C.: The Nutrition Foundation, Inc., 1984.

Recommended Dietary Allowances, rev. ed. Washington, D.C.: National Academy of Sciences, 1980.

Sourcebook on Food and Nutrition, 3rd ed. Edited by Joannis Scarpa, Ph.D., Helen Kiefer, Ph.D., and Rita Tatum. Chicago: Marquis Academic Media, 1982.

Steadman's Medical Dictionary, 24th ed. Baltimore: The Williams & Wilkins Co., 1982.

Suspected Carcinogens: A Subfile of the NIOSH Toxic Substance List. Rockville, Md.: Tracor Jitco, Inc., U.S. Department of Health, Education and Welfare, 1975.

Suspected Carcinogens: A Subfile of the Registry of Toxic Effects of Chemical Substances. Cincinnati: U.S. Department of Health, Education and Welfare, Public Health Services, Centers for Disease Control, 1976.

Toxicants Occurring Naturally in Foods, 2nd ed. Washington, D.C.: National Academy of Sciences, 1973.

Toxicity Testing: Strategies to Determine Needs and Priorities. Washington, D.C.: National Research Council: National Academy Press, 1984.

Watt, Bernice and Annabel Merrill, et. al., *Composition of Foods: Raw, Processed, Prepared.* Washington, D.C.: Agriculture Handbook No. 8, U.S. Department of Agriculture, 1963.

White, John Henry, *A Reference Book of Chemistry,* 3rd ed. New York: Philosophical Library, 1965.

Winter, Ruth, *Cancer-Causing Agents: A Preventive Guide.* New York: Crown Publishers, Inc., 1979.